T0378045

FIFA World Cup and Beyond

Soccer, the most popular mass spectator sport in the world, has long been a site which articulates the complexities and diversities of the everyday life of the nation. The imaging and prioritization of the game as a 'national' or an 'international' event in public opinion and the media also play a critical role in transforming the soccer culture of a nation. In this context, the FIFA World Cup remains the grand spectacle for asserting the identity of the nation. This book intends to offer eclectic perspectives and discourses on the FIFA World Cup, and to throw light on the changing dimensions of football and sports culture in terms of identity, race, ethnicity, gender, fandom, governance, and so on. On the one hand, it focuses on the significance of the FIFA World Cup for nations in terms of hosting, performance, playing style, and identity formation. On the other, it looks beyond the World Cup to highlight the growing importance of a host of perspectives in sport in general and football in particular with reference to art, fandom, gender, media, and governance.

The chapters in this book were originally published as a special issue of *Sport in Society.*

Kausik Bandyopadhyay is Professor of History at West Bengal State University, India. He was a former Fellow of the International Olympic Museum, Lausanne, Switzerland. A Deputy Executive Editor of *Soccer & Society* (Routledge), his most recent works include *Mahatma on the Pitch: Gandhi and Cricket in India* (2017) and *Sport, Culture and Nation: Perspectives from Indian Football and South Asian Cricket* (2015).

Souvik Naha has a PhD in History from the ETH Zurich, Switzerland. An Editor of *Soccer & Society* (Routledge), he has published his research in journals such as *International Journal of the History of Sport, Sport in Society, Soccer & Society, Sport in History,* and *Economic and Political Weekly,* as well as in various edited volumes.

Shakya Mitra is a post graduate in Sports Management from Stirling University, Scotland. He has worked in the Sports Management Industry as well as in the media in India for close to eight years. He has contributed articles to international journals and co-edited special issues of Routledge journals on sport.

Sport in the Global Society: Contemporary Perspectives

Series Editor: Boria Majumdar, *University of Central Lancashire, UK*

The social, cultural (including media) and political study of sport is an expanding area of scholarship and related research. While this area has been well served by the *Sport in the Global Society* series, the surge in quality scholarship over the last few years has necessitated the creation of *Sport in the Global Society: Contemporary Perspectives*. The series will publish the work of leading scholars in fields as diverse as sociology, cultural studies, media studies, gender studies, cultural geography and history, political science and political economy. If the social and cultural study of sport is to receive the scholarly attention and readership it warrants, a cross-disciplinary series dedicated to taking sport beyond the narrow confines of physical education and sport science academic domains is necessary. *Sport in the Global Society: Contemporary Perspectives* will answer this need.

For a complete list of titles in this series, please visit: https://www.routledge.com/series/SGSC

Recent titles in the series include:

Extraordinary Sportswomen
Edited by Susanna Hedenborg and Gertrud Pfister

FIFA World Cup and Beyond
Sport, Culture, Media and Governance
Edited by Kausik Bandyopadhyay, Souvik Naha and Shakya Mitra

Junior and Youth Grassroots Football Culture
The Forgotten Game
Edited by Jimmy O'Gorman

Gender in Physical Culture
Crossing Boundaries – Reconstituting Cultures
Edited by Natalie Barker-Ruchti, Karin Grahn and Eva-Carin Lindgren

DIY Football
The Cultural Politics of Community Based Football Clubs
Edited by David Kennedy and Peter Kennedy

A Social and Political History of Everton and Liverpool Football Clubs
The Split, 1878–1914
David Kennedy

Football Fandom in Italy and Beyond
Community through Media and Performance
Matthew Guschwan

Numbers and Narratives
Sport, History and Economics
Wray Vamplew

Healthy Stadia
An Insight from Policy to Practice
Edited by Daniel Parnell, Kathryn Curran and Matthew Philpott

Young People and Sport
From Participation to the Olympics
Edited by Berit Skirstad, Milena M. Parent and Barrie Houlihan

FIFA World Cup and Beyond

Sport, Culture, Media and Governance

Edited by
Kausik Bandyopadhyay, Souvik Naha and Shakya Mitra

Routledge
Taylor & Francis Group

LONDON AND NEW YORK

First published 2018
by Routledge
2 Park Square, Milton Park, Abingdon, Oxon, OX14 4RN, UK

and by Routledge
711 Third Avenue, New York, NY 10017, USA

Routledge is an imprint of the Taylor & Francis Group, an informa business

British Library Cataloguing in Publication Data
A catalogue record for this book is available from the British Library

ISBN 13: 978-0-8153-9633-8

Typeset in Minion Pro
by RefineCatch Limited, Bungay, Suffolk

Publisher's Note
The publisher accepts responsibility for any inconsistencies that may have
arisen during the conversion of this book from journal articles to book chapters,
namely the possible inclusion of journal terminology.

Disclaimer
Every effort has been made to contact copyright holders for their permission to
reprint material in this book. The publishers would be grateful to hear from any
copyright holder who is not here acknowledged and will undertake to rectify
any errors or omissions in future editions of this book.

Contents

Citation Information

The chapters in this book were originally published in *Sport in Society*, volume 20, issues 5–6 (May–June 2017). When citing this material, please use the original page numbering for each article, as follows:

Chapter 1
FIFA World Cup and beyond: sport, culture, media and governance
Kausik Bandyopadhyay, Souvik Naha and Shakya Mitra
Sport in Society, volume 20, issues 5–6 (May–June 2017), pp. 547–554

Chapter 2
A second 'Maracanazo'? The 2014 FIFA World Cup in historical perspective
Kevin Moore
Sport in Society, volume 20, issues 5–6 (May–June 2017), pp. 555–571

Chapter 3
Reporting the 2014 World Cup: football first and social issues last
Helton Levy
Sport in Society, volume 20, issues 5–6 (May–June 2017), pp. 572–582

Chapter 4
Risk and (in)security of FIFA football World Cups – outlook for Russia 2018
Donna Wong and Simon Chadwick
Sport in Society, volume 20, issues 5–6 (May–June 2017), pp. 583–598

Chapter 5
The language of football: a cultural analysis of selected world cup nations
Niels N. Rossing and Lotte S. Skrubbeltrang
Sport in Society, volume 20, issues 5–6 (May–June 2017), pp. 599–611

Chapter 6
Conflicting traditions: the FIFA World Cup, Australia and football identities
Binoy Kampmark
Sport in Society, volume 20, issues 5–6 (May–June 2017), pp. 612–626

Chapter 7
Amnesia and animosity: an assessment of soccer in the States
David Kilpatrick
Sport in Society, volume 20, issues 5–6 (May–June 2017), pp. 627–640

Chapter 8
The art of goalkeeping: memorializing Lev Yashin
Mike O'Mahony
Sport in Society, volume 20, issues 5–6 (May–June 2017), pp. 641–659

Chapter 9
Politics and international fandom in a fringe nation: La Albiceleste, *Maradona, and Marxist Kolkata*
Sarbajit Mitra and Souvik Naha
Sport in Society, volume 20, issues 5–6 (May–June 2017), pp. 660–674

Chapter 10
Soccer and the city: the game and its fans in Solo and Yogyakarta
Andy Fuller
Sport in Society, volume 20, issues 5–6 (May–June 2017), pp. 675–688

Chapter 11
Women's time? Time and temporality in women's football
Kath Woodward
Sport in Society, volume 20, issues 5–6 (May–June 2017), pp. 689–700

Chapter 12
Making sense of race/ethnicity and gender in televised football: reception research among British students
Rens Peeters and Jacco van Sterkenburg
Sport in Society, volume 20, issues 5–6 (May–June 2017), pp. 701–715

Chapter 13
FIFA, *the video game: a major vehicle for soccer's popularization in the United States*
Andrei S. Markovits and Adam I. Green
Sport in Society, volume 20, issues 5–6 (May–June 2017), pp. 716–734

Chapter 14
Stakeholder governance and Irish sport
David Hassan and Ian O'Boyle
Sport in Society, volume 20, issues 5–6 (May–June 2017), pp. 735–749

For any permission-related enquiries please visit:
http://www.tandfonline.com/page/help/permissions

Notes on Contributors

Kausik Bandyopadhyay is Professor of History at West Bengal State University, India.

Simon Chadwick is Professor of Sports Enterprise at the University of Salford, Manchester, UK.

Andy Fuller is based at the KITLV/Royal Netherlands Institute of Southeast Asian and Caribbean Studies, Leiden, The Netherlands.

Adam I. Green is Lecturer at the Department of Economics, University of Michigan, Ann Arbor, USA.

David Hassan is Associate Dean (Global Engagement) at the School of Sports, Ulster University, Belfast, UK.

Binoy Kampmark is Senior Lecturer at the School of Global, Urban and Social Studies, RMIT University, Melbourne, Australia.

David Kilpatrick is based at the Department of Literature and Language, Mercy College, New York, USA.

Helton Levy is based at the Department of Sociology, City University London, UK.

Andrei S. Markovits is Arthur F. Thurnau Professor and Karl W. Deutsch Collegiate Professor of Comparative Politics and German Studies at the University of Michigan, Ann Arbor, USA.

Sarabajit Mitra received his Masters in History from Jadavpur University, Kolkata, India.

Shakya Mitra is a post graduate in Sports Management from Stirling University, Scotland.

Kevin Moore was the Director of the National Football Museum, Manchester, UK.

Souvik Naha has a PhD in History from the ETH Zurich, Switzerland.

Ian O'Boyle is Senior Lecturer and Director of CERM PI at the University of South Australia.

Mike O'Mahony is Professor of History of Art and Visual Culture at the University of Bristol, UK.

Rens Peeters is a PhD candidate at the Erasmus Research Centre for Media, Communication and Culture, Erasmus University, The Netherlands.

Niels N. Rossing is based at the Department of Health Science and Technology, Aalborg University, Denmark.

Lotte S. Skrubbeltrang is based at the Department of Health Science and Technology, Aalborg University, Denmark.

Jacco van Sterkenburg is Assistant Professor at the Erasmus Research Centre for Media, Communication and Culture, Erasmus University, The Netherlands.

Donna Wong is Research Fellow at the Faculty of Business and Law, Centre for Business in Society, Coventry University, UK.

Kath Woodward is Emeritus Professor at the Faculty of Social Sciences, Sociology, Open University, UK.

FIFA World Cup and beyond: sport, culture, media and governance

Kausik Bandyopadhyay, Souvik Naha and Shakya Mitra

Soccer, the most popular mass spectator sport in the world (Goldblatt 2008), is a game where humanity comes alive with one goal.[1] Globally soccer has long been a site which articulates the complexities and diversities of the everyday life of the nation.[2] The game has always remained a marker of identities of various sorts. Behind the façade of its obvious entertainment aspect, it has proved to be a perpetuating reflector of cultural nationalism, distinctive ethnicity, community or communal identity, cultural specificity as well as representative of models of development and international status of post-colonial nation states. For those nations, which still remain at the periphery of the modern world, the game provides a platform to assert their national identity at the international stage through on-field performance or off-field fandom.[3] The imaging and prioritization of the game as a 'national' or an 'international' event in public opinion and the media also play a critical role in transforming the soccer culture of a nation into a developed one.[4] In this context, the FIFA World Cup remains the grand spectacle for asserting the identity of the nation. It also gives birth to heroes, icons and legends, who not only represent their national identity at the global stage, but float at a transnational global space, transcending the limits of space, identity or culture of a nation (Bandyopadhyay 2016).

It is the staggering mass following at all levels transcending age, space or time that makes soccer different from any other sports in the world. Yet, as in other sports, performance and non-performance are equally revealing in soccer as well. The craze and status of the game as well as the future of soccer is revealed through this graph of performances or non-performances in World Cups. In the developed, developing and underdeveloped nations, soccer has faced new challenges emanating from globalization: commercialization, professionalization and mediatization in the last three decades.[5] In the face of these, when growing competition among elite football clubs in developed soccer bastions has become obvious and when the FIFA, world's apex body of soccer, has recently put so much emphasis on the exercise on standardization, new priorities under globalization – access to capital, models of sports governance, competitive mass media and sponsorship, transnational fandom, gendered discourses on the game, and so on – all have altered the balance of power in international, national and local rivalries affecting the game across the world in the twenty-first century (Garland, Malcolm, and Rowe 2013).[6]

In trying to address some of these diverse issues mentioned above, the present volume intends to offer eclectic perspectives and discourses on the FIFA World Cup, and throw light on changing dimensions of football and sports culture in terms of identity, race, ethnicity, gender, fandom, governance, and so on. The initiative for this volume goes back to the International Conference on *FIFA World Cup and the Nation: Culture, Politics, Identity* jointly organized by the Taylor & Francis Group and the University of Central Lancashire and held at the University Club, Oxford on 23–24 July 2014. While the present work has incorporated some of the papers presented in the conference, it also includes essays primarily written to illuminate the theme of the volume. Apart from its predominant emphasis on the FIFA World Cup, the volume comprises a few essays that shift the focus in the end to some other football/sports-related issues, emerging in the field. The volume is divided into two sections apart from the Introduction. The first section 'FIFA World Cup and the Nation' focuses on the significance of FIFA World Cups for nations in terms of hosting, performance, playing style, and identity formation. The last and forthcoming editions of the Cup – Brazil 2014 and Russia 2018 are given particular attention by the authors in that context while case studies include those of Brazil, Italy, Australia and the United States. The second section looks beyond the World Cup to highlight the growing importance of a host of perspectives in sport in general and football in particular. These include art, fandom, gender, media, and governance.

The volume, i.e. the first section, unfolds with two intriguing perspectives on the 2014 Brazil World Cup. After the 2014 World Cup was concluded, various stakeholders started promoting the particular event as the best ever in the history of the tournament. The media circulated the event's positive aspects so successfully that in a public poll conducted by the BBC, 39% of the readers voted in favour of the best ever tag. Kevin Moore's narrative, which offers the first perspective, travels through the long history of the FIFA World Cups to show that such comparison between eras is not only invalid in terms of goal scoring and style of play, but also in the scale of organization. The event was pretty average in the number of goals scored per match, indicating how competitive global football has become. Both media coverage and public attendance have increased exponentially over the years. Even the widely reported social turmoil over the high costs of hosting the event was trifling compared to the political controversies to have taken place within the World Cup's contexts. Moore's chronological account also adequately captures the international and local politics at play behind every edition of the tournament. Since it is a tournament between nations, heads of states and other politicians naturally become involved in its organization. Their exercise of political motives plays a significant role in determining participation, which is evident in the inclusion and exclusion of various countries and preparation of first round groups over the years. War – both the Second World War and civil wars, refusal to compete against political enemies, non-acceptance of countries not diplomatically recognized by the host, ethnic tensions, boycott against FIFA rulings, and dictatorships have all played critical roles in shaping the tournament's fortunes. The much-criticized 2014 World Cup, in Moore's analysis, was far less controversial politically.

The second perspective on the 2014 World Cup comes from Helton Levy who discusses the significance of media coverage in bringing forth the narratives and counter-narratives about the preparations, problems and prospects of the tournament, and its role in prioritizing specific narratives in that context. As Brazil was engulfed by social turmoil and political tension in the year preceding the World Cup, issues such as poverty, protest and violence became pivotal in local media reportage. Yet, Levy shows through a frame analysis that these serious social issues were ultimately overshadowed by commercial interest and political agenda projected by the global media, particularly in England and elsewhere, which privileged the priorities of a global spectacle, thereby focusing on FIFA's narrative on the event. As a result, delays and infrastructure problems were given more consideration than crucial local issues, thereby pointing to the role of global media in the marginalization of local voices in case of international sports events. Levy's effort underlines the significance of the continuing debate around motivated mediatization of sporting events across the world.

With growing emphases on the bidding and preparation of, and build-up to global mega events in recent times, studies on the significance of hosting such events have become increasingly relevant and popular. The essay by Dona Wong and Simon Chadwick reflects upon the prospects of World Cup 2018 to be hosted by Russia in terms of risk-assessment. While hosting a grand spectacle of the magnitude of FIFA World Cup provides a great opportunity to showcase the nation, modernize the state's economy, and fast-track development, it also brings risks of various sorts. Wong and Chadwick first take stock of the risks faced by the last three World Cups and comment on the ability of the host nations to handle those risks. With this background, they proceed to identify the potential threats and challenges that can jeopardize the security of the 2018 World Cup to be hosted by Russia, particularly in a context where the planning and operational decisions for Russia 2018 are undertaken under conditions of high ambiguity and uncertainty. Terrorism, violence, racism, boycott, cost inflation, infrastructural problem and political unpredictability loom large before Russia as it prepares for the greatest football show. To combat such risks effectively and to secure the mega event, they suggest, it is important to chalk out and implement preventative and security measures.

The World Cup is undoubtedly dependent on the media's assessment of the turn of events and inclination of readers/viewers for establishing its legacy. The same can be said about national football cultures, the distinguishing features of which are largely disseminated through the media's appropriation. The essay by Niels N Rossing and Lotte S Skrubbeltrang uses Edgar Schein's framework for cultural analysis to examine to what extent action on the playing field corresponds to specific 'national football cultures' commonly quoted in the media and the public sphere. They analyse textual (research works and popular books) and visual (match videos) materials related to Brazil and Italy's campaign in the 2010 and 2014 World Cups. The evidence leads them to argue that the two national teams' playing styles were sometimes consistent with how their national football cultures are universally understood. They present an intriguing idea, comparing a nation's style of play to a dialect within the general language of football. Each national dialect, they contend, is supported by 'different basic assumptions and to some extent specific symbolic actions on the field'. However, this consistency was not so regular that a cultural identity could readily be imposed on each country at national level football. In the final analysis, they reveal divergences between the Brazilian and Italian national teams and their football culture in general, mainly because of how players are primed in their club career. Hence, they conclude, a national team doesn't always speak the same dialect as of its internal football culture.

While soccer is widely considered as the global game, but within two major regions of the world it was largely seen as an 'outsider' sport. Two following essays by Binoy Kampmark and David Kilpatrick examine the place of football in these regions – Australia and the United States respectively. Despite being the world's most popular sport, football for a long time struggled to make an impact in the sporting landscape of Australia, widely considered as one of the world's most sports loving countries. Perception towards the sport has been helped though by qualification for three consecutive Men's World Cups. Kampmark's essay accounts for football in Australia, the past indifference and a growing warmth towards it in recent times. One of the main reasons why soccer (as a lot of Australians refer to it) struggled to gain relevance in Australia for long periods of time was that it could not match the popularity of rival sports, the most prominent being Australian Rules Football. However with time for Australia to garner a more global identity, it became necessary to embrace football. Over the last decade, much of the indifference that football was subjected to in the past has reduced. One of the clearest manifestations of this growing significance of the game was seen in the outrage throughout the country when Australia was controversially eliminated in the round of 16 in the 2006 World Cup, or even more recently, when Australia missed out on hosting the 2022 World Cup. Despite the continuing cultural resistance towards the game, the essay argues, the experience of the 2014 World Cup hints at a more stable future for the game in Australia.

The United States also had similar issues coming to terms with soccer. Kilpatrick looks at the indifference and animosity with which the game has been viewed with in the United States. While the 1950 Cup was remarkable in that it witnessed USA's shock victory over England, but this upset victory did not really push the game further in the States as it was followed by a lull of 40 years as the Men's Football team failed to qualify for the World Cup between 1950 and 1990. The game retreated into an isolated, insular and mostly ethnic marginalized status on the periphery of the American sporting landscape. If Pelé's arrival in America to play for New York Cosmos was deemed to be soccer's arrival in the States, argues Kilpatrick, hosting the 1994 World Cup was the real big boost for the game in the USA, particularly in terms of audience reception, followed by the start of Major League Soccer. The performances of the Men's National Team have improved considerably since then with a concomitant rise in FIFA rankings. Despite this rising image of soccer in contemporary America, according to the author, the sport does not seem to completely break away from its amnesia probably due to the animosity which has always marked its struggle for relevance in American society. Soccer being a threat to hegemonic forces and discourses in American sporting landscape, it has always been criticized for its alleged 'foreignness', and hence its competition with ostensibly indigenous sports has been far from fair. More importantly, as Kilpatrick shows, the internal animosity in the organization and governance of the game continues to complicate the growth of the domestic game on stable footing. Yet, given the steady rise in mass interest in soccer visible during and post 2014 World Cup, the author predicts a brighter future of soccer in America.

The second section of the volume begins with Mike O'Mahony's nuanced attempt to explore the relational complexities among sport, art and society. Following the collapse of the Soviet Union, the urban landscape of the city of Moscow changed considerably with a host of new monuments springing up. Old Heroes once revered but later despised during the Soviet era acquired a new found status with their statues adorned on the streets of Moscow post the events of August 1991. Yet one man established as a hero during Soviet times continued to find pride of place, even in the aftermath of the collapse. Mike O'Mahony explores this legendary Russian – Lev Yashin, widely considered as the greatest goalkeeper of all time, with reference to him being immortalized in Moscow in the form of two sculptures by Alexander Rukavishnikov, one of the most prolific Russian sculptors of the post-Soviet era. O'Mahony through these sculptures looks at two issues, the connection between sport and art, and the role of the goalkeeper in Soviet society. Also in accounting for the greatness of Yashin, the author deconstructs the sculptural representations to reflect upon the career, status and reputation of Yashin. Yashin remains without doubt one of the greatest national heroes from the Soviet Union, and with Russia all set to host the 2018 World Cup, there is no doubt that his name will be used to build up publicity for the tournament.

The spread and significance of transnational fandom and its associated subcultures has become one of the core values and markers of contemporary sporting world primarily driven by commercial forces. Football being the most global of international sports, fandom has made strongest inroads to foment fan identities based on nation, club or personality, both singularly and plurally. The old Indian city of Kolkata has been a case in this regard, as Sarbajit Mitra and Souvik Naha examines roots and impact of the fan base *La Albiceleste* (the Argentine national football team) and its football legend Diego Maradona began to command since the mid-1980s. Their essay traces the fascinating story of Kolkata's transformation from a Brazilian football colony to an Argentinian one particularly during World Cups from mid-1980s to mid-1990s through a discussion of Maradona's footballing ability, personal life and political predilections. The trajectory of Bengalis' tryst with Maradona/Argentina between 1986, the year Argentina lifted the World Cup under his captaincy and 2008, when Maradona visited Kolkata, is explored analysing contemporary media representations and literary output. The study, by exploring the deeper significance of an international icon in the social and political world of an underdeveloped footballing nation like India, brings to fore the complexities of fandom as a global process.

Like transnational fandom, local fan cultures constitute an important area of enquiry in sports and cultural studies. Andy Fuller's essay explores the patterns of local football cultures in Indonesia, another underdeveloped footballing nation with a focus on two of its cities – Solo and Yogyakarta. While Indonesia cuts a sorry figure in the international soccer map, international soccer including European leagues and World Cups are hugely popular there commanding large fan bases and supporter groups. Yet, despite the consistent failure of the national team, as Fuller shows, local football rivalries and culture have been rich in tradition and intense enough to merit scholarly attention. Parallel to the popularity of the English Premier League, the author, through his painstaking ethnographic research, sheds light on the violent and tense rivalries in Solo and Yogyakarta in the broader context of Indonesian 'soccerscapes'. He links the urban fan culture in these cities to wider processes of politics and policies of decentralization in the post-New Order period (1998 onwards) as well as to the deeply contested identity politics across the state. The essay focuses on the experiences of identification with a particular club in case of Solo and an ex-player in case of Yogyakarta to understand how football culture plays a pivotal role in shaping urban identities.

'Time' is a crucial aspect in everyone's life and it is no different with football. Kath Woodward looks at the current state of women's football from the relational perspective of time and temporality. Taking 'Time' into context, Woodward argues that the legacy of memories of pivotal moments, record breaking displays and construction of heroes over a period of time have been absent in women's football. This is in complete contrast to the men's game. While the 2014 Men's World Cup did see some degree of incremental change in the way women are viewed, there still remains the feeling that gender in sport, particularly football, is dominated by masculinity rather than femininity. There were of course positive changes taking place, examples being Women being brought in as commentators as well as providing their expert opinion on the game during the Cup or the Women's Super League being launched in England. There have been, on the contrary, negative blogs questioning how much women can support football. Woodward also draws attention to sexist abuses to which women on and off the field are subjected to and the persistent need felt at all levels to rectify the discriminatory gendered attitude inherent in society in order to efface such abuses. Woodward argues that football should be enjoyed, and should become as socially inclusive as possible. While Women's Time is not an alternative to Men's Time, being able to address the inequalities of the past could help bring us a more equal future for Men's and Women's Football.

Football in England constitutes an important part of what constitutes the nation's cultural identity. Televised football is a key arena where prominent ideas of race, identity and gender and the differences they entail are reproduced and naturalized. These ideas have become all the more important in a multicultural society like England which has begun to question the lack of Englishness in its highest league, due to the influx of foreign players. The football media is one of the most powerful institutions through which ideas of races are dispersed. It is also one of the few arenas in our modern society where segregation across gender lines takes place. In their essay, Rens Peeters and Jacco Van Sterkenburg, through a focus group research conducted with students of two London universities, viz. Brunel University and Croydon College, discuss how ideas of nationality, race/ethnicity and gender are made through the prism of televised football. In doing so, they try to explore on the one hand the discourses television viewers of various ethnic and gender groupings draw on to give meaning to race/ethnicity and gender, and on the other how viewers' individual reception and discourses overlap with hegemonic media discourses and strengthen or challenge wider hegemonic media discourses in a multi-ethnic society. However, as the authors argue, a fuller understanding of a participant's sense of belonging that includes various domains of social experience such as national and/or local belongings would require more complex approach in both the focus of the interviews as well as in the analysis of the data as the researcher in that case would have to negotiate with new and politically infused questions about groupings and racial hierarchies in and through (mediated) football.

It has already been shown in an earlier chapter that despite resistance from competing sections soccer in the United States – both Men's and Women's – is making steady strides to become a popular and commercially viable mass consumed sporting activity. In that process, along with real time soccer play and its telecast, in the last one decade or so, a new element of multimedia has become an influential vector in generating tremendous interest in the game particularly among the younger sections of American society. This burgeoning development in the field of soccer has been due to EA Sports' *FIFA* video game series, launched globally in 1993. As the essay of Andrei S. Markovits and Adam I. Green has tried to argue, while soccer still lags behind America's 'Big Four' of football, baseball, hockey and basketball in terms of following, the recent proliferation of FIFA the video game has the potential to transform soccer's cultural presence in American society in coming years. The authors discuss the origins, growth and impact of this unique audiovisual instrument of soccer's global popularization in the context of soccer's social and cultural presence in the United States over the last one decade or so. By offering an in-depth analysis of video game users and their narratives, they conclude that this video game, a non-reality, has become a new lived cultural experience that has the ability to transform the 'real' social and cultural status of soccer in the United States.

The last essay of the volume turns attention to the crucial issue of governance in contemporary sports world with focus on the Gaelic Athletic Association (GAA) of Ireland, the largest Irish sporting body, in the context of growing significance of corporate business and stakeholder management in the realm of sport. Traditionally being an amateurish and community-based institution, the GAA's transition to modern day professional and commercial stage has been the subject of enquiry by the authors – David Hassan and Ian O Boyle. They situate this transition against the backdrop of a changing reality within global sport – the pressing need for effective management of the interdependency of national governing bodies, individual clubs and a network of stakeholder interests. While the GAA as a self-regulatory body employed both volunteerism and financial altruism as also stewardship for administering good governance, the main challenge it now faces is how to manage a vibrant, professional and modern sporting body within the confines of a historically determined and fundamentally amateur context. The essay argues that only through the introduction of a meaningful stakeholder model can the governance of an organization like the GAA even attempt to respond to this challenge.

The present volume has in no way pretended to present any holistic understanding of events, processes and discourses in relation to FIFA World Cups and other sporting issues enshrined in the title. Neither does it claim to offer an equitable spatial representation of global perspectives, as evidenced in the virtual absence of Africa in its coverage. The volume is rather an attempt to explore and understand some emerging issues in the realm of modern sport/football with two focal points of attention. The first looks at the FIFA Men's World Cup in relation to nations who host, take part in, or simply consume it. Representations of the nation through the World Cup in myriad forms have been discussed with reference to history, culture, identity, security, media and commerce. The second goes beyond the World Cup to look at more general yet important issues of sports/soccer culture, media representation and sports governance. Here, the essays aim to reflect upon a range of diverse themes including footballing art, fan culture, women's football, mediatization, video game and stakeholder governance.

Notes

1. Throughout this introduction and the volume, soccer and football have been used almost interchangeably, unless otherwise specified as in the cases of the United States or Australia.
2. Numerous studies have discussed the role of soccer/football in the everyday life of nations. For a most recent example, see Goldblatt (2014).
3. For a case study on this, see Crolley and Hand (2006).
4. For a general study of the significance of national identity around the two most significant global sporting spectacles, viz. Olympics and FIFA World Cup, see Tomlinson (2012).
5. A number of works have dealt with the impact of globalization on sports in general and football in particular. For example, see Sandvoss (2003).
6. Many of these emerging issues in world football have found their way through the articles published in the last few years in a host of scholarly journals on sport, and most notably in *Soccer & Society* (London: Routledge).

Disclosure statement

No potential conflict of interest was reported by the authors.

References

Bandyopadhyay, Kausik, ed. 2016. *Heroes, Icons, Legends: Legacies of Great Men in World Soccer*. London: Routledge.

Crolley, Liz, and David Hand. 2006. *Football and European Identity: Historical Narratives through the Press*. London: Routledge.

Garland, Jon, Dominic Malcolm, and Mike Rowe. 2013. *The Future of Football: Challenges for the Twenty-First Century*. London: Routledge.

Goldblatt, David. 2008. *The Ball is Round: a Global History of Soccer*. London: Penguin.

Goldblatt, David. 2014. *Futebol Nation: The Story of Brazil through Soccer*. New York: Penguin.

Sandvoss, Cornel. 2003. *A Game of Two Halves: Football, Television and Globalization*. London: Routledge.

Tomlinson, Alan. 2012. *National Identity and Global Sports Events: Culture, Politics, and Spectacle in the Olympics and the Football World Cup*. New York: Sunny Press.

A second 'Maracanazo'? The 2014 FIFA World Cup in historical perspective

ABSTRACT

This paper seeks to evaluate the 2014 FIFA World Cup in relation to the World Cup tournaments since the first in 1930, in terms of the success of the tournament, both on and off the pitch. The 2014 FIFA World Cup was characterized in the international media for several years prior to the tournament as one which was highly problematic in terms of its organization in Brazil, as to whether the stadia and other infrastructure would be ready. This negativity was compounded after the street protests around the 2013 FIFA Confederations Cup, leading to fears that the 2014 tournament would be marred by significant popular political opposition. Once the 2014 World Cup began and it was clear that the infrastructure was sufficiently in place and the protests would in fact be very minimal, the international media did a swift volte-face and instead portrayed the tournament as a great success. As an historian I take the long view, evaluating the 2014 tournament in the full historical perspective. In doing so, I debunk the media myths about the 2014 FIFA World Cup.

With a year to go, there were great concerns about the cost, with the country facing major economic and social problems. There were protests and then riots on the streets. Even just days before it began, there was negative media coverage, with the population split on whether it was all just a big waste of money, a distraction from the real issues facing the country. But once it began, the event was proclaimed a great success by the international media.

No, this is not the FIFA World Cup in Brazil 2014, but the London 2012 Olympics and Paralympics. London 2012 showed how a negative image and mood, partly created by the media, can very quickly be turned around. London 2012 is generally accepted to have been a great success, even by the hyper-critical UK media. Parts of the British media were still being negative after the games began, but then quickly changed when they realized the public mood was overwhelmingly positive. In many ways the same can be said of the 2014 FIFA World Cup in Brazil, in the sense that an event which was being portrayed very negatively in the media before it began is now generally regarded to have been a success. World Cups and Olympic Games are now reported and judged in the context of 24-hour rolling news channels and social media, with instant reactions and the possibility of the smallest negative incident becoming a major international news story.

This paper seeks to evaluate the 2014 FIFA World Cup in relation to the World Cup tournaments since the first in 1930, in terms of the success of the tournament, both on and off the pitch. To do so we need to get beyond the instant reactions of journalists and take a longer, historical view. The 2014 FIFA World Cup was characterized in the international media for several years prior to the tournament as one which was highly problematic in terms of its organization in Brazil, as to whether the stadia and other infrastructure would be ready. This negativity was compounded after the street protests around the 2013 FIFA Confederations Cup, leading to fears that the 2014 tournament would be marred by significant popular political opposition. Once the 2014 World Cup got under way and it was clear that the infrastructure was sufficiently in place and the protests would in fact be very minimal, the international media did a swift volte-face and instead portrayed the tournament as a great success, with some forecasting after the first round of group games that this could be the 'best World Cup ever'. Such is the nature of the modern global news media. As an historian, in this paper I will take the long view, evaluating the 2014 tournament in a historical perspective, from 1930 onwards. In doing so, I will debunk the media myths about the 2014 FIFA World Cup, some of which had been propagated even before it began.

Despite being the most successful World Cup nation, with five wins, Brazil had not hosted the finals tournament since 1950. Despite this success, deep in the Brazilian football psyche is the scar of the highly unexpected (by Brazilians) defeat in the deciding match in 1950 in the Maracana Stadium, known as the 'Maracanazo', the 'Maracana blow'. Hosting in 2014 would give the opportunity to finally expunge this by Brazil winning in the final in the new Maracana. However, given the protests around the Confederations Cup in Brazil in 2013, it seemed a real possibility that this dream could have turned into something of a nightmare, with unfinished stadia and street protests. The major fears were unfounded. It went from potentially a question of what went wrong for Brazil into a question of how it went right. But there was a genuine sense of trepidation before the tournament began, which cannot be put down purely to modern media hyperbole.

How in retrospect can we evaluate the FIFA 2014 World Cup? It is a moot question as to how long after an event can a historian make a composed and objective analysis? When asked in 1972 about the impact of the French Revolution, Chinese premier Zhou Enlai said it was 'too early' to say. This story turns out to be apocryphal, that he was referring to turmoil in France in 1968 and not – as is commonly thought – to the more distant political upheaval of 1789 (Campbell 2011). But as an historian I am still going to attempt the very difficult if not impossible task of evaluating the 2014 tournament after a few months, rather than years. To do so, it is essential to take an historical perspective, from the first FIFA World Cup in 1930 onwards. This paper does not consider the development of the women's FIFA World Cup or any of the other World Cup tournaments organized by FIFA. It will demonstrate that we can only understand and evaluate the FIFA World Cup Brazil 2014 if we consider it in relation to the FIFA World Cup from its inception. From this historical perspective, the 2014 tournament was one of the *least* controversial, in political terms.

The 2014 tournament was rapidly acclaimed around the world as potentially the best ever World Cup. But by which criteria? How can one measure the success or failure of a World Cup? Clearly the tournament is polysemantic, it means different things to different persons, no two views are the same. More than 3.2 billion people watched at least some television coverage of the tournament. In an increasingly globalized world, even most of those who did not watch would have an awareness and an opinion. During the tournament, the world was 'footballised'. Completely unrelated media stories were given a link to football, however tenuous, or even non-existent. For example, when experts found the largest ever fossilized skeleton of a bird, the story was that it would have made a great goalkeeper (Myles 2014).

Is it possible to quantify a World Cup? Joseph S. Blatter, then the president of FIFA, believes it is. At a press conference the day after the tournament ended, he gave it a score of 9.25, out of 10. 'We have improved on four years ago in South Africa,' said Blatter, who awarded the 2010 World Cup 9 marks out of 10 – for organization, not the quality of the football. Smiling broadly, he told reporters that 'We consulted all our computers and our Facebooks (*sic*) and decided on 9.25 out of 10 because perfection does not exist in football' (Collett 2014). Immediately after the rather disappointing – in football terms – World Cup in South Africa, Blatter said that FIFA should consider making the goals bigger, or have just 10 players in each team, as the great Brazilian player Socrates had suggested, given that modern players were so much fitter and faster, but that pitches were still the same size (McOwan 2011).

The one obvious quantitative measure for a World Cup is goals scored. In contrast to at least the two previous tournaments, the initial group games were not low scoring draws, but saw plenty of goals, not least the Netherlands' shock 5–1 defeat of the reigning champions Spain. There were 53 goals in the 12 initial group games, at an average of 4.42 per game, with only one 0–0 draw. The media started to talk about how this might be the best World Cup 'ever'. But by the end of the tournament, the number of goals per game had fallen to 2.67. This was the best since France in 1998, which it exactly matched. However, taking an historical perspective of all the World Cup tournaments from 1930 onwards, the number of goals per game at Brazil 2014 was lower than ten previous World Cups, as Table 1 demonstrates. More goals do not necessarily mean better football, as they can be the result of poor defending or bad goalkeeping, and a 0–0 draw can sometimes be as exciting as a high-scoring game, but in general the greater the number of goals, the more exciting the tournament. Brazil 2014 by this measure was average at best. The public at large, however, lack historical perspective, and in a BBC poll carried out immediately the tournament had ended, Brazil 2014 was voted the best World Cup ever, with 39% of the vote (BBC 2014).

Historical comparison between World Cups beyond goals scored becomes extremely difficult, not least because the early tournaments are on a completely different scale to the most recent. Take, for example, the number of teams entering and competing in qualification matches, as outlined in Table 2. The 1930 World Cup required no qualification because it had places for 16 teams, but only 13 turned up to compete. The first tournament to require qualification matches was in 1934, but as only 22 teams were competing for 16 places, the largest qualification groups were only three, with two teams qualifying from these groups. Some groups were only two, so teams only played each other home and away. Further, Peru and Chile withdrew, so Brazil and Argentina qualified automatically. In 1938, several teams qualified without playing a game, due to withdrawals. For example, Colombia, Costa Rica, Dutch Guiana, El Salvador, Mexico, and the United States all withdrew, so Cuba qualified automatically. In 1938 71% of teams competing reached the finals, as Table 2 demonstrates. In 1950, with only 34 teams initially entering for 16 places, and 13 then withdrawing, some teams again qualified without playing a game. Nineteen teams in qualification were competing for 14 available places. 1954 was the first World Cup where no team qualified without playing a game, but teams in qualification had a 48% chance of reaching the finals.

Table 1. Goals per game at FIFA World Cup Finals.

Year	Teams competing	Matches	Goals	Average goals per game
1930	13	18	70	3.89
1934	16	17	70	4.12
1938	15	18	84	4.67
1950	13	22	88	4.00
1954	16	26	140	5.38
1958	16	35	126	3.60
1962	16	32	89	2.78
1966	16	32	89	2.78
1970	16	32	95	2.97
1974	16	38	97	2.55
1978	16	38	102	2.68
1982	24	52	146	2.81
1986	24	52	132	2.54
1990	24	52	115	2.21
1994	24	52	141	2.71
1998	32	64	171	2.67
2002	32	64	161	2.52
2006	32	64	147	2.30
2010	32	64	145	2.27
2014	32	64	171	2.67

Source: FIFA, 2014a, 'FIFA World Cup Tournament Statistics', http://www.fifa.com/worldfootball/statisticsandrecords/tournaments/worldcup/organisation/.

Table 2. Teams entering and competing in qualification matches at the World Cup.

Year	Teams initially entering	Teams qualifying as hosts or holders	Teams withdrawing before qualification matches	Teams competing in qualification matches	Teams at finals	% of teams in qualification appearing at finals
1930	13	0	n/a	n/a	13	n/a
1934	32	0	5	27	16	59
1938	37	2	14	21	15	71
1950	34	2	13	19	13	68
1954	45	2	10	33	16	48
1958	55	2	7	46	16	35
1962	56	2	5	49	16	33
1966	74	2	21	51	16	31
1970	75	2	5	68	16	24
1974	99	2	7	90	16	18
1978	107	2	10	95	16	17
1982	109	2	4	103	24	23
1986	121	2	9	110	24	22
1990	116	2	11	103	24	23
1994	147	2	15	130	24	18
1998	174	2	4	168	32	19
2002	199	3	3	193	32	17
2006	198	1	3	194	32	16
2010	206	1	5	200	32	16
2014	203	1	2	200	32	16

Sources: FIFA. 2006. 'FIFA World Cup Qualifiers in a Nutshell', http://www.fifa.com/mm/document/fifafacts/mcwc/ip-301_11a_fwc-prelstats_8828.pdf; FIFA. 2013. 'Recap of the FIFA World Cup Preliminary Competitions 1930–2014, Statistical Kit', http://www.fifa.com/mm/document/fifafacts/mencompwc/51/97/68/2014fwc_kit_recap_fwc_prel_neutral.pdf.

Withdrawals also affected the finals tournament after 1930. In 1938, only 15 teams were at the finals instead of 16, because Austria withdrew. In 1950, there were only 13 teams, because India, Scotland and Turkey withdrew.

Only in 1970 did less than one in four teams seeking qualification get to compete in the finals. In many other ways, the early tournaments (pre-1970) bear no comparison with the later ones, in cost, media coverage and commerciality. One measure of the value of a World Cup could be how much each goal cost in terms of the budget for the tournament, but establishing the total costs is difficult, if not impossible. The economic impact of hosting the tournament is also difficult to estimate and potentially hosting a World Cup produces a significant net loss (Baade and Matheson 2004; Lee and Taylor 2005; Matheson 2014; Preuss and Schnitzer 2012). Media coverage has changed immeasurably, with no television coverage until 1954. The only way in which the scale of the tournament has not changed as disproportionately is in the average attendance at each match. While there were only 18 matches in 1930, the average attendance was 32,808. At the 64 games in Brazil, the average attendance was 53,592. The record average was 68,991 in the USA in 1994, as Table 3 below demonstrates. However, this does not take into account the capacity of the stadia. A better measure might be how full the stadia were in percentage terms, but this has not been quantified.

The early World Cups – up to and including 1966 – are arguably not World Cups in the current form; there is a discontinuity. We cannot compare the two eras. While there is no sharp break between 'early' and 'modern' World Cups, there is a strong sense in which they are so different as to make comparison impossible (Frawley and Adair 2014).

In March 2003, FIFA announced that the 2014 tournament would be held in South America for the first time since 1978, in line with its then active policy of rotating the right to host the World Cup among the different confederations. Only Brazil and Colombia formally declared their candidacy but, after the withdrawal of the latter from the process, Brazil was officially selected as host nation unopposed in October 2007. Brazil had its chance to expunge the 'Maracanazo'. However, the build-up to 2014 was marred by a succession of problems. Stadium construction was plagued by cost overruns, delays and accidents, with eight workers dying while building the tournament's twelve arenas. Despite these tragic deaths we should see this in the context that construction is a dangerous industry, and that

Table 3. Attendances at World Cup Finals matches.

Year	Matches	Total attendance	Average attendance
1930	18	590,549	32,808
1934	17	363,000	21,353
1938	18	375,700	20,872
1950	22	1045,246	47,511
1954	26	768,607	29,562
1958	35	819,810	23,423
1962	32	893,172	27,912
1966	32	1,563,135	48,848
1970	32	1,603,975	50,124
1974	38	1,865,753	49,099
1978	38	1,545,791	40,679
1982	52	2,109,723	40,572
1986	52	2,394,031	46,039
1990	52	2,516,215	48,389
1994	52	3,587,538	68,991
1998	64	2,785,100	43,517
2002	64	2,705,197	42,269
2006	64	3,359,439	52,491
2010	64	3,178,856	49,670
2014	64	3,429,873	53,592

Source: FIFA, 2014a, 'FIFA World Cup Tournament Statistics', http://www.fifa.com/worldfootball/statisticsandrecords/tournaments/worldcup/organisation/.

there will no doubt have been deaths in the construction of stadia for all the World Cups. There were also accusations of corruption regarding some of the construction projects. In March 2012, amid growing allegations, Ricardo Teixeira, head of the organizing committee for the 2014 World Cup in Brazil, resigned his positions as head of Brazil's Football Confederation (CBF) and from FIFA's 24-person Executive Committee, and moved to Miami for unspecified 'health reasons' (Radnedge 2014). Prior to the opening ceremony of the 2013 FIFA Confederations Cup staged in Brazil, crowds demonstrated in part about the amount of public money being spent on hosting the World Cup. Both the Brazilian president Dilma Rousseff and FIFA president Sepp Blatter were heavily booed as they were announced to give their speeches at the 2013 tournament's opening, which resulted in FIFA announcing that the 2014 FIFA World Cup opening ceremony would not feature any speeches. Further significant protests took place during the Confederations Cup (Winters and Weitz-Shapiro 2014).

There was therefore trepidation in Brazil in the months before the tournament, principally regarding potential protests. There were still some construction problems in and around the stadiums, such as an unstable makeshift staircase at the Maracana Stadium, a monorail collapse, and the collapse of an unfinished overpass in Belo Horizonte. The houses of thousands of families in Rio de Janeiro were cleared for redevelopments for the World Cup in spite of protests and resistance. Favela do Metro, near the Maracana Stadium, was completely destroyed as a result, having housed 700 families in 2010 (Gibson and Watts 2013). Protestors argued that the money spent on the World Cup would be better spent on welfare and education, whereas a *Washington Post* analysis showed how little the expenditure actually was in relation to this (von Vacano and Silva 2014).

However, while there were protests just before the tournament and as it began, with violent clashes with police, these were fairly minimal (CNN Staff 2014). Some potential protestors were detained before the final, but despite the perhaps heavy-handed nature of this, there clearly wasn't an appetite for mass protests. The protest of 2014 – and more particularly 2013 – should in any case not be seen as a negative for Brazil. It shows that Brazil is a democracy; people were free to protest against the cost of the World Cup. But the protests were about much wider issues. To an extent, the Confederations Cup and World Cup were a catalyst for protests, with the eyes of the world on Brazil. There were other problems in the build-up and during the tournament, such as the high cost of tickets, that too many tickets were going to sponsors, that some seats were empty for games. It was also noted that those in the stadiums – particularly for Brazil's matches – were largely white, in such a multi-ethnic society. The deaths of construction workers before the tournament began remained an issue, in part because of a campaign by the families through a global online petition to have this marked (Barton 2014).

However, if we take an historical perspective, the 2014 FIFA World Cup in Brazil is one of the *least* controversial tournaments in the history of the competition. This is not to play down the controversies in the build-up and during the 2014 tournament. But if we examine the past World Cups in terms of the selection of the hosts, the qualification process and the finals tournament, the political scandals and controversies at many if not most surpass 2014. This does not relate to controversies on the pitch, which are part and parcel of the game, such as dismissals, dives, and wrongly disallowed goals; or controversies relating to players off the pitch, such as bans for drug-taking. Despite FIFA's best efforts, every World Cup has had these, and will continue to do so. For example, how could Suarez's bite have been prevented? The increasing professionalization and organization of the competition has prevented some of these issues from reoccurring. It is unthinkable now, for example, that a World Cup Final would see a different ball used in each half, because the teams could not agree on which one to use, but this happened in 1930, with an Argentinian ball used in the first half and a Uruguayan in the second (Spurling 2010). Both balls are now on display at the National Football Museum for England. At the 2010 World Cup, because of the lack of goal line technology England had a goal disallowed against Germany, when it was clearly about a metre over the line. In the future, this event will no doubt seem as laughable as the two different balls in the 1930 final does to us now.

Beyond the inevitable controversies relating directly to the game, there is a long history of *political* controversy relating to the competition. An argument can be made that due to FIFA's increasingly successful political management, these controversies have significantly *decreased* over time. FIFA still creates its own political problems, as in the awards of the World Cups in 2018 and 2022. But other political controversies are the result of wider global events, and so FIFA cannot always control them. While there have been a plethora of publications on the history of the World Cup by journalists and academics, there has been no comparative study of the politics of the tournament. Yet, political controversy can be found throughout its history. In broad terms this can be categorized as being caused by: war; states refusing to play each other for political reasons; qualification by countries not diplomatically recognized by the hosts; ethnic tensions within states; states splitting; and civil wars. These will be explored through a chronological analysis.

Uruguay seemed a natural choice to host the first World Cup Finals in 1930, as the highly convincing winners of the Olympic football tournaments in 1924 and 1928 and with the country due to celebrate the centenary of its independence in 1930. However, the cost and time needed to send a team by ship from Europe meant that only five European teams were convinced by Jules Rimet to take part, despite Uruguay offering to contribute to travel expenses. In an attempt to gain some European participation, the Uruguayan Football Association sent a letter of invitation to the Football Association (FA), even though the British Home Nations were not members of FIFA at the time, but this was rejected (Anon 2009; Lanfranchi et al. 2004). As a result, the tournament had only 13 participants out of a possible 16. In the first example of national ethnic conflicts impacting on participation, there were doubts about the participation of Yugoslavia at first. The Croatians decided to boycott the national team and as a result the Yugoslavian team was exclusively made up of Serbian players. The Uruguayans built a new stadium to host the major matches in the tournament, the 90,000-capacity Estadio Centenari. It was the largest football stadium outside the British Isles at the time. However, in a major embarrassment for the organizers, it was not ready for use until five days into the tournament, and thus the first two matches had to be moved to a smaller stadium in Montevideo (Glanville 2011; Goldblatt 2007).

There is no doubt that Mussolini was determined to secure the 1934 World Cup Finals for Italy for propaganda purposes. But to what lengths his regime went is unclear. It is simple but inaccurate psychology to assume that because Mussolini was an evil dictator then therefore he *must* have fixed the tournament. Before the 1938 finals, Mussolini sent a telegram to the Italian team which read 'Vincere o morire!' – 'Win or die!' However, this was not a literal threat, but instead an encouragement to win (Mehrotra 2014). To an extent all host nations manipulate the tournament as far as possible in their favour. Mussolini clearly expected victory, as he commissioned a second winner's trophy, the 'Coppa Del Duce', which was six times taller than the Jules Rimet trophy (Spurling 2010). But what can we say with any confidence about Mussolini's manipulation?

There may have been undue influence in the host selection process. After a lengthy decision-making process in which FIFA's executive committee met eight times, Italy was chosen as the host nation at a meeting in Stockholm in October 1932. The decision was taken by the executive committee without a ballot of members. The Italian bid was chosen in preference to one from Sweden, possibly because Italy assigned a budget of 3.5 million lire to the tournament (Goldblatt 2007). The most significant factor in host selection is therefore that FIFA was happy to award the tournament to a fascist dictatorship, over a bid from a democracy. The tournament was significantly devalued when Uruguay, the champions from 1930, still apparently upset about the poor European attendance at its World Cup in 1930, boycotted. But this would work in Italy's favour, with the favourites not participating. The Italians bent the rules by using several 'oriundi', South Americans of Italian ancestry. Since they were eligible for military service, the Italian coach Pozzo's logic was 'if they can die for Italy, they can play for Italy', although when Italy entered the war in 1940 some of the oriundi were caught trying to get across the border to neutral Switzerland (Mehrotra 2014; Spurling 2010). Italy had to qualify for the finals – the only hosts in World Cup history compelled to do so. Italy had to play Greece over two legs, home and away. The Italians won the home leg 4–0. The Greeks, who had already sold 20,000 tickets for the return leg in Athens, suddenly withdrew from the competition. The Italians were spared an awkward and lengthy trip to Athens a month before the tournament, and were able to focus on preparing for it at home. According to FIFA's website, the Greek team withdrew because they were 'discouraged by the heavy loss', but there is evidence that the Greeks were incentivised by the Italians to withdraw. All the gate receipts would have been kept by the federation hosting the game, so abandoning it would have been a major financial blow for the Greeks, especially after the expense of sending a team to Italy for the first leg. It was alleged that the Italian FA compensated the Greek FA by buying it a new headquarters building in Athens, and that key figures and players in Greek football were paid for their silence (Katwala 2014).

During the final tournament itself, there is circumstantial evidence that Mussolini interfered, particularly as regards the referees. Certainly the referees seemed to very strongly favour Italy, in wins over Spain and Austria. The referee for the final was Ivan Eklind, who had refereed Italy's semi-final against Austria, and one of his linesmen was Louis Blaert, who had taken control of Italy's match against Spain. It is widely understood that the refereeing appointments were now being made by Mussolini himself and that Eklind dined with Mussolini the night before the final. Certainly the referee favoured Italy in the final, as they beat Czechoslovakia (Spurling 2010; Mehatra 2014).

Football politics and wider international politics overshadowed the 1938 World Cup. France was chosen as host ahead of Argentina and Germany. When FIFA chose that the tournament was to be held in Europe, rather than rotating back to South America, Uruguay and Argentina again boycotted, though there were protest riots at the failure to send a team outside the headquarters of the Argentina Football Association in Buenos Aires (Delaney 1965). Following a play-off match against Latvia, Austria had officially qualified for the finals, as had Germany, but because of the Anschluss (the annexation of Austria by Nazi Germany in March 1938), the Austrian national team withdrew, with some Austrian players being added to the German squad. Austria's place was not offered to Latvia but to England, but the FA declined, which left the Finals one nation short, with 15 competing. Spain became the first country to be prevented from competing due to its civil war. Germany went out after losing 2–4 to Switzerland. This loss, which took place in front of a hostile, bottle-throwing crowd in Paris, was blamed by German coach Sepp Herberger on a defeatist attitude by the five Austrian players he had been forced to include. A German journalist later commented that 'Germans and Austrians prefer to play against each other even when they're in the same team' (Hesse-Lichtenberger 2003, 85).

The ultimate political interruption to the FIFA World Cup then occurred – the Second World War. Germany applied to host the 1942 FIFA World Cup at the 23rd FIFA Congress in August 1936 in Berlin. In June 1939, Brazil also applied to host the tournament. However, after the beginning of the war, further plans for the 1942 tournament were cancelled, before a host country was selected. The Italian Vice-President of FIFA hid the Jules Rimet trophy in a shoe-box under his bed throughout the Second World War (Atherton 2008).

During the War, FIFA struggled to keep itself afloat, and it had no financial or personnel resources with which to plan the next tournament. When the War ended in 1945, it was clear that there could not be a World Cup in line with the existing four-year schedule in 1946. In fact, FIFA's first meeting was on July 1, 1946 – around the time the 1946 World Cup would ordinarily have been played – and when it planned the next World Cup for 1949 no country, in this period of post-war austerity and rebuilding, was prepared to host it. Brazil presented a bid at the 1946 FIFA Congress, offering to host the event on condition that the tournament would take place in 1950, rather than 1949, and this was accepted (Fabian and Green 1960).

Initial signs for the 1950 tournament were very positive. The four British nations had re-joined FIFA in 1946 and would therefore be competing in qualification for the first time. The tournament also saw the return of 1930 champions Uruguay, who had boycotted the previous two World Cups. However, Germany (still occupied and partitioned) and Japan (still occupied) were not permitted to enter for qualification. The French-occupied Saarland had been accepted by FIFA two weeks before the World Cup, several months before the German Football Association (DFB) was reinstated, while Soviet-occupied East Germany had not yet founded a football association. Italy, Austria, and other countries involved in the Second World War as allies of Germany, were not subject to international sanctions. However, a number of teams refused to participate in the qualifying tournament, including most nations behind the Iron Curtain, such as the Soviet Union, 1938 finalists Hungary and 1934 finalists Czechoslovakia (Lisi 2007).

Before the qualification competition, George Graham, chairman of the Scottish Football Association (SFA), said that Scotland would only travel to Brazil as winners of the Home Championship, the annual tournament between England, Scotland, Wales and Northern Ireland. England, by contrast, had committed to attending, even if they finished in second place. After Scotland ended up in second place behind England, Scotland withdrew from the tournament (Fabian and Green 1960). Turkey also withdrew, citing financial problems and the cost of travelling to South America. Peru also withdrew at the last minute, due to a dispute with FIFA and CONMEBOL. FIFA invited the United States, Portugal and France, which had been eliminated in qualifying, to fill the gaps left by Peru, Scotland and Turkey. Portugal refused, but France initially accepted, and was entered into the draw. After the draw, the All India Football Federation decided against going to the World Cup, citing travel costs (although FIFA had agreed to bear a major part of the travel expenses), lack of practice time, team selection issues and valuing the Olympics over the World Cup. Although

FIFA had imposed a rule banning barefoot play following the 1948 Olympics, where India had played barefoot, it appears to be a myth that India withdrew from the 1950 World Cup because of this. France also withdrew, citing the amount of travel that would be required in their group in Brazil. There was not enough time to invite further replacement teams or to reorganize the groups, so the tournament featured only thirteen teams, with just two nations in one group. So Brazil's triumph in 1950 has to be seen in the context of a much reduced tournament in terms of the number and quality of the teams competing.

Switzerland was awarded the 1954 tournament unopposed in July 1946, at the same time that Brazil was selected for the 1950 World Cup. Switzerland had the economic and political advantage over most countries in Europe in that it had been neutral in the Second World War. The tournament was dogged by much fewer problems than 1950. German teams were allowed to qualify again, after having been banned from the 1950 FIFA World Cup. West Germany qualified against fellow Germans from the Saarland (which was still then a French protectorate). Argentina declined to participate for the third World Cup in succession. Teams from the Soviet Bloc, most notably Hungary, agreed to take part. However, East Germany had not entered, cancelling international football games after the East German uprising of 1953.

Argentina, Chile, Mexico and Sweden expressed interest in hosting the 1958 tournament, but Sweden was awarded this unopposed in 1950. This World Cup saw the entry and qualification of the Soviet Union for the first time, but international politics again marred the qualification process. Israel won its group by default because its three opponents, Turkey, Indonesia and Sudan, refused to play. As FIFA had imposed a rule that no team would qualify without playing at least one match, Wales, which had failed to qualify after finishing second in its group behind Czechoslovakia, was drawn into a play-off with Israel. Wales won the play-off against Israel and qualified (Fabian and Green 1960).

After Europe hosted two consecutive World Cups, the South Americans claimed that the 1962 tournament must be held in the continent or face a complete boycott, similar to 1938. Argentina, after previously failed candidacies, was the favourite, but Chile also expressed interest. It has been suggested that FIFA did not want Argentina to run alone, requesting the participation of Chile as almost symbolic. Chile registered its candidacy in 1954 alongside Argentina and West Germany, the latter withdrawing at the request of FIFA. Argentina had the infrastructure in place, Chile had not, but Chile invoked Article 2 of the FIFA statutes that addressed the tournament's role in promoting the sport in countries deemed 'underdeveloped'. Chile won 32 votes to Argentina's 11, with 13 members abstaining from voting (FIFA 2014b). In May 1960, as the preparations were well under way, Chile suffered the largest earthquake ever recorded (9.5 magnitude), which caused enormous damage. With over 50,000 casualties and more than 2 million people affected, the earthquake forced the organizing committee to completely modify the World Cup's calendar. Originally, eight stadiums were selected to host the World Cup matches in eight different cities. Four were severely damaged and discarded as venues and a further two cities declined to host any matches as their venues were not financially self-sustainable. Four stadiums in four cities were finally available with two rather sub-standard existing stadiums brought into use (Glanville 2011).

England was chosen as the host of the 1966 World Cup in Rome in 1960, ahead of West Germany and Spain. While in England the tournament is remembered nostalgically as the country's only World Cup triumph, it is much less fondly recalled in many other countries.

The tournament was marred by the biggest withdrawal to date. Sixteen African nations boycotted in protest at a 1964 FIFA ruling that required the three second-round winners from the African zone to enter a play-off round against the winners of the Asian zone in order to win a place at the finals. The Africans felt that winning their zone was enough in itself to merit qualification for the finals (FIFA 2007, 2013). The qualification of North Korea was a further problem. The UK Government considered refusing to grant visas to the team as a means of solving the diplomatic problem. Britain did not officially recognize North Korea – officially known as the Democratic People's Republic of Korea – and officials worried that allowing the country to attend would cause diplomatic shock waves, particularly with South Korea. A Foreign Office memo written in the months before the World Cup stated:

> The simplest way to solve the problem might be to refuse visas to the North Korean team. But if we do this the consequences could be very serious. Apparently FIFA has made it very plain to the FA that if any team that has won its way through to the finals is denied visas then the finals will take place elsewhere. This would be a disaster for the FA. You can imagine what the papers would make of this. We would be accused of dragging politics into sport, sabotaging British interests and so on. (Anon 2010).

The Foreign Office also envisaged problems arising if it imposed restrictions on the North Koreans during the tournament. Another memo explains: 'The North Koreans will probably object very strongly if they are prevented from playing their National anthem, displaying their National flag etc., when the other 15 countries taking part in the finals are all permitted to do so.'(Anon 2010). It was decided to allow the North Korean flag to be flown at all matches alongside the flags of other competitors, but national anthems would only be played for the two teams playing in the opening game and the two teams at the final. The Government insisted that the state be referred to as North Korea (Anon 2010). North Korea's presence passed without major incident, the team performed heroically to beat Italy and qualify from its group, losing 5–3 to Portugal in the quarter finals, after leading 3–0, and they were very much taken to the hearts of the English crowds.

The biggest controversy of the finals tournament itself was not England's controversial third goal in the final, but when Argentina's Antonio Rattin became the first player to be sent off in a senior international football match at Wembley. He at first refused to leave the field and eventually had to be escorted off by several policemen. After 30 minutes, England scored the only goal of the match. This game is called 'el robo del siglo' (the robbery of the century) in Argentina. This dismissal appears to have been very harsh – he was sent off for 'violence of the tongue', despite the referee speaking no Spanish. The Argentinian team were welcomed as heroes on their return home (Goldblatt 2007). The treatment of South American teams in the tournament has led to accusations, most notably by former FIFA President Joao Havelange, that the 1966 World cup was fixed for England to win – and that 1974 was fixed for West Germany to win (Ladyman 2008). While the evidence for such a claim does not stack up, the English in 1966 did act in a high-handed, quasi-imperialist manner. The referee for the England v. Argentina game was a German, while the official in Germany's quarter final win over Uruguay was English. The England manager Alf Ramsey described the Argentinians after the game as 'animals'. The West Germany v. Uruguay match had a British referee and two Uruguayans were sent off. In the three matches that the Brazilian national team played in 1966, of the three referees and six linesmen, seven were British and two were Germans. The English left themselves open to the perception that they had shown bias against South America, when the President of FIFA was the Englishman, Sir Stanley Rous.

Strong anti-British feeling was demonstrated all over South America. A confidential letter sent to eighteen British embassies in South and Central American countries on 12 August 1966 stated:

> There is no need for me to tell you (indeed some of you have already told us) that we have had an extremely bad press in some countries over the World Cup, mainly, we believe, in Latin America but also in other parts of the world, including Italy. Many accusations have been levelled against the organisers of the competition, and the fact that Sir Stanley Rous, the President of FIFA, is British and that the finals were held in England, has meant that Britain as a whole and not merely FIFA has incurred a good deal of odium ... We have come round to the conclusion, expressed to us forcibly by H.M. Ambassador in Buenos Aires (where the furore has been greatest) that the wisest course is just to sit quiet and let the storm blow itself out. (National Archives 2014).

A letter from the British Embassy in Uruguay to the Foreign Office stated:

> 27 July 1966
>
> La Copa Mondial or The Twist in Willie's Tale
>
> The Residence, Chancery and Consulate were now bombarded by anonymous telephone calls, often of an extremely abusive nature, asking, among other things, how much we had paid the German referee. There have been about 300 calls in all. Groups gathered outside the residence (empty except for the servants), pulled the street-bell out of its socket and threatened the servants ... It would be comforting to say that the only moral of the story is, never let a South American team lose a football game. But unfortunately the net result has been to raise doubts in the minds of many normally friendly people as to whether the traditional British 'fair play' really exists now. (National Archives 2014).

International politics – and even a war – marred the qualification and the finals of the 1970 World Cup. Mexico was chosen as the host nation for 1970 in 1964, ahead of the only other submitted bid from Argentina. North Korea, quarter-finalists at the previous tournament, were disqualified after refusing to play in Israel for political reasons (Glanville 2011). El Salvador qualified for the finals after beating Honduras in a play-off match, which was the catalyst for a four-day conflict in July 1969 known as the Football War, in which over 5,000 people were killed (Kapuscinski 1990). The qualification of Israel caused a major political problem for FIFA. Although it was reported in the build-up to the draw for the groups in the finals tournament that seedings would be used, as had been the case at the previous two World Cup Finals, the FIFA Organizing Committee ultimately announced that there would be no seeding of teams. Instead the sixteen teams were divided into four 'geographical groupings', which also took into account the teams' strengths and even political consider-ations. This convoluted system ensured that Israel and Morocco would not be drawn to face each other, after Morocco had earlier threatened to withdraw from the tournament, just as they had done from the Olympic football tournament two years earlier, if that were the case (FIFA 2010).

West Germany was chosen as the host nation for the 1974 World Cup by FIFA in London in July 1966. Hosting rights were awarded to Argentina in 1978 and Spain in 1982 at the same time. Qualification for the 1974 World Cup was again marred by a major controversy, in the 1973 play-off between the Soviet Union and Chile. Following a 0–0 draw in the first leg in Moscow, the second leg was scheduled to take place in the Estadio Nacional de Chile in Santiago, the Chilean capital. There had been a *coup d'état* in Chile two months before, immediately after which people deemed undesirable to the new regime of Augusto Pinochet had been held captive and even executed in the stadium. The Soviet Union asked

FIFA to find a different venue in Chile. When agreement could not be reached, the Soviet team did not attend and was disqualified from the tournament, giving the Chilean team a victory by walk-over and a place at the 1974 World Cup Finals. In a piece of propaganda, the match 'went ahead' with the Chilean team passing the ball into the net in the absence of the Soviet players (Goldblatt 2007).

Zaire was the first sub-Saharan African team to participate in a FIFA World Cup Finals, but the team participated in fear of the reaction of the country's dictator Mobuto should they fail. After Zaire had lost 2–0 to Scotland and 9–0 to Yugoslavia (still a World Cup Finals record), Mobuto sent them a message: 'You're scum and sons of whores. ... if you concede more than three against Brazil in the final match, you will never see Zaire or your families again' (Spurling 2010, 28). With Brazil leading 2–0, the Brazilian free-kick specialist Rivelino was ready to take a kick from just outside the penalty area, when the Zaire player Ilunga came out of the defensive wall and kicked the ball away, before the referee blew his whistle. At the time British journalists and commentators put this down to 'naivety', with more than a hint of racism in their reaction. In reality, Ilunga kicked the ball away in fear of going 3–0 down with so much time left in the match. Zaire lost only 3–0, but Mobuto saw to it that their careers were ruined on their return home (Spurling 2010).

Argentina had a military coup in June 1966, so it was not a democracy when it was chosen as the host for 1978. The country remained politically unstable until a further military coup in 1976. Under this murderous new regime, thousands of people were imprisoned, killed, or simply 'disappeared'. Because of the political turmoil, some countries, most notably the Netherlands, considered publicly whether they should participate in the event. Despite this, all teams eventually took part without restrictions. Allegations that Dutch star Johan Cruyff refused to participate because of political convictions were denied by him 30 years later, but it appears that West Germany's Paul Breitner did withdraw for political reasons (Keeley 2008; Spurling 2010). Controversially, all Argentina's games in the first round kicked off at night, giving the Argentines the advantage of knowing where they stood in the group.

Further accusations surround the game Argentina and Peru played in the second round of the tournament. Argentina needed to win by a margin of four goals to proceed to the final and did so by defeating Peru 6–0. However, claims that the Argentine military dictatorship interfered to ensure Argentina won were denied by the Peruvian captain and several Peruvian players. Some accusations originated in the Brazilian media and pointed to the fact that the Peruvian goalkeeper had been born in Argentina. There is also an alleged deal, reported by the British media, which involved the delivery of a large grain shipment to Peru by Argentina and the unfreezing of a Peruvian bank account that was held by the Argentine Central Bank (Kuper 1996). When Argentina won the final, political prisoners were let out for the evening by their guards to celebrate: 'But if you try to run we'll put a bullet in you. With all the fireworks no one will notice' (Spurling 2010, 64).

Spain was under the dictatorship of Franco when it was awarded the host status for the 1982 World Cup in 1966. It only moved back to democracy in 1977. A war overshadowed the 1982 finals in Spain. There was some consideration given by the British Government as to whether England, Northern Ireland and Scotland should withdraw from the tournament due to the Falklands War between Argentina and the UK, which was between 2 April and 24 June 1982. The World Cup Finals was held from 13 June to 11 July. A directive issued by the British Sports Minister Neil Macfarlane in April, at the start of the conflict, suggested that there should be no contact between British representative teams and Argentina. This directive was not rescinded until August, following the end of hostilities. Macfarlane reported to Prime Minister Margaret Thatcher that some players and officials were uneasy about participating due to the casualties being suffered by British forces. FIFA advised the British Government that there was no prospect of Argentina (the defending champions) being asked to withdraw. It also became apparent that no other countries would withdraw from the tournament. It was decided to allow the British national teams to participate because withdrawal could have been used for propaganda purposes by Argentina (BBC 2012).

The 1986 World Cup was marred by perhaps the ultimate problem – the withdrawal of the host country. Colombia was chosen as host for the 1986 World Cup Finals by FIFA in June 1974. However, the Colombian authorities announced in November 1982 that they could not afford to host the World Cup under the terms that FIFA demanded because of political and financial turmoil and the emergence of powerful and ruthless drug cartels (Ogden 2014). The United States, Canada, Brazil and Mexico all offered themselves as replacements for Colombia, but the decision was ultimately between the Americans and Mexicans, who had hosted the tournament as recently as 1970. The Americans, backed by Pele and Franz Beckenbauer, appeared to have the most influential support, but FIFA president Joao Havelange, apparently angered by the North American Soccer League's refusal to abandon gimmicks such as penalty shoot-outs for drawn games and a 35-yard offside line, pushed for Mexico. FIFA and Havelange were also made aware of a potential South American boycott of the tournament should it be handed to the United States, given the long-standing political distrust of the USA in Latin and South America. It is claimed that it ultimately came down to money and the opportunity for FIFA to make substantial financial gains by awarding the tournament to Mexico. Guillermo Caneda, the head of Mexican media giant Televisa, was a FIFA Vice-President and was apparently able to persuade Havelange that his commercial blueprint – including the inflated sale of television rights to European broadcasters – would transform FIFA's finances. Mexico's staging of the tournament just 16 years previously was conveniently overlooked (Ogden 2014). FIFA stated that 'A special Committee entrusted with examining the bidding file and making a confidential report gave the recommendation to assign the 1986 FIFA World Cup to Mexico which was unanimously approved' (FIFA 2014b).

In 1984, the FIFA Executive Committee chose Italy ahead of the only rival bidder, the USSR, to host the 1990 World Cup Finals, by 11 votes to 5. The Soviet boycott of the 1984 Olympic Games, announced on the eve of the World Cup decision, was speculated to have been a major factor behind Italy winning the vote so decisively, although this was denied by FIFA. The USA was chosen as the host for 1994 by FIFA in July 1988. Again, international politics marred the qualification process. The nation of Czechoslovakia dissolved in 1992, and the team completed its qualifying group under the name 'Representation of Czechs and Slovaks', but failed to qualify for the finals. Yugoslavia was suspended from international competition in 1992 as part of the United Nations' sanctions against the country as a result of the wars in the break-up of Yugoslavia. The sanctions were not lifted until 1994, by which time it was no longer possible for the team to qualify.

However, the selection of developed nations for the tournaments in 1990 and 1994 meant that the finals themselves were free from any major organizational issues. The tournaments in France (1998), Japan and South Korea (2002) and Germany (2006) were relatively free from controversy in the process of the selection of host nation, qualification and the finals tournament. Having pushed hard for the selection of South Africa in 2006, FIFA was accused of fixing its selection for 2010. As part of a short-lived policy, abandoned in 2007, to rotate the event among the football confederations, only African nations could bid to host, and having come so close for 2006, there was little question South Africa would be selected for 2010. During 2006 and 2007, rumours circulated in the international media that the 2010 World Cup could be moved to another country, due to concern over preparations, but ultimately these concerns proved to be groundless.

Seen from this historical perspective, the controversies of the 2014 World Cup were relatively minor. What would today's global media have made, for example, of the World Cups in Italy in 1934 or Argentina in 1978? The 2014 tournament was not a dream for Brazil. It did not win, and expunge the memory of 1950, and Brazil has a new footballing humiliation to replace that of 1950 – the 7–1 defeat to Germany. So in *football* terms Brazil has a second Maracanazo, though at least Brazil's great football rival Argentina did not win the tournament. But in every other sense, the 2014 was not the nightmare that was feared in advance, with no major issues with infrastructure, and no significant protests. The tournament was viewed internationally as a success. But what impact the finals had within Brazil is harder to tell. Football may not be that important, even in Brazil. After the Confederations Cup of 2013, FIFA must have been fearful of 2014, but surely emerged stronger as a result of the success of the tournament. Having carefully stage-managed the politics of the World Cup from 1990 to 2014, FIFA has brought on itself the problems of 2018 and 2022. However, the success of the 2014 World Cup may enable FIFA to ride out the continuing controversy of the process of the award of the 2018 and 2022 tournaments. After 2014 for Brazil, and especially for Rio de Janeiro, a bigger challenge lay ahead – the 2016 Olympics and Paralympics.

This paper has shown just how different in scale and scope a World Cup is today compared to that of 1930, which makes comparisons difficult. But, that the discontinuity is greater than the continuity is fundamental to our understanding of World Cup history. It has been beyond the bounds of this study to consider the changing meaning of hosting the FIFA World Cup for national football associations and nation states. Their motivations to act as hosts are worthy of further study. The changing meaning and significance of the World Cup to FIFA itself also needs to be considered further. FIFA's fortunes as an organization are now inextricably linked with the tournament, as it is economically and politically reliant on its success. As I have tried to show, politics has been inextricably linked with the World Cup since its inception, but its rapidly increased commercialization adds a very significant further dimension. The World Cup is now a global political, commercial and cultural event. Managing these sometimes competing demands is becoming increasingly challenging for both FIFA and host nations. Ultimately, Brazil and FIFA managed these challenges relatively successfully in 2014. The 2018 and 2022 tournaments already offer a new set of challenges.

Disclosure statement

No potential conflict of interest was reported by the author.

References

Anon. 2009. "Uruguay 1930." *FourFourTwo.Com*. http://web.archive.org/web/20070819173027/http://www.fourfourtwo.premiumtv.co.uk/page/BigRead/0,11442~1034860,00.html.

Anon. 2010. "World Cup: 'Political Headache' of North Korea in 1966." http://www.telegraph.co.uk/sport/football/world-cup/7825219/World-Cup-Political-headache-of-North-Korea-in-1966.html.

Atherton, M. 2008. *The Theft of the Jules Rimet Trophy: The Hidden History of the 1966 World Cup in England*. Aachen: Meyer and Meyer.

Baade, R., and V. Matheson. 2004. "The Quest for the Cup: Assessing the Economic Impact of the World Cup." *Regional Studies* 38 (4): 343–354.

Barton, A. 2014. "50,000 Signatures for FIFA Memorial Petition." http://www.touchlinetalk.com/50000-signatures-fifa-memorial-petition/95379.

BBC. 2012. "World Cup Withdrawal Considered amid Falklands War." http://www.bbc.co.uk/news/uk-20856004.

BBC. 2014. "World Cup 2014: Brazil is Greatest Tournament in BBC Vote." http://www.bbc.co.uk/sport/0/football/28268842.

Campbell, W. 2011. "'Too Early to Say': Zhou Was Speaking about 1968, Not 1789." https://mediamythalert.wordpress.com/2011/06/14/.

CNN Staff. 2014. "Brazilian Police Fire Tear Gas at World Cup Protesters." http://edition.cnn.com/2014/06/12/world/americas/brazil-world-cup-protests/.

Collett, M. 2014. "Blatter Gives World Cup 9.25 out of 10." http://uk.reuters.com/article/2014/07/14/uk-soccer-world-blatter.

Delaney, T. 1965. *A Century of Soccer*. London: The Sportsmans Book Club.

Fabian, A., and G. Green. 1960. *Association Football*. Vol. 4. London: Caxton.

FIFA. 2006. "FIFA World Cup Qualifiers in a Nutshell." http://www.fifa.com/mm/document/fifafacts/mcwc/ip-301_11a_fwc-prelstats_8828.pdf.

FIFA. 2007. "History of the FIFA World Cup Preliminary Competition." http://www.fifa.com/mm/document/fifafacts/mcwc/ipfwc_preliminaryhistory(byyear)_36285.pdf.

FIFA. 2010. "World Cup Seeded Teams." FIFA Fact Sheet. http://www.fifa.com/mm/document/fifafacts/mencompwc/82/40/89/fs-201_12a_fwc-seeding.pdf.

FIFA. 2013. "Recap of the FIFA World Cup Preliminary Competitions 1930–2014, Statistical Kit". http://www.fifa.com/mm/document/fifafacts/mencompwc/51/97/68/2014fwc_kit_recap_fwc_prel_neutral.pdf.

FIFA. 2014a. "FIFA World Cup Tournament Statistics." http://www.fifa.com/worldfootball/statisticsandrecords/tournaments/worldcup/organisation/.

FIFA. 2014b. "FIFA World Cup Host Announcement Decision." http://www.fifa.com/mm/document/fifafacts/mencompwc/51/97/81/fs-201_13a_fwc-bidding.pdf.

Frawley, S., and D. Adair, eds. 2014. *Managing the Football World Cup*. London: Palgrave MacMillan.

Gibson, O. and J. Watts. 2013. "World Cup: Rio Favelas Being 'Socially Cleansed' in Run up to Sporting Events." http://www.theguardian.com/world/2013/dec/05/world-cup-favelas-socially-cleansed-olympics.

Glanville, B. 2011. *The Story of the World Cup*. London: Faber and Faber.

Goldblatt, D. 2007. *The Ball is Round: A Global History of Soccer*. London: Penguin.

Hesse-Lichtenberger, U. 2003. *Tor! the Story of German Football*. London: WSC Books.

Kapuscinski, R. 1990. *The Soccer War*. London: Granta Books.

Katwala, A. 2014. "World Cup 1934: Did Italy Fix a World Cup Qualifier?" http://talksport.com/football/world-cup-1934.

Keeley, G. 2008. "After 30 Years, the Truth behind Cruyff's World Cup Absence." http://www.theguardian.com/football/2008/apr/17/newsstory.sport.

Kuper, Simon. 1996. *Football against the Enemy*. London: Phoenix.

Ladyman, B. 2008. "England's World Cup '66 Win Was Fixed by Referees, Claims Ex-FIFA President Havelange." Accessed June 27, 2008. http://www.dailymail.co.uk/sport/football/article-1029687/Englands-World-Cup-66-win-fixed-referees-claims-ex-FIFA-president.html#ixzz3UkuQRSyb

Lanfranchi, P., C. Eisenberg, T. Mason, and A. Wahl. 2004. *100 Years of Football: The FIFA Centennial Book*. London: Wiedenfeld and Nicolson.

Lee, C., and T. Taylor. 2005. "Critical Reflections on the Economic Impact Assessment of a Mega-Event: The Case of 2002 FIFA World Cup." *Tourism Management* 26 (4): 595–603.

Lisi, C. 2007. *A History of the World Cup: 1930–2006*. Lanham, MD: Scarecrow Press.

Matheson, V. 2014. "Were the Billions Brazil Spent on World Cup Stadiums worth It?" http://fivethirtyeight.com/features/were-the-billions-brazil-spent-on-world-cup-stadiums-worth-it/.

McOwan. 2011. "Disarming, Friendly and a Football Sage – Socrates Was the Real Deal." http://www.theguardian.com/football/blog/2011/dec/04/socrates-football-sage.

Mehrotra, A. 2014. "Fascism and Football: How Italy Won the 1934 and 1938 World Cup." http://outsideoftheboot.com/2014/05/20/fascism-and-football-how-italy-won-the-1934-and-1938-world-cup/.

Myles, R. 2014. "Largest Ever Flying Bird Had Wingspan as Wide as Soccer Goalmouth." http://www.digitaljournal.com/science/largest-ever-flying-bird-had-wingspan-as-wide-as-soccer-goalmouth/article/388918.

National Archives. 2014. "World Cup 1966. Did England Rig the Result?" http://www.nationalarchives.gov.uk/education/resources/world-cup-1966/.

Ogden, M. 2014. "Shadow of 'World Cup That Never Was' Now Hangs over Qatar after Bribery Fears, Just as It Did Colombia in 1986." http://www.telegraph.co.uk/sport/football/world-cup/10889437/Shadow-of-World-Cup-that-never-was-now-hangs-over-Qatar-after-bribery-fears-just-as-it-did-Colombia-in-1986.html.

Preuss, H. and M. Schnitzer. 2012. "Budgeting the FIFA World Cup. a Benchmark Analysis for the Local Organising Committee Budgets." *Working Paper Series, Mainzer Papers on Sports Economics & Management* 6. Mainz: Johannes Gutenberg-University.

Radnedge, K. 2014. "Ricardo Teixeira: How 25 Years of Absolute Power Came to an End." http://www.worldsoccer.com/columnists/keir-radnedge/ricardo-teixeira-how-25-years-of-absolute-power-came-to-an-end-344414.

Spurling, J. 2010. *Death or Glory. The Dark History of the World Cup.* Surrey: Vision Sports Publishing, Kingston upon Thames.

von Vacano, D., and T. Silva. 2014. "Brazil's Protest Paradox." http://www.washingtonpost.com/blogs/monkey-cage/wp/2014/06/10/brazils-protest-paradox/.

Winters, M., and R. Weitz-Shapiro. 2014. "Partisan Protesters and Nonpartisan Protests in Brazil." *Journal of Politics in Latin America* 6 (1): 137–150.

Reporting the 2014 World Cup: football first and social issues last

Helton Levy

ABSTRACT

Delays and infrastructure problems appeared as key issues in numerous media reports on the preparations for the 2014 World Cup in Brazil. This paper analyses to what extent the media coverage of this period helped to overshadow serious existent social issues, such as poverty and violence, and how this has meant the privilege of FIFA's narratives over these issues. A frame analysis shows that while the FIFA is quoted as a major source of the news on the event, a stereotyped portrait of Brazil has been constantly offered. As far as as protests led by ordinary citizens and social movements have appeared as disruptors of the tournament's safety. This case yet illustrates not only the priority given to commercial interests in the news, but the necessary debate around the media coverage of global events, in which the media are expected to side with international bodies, as local voices remain marginalized.

Introduction

Since the last decade, developing countries such as South Africa, Brazil and Russia have been chosen by the International Federation of Association Football (FIFA) as World Cup hosts. What has been sold as political strategy has actually sought to boost these countries' economy and contribute for the development of these nations (Cornelissen and Swart 2006; Ngonyama 2010). During the preparations for the 2014 World Cup in Brazil, the media in Britain and elsewhere had focused on the readiness of infrastructure projects, while highlighting also on moments of civil unrest in Brazilian metropolises. This essay analyses news articles published since 1.5 years before the World Cup kick-off ($n = 100$), verifying to what extent those reports privileged international organizers' accounts, such as FIFA, and whether this has meant a less socially sensitive approach. Yet, we can also see the extent to which the international media reporting have failed the expectations that Brazil, and to some extent South Africa, had of boosting their global insertion by hosting a World Cup.

It is known that international media discourses can result in powerful representations when relating to foreign countries, given the often impossibility of direct interaction between groups from different countries (Kashima 2013). Barnett and Kim (1996, 324) underline an economic bias of this asymmetry, as news flows between developed and developing regions vary in different proportions. In addition to that, World Cups have historically received a particular problematic coverage by each country's media. Tudor (1992, 393) has identified racial stereotyping from the British TV punditry during the 1990 World Cup. During the 2002 World Cup, media outlets offered distorted the representations which audiences in the US and South Korea received of each country (Lee and Choi 2009; Yang et al. 2008). The 2010 South African edition has been represented as a political achievement and as a development ally, while marginalizing or commoditizing voices from social movements (Cornelissen and Swart 2006; Duvall and Guschwan 2013).

The so-called media events have been nevertheless grounded on the discourse of 'sharing human values'. In the case of the World Cup, a call for fair competition among nations, as a viable idea, has grown stronger after many waves of globalization (Dayan and Katz 2009, 101; Tomlinson and Young 2012). The bureaucratic nature of the international coverage, punctuated by a non-diversified profile of newsroom staff, and the competitive reality of news businesses are factors that can also constrain a more balanced representation of foreign countries. However, on top of that, it is important to clarify subtle news values pursued by the major organizations, which are undoubtedly result of culturally-oriented discourses (Cottle 1999; Hall 1997). It is worth saying that Latin America has been a neglected region in the media, at least judging by the newsworthiness criteria which the British press comes adopting since decades (Aguirre 1985). Still, the international news agenda has rather been negative towards Brazil in specific (Paganotti 2009; Wanta, Golan, and Lee 2004).

In an agenda-setting perspective, the literature shows how many layers of interest make the news agenda, including the competitive relations among media organizations, and the urgency of sources, turning patterns of news coverage into actual concerns of the public (McCombs 2014). The *salience* in the context of the media happens when certain angles are prioritized, and as a result, they can lead to a poor exploration of other important issues, as others remain overexposed. That explains why only considering media portraits as negative or positive is rather a limited approach (Dearing and Rogers 1996). Therefore, studying the salience of some angles or of some sources appears as good path to study how a news agenda is constructed.

Having said that, by adopting some of the agenda-setting concepts, we can situate the coverage of Brazil's 2014 World Cup in the context of developing countries that have sought to capitalize that global coverage in favour of their own geopolitical insertion. They however might have failed to boost local projects that could benefit local populations, and promote social equality (Conchas 2014; Gaffney 2010). Even at times matching the Brazilian mainstream journalism discourse, which has historically pursued a cultural maximization of football (Gastaldo 2014), it is not possible to deny the inclusion of Brazil's social deficits in the news agenda, which included striking scenes of slums, and the constant depiction of poverty. However, I argue that the approach of social issues that could have served to attack the host country's precarity, ultimately served to either detach FIFA's interests from the burden of investment demanded in Brazil, or to represent social issues as if they were at odds with the interests of the football business. In that sense, verifying media discourses allow a better perception on the extent of this hierarchy and the clarification on what the 2014 World Cup really meant in terms of a socially-committed coverage, despite the pressure to comply with commercial agreements and sponsors.

Methods

Frame analysis remains a useful tool to understand to what extent media agents can shape basic ideological senses, acting as ultimate mediators of political power (Entman 2007; Goffman 1974). Studies have used frame analysis to measure the level of plurality of media discourses worldwide (Benson et al. 2009; Gerhards and Schäfer 2010). The diversity of media frames can be considered as indicative of news quality (Porto 2007). The frame built for this paper is first aimed at analysing the possibility of a socially preoccupied discourse amid the news on the World Cup preparations. Examples of social issues have consisted in any type of civil unrest, poverty and urban violence. Secondly, it intends to look at how media discourses situate FIFA's accounts by placing FIFA's versions on top of the local sources, or still, whether has FIFA been detached, engaged or taken into account for those issues. There are questions on how efficient the media's scrutiny can be towards FIFA, taking the case of past World Cups, in which host countries were the only ones led to respond for potential disruptions or risks (Alegi 2008; Cornelissen and Swart 2006). The role of the news media continues appearing as an essential component of global events (Rojek 2013; Wark 1994). Considering that some outlets that are part of the mainstream British press, such as the *Financial Times*, represent the so-called 'global media', one should verify whether the latter is today more an agent to entertain, than one to attend citizens' needs (Hermann and McChesney, 2001, 9).

The sample has been composed of 100 reports randomly chosen from 1.5 years for the tournament kick-off. Articles have been analysed according to their frame of FIFA's statements on World Cup on top of accounts extracted from Brazilian officials, specialists and other local actors. Brazilian authorities or institutions would be thus framed as if they had to fulfil obligations with FIFA, as far as the news coverage of social issues, such as poverty and violence, would be less emphasized. The following checks have also considered how the urgency of underprivileged groups and social movements have been described. The coding strategy has assigned 'yes' or 'no' according to their compliance to the frame. The choice for a straightforward framing filter tries to avoid subjectivity (Van Gorb 2010). A final step was to select parts of this coverage, and then perform a critical discourse analysis (Van Dijk, 1993:252), and check the articulation of text and image as visual resources may also play a role in reinforcing frames of news stories (Coleman 2010). The use of a mix of qualitative and quantitative methods can be beneficial to complement both the analyses (Holsti 1969; Riffe, Lacy, and Fico 2013).

Following the criteria mentioned by McNair (2003, 16), the sample included *The Daily Mirror* (tabloid), *The Guardian* (centre-left), *Telegraph* (Conservative), *BBC* (Public), and the *Financial Times* (newspaper). Only articles specifically related to the preparations for the 2014 World Cup have been selected, including those which have mentioned debates on venues, funding, and opinion pieces. Stories featuring specific actors, such as footballers, or national teams, were not considered. The term 'World Cup Brazil' was used as a keyword in searches performed directly in each outlet's website, collecting data from 1 January 2013 until 11 June 2014, the first day of the World Cup.

The content was retrieved in to a content analysis sheet. The intercoder reliability test involved 20% ($n = 20$) of the sample (Lombard, Snyder-Duch, and Bracken 2002). Cohen's (1968) *kappa* was calculated, achieving a coefficient of 0.714. In order to reinforce this index, Krippendorff's (2007) *alpha* was also calculated, reaching to 0.743. Both indices could be justified by considering the low complexity of the coding procedure as well as by the variety of styles of the publications, as both aspects could lead to different conclusions among

Table 1. Number of articles emphasizing FIFA's accounts.

Outlet	Results
The Guardian	11
Telegraph	10
Financial Times	13
The Mirror	8
BBC	18
Total	60

coders, while still agreeing with the overall result. Indices close to 0.7 should represent a good mark for exploratory research (Lombard, Snyder-Duch, and Bracken 2002), as indices inferior to 0.8 can yet be in accordance with tentative research (Riffe, Lacy, and Fico 2013).

Results

From 100 articles analysed, 60 (60%) articles from the 5 broadsheets in scope were framed as holding FIFA's agenda over social issues. Reports gave a continuous emphasis on the high chances of stadia, or airports not being ready on time or to the non-compliance with FIFA's requirements, while giving little space for the country's accounts. Six months ahead of the event, *The Guardian*'s headline of 16 February 2014 summarized the tone of most reports: 'Brazil's World Cup courts disaster as delays, protests and deaths mount.' (Table 1).

Amid the main British broadsheets, left-wing *The Guardian* did not present any substantial variation in framing Brazil's social reality if compared to the more conservative *Telegraph*. *Telegraph*'s approach was rather less critical on the issue of accountability, which might have happened perhaps because of its focus on entertainment, travel and leisure. BBC's coverage on the other hand offered more articles directly quoting FIFA's versions in the headlines (18). This did not happen in the case of *Daily Mirror*'s approach, which gave a much more personalized tone, while using tabloid language (8). That summary means that no direct link was found between the kind of media business (commercial, financial, public funded) and the priority given to the FIFA in news reports. 40% of the articles did not approach social problems in Brazil at all, and even when they came to approach the problems, those issues appeared parallel to the event, i.e. not reported within World Cup news sections. There was a clear tendency to detach issues that have offered negative impacts over the poor, such as evictions, or those that addressed public concerns with budget constraints from the main reports. Those reports have otherwise covered engineering progresses and the opening of new venues albeit without any reference to their socioeconomic impact.

Discussion

Even not figuring as a high majority in the articles, the frame that points to FIFA's accounts first had been constant in news reports on the World Cup preparations. These accounts were those to generally place FIFA's accounts as the most important sources, and which have generally presented a range of risks to be faced by potential attendees. For example, those stories criticized the high prices for consumers in Brazil, its vast geographic distances,[1] urban violence, and, more importantly, the frequent association of poverty as a threat. Nevertheless, the 2014 World Cup has been considered a marketing success. The event reached record levels of social media audience,[2] and a great acceptance in the United States.[3]

It is not the purpose here to discuss the damage or boost of *Brazil* as an international brand. Yet, other studies have come out to increasingly scrutine media constructions in which the FIFA appeared as the 'owner' of the World Cup, as the burden of the works and investment always stayed with the host country. The event organizer has left generally fortified after the event (Tomlinson 2014). As I understand, the role of an engaged and independent journalism should be one of contesting this supremacy, tackling the consequences of FIFA's entrepreneurial ties, which in this case were only made possible with the use of public funds.[4]

While focused on political communications according to the American context (Dearing and Rogers 1996; Galtung and Ruge 1973; McCombs and Shaw 1972), studies on agenda-setting can enlighten on the reasons why the World Cup build-up has been marked by a narrative of risk, while FIFA appears in a non-scrutinized position. McCombs (2014, 112) argues that an amalgam of factors, including not only the interest from the public, but also the take from other news media groups and organizations, plus the urgency of sources, can affect the first layer of the media agenda, as others remain unexplored. In our case, if a first layer is completely dominated by the unequivocal appeal of the World Cup, the second one is dedicated to provide *salience* of the different risks posed to the event. Reports touched mostly on what could prevent the event from and its organizers from profiting, but rarely dealt with the impact over the host place. Two of these points of *salience* are more than missing parts of the conversation. By looking only at Brazil's responsibilities, the British press has obfuscated the constraints imposed and reinforced stereotypes against the poor, likewise as it criminalized democratic demonstrations. Both issues ended up as efficient shields which prevented further criticism against FIFA, whereas that criticism could have been leveraged on a worldwide basis.

The problem with Brazil

The headline 'Brazil's frantic eleventh hour World Cup preparations' (*BBC News*, May 6, 2014) is an example of the pressure that the media created around Brazilian authorities, as FIFA was portrayed as a creditor. The image of an incompetent host country was repeatedly constructed here but was not, for instance, applied to South Africa (Cornelissen 2006, 120). Wanta et al. (2004, 369) note that the use of known 'attributes' of news actors is enough to boost second layers in the agenda, to which the audience will always refer more easily, increasing the interest for the news. Instead of traditional and impactful agenda-setters, such as unemployment, economics or natural disasters (Dearing and Rogers 1996), we have in reality the possibility of 'disasters' that can undermine the FIFA, which are otherwise presented as public harm, as it is the case of the delayed infrastructure, for which the FIFA and its sponsors should are not accountable agents. As a developing country, Brazil appeared as courting delays, feeding an incompetent management, and perpetuating poverty, while the FIFA, the European institution, was excused from giving any explanation on its demands and expensive construction standards.

Such discussions have held the country under permanent scrutiny, which led to consequences. Previous World Cups promoted the temporary extolling of 'national' values by the media (Nicholson 2014; Tomlinson 2007), in which the stir of sensitive questions pushed the nation to undertake discussions that could be otherwise object of a more serious and deep debate (Bonthuys 2012; Kennelly and Watt 2013; Stehle and Weber 2013). This research confirms both trends on the 2014 World Cup. The pressure to comply with FIFA's demanded that Brazilians discussed their ability to build nationwide projects. The rush for approving tenders and legislations reflected this artificial prioritization, as old bills remained in stand-by. One example is the troubled review of laws that used to benefit the locals, but not the FIFA, such as half-priced tickets for students, the reversal of alcohol bans within stadia, and the eviction of poor families for new football venues. Only a smaller part of the coverage found in the British press in reality addressed those issues from the perspective of an ordinary Brazilian citizen.

However, this frame analysis shows a paradox of not denying a congratulatory sense when referring to the FIFA, as it did with the stadia, facilities, and the competitors, on the other hand allowing graphic imagery of poverty, inequality, and disruption when the focus was only at Brazil. Appropriately, authors have argued that media events have traditionally resulted in a ritual of self-importance, even though the news coverage tries to confirm its serious nature, removing any sense of futility (Dayan and Katz 2009, 103). Before the FIFA 2014 kick-off, the media's occasional portrait of social issues confirmed this ambiguous detachment. At one level, the World Cup was a great achievement. At another, there were 'national' de-stabilizing factors. In other words, as the country suffered the consequence of megalomaniac projects, the event in itself was still presented as desirable and proportional.

World Cup, poverty, and inequality

The British press has frequently mixed poverty, violence and technical incompetence as weaknesses of the Brazilian World Cup. 'Police warn visitors "Don't scream if robbed"' (*The Guardian*, May 12, 2014) or 'Gunfights and killings in shanty towns have escalated just weeks before the World Cup begins in Brazil' (*The Telegraph*, April 27, 2014) are examples of this generalizing approach. The *Financial Times* sought a more socially sensitive coverage, although the newspaper had at many times given FIFA the entitlement to question the Brazilian government, with no consideration to the role of each of them in the process of hosting the World Cup, e.g. 'FIFA questions Brazil as 2014 World Cup host' (July 18, 2013).

On June 4, 10 days before the kick-off, *The BBC* broadcast *Under the Shadow of the Stadiums*, a 40-minute *Panorama* documentary telling the story of child prostitution around the city of *Fortaleza*. The programme compiled shock-effect signifiers of poverty and social tragedy that at some point became disconnected from the World Cup. The struggle for social justice is a desired agenda when it comes to Brazil's flaws, but this documentary went further by insisting in a sense of moral condemnation that lay beyond the discussion of the World Cup. Other headlines of this period confirmed the same intent of other outlets: 'Brazil is dangerous, deprived and the beautiful game's spiritual home' (*Daily Mirror*, October 16, 2013). Exaggeration seems to be an increasingly common resource in the media in order to provoke moral panics (Goode and Ben Yehuda 2009, 100). Yet, the use of poverty and inequality as a counter-narrative for the World Cup was not necessarily a new type of framing. Bonthuys (2012) argues that the media rushed to discuss child abuse and sexual exploitation during the preparations for the South Africa World Cup more as an impediment for tourism, and less for addressing issues on public policy.

On the other hand, it is known that moral discourses (e.g. global warming, fight against hunger, HIV) have generally sought to add cohesion and mobilization for global events (Rojek 2013). It is fair to say that the use of the inequality in Brazil as a moral weapon discourse was not in fact linked to any bona fide purpose, not even to promote FIFA's charitable activities, which include child protection and racism[5]. 'The beautiful game exposes Brazil's ugly flaws' (*Financial Times*, April 20, 2014), and 'Brazil's battle to upgrade airports for the

World Cup' (*BBC*, May 19, 2014) underline the World Cup as a modernizing agent, never as a burden to development. To a certain extent, the same 'redemption to modernization' argument was also used during the 2010 World Cup, in which the sub-text was 'the first World Cup in Africa' (Tomlinson and Young 2010, 3). In that same moment, the developmental issue was a trigger to 'conscious consumerist' campaigns, as seen at RED campaign (Duvall and Guschwan 2013). In Brazil, this sort of commodification of poverty have had the *favelas* as a worldly recognizable postal card of Rio de Janeiro, a place for movies and TV shows, it is nonetheless not possible to assume that aspect as an exclusive feature of the World Cup.

Disrupting the FIFA

A large part of the reports dwelt on the massive protests that occupied the streets of São Paulo in July 2013. These reports have described the imminent threat to the World Cup, framing demonstrators as a non-organized, anonymous, and often-deviant group. Stories such as 'Anti-World Cup protests across Brazil' (*The Guardian*, May 16, 2014), and 'Sorry FIFA, protests in Brazil will go on' (*Financial Times*, July 18, 2013) brought in their covers the massive crowds that marched on Brazil's biggest metropolises. Protest participants have been historically portrayed in the media more as violent disrupters than as a group with legitimate claims (Boykoff 2006). In the second semester of 2013, the British press shifted from denial to finally confirm the civil unrest as a World Cup consequence. The mass demonstrations were nonetheless oversimplified or not correctly captured. The BBC home page (May 28, 2014) used a man in an indigenous cockade and yellow t-shirt to headline 'Anti-World Cup protest' what was actually a protest for indigenous rights.[6]

In spite of the popularity of demonstrations that indeed rejected FIFA's demands such as high standard stadia, the Brazilians were mostly in favour of the World Cup in 2013, and in 2014.[7] On the other hand, little had been reported to understand the crisis of political representation that most likely are in the roots of those demonstrations (Saad-Filho 2013; Sweet 2014). Local protesters adopted 'Padrão FIFA' (or FIFA Standard) as a jargon to demand the same standards of construction adopted for the stadia, deemed as luxurious, at new schools, and hospitals in Brazil. This was a far more complex issue than the fierce opposition to the World Cup that was usually reported, and a debate largely absent from the coverage.

Not limited to civil unrest, the disruption narrative still counts with stories on water scarcity in São Paulo (*The Telegraph*, May 1, 2014), chaos in the metro (*Financial Times*, February 5, 2014), failed construction projects (*BBC News*, May 29, 2014), and widespread drug traffic (*The Mirror*, May 31, 2014).

A similar environment of tension and threat has appeared in the media reports of the 2010 World Cup in South Africa. There were clashes between demonstrators, the FIFA, and local government authorities. As in Brazil, the media targeted South African striking construction workers, and members of social movements as potential disrupters. The bottom line of the dissent on the 2010 World Cup was at the failure of the whole World Cup project in bringing more prosperity (Ngonyama 2010). Though it is possible to confirm the same kind of political disillusion in the Brazilian protests, this has not meant a complete unfeasibility of the event or its complete rejection, as many reports did announce. *The Guardian* was one of the British broadsheets to give more voice to the Brazilians in this period, as it happened in this piece, 'The world is looking to Brazil, and we are showing that the World

Cup doesn't represent us' (May 16, 2014). These brief spaces, mostly occupied by Brazilian authors and academics, were not enough to push for more balance, surprisingly found in the tabloid-style press 'Our Brian discovers people who loathe FIFA almost as much as they love football itself' (*Daily Mirror*, December 7, 2013).

Global events and media coverage: some brief conclusions

Evidences discussed in this essay present a series of media discourses that not only have accredited the FIFA as a primary source of news stories, but also created an agenda that regarded social issues as threats to the 2014 World Cup, most of which overshadowed important discussions that happened on the local public sphere. It is not the case to state that all stories, articles, and opinion pieces were wrong or inaccurate, particularly on urban violence (Waiselfisz 2013). Amid the 40% of the sample that did not comply with the frame proposed here, there were minor, but relevant contributions to the understanding of the local reality. For example, during the boycott of the later banned Adidas t-shirts, which represented sexualized images of Brazilian women, the *Financial Times* argued against it in 'sexualised Brazilian t-shirts' (February 26, 2014). Stories such as 'FIFA World Cup "hits the poorest hardest"' (*BBC News*, September 9, 2014) showed how the media could campaign for the rights of the poor on a fair basis.

The final goal of this research is to denounce the reduction of socially sensitive journalism during the World Cup, along with the diversion towards the interests of powerful institutions, such as the FIFA. Different from the traditional media strategy aimed at exhibiting beautiful images during global events (Dayan and Katz 2009; Rojek 2013), the coverage of the 2014 World Cup has particularly allowed images of disruption and the 'aesthetics of poverty'. However, such graphic materials were exposed up to a point of no serious disruption of the event's brand, and conveniently labelled as Brazil's internal problems. It is no surprise that the so-called 'global' media have been partners of a global financial elite, leading to questions on the real commitment to democratic values and to a stronger public sphere (Hermann and McChesney 2001). The political economy of journalism continues to remain much grounded in how power holders set their definitions of the world (Schudson 1989: 267).

One of the consequences of this commercial interference is the overlook of disadvantaged groups. During the 2010 World Cup in South Africa, marketing campaigns linked charity campaigns to consumerism, while victims remained voiceless in the media (Duvall and Guschwan 2013; Ngonyama 2010). In Brazil, while exaggerating on its reports of civil unrest, or *viralizing* graphic imagery of poverty, the media failed to use the particular moments of global influence to scrutinize FIFA's self-assigned mission to become partner in the host country's development and economic growth.[8] New case studies could expand the position of professional journalism in global events, examining the extent to which a reliable coverage amidst a strong advertising machine could be restored in a sustainable basis or at least how can the alternative media complement that coverage.

Finally, this paper recognizes the limitation of not considering the voices of journalists and media agents who worked during the 2014 World Cup, which could have opened the reality of news production. The extent to which Latin America is newsworthy in Britain could yet clarify why international correspondents still show little grasp of local politics, as observed by the lack of context offered during the World Cup protests. However, it is clear that there should be no expectations that global events can approximate countries and reorganize geopolitics (Cornelissen 2004). Even having more correspondents now than 30 years ago, British news organizations still preserve the colonial and stereotypical outlook with regard to South and Central America (Boyd-Barrett, 1977; Aguirre 1985; Ramirez 2007). A balanced coverage should be able to independently criticize global events, that is, going beyond the US corporate media narrative, pursuing news values that are more suited to a multipolar geopolitics. That would enable socially committed reports, which would be able to criticize capitalist institutions to the extent they can undermine the democratic debates that happen in emerging urban societies from the Global South.

Notes

1. *The Guardian* published in December 2013 the cost of £6.000 lb and 13.000 miles for a countrywide trip. Available at http://www.theguardian.com/football/2013/dec/04/world-cup-2014-fans-england. Accessed on July 4, 2013.
2. http://www.theguardian.com/media/2014/jun/08/social-media-winner-world-cup-advertising. Accessed on July 4, 2014.
3. http://www.nytimes.com/2014/06/29/sports/worldcup/a-new-york-odyssey-through-world-cup-fandom.html. Accessed on July 4, 2014.
4. According to this report, public funds in Brazil have subsidized stadia and infrastructure only used for the event. Available at http://stadiumdb.com/news/2014/07/report_how_much_did_brazil_spend_on_world_cup_stadiums. Accessed on July 4, 2014.
5. FIFA's official website has a sub-section named as 'Development' in which the organization lists many of its activities related to bona fide causes, including, but not limited to, gender inclusion, racism and education.
6. The protest was motivated by the World Cup, but other groups gathered at the site for numerous other reasons. However, images of these groups were used by the global media to illustrate World Cup anger. More information on this is available at http://www1.folha.uol.com.br/poder/2014/05/1461052-indio-fere-pm-com-flechada-em-ato-anti-copa-em-brasilia.shtml. Accessed on July 4, 2014.
7. As reported by a Datafolha Survey, available at http://datafolha.folha.uol.com.br/opiniaopublica/2014/06/1467905-51-dos-brasileiros-aprovam-realizacao-da-copa-no-brasil.shtml. Accessed on July 12, 2015.
8. According to 'FIFA Sustainability Plan', it has avowed objectives that involve social programmes and poverty reduction. Available at http://www.fifa.com/mm/document/tournament/loc/01/65/19/25/sustainability_strategy_e_web.pdf. Accessed on July 13, 2015.

Acknowledgment

I would like to thank Professor Eugene McLaughlin for some fruitful discussions on the British Press during the first phase of this project.

Disclosure statement

No potential conflict of interest was reported by the author.

References

Aguirre, P. 1985. "The Coverage of Latin America by the British Press." PhD diss., City University.
Alegi, P. 2008. "A Nation to Be Reckoned with: The Politics of World Cup Stadium Construction in Cape Town and Durban, South Africa." *African Studies* 67 (3): 397–422.

Barnett, G. A., and K. Kim. 1996. "The Determinants of International News Flow: A Network Analysis." *Communication Research* 23 (3): 323–352.

Bonthuys, E. 2012. "The 2010 Football World Cup and the Regulation of Sex Work in South Africa." *Journal of Southern African Studies* 38 (1): 11–29.

Boyd-Barrett, O. 1977. "Media Imperialism: Towards an International Framework for the Analysis of Media Systems." *Mass Communication and Society* 116–135.

Boykoff, J. 2006. "Framing Dissent: Mass-media Coverage of the Global Justice Movement." *New Political Science* 28 (2): 201–228.

Cohen, J. A. 1960. "Coefficient of Agreement for Nominal Scales." *Educational and Psychological Measurement* 20: 31–46.

Cohen, J. 1968. "Weighted Kappa: Nominal Scale Agreement Provision for Scaled Disagreement or Partial Credit." *Psychological Bulletin* 70 (4): 213.

Coleman, R. 2010. "Framing the Pictures in Our Heads: Exploring the Framing and Agenda-Setting Effects of Visual Images." In *Doing News Frame Analysis: Empirical and Theoretical Perspectives*, edited by P. D'Angelo and J. A. Kuypers. p. 233–246 London: Routledge.

Conchas, M. 2014. "Research Possibilities for the 2014 FIFA World Cup in Brazil." *Soccer & Society* 15 (1): 167–174.

Cornelissen, S. 2004. "'It's Africa's Turn!' the Narratives and Legitimations Surrounding the Moroccan and South African Bids for the 2006 and 2010 FIFA Finals." *Third World Quarterly* 25 (7): 1293–1309.

Cornelissen, S., and K. Swart. 2006. "The 2010 Football World Cup as a Political Construct: The Challenge of Making Good on an African Promise." *The Sociological Review* 54: 108–123.

Cottle, S. 1999. "Ethnic Minorities and the British News Media: Explaining (Mis)Representation." In *The Media in Britain: Current Debates and Developments*, edited by J. C. Stokes and A. Reading. p. 191–200. Basingstoke: Palgrave Macmillan.

Dayan, D., and E. Katz. 2009. Media events. Cambridge: Harvard University Press.

Dearing, J. W, and E. M. Rogers. 1996. *Agenda-setting*. Thousand Oaks, CA: Sage.

Duvall, S. S, and M. C. Guschwan. 2013. "Commodifying Global Activism and Racial Unity during the 2010 FIFA World Cup." *Communication, Culture & Critique (1753–9129)* 6 (2): 298–317.

Entman, R. M. 2007. "Framing Bias: Media in the Distribution of Power." *Journal of Communication* 57 (1): 163–173.

Gaffney, C. 2010. "Mega-events and Socio-spatial Dynamics in Rio De Janeiro, 1919–2016." *Journal of Latin American Geography* 9 (1): 7–29.

Galtung, J., and M. Ruge. 1973. "Structuring and Selecting News." *The Manufacture of News.* 1 (62) 62–72.

Gastaldo, E. 2014. "Soccer and Media in Brazil." *Soccer and Society* 15 (1): 123–131.

Gerhards, J., and M. Schäfer. 2010. "Is the internet a better public sphere? Comparing old and new media in the US and Germany." New media & society.

Goffman, E. 1974. Frame analysis: An essay on the organization of experience. Cambridge: Harvard University Press.

Goode, E., and N. Ben-Yehuda. 2009. Moral panics: The social construction of deviance. John Wiley & Sons.

Hall, S. 1997. *Representation: Cultural Representations and Signifying Practices*. London: Sage.

Herrmann, E., and R. McChesney. 2001. *Global Media: The New Missionaries of Global Capitalism*. A&C Black.

Holsti, O. R. 1969. *Content Analysis for the Social Sciences and Humanities*. Addison-Wesley Pub Co.

Kashima, Y. 2013. "Cultural Dynamics of Inter-group Relations." In *Stereotyping and Prejudice*, edited by C. Stangor and C. Crandall. London: Psychology Press. p.119–150.

Kennelly, J., and P. Watt. 2013. "Restricting the Public in Public Space: The London 2012 Olympic Games, Hyper-securitization and Marginalized Youth." *Sociological Research Online* 18 (2): p. 19.

Krippendorff, K. 2007. "Computing Krippendorff's Alpha Reliability." *Departmental Papers (ASC)*: 1–43.

Lee, J. H., and Y. J. Choi. 2009. "News Values of Sports Events: An Application of a Newsworthiness Model on the World Cup Coverage of US and Korean Media." *Asian Journal of Communication* 19 (3): 302–318.

Lombard, M., J. Snyder-Duch, and C. C. Bracken. 2002. "Content Analysis in Mass Communication: Assessment and Reporting of Intercoder Reliability." *Human Communication Research* 28 (4): 587–604.

McCombs, M. E., ed. 2014. *Setting the Agenda: The Mass Media and Public Opinion.* 2nd ed. Cambridge: Polity.

McCombs, M. E., and D. Shaw 1972. "The agenda-setting function of mass media." *Public opinion quarterly* 36 (2): 176–187.

McNair, B. 2003. *News and Journalism in the UK.* London: Psychology Press.

Ngonyama, P. 2010. "The 2010 FIFA World Cup: Critical Voices from below." *Soccer and Society* 11 (1–2): 168–180.

Nicholson, M, E. Sherry, and A. Osborne. 2014. "Negotiating National Identity through Loss: Australian Newspaper Coverage of the 2010 FIFA World Cup." *Soccer and Society*: 1–15.

Paganotti, I. 2009. "Images and stereotypes of Brazil in articles written by international corrrespondents". Imagens e estereótipos do Brasil em reportagens de correspondentes internacionais. *Rumores-Revista de Comunicação, Linguagem E Mídias*: 1 (1).

Porto, M. P. 2007. "Frame Diversity and Citizen Competence: Towards a Critical Approach to News Quality." *Critical Studies in Media Communication* 24 (4): 303–321.

Ramirez, L. E. 2007. *British Representations of Latin America.* Miami, FL: University Press of Florida.

Riffe, D., S. Lacy, and F. Fico. 2013. *Analyzing Media Messages: Using Quantitative Content Analysis in Research.* New York: Routledge.

Rojek, Chris. 2013. *Event Power: How Global Events Manage and Manipulate.* London: Sage.

Saad-Filho, A. 2013. "Mass Protests under 'Left Neoliberalism': Brazil, June–July 2013." *Critical Sociology* 39 (5): 657–669.

Schudson, M. 1989. "The Sociology of News Production." *Media, Culture and Society* 11 (3): 263–282.

Stehle, M., and B. M. Weber. 2013. "German Soccer, the 2010 World Cup, and Multicultural Belonging." *German Studies Review* 36 (1): 103–124.

Sweet, C. 2014. "Brazil Woke up Stronger? Power, Protest, and Politics in 2013." *Revista De Ciencia Politica* 34 (1): 59–78.

Tomlinson, A. 2007. "Lord, Don't Stop the Carnival: Trinidad and Tobago at the 2006 FIFA World Cup." *Journal of Sport &Amp; Social Issues* 31 (3): 259.

Tomlinson, A. 2014. *FIFA (Federation Internationale de Football Association): the Men, the Myths and the Money.* New York: Routledge.

Tomlinson, A., and C. Young. 2012. *National Identity and Global Sports Events: Culture, Politics, and Spectacle in the Olympics and the Football World Cup.* New York: SUNY Press.

Tudor, Andrew. 1992. "Them and Us: Story and Stereotype in TV World Cup Coverage." *European Journal of Communication* 7 (3): 391–413.

Van Dijk, T. A. 1991. "Principles of Critical Discourse Analysis." In *A Handbook of Qualitative Methodologies for Mass Communication Research*, edited by K. B. Jensen and N. Jankowski. New York: Routledge.

Van Gorb, B. 2010. "Strategies to Take Subjectivity out of Framing Analysis." In *Doing News Framing Analysis: Empirical and Theoretical Perspectives*, edited by Paul D'Angelo and Jim A. Kuypers, 84–109. London: Routledge.

Waiselfisz, J. J. 2013. "Violence Map 2013: Murder and Youth in Brazil". Mapa da violência 2013: homicídios e juventude no Brasil. Accessed July 4, 2014. http://www.mapadaviolencia.org.br/pdf2013/mapa2013_homicidios_juventude.pdf

Wanta, W., G. Golan, and C. Lee. 2004. "Agenda Setting and International News: Media Influence on Public Perceptions of Foreign Nations." *Journalism & Mass Communication Quarterly* 81 (2): 364–377.

Wark, M. 1994. *Virtual Geography: Living with Global Media Events.* Indianapolis: Indiana University Press.

Yang, H., S. Ramasubramanian, and M. B. Oliver. 2008. "Cultivation Effects on Quality of Life Indicators: Exploring the Effects of American Television Consumption on Feelings of Relative Deprivation in South Korea and India." *Journal of Broadcasting & Electronic Media* 52 (2): 247–267.

Risk and (in)security of FIFA football World Cups – outlook for Russia 2018

Donna Wong and Simon Chadwick

ABSTRACT

Preparing and hosting a FIFA World Cup has often been perceived to bring tremendous opportunities to the host country. These include stimulating a sense of patriotism and fostering nation-building to help further modernize and fast-track infrastructural development within the country. Nevertheless, as with any sporting mega-events, hosting an event of such magnitude and international interest comes with exceptional risks. This essay presents an assessment of risks relating to previous FIFA football tournaments, namely – 2006 FIFA World Cup Germany; 2010 FIFA World Cup South Africa and the 2014 FIFA World Cup Brazil, to reflect upon a number of threats and challenges associated with the hosting of the 2018 FIFA World Cup Russia. With a lapse of eight years from the award to the tournament, the planning and operational decisions for Russia 2018 are undertaken under conditions of high ambiguity. The essay aims to identify the effects of uncertainties that may compromise the Russian World Cup through the assessment of potential and emerging threats that hold the potential to jeopardize the safety and security of the tournament.

Introduction

The staging of sport mega-event often results in a unique mix of sporting and non-sporting benefits which are hard to generate by any other means. The biggest challenge for any host country is to deliver an event that is considered as 'the best ever', where there is not one individual plan that can guarantee its success. The staging of the FIFA Football World Cup (hereafter 'FWC'), as the world's most widely viewed sports mega-event, represents a venue of exceptional risk profile. It is after all an event with a high visibility attracting television audiences of millions globally, live spectators, as well as wider public and media interest. Although concerns with security and risk have been prominent themes at sports mega-events since the 1960s (Houlihan and Giulianotti 2012), the world of sports mega-events entered a new era of a heightened perception of insecurity and risk following the attacks in the United States on 11 September 2001. Risk became the dominant discourse of sport mega-events, for especially the Olympic Games and the FWC (Giulianotti and

Robertson 2009). As the Brazilian FWC have passed without major incidents, attention now inevitably shifts to the next FWC to be held at Russia. With allegations of corruption in the bid process for securing the hosting right as the latest issue, among the long list of controversies surrounding the Russian FWC, it certainly warrants a close attention to the risks associated with the organizing of the tournament.

This essay seeks to carry out a risk assessment based on the FWCs held within the last decade – Germany 2006 FWC (hereafter 'Germany 2006'), South Africa 2010 FWC (hereafter 'South Africa 2010') and Brazil 2014 World Cup (hereafter 'Brazil 2014') – to reflect upon a number of threats and vulnerabilities associated with the hosting of the Russia 2018 FWC (hereafter 'Russia 2018'). It aims to identify the effects of uncertainties that may compromise Russia 2018 through the assessment of potential and emerging threats that may impact on the tournament. With a lapse of eight years from the award to the tournament, the planning and operational decisions for Russia 2018 are undertaken under conditions of high ambiguity. Identifying the 'known unknowns' of sport mega-events is a step forward to reduce such uncertainties. It justifies and encourages the early preparation for the 'unknown unknowns' (Horne 2007). This enables the organizations involved to develop strategies and implement measures to mitigate potential threats and challenges that might arise before and during the tournament.

Scope and methodology

In all types of undertaking, there is the potential for events and consequences that constitute threats to success. These threats pose a risk to the event. This essay seeks to review the various facets of risks associated with the organization of a FWC, where the outcome will be extrapolated to identify, analyse and describe Russia 2018's exposure to risk. This is carried out through the collation, review and synthesis of information related to risks and challenges of football mega-events. It focuses specifically on three recent FIFA events – Germany 2006, South Africa 2010 and Brazil 2014. Although the risks differ in their main causes, forms and effects, FWCs are often exposed to similar security threats (Jennings 2012). Conditions of risk and uncertainty are shared between the respective editions of the FWCs; it might therefore be expected that security risks would tend to resemble one another across events and over time. The assessment of these tournament-specific risks security plans and operations of the past FWCs therefore provides leverage for possible insights into the risk profile of the Russia 2018.

This assessment also seeks to integrate analyses of security risk with insights from academic literature on sporting events risk management and public administration documentation. To explore narratives of risks, documentary analyses of official documents, content analysis of media coverage, interviews with key personnel (event directors, senior management and consultants responsible for event security planning) directly associated with these events were carried out. Official documents scrutinized include reports, debriefs, event evaluations, marketing publications and media releases pertaining to the aforementioned events. Media are acknowledged as a cultural force in sport; media reports provide a new perspective to the study, providing representation of external opinions on the subject. This additional source of information adds depth to the scrutiny of data to identify alternative perspectives, and most importantly to confirm and/or contradict data collected from official sources. A media analysis of the newspaper articles, web pages associated with risks and security at these events was undertaken to complement the data analysis.

Germany 2006

Held from 9 June to 9 July 2006, the Germany 2006 was its first since its reunification in 1990. As a country suffering from a poor international image for decades since the World Wars, the FWC was intended to be used as a platform to ameliorate its reputation on a global scale. A secured tournament that ensured the safety and enjoyment of the fans was adopted as its hosting strategy (Federal Ministry of the Interior 2006). The securitization of the tournament remained its top priority where the threat of football violence and politically motivated terrorism were identified as key risks to the tournament (BDI 2006). The risks were not unfounded, particularly with the history of previous FWC played in Europe (France 1998) where it was marred by English hooligans and clashes between German fans and the police.

Football violence

With the successful management of security risks for the tournament, Germany 2006 is often hailed as one of the more successful FWCs in recent years (Grix 2013; Klauser 2008). Although the tournament passed without any major incident, disturbances were recorded in three matches (Poland vs. Germany, England vs. Sweden and England vs. Ecuador) (BDI 2006). Traditionally, the risk of football violence has come from English, Dutch and German fans (Carnibella et al. 1996; Ingle 2013; Spaaij 2007). However, intelligence obtained by the Central Sports Intelligence Unit (ZIS) prior to the FWC suggested a radical hooligan fringe is on the rise in Poland (BDI 2006). Hooliganism problem in Germany appeared to be especially acute given the strains of re-unification and the alleged involvement of neo-fascist groups in football disorder in the country. During the lead up to the tournament, the right-wing scene announced several campaigns and events intended to gain media and public attention (Alexander 2006). This is exemplified by the traditional rivalry between the far-right German fan groups and the Polish fans. It was impossible then to rule out the threat of such groups considering the fact that Poland is one of Germany's neighbours and the two nations had been drawn to play each other in the first round of the tournament in Dortmund. Despite the restriction placed on the entry of numerous violent Polish fans into Germany prior to the start of the FWC, with targeted groups of German and Polish fans were taken into preventative custody ahead of the match, violent clashes took place nonetheless between German and Polish fans in Dortmund's city centre (BDI 2006).

Many violent offences are frequently linked to the use of alcohol (Frosdick and Marsh 2005). Football tournaments, in particular, often sponsored by breweries, seem to be associated regularly with male fans drinking heavily together pre- and post-event. Although the FWC in Japan and South Korea in 2002 were trouble-free, observers attributed that to the fact they were staged far from the traditional European 'centres' of hooliganism, such as England. With wide availability of cheap beer in Germany, the fact that the country is served by cheap flights from all over Europe and its many shared borders made football violence potentially a high risk for the 2006 tournament (Klauser 2008). The second football violence that took place was generally attributed to the excessive consumption of alcohol which resulted in violent clashes between aggressively English hooligans and the police after the Sweden versus England match.

A similar incident took place in Stuttgart which involved a match between England and Ecuador. There were already repeated clashes between English fans and police officers in Stuttgart city centre prior to the match, which saw attempts by intoxicated English fans provoking other groups of fans. Despite huge police presence on the eve of the match, clashes still took place between huge groups of violent English and German fans. The UK liaison officers categorized the great majority of English troublemakers as typical 'event rowdies' who tended to become violent when under the influence of alcohol (Spiegel Online 2006).

Threat of terrorism

Although historically international football tournaments have not been associated with acts of domestic or international terrorism like the Olympic Games, given the general security situation and threat of international terrorism then, it still presented a key risk to all FWCs. The possibility that extremist, terrorist groups or individuals might try to use Germany 2006 as a stage for propaganda remained one of the key focuses for the tournament's security risk management. Extremism, xenophobia and anti-Semitism were identified as key threats behind acts of terrorist attack (BDI 2006). Given the terrorist attacks which took place during the summer of 2005 in London[1] and Sharm el Sheik,[2] preparations were undertaken to deal with the possibility of radical Islamist terrorist attacks. There was also a reported neo-Nazi surge during the build-up to Germany 2006 where these far-right groups intended to use the tournament as a platform to win publicity (see discussion earlier). Despite these threats to the tournament, none came to fruition during the run-up to the FWC or during the tournament itself.

South Africa 2010

The South Africa 2010 was the first FWC to be hosted in Africa. Although officially declared by FIFA a success (Robbins 2012), there was a discernible level of scepticism over the authorities' capacity to complete all organizational and logistical preparations on time, and particularly to adequately securitize the event prior to tournament (Cornelissen 2011). The fact that the country carries the reputation for being among the world's most violent and crime ridden in the world amplified scepticism in the international arena about the country's ability to host a 'secure' and risk-free tournament (Donaldson and Ferreira 2009).

Crime

South Africa's status as a developing country and it being the first African country to host an event of the magnitude of a FWC – raised to prominence the question of organizational ability more than usual (Cornelissen 2011). The primary safety concern for FWC visitors was the prevalent criminal activity in South Africa. High levels of crime and the apparent ineffectiveness of national policing were perceived to be one of the key risks for the tournament. The host cities of Johannesburg, Durban, Cape Town and Pretoria were rated as 'critical' for crime threat (Overseas Security Advisory Council 2010). Crime in South

Africa ranged from petty muggings to ATM scams to armed residential home invasions. These crimes occurred with high frequency and increasing sophistication on the part of well-armed criminals. Police reports disclosed staggering statistics of business robberies and carjacking. The influx of tourists and visitors for the FWC was seen to provide increased opportunity for criminals, making street or contact crimes the biggest potential threat to visitors.

The perception of South Africa being a dangerous country for tourists lingered, and was powerful. This was considered a potentially strong deterrent for many prospective international visitors. Attempts were made by South Africa's authorities to mitigate the reputational risk by visibly and concretely managing the country's crime problem prior to the tournament. The government boosted surveillance technologies and implemented new governance arrangements through which they could enforce public order and safety during the FWC. As a result, crime at FWC locations was lower than average during the tournament, which proceeded with few major incidents, contrary to initial concerns about visitors' safety (Cornelissen 2011).

Terrorism

As with Germany 2006, while no specific or credible terrorist threats have been identified by the South Africa 2010 organizers, terrorism remained a risk for the tournament. Online postings on jihadist websites prior to the tournament highlighted the threat. In April 2010, a threat was posted on a jihadist website in which one of the al-Qaeda franchises – al-Qaeda in the Lands of Islamic Maghreb (AQIM) reportedly threatened to attack the 12 June England versus USA match in Rustenburg using undetectable explosives (Overseas Security Advisory Council 2010). The credibility of the threat was questionable as AQIM has not demonstrated the capability to execute such an operation and it was uncharacteristic for the group to publicly announce the target, timing and method of an attack well in advance. Although the South African authorities doubted the credibility of this threat, the threat could not be ignored (Botha 2010). Extra security measures were put in place by South African security authorities to secure the match in Rustenburg, although the authorities were unable to elaborate on what the increased precautions entailed. The threat was largely unfounded and not followed up by the terrorist group.

Domestic extremists

Violence arising from domestic tensions was also identified as a key risk to the tournament. The post-apartheid tensions caused great concern within the international arena that it would escalate during the tournament and that it would be particularly tourists who would be affected (Botha 2010). The murder of Eugene Terre'Blanche, white supremacist leader of the Afrikaner Resistance Movement (AWB), months before South Africa 2010 highlighted existing tensions between black and white South Africans. The AWB, an extreme right-wing group, threatened to avenge Terre'Blanche's death. Although the AWB does not enjoy extensive popular support, the incident could have been used as a rallying event for the AWB and other far-right groups. There was the risk that some right-wing groups would use the platform of FWC to bring attention to their cause and try to embarrass the South African Government. The South African Police Force made several arrests of individuals with ties to right-wing groups around the country in April and May 2010, seizing weapons caches which reportedly included arms, ammunition and explosives (Blazkiewicz 2010). While media reports claimed some of the suspects planned to bomb townships and possibly sabotage the FWC (Solomon 2011), these did not materialize.

Unruly crowds

While football violence is not a common problem in South Africa, crowd stampedes, particularly at the start of a match, were a top concern expressed by FIFA. The previous incidents in 2001 at the Ellis Park stampede killed 43 people before a match (McGreal 2001); and in 2009, the World Cup qualifier at Ivory Coast saw ticketless spectators starting a last-minute stampede when provoked by the security forces who threw tear gas. The Ivory Coast stampede resulted in 19 deaths (BBC 2009; Blazkiewicz 2010). These were reminders of the risk of a crowd stampede. The South African Police Force acknowledged the risk and conducted numerous crowd control exercises to test out their readiness. The authorities had an opportunity to test their crowd control skills following the murder of Terre'Blanche (see earlier discussion) shortly before FWC. Volatile crowds of black and white South Africans gathered at the courthouse on 6 April where the two suspects were being tried. With sufficient preparation, the police force was able to maintain order and keep the crowd separated despite high tensions and rancorous verbal exchanges (BBC 2009; Blazkiewicz 2010). Although crowd stampede was identified as a key risk for South Africa 2010, it failed to materialize into any incidents during the tournament.

Strikes and protests

The risk of strike and protest, a common theme during high-profile event, was one of the key threats identified for South Africa 2010 (Botha 2010). South Africa regularly experiences protests and strike activities over wage disputes. Most wage disputes in South Africa occur between the months of April and July, which coincided with the hosting of FWC. There was the concern that activists would attempt to gain leverage from the tournament to pressure the government to give in to their demands. One of the notable strikes took place in July 2009, where an estimate of 70,000 workers went on strike which lasted for a week. Construction work on stadiums, airports, freeways and Johannesburg's new high-speed rail link came to a standstill. At one stage, these strikes and protests threatened to derail the completion of already tightly scheduled projects for South Africa 2010.

In the context of deep and extensive poverty in some of the FWC host cities where close to half of the households live in informal settlement, the funding and resources allocated from the public purse to the organizing of South Africa 2010 was a major cause for resentment among South Africans. Friction was caused by the reality of high spending on the tournament against South Africans who strongly believed that the money should be spent on poverty reduction. The perceived lack of governmental assurance of citizens' needs and concerns over poverty produced a spark that kicked off a protest March in March 2010. It involved 3000 campaigners in Durban protesting against the resource allocations and cost escalations on the FWC (International Regional Information Network 2010). Although rubber bullets and teargas were used to quell the protest, no major injuries were sustained.

The risk of additional protest activity surrounding the FWC remained throughout the duration of the tournament.

In June 2010, a pay dispute among stewards and security workers resulted in a series of demonstrations and strikes during the tournament. These workers, hired by a private security company, were working in FWC stadiums in Durban, Cape Town and Port Elizabeth and Johannesburg. It appears that many workers were employed on a temporary basis under conditions without written contracts (Smith and Gibson 2010). These protests affected security operations at more than half the FWC stadiums and prompted the South African Police Force to deploy their own officers to assume security in these stadiums. The deployment helped to resolve an impending crisis, but left an additional World Cup cost of R90 m (£7.8 m) for the South African Police Services (Blazkiewicz 2010). Police in the host cities remained on high alert for the duration of the tournament to prevent further escalation of these protests into riots.

These strikes caused, to a certain extent, disruption to the event (eg lost construction time due to strikes during stadium construction). Progress of infrastructural construction was intermittently halted by these strikes and pay disputes, which ran into the risk of delays in operational readiness. The stadiums, together with major event infrastructure (eg roads, airport terminal buildings and newly developed urban transport system), were eventually completely on time albeit in a hurry. The late finalization of infrastructure had ramifications for security planners as safety systems could only be piloted when the tournament got underway.

Brazil 2014

The hosting of Brazil 2014 was a significant part of Brazil's strategy to secure a positive image of the country apart from the traditional developing nation that the Brazil brand represented in the past. Brazil 2014 was, however, embroiled in disputes, delays and demonstrations since the preparation phase of the tournament. The tournament was overshadowed by a rapid and unexpected display of discontent during the Confederations Cup, a test event that took place in June 2013. The protesters, which drew over one million in more than 100 cities at their peak, used the tournament as a platform from which to vent their grievances. The stark realities of protests, the police brutality and violent reaction to it have in fact affected Brazil's attempt to rebrand itself as a modern and vibrant democracy. The following section discusses major risk issues which plagued Brazil 2014.

Terrorism

Where the FWC is concerned, the risk of terrorism was considered low for Brazil (Aon 2014). No terrorist threats were expected for Brazil 2014 as Brazil is not a major target or focal point for the world's more capable and funded terrorist organizations. The country lacks the types of political and ethnic tensions that have led to terrorist attacks in other countries. Brazil presents a challenge for international terrorist networks due to cultural and linguistic issues. Few of the world's major terrorist groups have ethnic, religious or cultural counterparts in the country to use for cover while planning an attack, making the Portuguese language and criminal underground even harder to navigate than usual.

Football violence

Football violence caused by local hooligans was not identified as one of the key risks to Brazil 2014. Brazil's local fan bases (*Torcidas Organizadas*) are organized around local teams, not the national team. Their demonstrations do not focus on the national team and they do not look at other country's fans as rivals (Raspaud and da Cunha Bastos 2013). However, foreign football fans – including English hooligans, Italian and Croatian ultras, and Argentine *barras bravas* (*barras* in short) was thought to be a challenge for Brazilian law enforcement. While the Europeans may easily be screened, detained and returned to their countries before entering Brazil with border control, the Argentines have relatively easy access into Brazil. A long continuous border and no visa process, the Argentines have freedom to move in and out of Brazil without visas, which made it easy for the *barras* to avoid detection when crossing the border. The Argentine *barras* are notorious ultra-violent football supporter groups that have played a disruptive role at many FWC (Piette 2010). Financed by their national confederation and local football clubs, the Argentine *barras* have a long history of looking towards FWC as an opportunity to prove their superiority to other hooligans, especially the English. The Argentine *barras* were absent from the Confederations Cup since Argentina did not play. However, with Argentina's presence in the FWC, intelligence predicted that the *barras* would commit acts of public disorder, engage in acts of violence and provoke conflict with fans of opposing teams and other groups from Argentina (Soto 2014). Although there was no instance of football violence by the *barras* during Brazil 2014, a minor incident involving a spontaneous attack of English fans by local Brazilian fans took place while the tournament was underway (Watts 2014). Drawing the lesson learnt from the Confederations Cup, the Brazilian police force was well-prepared for any eventuality for such acts to take place during the tournament and the attack was swiftly put down. All forms of disorder were minimal during the FWC and there was much less of an issue than many analysts had predicted (Davies 2014).

Protests

Brazilians have protested throughout the country's contemporary history. There is no lack of examples of protests or massive rallies held and led by communities and social movements throughout Brazil's history. However, the wave of unrest that took place during the Confederations Cup was distinct. Held as a prelude to the FWC from 15 to 30 June 2013, it served as a warm-up competition for the FWC to test out security, stadiums and transport. The protest started in early June 2013 when a group of São Paulo citizens protested against an increase in bus fares. Brazilian bus fares typically increase in January when most people are away on vacation. Previous fare hikes have come and gone with little or no accompanying civil disobedience. However, in early 2013, the perennial January increase was suspended until May, to ease government concerns over inflation in January.

The unintended consequence of the change was a tide of protest when bus fare increases snapped into place at an unusual time (ie May). Commuters travelling to work, and not on vacation, were immediately affected by this otherwise routine policy. These protests later spread to the rest of Brazil, as the demonstration resonated with struggling middle-class commuters concerned with escalating bus fares right across the country. The protests continued to grow as hundreds of thousands of Brazilians across the country organized crowds on social media, among other platforms, to exercise their right to denounce the government for a range of other perceived injustices. Themes ranged from corruption to gay rights, which exposed the core of this social movement: discontent over perceptions of excessive spending in preparation for the FWC and the 2016 Olympic Games. This contrasted with the reality of hunger, poverty, insecurity and squalor that the majority of the Brazilians face daily, exacerbated by tournament preparations. The Confederations Cup attracted protestors eager for the attention of national and international media to express their grievances in protests, which reached their peak on 20 June 2013 when a semi-final match was taking place (Withnall 2013).

The protests took the authorities by surprise. The Brazilian government reacted to the protests with extreme violence as the wave of protests swept across several Brazilian cities in June 2013. Protesters took advantage of the enhanced media coverage as scenes of violence were shared real time with a global viewing public. With the combination of citizen journalism and social media, it accelerated the velocity at which the portrayal of excessive use of force and human rights violations were presented across international media. These were the very images that the Brazilian government most wanted to avoid. It was more reminiscent of Brazil's military dictatorships than the modern country the current government wished to promote on the global stage through Brazil 2014. Learning from the protests of Confederations Cup, the Brazilian government intensified its security measures to prevent any outbreak of protests during the FWC. A 10,000 strong anti-protest police force was dispatched across all 12 host cities, in addition to the battalion of 20,000 men from the Brazilian Army devoted to guaranteeing security of the tournament (Tynan 2014). To avert further risk of embarrassment at security failures, the Brazilian government also worked with other international agencies (eg US Federal Bureau of Investigation), in a number of areas ranging from organized crime, peacekeeping and maintaining respect for human rights (Masters 2014). With fortified efforts in prevention measures, although protests did take place during the FWC, they were smaller in scale. The Brazilian security forces effectively contained these smaller scale protests and carefully avoided the heavy-handed tactics that aggravated matters in during the Confederations Cup.

Stadiums

Infrastructure is the most significant legacy the Brazilian authorities have envisioned from the FWC. New and modernized airports, significant investment in public transportation and urban renewal were the focus of the preparations for the FWC beyond renovated or new stadiums, leading to tangible gains in quality of life for Brazilian citizens. However, these projects presented most risks involving operational preparation for Brazil 2014. Out of the 12 FWC stadiums (four more than the eight required by FIFA), five are new venues constructed specifically for the FWC, with one in the capital Brasilia demolished and rebuilt, and the remaining six extensively renovated. Six of these stadiums were delivered within the FIFA required dates for the Confederations Cup; while six other stadiums missed FIFA's original 31 December 2013 deadline for completed works. Poor safety working conditions, resulting in frequent accidents were the key reasons impacting on the late completion of some of these stadiums (BBC 2013). The first major accident took place on 27 November 2013 when a crane collapsed while workers were finishing the roof installation at the *Itaquerão* Stadium (*Arena de São Paulo*), which resulted in the loss of two construction workers. Fatalities also occurred in other stadiums. A total of eight workers were killed in accidents during the building of Brazil's 12 FWC stadiums (BBC 2014b).

The severe disruption in stadiums completion was compounded by workers' strikes. Mirroring South Africa, workers went on strikes to demand for better wages and benefits. In addition, funding issues such as state governments' slow procurement processes, constant increasing costs due to missed deadlines and poor planning for weather issues (eg intense tropical rain). An ultimatum was issued in January 2014 by FIFA to the Brazilian authorities accelerate its stadium construction. With sufficient progress being made, these stadiums were eventually completed merely weeks before the tournament kick-off. The delay in the completion of infrastructure resulted in a knock-on effect on the conduct of safety inspection of structures, buildings and plans prior to the tournament. The FIFA regulation stipulates that three trial events should be held at each venue before the FWC. However, the *Itaquerão* stadium, where the opening ceremony was held, only had one (Watts 2014). The rush to complete the infrastructure has risked compromising the safety requirements and quality necessary to host the tournament. It also risked the safety of both participating teams and fans. While the FWC was underway in July, an unfinished overpass in the FWC host city of Belo Horizonte collapsed onto a busy carriageway below, where the incident left two people dead and 22 others injured (BBC 2014a). As part of the FWC infrastructure projects, the overpass was supposed to have been completed in time. In a bid to achieve readiness for the 12 host venues, secondary infrastructural projects were marginalized while the Brazilian government focussed its resources to meet construction schedules in time for the tournament. Critiques claimed that this fatal accident was a result of a knock-on impact of rushed preparations where safety standards have been compromised (Winter 2013).

Russia 2018

With the conclusion of Brazil 2014, attention has now turned to Russia 2018. Russia secured the hosting right to the FWC in 2010. The tournament will be held in 12 stadiums in 11 host cities spread 2500 km across the country, from 8 June to 8 July 2018. With the ambition to build 'a new Russia', as reiterated by the First Deputy Prime Minister Igor Shuvalov in his presentation to FIFA in 2010, the intention is to leverage the event for the modernization of Russia (Müller 2014). The benefits Russia expects from holding the FWC range from improving Russia's international standing and instilling a sense of national pride to turning around the country's standing in the international arena. Yet, as with all FWCs, the local geographical, economic and political factors external to the execution of the tournament generate a set of risks unique to Russia 2018. While less civil unrest and fewer concerns that the stadiums will not be completed on time are expected, other risks and challenges identified have been – terrorism, violence, racism, cost, associated infrastructural developments and boycotts.

Terrorism

The threat of international terrorism is perhaps the most prominent and recurring risk that the FWC is subjected to. The prominence of the tournament provides a platform for terror groups, dissidents and civic protests. The risk to Russia is made more prominent given some of the locations of host cities (eg Sochi and Volgogard) which are on the edge of the volatile Caucasus region. These cities are in close proximity to republics most affected by Islamic groups fighting for independence from the Russian Federation and creation of a wider Caucasus Emirate. The militants, recognizing that the value of increased media coverage and impact which could be obtained by attacking Russia, have carried out a number of high profiles in recent years. These include the suicide attacks against the metro system in 2010, the Domodedovo airport in Moscow in 2011 and three more attacks in Volgogard in 2013. The militant has also proven itself to be innovative in its approach where an attack was carried out in a stadium in Grozny in 2004.[3] A threat was also issued by the leader of the Caucasus Emirate militancy, Doku Umarov in January 2014, to disrupt the Winter Olympic Games. This threat, however, did not come to fruition. Analysts have suggested the possibility that the militancy did not believe it has the capability to launch any attack or it was simply making references to the Games to gain international media attention and/or to create a climate of fear around the Games (Allen-Vanguard 2014).

Political situation may change before and during the FWC period that can pose a significant risk of resulting in terrorist acts. No doubt layers of physical security measures will be put in place (dubbed the 'ring of steel') as witnessed during the Winter Olympic Games; but actions of militants conducting terrorist attacks are difficult to predict. The threat of terrorism hence could not be ruled out and remains high for Russia 2018. Given the history of recent successful attempts, attacks against transport infrastructure are very likely. Security efforts are often focused on premium sporting assets such as stadiums and athlete accommodations, the nation's transport infrastructure can be especially vulnerable. Security measures often do not extend to the outlying area, thus greatly increasing the possibility of an attack outside the 'ring of steel' where security is lacking. To add on to the challenge, securing the transport infrastructure and outside the host venues can be problematic with their complexities and cost. It is expected that security budgets for anti-terrorism measures will be at all-time high for Russia 2018, to reflect the challenges particular to Russia.

Costs and associated infrastructural development

Treading a familiar path to recent FWCs, the projected cost for the 2018 FWC has already nearly doubled the original budget halfway through its preparation. At more than US$20 bn (£13.1 bn), which only accounts for the hosting of the tournament, scholars have estimated Russia 2018 to be the most expensive FWC yet (Chadwick 2014; Müller and Wolfe 2014). The 12 stadiums have been budgeted separately at US$ 6.9 bn (£4.5 bn),[4] with six constructed anew and the rest renovated. Construction on most venues has not even started, which raised concerns over the tournament preparations (Butler 2014). With a non-negotiable deadline of the tournament's opening, this suggests that the final cost will escalate the expense which inevitably will be borne by the public. Analysts have forecasted that Russia's economy is stalling (Müller 2014); such massive state spending is likely to strain the country's scarce resources further. Spiralling costs aside, the stadiums construction creates the risk of 'white elephants' where these venues will be under-utilized or see no use after the tournament. The overcapacity of several stadiums in South Africa from the FWC is a risk Russia will face. Prior to the new construction, stadiums in Russia had an estimated seating capacity of 1.4 m, which is adequate for existing demand. The new and renovated FWC stadiums will expand the capacity by almost a third (Müller 2014). This potentially creates the situation where supply outstrips demand – the minimum capacity for FWC stadium is 45,000 while the average attendance for the Russian Premier League is 11,500, which is among the lowest in Europe. Despite rising disposable income and the regular upgrading of stadiums, match attendance has stagnated since 2007 (Müller 2014; Riordan 2007). These new stadiums are thus unlikely to attract enough number of visitors that will enable the owners and/or the Russian government to recoup their construction and maintenance costs.

Violence and racism

The risk of overcapacity aside, a bigger challenge inside the stadium will be its security – keeping out fans with violence and/or racist tendencies. Security concerns were raised when Russian fans displayed extreme nationalist banners during the country's opening match in Brazil 2014. The use of pyrotechnics, smoke grenades and display of offensive banners have become commonplace among Russian fans in recent years (Agapov 2013). Recent incidents include EURO 2012 and the championship game between the Moscow Dynamo and Torpedo in 2012, where fans threw fireworks onto the pitch and displayed offensive banners. Fans clashes and brawls with police force during matches are by no means unheard of (Golubock 2014). Although a new law, dubbed the 'Fans Law' aimed at curtailing football violence, has been in place since January 2014, the effect of the measure has yet to be seen.

Dealing with football violence is by no means the only challenge for the organizer. The racist football culture is another major area of concern, which the Russia organizing committee vowed to combat prior to the award of hosting right (Agapov 2013). After repeated racist incidents by fans, Russian champions CSKA Moscow have been sanctioned by UEFA to play all of their Champions League home group games for the 2014/2015 season behind closed doors as punishment. Former Brazilian defender Robert Carlos and Congolese international Christopher Samba, both who played for a Russian football club, as well as Manchester City's Ivorian midfielder Yaya Toure, are among those who have been racially abused in Russia in recent years (Saakov 2014). Toure has openly suggested a boycott of Russia 2018 for black players. A warning has also been issued by Piara Powar, a member of FIFA's anti-discrimination task force, that African teams may boycott the matches at Russia 2018. Powar, who is also the executive director of Football Against Racism in Europe (FARE) has commented that 'the levels of racism and attacks that are taking place […] are at levels completely unacceptable in a country that is going to host the World Cup' (cited in Etchells 2014).

Any outbreaks of violence or racist incidents will not only exacerbate security issues, they can cause political embarrassment for host nations and organizers. Instead of securing a positive image of the country apart from the communist image that the Russian brand represented in the past, any failure in policing and security approaches can lead to potential reputational damage of the host country. It can result in long-term economic loss from business opportunities. As global corporations seek to protect their own brands from negative associations with violence and public unrest, the prospect of brand damage from negative images associated with an event may deter sponsors, as they might find themselves embroiled involuntarily in negative press associated with a host country witnessed during the Brazil Confederations Cup. As it is, recent report (IEG 2014) suggests that there has been a cutback on sponsorship activation and marketing by the Olympic partners for the recently concluded 2014 Sochi Winter Olympic Games over Sochi's negative press.

Boycotts

Major sporting events are increasingly used as platforms for political activists of all types to communicate their message and promote campaigns of all kinds. As sports and politics become increasingly intertwined, the host country's geopolitical environment poses possible risks for the tournament. Any discord between ruling parties, governments and nations raises political issues which poses threat to the impending event. The annexation of Crimea into the Russian Federation, Russia has already led to calls among Western countries to boycott Russia 2018 (Spiegel and Olivier 2014). This call for boycott over the territorial dispute in Russia is an added risk to the earlier threat of boycott over its racist football culture. Britain's Deputy Prime Minister Nick Clegg has reportedly called for the revoke of hosting right from Russia, justifying the action as 'a very potent political and symbolic sanction' (Cited in BBC 2014c). Notwithstanding international alienation and reputational damage, the range and scope of risks for the tournament over the political actions are multi-fold – terrorist acts, protest activities with possibility of violence and demonstrations pre- and post-tournament period, to name a few. Financially, in addition to economic sanctions, Russia's action risks affecting relations with commercial partners, in particular, sponsors for the tournament.[5] As the crisis in Ukraine continues, repercussions from Russia's actions are still unfolding although it will take a while to have any tangible effect on the tournament.

Conclusion

Sports mega-events like the FWC have often been staged for their perceived economic benefits and values. High stakes are involved for host organizations and governments to ensure a successful and memorable event, where failure to deliver can lead to long-term reputational damages. As the world's most watched sporting event, hosting the FWC carries exceptional risks including terrorists incidents, football violence, protests, budget over-spends, operational failures and protests. Many of these risks have been recurring for every edition of the FWC and at the same time as generating its own set of risks along with the change of location for each FWC. As with the security concerns preceding Germany 2006, South Africa 2010 and Brazil 2014, Russia 2018 faces its unique set of risks which differs in the main causes, forms and effects. However, the socio-political environment and seeming lag in adequate preparation in Russia intensified concerns of catastrophic risks. The key risks for Russia 2018 that have emerged through the analysis of previous FWCs are delineated within the broad categories of: terrorism, inflating costs, football violence, racism as well as boycotts of the tournament. The biggest risk yet to be encountered in organization of the tournament, nevertheless, will be the unpredictability of the political, economic and social development in the years leading up to 2018. Although Russia's geopolitical environment is likely to change by 2018, political observers predict that the Russia will still be experiencing turmoil over the Crimea situation for years to come (Wright 2014). Given the Russian determination to demonstrate itself as a successful, modern nation through Russia 2018, no doubt massive capital will be invested to ensure a safe and smoothly running event. This too, may run into the risk of security arrangements eclipsing the tournament itself. Regardless, with the successful staging of the recently concluded Sochi Winter Olympic Games, the challenges of mitigating the risks of organizing a FWC in Russia are in effect no higher. Risk can never be totally eliminated but can be minimized. Ultimately, the early preparation and implementation of preventative and security measures remains the key to securing the tournament.

Notes

1. A series of coordinated suicide attacks was carried by four Islamist home-grown terrorists in central London on 7 July 2005 which targeted civilians using the public transport system during the morning rush hour. It coincided with the G8 summit which was taking place in Gleneagles, Scotland.
2. Two car bombings, allegedly carried out by the al-Qaida group, were carried out in the Egyptian resort of Sharm el-Sheik allegedly carried out in 23 July 2005.
3. A bomb was planted in the Dynamo stadium in the Chechen capital of Grozny during its construction phase. The bomb was set off during the Victory Day parade, killing the Russian backed Chechen president, Akhmad Kadyrov.
4. This budget accounts only for the hosting of the tournament. The cost per seat of Russia stadiums is estimated at US$11,600; double those in Brazil.
5. Emirates has recently ended its sponsorship with FIFA which started since 2006, allegedly over FIFA's tainted image over corruption. This indicates the delicate nature of corporate concerns on adversity of brand image.

Disclosure statement

No potential conflict of interest was reported by the authors.

References

Agapov, E. 2013. "The Problem of Football Hooliganism in Russia." *Proceedings of the 1st Global Virtual Conference*, 119–120, April 8–12. Accessed June 16, 2014. http://www.gv-conference.com/archive/?vid=1&aid=3&kid=40101-47&q=f1

Alexander, B. 2006. "World Cup Threat." *BBC* [Online], March 30. Accessed June 18, 2014. http://news.bbc.co.uk/sport1/hi/football/world_cup_2006/4860986.stm

Allen-Vanguard. 2014. "Russia: Security Challenges and Threats to the 2014 Sochi Winter Olympics." *Allen-Vanguard International Corporation* [Online], February 10. Accessed March 15, 2014. https://portal.allenvanguard-uk.com/DesktopModules/AllenVanguardModule/Media.ashx?Id=39&type=p

Aon. 2014. *Aon Terrorism and Political Violence 2014 Map*. London: Aon Risk Solutions.

BBC. 2009. "Fans Blamed for Ivorian Stampede." *BBC News* [Online], March 30. Accessed September 12, 2014. http://news.bbc.co.uk/1/hi/world/africa/7971596.stm

BBC. 2013. "Brazil World Cup: Six Stadiums to Miss FIFA Deadline." *BBC News* [Online], December 5. Accessed December 15, 2013. http://www.bbc.co.uk/news/world-latin-america-25226088

BBC. 2014a. "Flyover Collapses in Brazil World Cup Host City." *BBC News* [Online], July 4. Accessed August 1, 2014. http://www.bbc.co.uk/news/world-latin-america-28155216

BBC. 2014b. "World Cup 2014: Curitiba Stadium Earns FIFA Reprieve." *BBC News* [Online], February 18. Accessed February 18, 2014. http://www.bbc.co.uk/sport/0/football/26249123

BBC. 2014c. "World Cup Should Not Be Held in Russia, Nick Clegg Says." *BBC* [Online], July 27. Accessed July 28, 2014. http://www.bbc.co.uk/news/uk-28508509

BDI (Bundesministerium des Innern). 2006. *Evaluation Report: The National Security Strategy for the 2006 FIFA World Cup*. Berlin: BDI.

Blazkiewicz, S. 2010. "South Africa 2010 FIFA World Cup – Security Assessment." *SASMA* [Online]. Accessed December 30, 2013. http://sas-ma.org/eng/index.php/edition-july-2010/229-south-africa-2010-fifa-world-cup-security-assessment-sebastian-blazkiewicz

Botha, A. 2010. *Preparations for the 2010 FIFA World Cup: Vulnerability and Threat of Terrorism – Working Paper*. Madrid: Elcano Royal Institute.

Butler, N. 2014. "Moscow to Spend $8 Billion on Hosting 2018 FIFA World Cup." *Inside the Games* [Online], April 21. Accessed June 2, 2014. http://www.insidethegames.biz/sports/summer/football/732-world-cup/1019595-moscow-to-spend-8-billion-on-hosting-2018-fifa-world-cup

Carnibella, G., A. Fox, K. Fox, J. McCann, J. Marsh, and P. Marsh. 1996. *Football Violence in Europe: A Report to the Amsterdam Group*. Oxford: The Social Issues Research Centre.

Chadwick, S. 2014. "Assessing Risk in Sport – Will Russia 2018 Go Ahead?" *The Scorecard* [Online], July 31. Accessed August 1, 2014. http://thescorecard.org/post/832

Cornelissen, S. 2011. "Mega Event Securitisation in a Third Word Setting: Global Processes and Ramifications during the 2010 FIFA World Cup." *Urban Studies* 48 (15): 3221–3240.

Davies, W. 2014. "How Brazil Silenced Its Critics." *BBC News* [Online], July 16. Accessed August 1, 2014. http://www.bbc.co.uk/news/world-latin-america-28322375

Donaldson, R., and S. Ferreira. 2009. "(Re-)Creating Urban Destination Image: Opinions of Foreign Visitors to South Africa on Safety and Security?" *Urban Forum* 20: 1–18.

Etchells, D. 2014. "African Teams Could Boycott 2018 FIFA World Cup Matches If Russian Racism Continues, Warns Top Official." *Inside the Games* [Online], October 26. Accessed October 27, 2014. http://www.insidethegames.biz/sports/summer/football/732-world-cup/1023452-african-teams-could-boycott-2018-fifa-world-cup-matches-if-russian-racism-continues-warns-top-official

Federal Ministry of the Interior. 2006. *Review by the Federal Government on the 2006 FIFA World Cup*. Berlin: Bundesministerium des Innern.

Frosdick, S., and P. Marsh. 2005. *Football Hooliganism*. Devon: Willan Publishing.

Giulianotti, R., and R. Robertson. 2009. *Globalization and Football*. London: Sage.

Golubock, D. G. 2014. "Russian Football Violence Reinforces Concerns about 2018 World Cup." *The Moscow Times* [Online], May 15. Accessed June 16, 2014. http://www.themoscowtimes.com/arts_n_ideas/article/russian-football-violence-reinforces-concerns-about-2018-world-cup/500176.html

Grix, J. 2013. "The Risks and Rewards of Hosting Sports Mega-events." *International Centre for Sport Security Journal* 1 (1): 22–27.

Horne, J. 2007. "The Four 'Knowns' of Sports Mega-events." *Leisure Studies* 26 (1): 81–96.

Houlihan, B., and R. Giulianotti. 2012. "Politics and the London 2012 Olympics: The (in)Security Games." *International Affairs* 88: 701–717.

IEG. 2014. "Sochi 2014 Olympics Sponsorship Insights." *IEG Consulting* [Online]. Accessed August 1, 2014. http://www.sponsorship.com/Sponsorship-Consulting/Sochi-2014-Olympic-Sponsorship-Insights.aspx

Ingle, S. 2013. "Football Hooliganism, Once the English Disease, is More like a Cold Sore Now." *The Guardian* [Online], November 4. Accessed January 12, 2014. http://www.theguardian.com/football/blog/2013/nov/03/english-football-hooliganism

International Regional Information Network. 2010. "South Africa: Poor People's Movement Draws Government Wrath." *UN Office for the Coordination of Humanitarian Affairs* [Online], April 21. Accessed October 12, 2014. http://www.irinnews.org/report/88883/south-africa-poor-people-s-movement-draws-government-wrath

Jennings, Will. 2012. *Mega-events and Risk Colonization: Risk Management and the Olympics*. Discussion Paper 71. London: London School of Economics and Political Science.

Klauser, F. 2008. "FIFA Land 2006™: Alliances between Security Politics and Business Interests for Germany's City Network." In *Architectures of Fear*, edited by S. Graham, 173–188. Barcelona: Centre of Contemporary Culture of Barcelona.

Masters, J. 2014. "World Cup 2014: Can the FBI Help Stop Brazil's World Cup Protesters?" *CNN* [Online], May 13. Accessed June 1, 2014. http://edition.cnn.com/2014/05/13/sport/football/world-cup-brazil-security-football/

McGreal, C. 2001. "Families Mourn 43 Killed in Football Stampede." *The Guardian* [Online], April 12. Accessed October 1, 2014. http://www.theguardian.com/world/2001/apr/12/football

Müller, M. 2014. "Event Seizure: The World Cup 2018 and Russia's Illusive Quest for Modernisation." *Social Science Research Network* [Online], June 1. Accessed August 1, 2014. http://dx.doi.org/10.2139/ssrn.2368219

Müller, M., and S. D. Wolfe. 2014. "World Cup Russia 2018: Already the Most Expensive Ever?" *Russian Analytical Digest* 150: 2–6.

Overseas Security Advisory Council. 2010. "South Africa 2010 Crime & Safety Report." *United States Department of State Bureau of Diplomatic Security* [Online], June 9. Accessed August 10, 2014. https://www.osac.gov/pages/ContentReportPDF.aspx?cid=9474

Piette, C. 2010. "South Africa Deports Argentine Football 'Hooligans." *BBC News* [Online], June 7. Accessed June 16, 2014. http://www.bbc.co.uk/news/10257163

Raspaud, M., and F. da Cunha Bastos. 2013. "Torcedores de futebol: Violence and Public Policies in Brazil before the 2014 FIFA World Cup." *Sport in Society* 16 (2): 192–204.

Riordan, J. 2007. "Football: Nation, City and the Dream. Playing the Game for Russia, Money and Power." *Soccer & Society* 8 (4): 545–560.

Robbins, G. 2012. *Major International Events and the Working Poor: Selected Lessons for Social Actors Stemming from the 2010 Soccer World Cup in Africa.* Cambridge, MA: Women in Informal Employment: Globalising and Organising.

Saakov, R. 2014. "Russia 2018: Major Challenges for Next World Cup Hosts." *BBC* [Online], July 22. Accessed August 1, 2014. http://www.bbc.co.uk/news/world-europe-28409784

Smith, D., and O. Gibson. 2010. "World Cup Stewards Strike over Pay." *The Guardian* [Online], June 16. Accessed August 10, 2014. http://www.theguardian.com/football/2010/jun/16/world-cup-stewards-strike-pay

Solomon, H. 2011. *Playing Ostrich: Lessons Learned from South Africa's Response to Terrorism.* Washington, DC: Africa Center for Strategic Studies, National Defense University.

Soto, A. 2014. "Brazil Braces for Argentine Hooligans During World Cup." *Reuters* [Online], June 9. Accessed June 16, 2014. http://in.reuters.com/article/2014/06/09/us-soccer-world-hooligans-idINKBN0EK18N20140609

Spaaij, R. 2007. "Football Hooliganism as a Transnational Phenomenon: Past and Present Analysis: A Critique – More Specificity and Less Generality." *The International Journal of the History of Sport* 24 (4): 411–431.

Spiegel, P., and C. Olivier. 2014. "Western Diplomats Consider Boycott of Russia 2018 World Cup." *The Financial Times* [Online], September 2. Accessed September 6, 2014. http://www.ft.com/cms/s/0/26f10494-32b9-11e4-b86e-00144feabdc0.html#axzz3K08Pij00

Spiegel Online. 2006. "Violence in Stuttgart: German Police Confront English Hooligans." *Spiegel Online International* [Online], June 25. Accessed July 18, 2014. http://www.spiegel.de/international/violence-in-stuttgart-german-police-confront-english-hooligans-a-423490.html

Tynan, G. 2014. "World Cup 2014: Brazil Creates 10,000-Strong Elite Security Force to Deal with Expected Protests." *The Independent* [Online], January 3. Accessed January 4, 2014. http://www.independent.co.uk/sport/football/international/world-cup-2014-brazil-creates-10000strong-elite-security-force-to-deal-with-expected-protests-9037996.html

Watts, J. 2014. "World Cup Diary: Brazil's Hooligans Cut Loose after Attack on England Fans." *The Guardian* [Online], June 20. Accessed July 1, 2014. http://www.theguardian.com/football/2014/jun/20/world-cup-diary-brazil-hooligans-england-fans

Winter, B. 2013. "Insight: Brazil's Opening World Cup Stadium: Troubled from the Start." *Reuters* [Online], December 11. Accessed February 2, 2014. http://www.reuters.com/article/2013/12/11/us-brazil-worldcup-stadium-insight-idUSBRE9BA0ZW20131211

Withnall, A. 2013. "Confederations Cup Final Marred by Violent Clashes between Protesters and Riot Police after Brazil Beat Spain 3-0 in Rio." *The Independent* [Online], July 1. Accessed January 6, 2014. http://www.independent.co.uk/news/world/americas/confederations-cup-final-marred-by-violent-clashes-between-protesters-and-riot-police-after-brazil-beat-spain-30-in-rio-8680899.html

Wright, C. 2014. "Russia's World Cup Hosting in Jeopardy as Ukraine Escalates." *Forbes* [Online], August 29. Accessed September 1, 2014. http://www.forbes.com/sites/chriswright/2014/08/29/russias-world-cup-hosting-in-jeopardy-as-ukraine-escalates/

The language of football: a cultural analysis of selected world cup nations

Niels N. Rossing ⓘ and Lotte S. Skrubbeltrang ⓘ

ABSTRACT

This essay aims to describe how actions in the football field relate to the different national teams' and countries' cultural understanding of football and how these actions become spoken dialects within a language of football. Inspired by Edgar Schein's framework of culture, the Brazilian and Italian national team football cultures were examined. The basis of the analysis was both document and video analysis. The documents were mostly research studies and popular books on the national football cultures, while the video analysis included all matches including Italy and Brazil from the World Cup in 2010 and 2014. The cultural analysis showed some coherence between the national football cultures and the national teams, which suggested a national dialect with the language of the game. Each national dialect seemed to be based on different basic assumptions and to some extent specific symbolic actions on the field. The actions were found to be quite dynamic, which questions the cultural stability at the national team level. Furthermore, the analysis also revealed some incoherence between the national teams and the Brazilian and Italian football culture in general. The results question the idea of the national team as a symbol of a particular national football culture.

Introduction

Even though football has been called a major cultural phenomenon, there seem to be numerous ideas of what kind of phenomenon football actually is (Tomlinson, Markovits, and Young 2003). The historian Richard Holt argues that football is a mirror for its spectators (Holt 1989), while Janet Lever argues that football fosters social integration through the ritualization of conflict (Lever 1995). The anthropologist Eduardo Archetti considers football as a 'rich, complex, open scenario that has to be taken seriously' (Archetti 1992). Inspired by system theory, sport can also be viewed as a functional communication system of a society, because modern society needs a system capable of representing distinctions (Wagner and Storm 2013). Wagner and Storm argue that the body is a fundamental communication medium in sport (Wagner and Storm 2013). Tangen connects these characteristic distinctions to sport codification that reveals the core value of the game such as win/lose and progress/regress, which vehicles the development in sport (Tangen 2004). In essence, it seems that football is a field of communication for both players and spectators. From an interactionist approach, football as an activity and cultural phenomenon therefore can be seen as a symbolic system, which is primarily mediated and communicated through bodies.

Traditionally, we understand verbal communication as language. This tendency might be inspired by the philosopher George Herbert Mead (Brandt 2004) who advocated that the verbal language is the mechanism by which the mind is socially constituted (Mead 1967). Human ability to verbalize thoughts is seen as the starting point for language, but the body is often forgotten as a medium of communication of thoughts and social constitution of the mind, which challenges the privileged status of verbal language.

With inspiration from the German poet Bertold Auerbach, who wrote, 'Music is the universal language, the only one that requires no translation' (Auerbach 2013), we argue that like music, football can also be understood as a universal language. The philosopher Ludwig Von Wittgenstein, who is famous for his analogy with language as a game, an analogy he presumably thought of when passing a field where a football game was in play (Chihara and Fodor 1965). Wittgenstein explains his language game using chess as an example. Chess is played using a set of rules, much like language is spoken with a certain set of grammar rules, each draw can be seen as an argument in a discussion, and it exists because of the individual player, the one speaking the language. Much like Wittgenstein, the linguist Saussure also used chess as an analogy for language, adding that each piece in itself is not a part of the game, but only becomes part of the game, when it is recognized as valuable in or to the game (Harris 1988). In the same sense, Saussure argues that a word is only given meaning when used in the right way in the language system. We argue that a passing in itself does not contain any value outside the system, but is recognized as valuable inside the football system. Saussure defines any language to have two components: a language system and language users (Danesi 2003). Consequently, football can be characterized as a language that contains a system with standardized, specific rules of the game across national boundaries and users with actual choices and actions within the game. All football participants such as players, coaches, spectators and media can be considered language users embedded in different collective social institutions such as national cultures that affect their choices in game playing situations.

The writer Eduardo Galeano comments: 'a style of play is a way of being that reveals the unique profile of each community and affirms its right to be different' (Galeano 2013). Thus, considering football as a language means that the distinct dialects are expressed in actions on the field such as the shifting tempo, centre of mass and directions in space and all reveal an individual's attachment and identification with a certain community, which Maguire named *anchors of meaning* (Maguire 2000). However, national football cultures are experiencing the effect of global time – space compression, which the Bosman ruling of the European Court of Justice in December 1995 may have increased by allowing professional soccer players to frequently migrate between countries (Maguire and Pearton 2000). Although a study concluded that the rule did not affect the competitive balance at national level across countries, the style and meaning of playing may have been affected (Frick 2009). The rule together with the global time – space compression may have standardized the actions and meanings on the field towards a homogenization trend (Wagner 1990), and as a result the dialects of the language of football might die out. To our knowledge, this has not been empirically studied even though such studies can unfold important knowledge on the global processes between different national football cultures.

This essay aims to describe how actions in the football field relate to the different national understandings of football and how these actions become spoken dialects within a language of football. Furthermore, we aim to analyse the consistency between the national football team culture and the espoused national football culture. We argue that a deeper analysis is required to understand *how* and *why* football dialects differ between selected national teams and football cultures. This provides us with a better understanding of how national teams function and what they represent in a globalized world. In our study, we examine two national football teams and football cultures through empirical research in a systematic, but not exhaustive cultural analysis. We allude to qualitative data in the form of document and video to support our cultural analysis.

The following section offers atheoretical framework for the study. The second section presents the study's research design and methodology. The main findings and results are illustrated in the third section, and the final section presents the conclusions and provides directions for future studies.

Theoretical framework

Culture in an organizational perspective

In this essay, we are inspired by a functionalist view upon organizational culture theory, which is understood as a collective phenomenon, an independent, stable and social unity (Schein 1990). We have chosen to include this theoretical standpoint, because we believe it unites the idea of football as a language and the functionalist cultural theory. Edgar Schein argues that any culture consists of three levels, namely artefacts, espoused values and basic assumptions. *Artefacts* refer to physical appearance and communication, but also to central verbal artefacts such as notions or statements of philosophy. This level is easy to observe, but difficult to decipher. *Espoused values* are less visible and found as social principles, norms, goals, and in the way members of culture describe their culture to others. *Basic assumptions* are underlying reasons for actions that usually exist at an unconscious level, but are taken for granted and are therefore derived by the researchers (Schein 1990). In a football setting, each player and his or her actions can be considered as an artefact – a concrete symbol in motion embedded in espoused values and basic assumptions. The basic assumptions are essential for the obvious differences for the actions in the football field, and allow us to understand the reasons for distinct actions in the field.

We have advocated that football can be defined as a language system that operates with actions as words, thus the dialects within the language system become a specific symbolic system, because the symbols imply different meanings to different recipients. In this case, the dialects within football probably contain various symbolic systems that are based on different assumptions. We find that the basic assumption is the root of the football dialects within different national systems, with more or less variations on the national team and clubs within the system. We consider both national teams and national sport cultures as stable social unities. These units or groups have a distinct culture, that can be defined as '... what a group learns over a period of time as that group solves its problems of survival in an external environment and its problems in internal integration' (Schein 1990). Internal integration creates unity among group members with respect to values of the organization. For instance, when young footballers are integrated into any respective football culture, they are taught to both play *and* perceive football from a certain cultural understanding. External adaptation on the other hand refers to the cultures' required adaptation to its surrounding. For example, when a national team experiences failure, the playing style may be revised leading to new espoused values or even basic assumptions of playing, thus changing the culture.

Methodology

Research methods and instruments

Most studies in organizational culture use written or verbal content as units for analysis (Martin and Siehl 1983). However, according to Bryman, documents should be recognized as a broad term containing physical objects, photographs and technologies (Bryman 2012). A broad selection of research has studied physical symbols by linking them to patterns of meaning through 'the hermeneutic dimension' (Gagliardi 1990). For instance, a study on customers contained photographs as an empirical source revealing cultural assumptions in a non-verbalized but substantive way (Gagliardi 1990). Larsen and Schultz found that the emergent physical symbols within an organization serves as an unintended pathway to highlight the culture of the organization (Larsen and Schultz 1990), while Berg and Kreiner showed how corporate architecture served as symbols of strategic profile and status (Berg and Kreiner 1990).

In this paper we use a combination of written documents and videos of selected football matches as units for analysis. Therefore, data were collected from document analysis, which included both text analysis and video analysis of each national football culture and national team. In order to grasp all three cultural levels (Schein 1990) of the national teams, specific actions on the field have been included as these indicate the actual culture in action, the artefacts, of the national teams. Furthermore, the written documents provide us with insights to the espoused values.

As mentioned in our theoretical framework, basic assumptions are not easily derived. We did not have the opportunity to study different football cultures through extensive observational studies, which would be preferable when doing a cultural analysis. Instead we looked towards both scientific articles and popular books available in English all focusing on football culture and playing style. Because we had to derive our basic assumptions from document analysis, we chose two of the best-described football nations in popular and scientific publications with regard to playing style and national football culture – Brazil and Italy. Furthermore, both nations participated in the last two World Cups. We derived the basic assumptions through structured meaning coding (Huberman and Miles 2002) of the scientific articles and popular books available in English. In our coding, we asked several questions leading to our description of the basic assumptions that can be found in the scheme for the document analysis. In the coding phase, inter-rater reliability (Armstrong et al. 1997; Huberman and Miles 2002) is enhanced through a third researcher coding samples of documents and through discussions of differences in codes (Kvale 1996).

We used videos of World Cup football matches in 2010 and 2014 to capture the action artefacts of the national teams and the documents to analyse the national team cultures of Brazil and Italy. The video analysis was performed on all World Cup matches that each nation played in 2010 and 2014 because they represent central physical and action-oriented artefacts. The rationale was that data gathered from higher-level competitive settings are more reliable than data obtained from lower-level settings (Ericsson 1996), since all stakeholders, especially players and coaches and nations as such, highly prioritize and value the tournament. Examining data collected from online sources is among the methodological approaches adopted by scholars interested in examining playing styles (Pollard and Gómez 2009). The material on the matches was retrieved from an online Danish library (http://www.statsbiblioteket.dk, 2014). We analysed three Italy matches and five Brazil matches of the 2010 World Cup and three Italy and seven Brazil matches of the 2014 World Cup.

We do acknowledge that no culture can be empirically analysed objectively because every description of human interaction contains a degree of social construction (Gullestrup 2007). In doing so, we are aware that we are embedded within a Danish football culture, and that is our cultural standpoint. In our effort to reach inter-rater reliability, we have developed an analysis scheme with inspiration from a Danish study on footballers in Trinidad and Tobago and revised accordingly to the purpose of the present study (Almind and Madsen 2003). The scheme includes actions such as high, low or changing tempo and directions in space such as playing the ball pluralistically or mostly directly to the opponent's goal. These categories were selected, since they all in various ways try to grasp different actions within the game. These actions are thought of as action artefacts that are central to understand the culture within the actions.

All matches were coded using the scheme for analysis. Each researcher found a collective pattern in each category to find the action artefacts mostly observed. Mostly only nuances to the categories were found, with a few exceptions. One is Brazil in 2014 that changed their action artefacts drastically in both their semi-final and third place play-off. Since the pattern of action artefacts differed greatly from the rest of the matches, we relied on the former matches, since the actions on the field in these matches seemed more intentional. Furthermore, smaller incongruences between the researchers were found in few categories. Both researchers presented the categories and discussed the differences in order to reach intersubjective consensus (Gillespie and Cornish 2010).

Table 1 presents the action artefacts of the national teams in the World Cup 2010 and 2014, whereas Table 2 illustrates the cultural analysis of espoused values and basic assumptions for each national team and national football culture. The tables will not be discussed in detail, but they provide an overview of our analytical approach and results of the video and document analysis.

Analysis

Organization football culture: Italian football culture and the national team

Artefacts

What especially stands out in the video analysis of the Italian national team is changes in nearly all categories regarding the action artefacts from the World Cup 2010 to World Cup 2014. We found the external communication to be *somewhat hard* in 2010, which is altered in 2014 to a *shifting tendency*. Other altered central action artefacts are the movements of the ball, the movement of the players and the tempo. Interestingly, the only category in which the characteristics from the two World Cups are similar is the collective rhythm of the players.

Table 1. Analysis on action artefacts of Brazil and Italy in the World Cup.

Themes		Brazil 2010	Brazil 2014	Italy 2010	Italy 2014
Space					
Primary playing areas	*Small or large*	Mostly small areas	Mostly small areas	Relatively large areas	Small- to middle-sized areas
Movement of the ball	*Ground/air*	Mostly ground	Ground	Ground, but mostly air when on the attacking third[a]	Shifting between ground and air
Time					
Tempo	*Slow/Changing/Fast*	Changing	Mostly fast	Relatively slow	Changing
Rhythm	*Individually/Collective*	Mostly collective	Mostly individually	Collective	Collective
Communication internal					
Movement of the players	*Sideways/towards goal*	Both sideways and towards goal	Mostly towards goal	Mostly towards goal	Mostly sideways
Communication external					
Interaction with opponents	*Hard/soft*	Medium	Hard	Somewhat hard	Shifting between hard and soft

[a]The attacking third means the last third of the pitch closest to the opponents.

Table 2. The table illustrates the two levels of the national football culture of the two nations: Italy and Brazil.

	Italy	Brazil
Espoused values	'Our first priority is a clean sheet'	'The best defence is a good offense'
Basic assumptions		
How is football played?	Football is played with rationalism	Football is played with aesthetics
What characterises a winning team?	• A winning team is a good defensive team • A winning team wins by any means necessary	A winning team is a good offensive team
What is football about?	Football is about winning	Football is about displaying skills
What is most important in the game?	The result of the game	The beauty of the game
A team is characterised by	Collectivism	Individual qualities

Espoused values

We find the key value expressed by different insiders and outsiders in the environment includes the term *Catenaccio*. This term refers to a defensive playing style, but also a state of mind among the participants of the game. It leads us to the most outspoken Italian football cliché: 'Our first priority is a clean sheet' (Foot 2007), that again points to the defensive tactical position within the game. The defensive state of mind may be expressed through the observed collective rhythm, since this characteristic can be the result of the state of mind.

Basic assumptions

We find the national football culture in Italy to be characterized by a cultural paradigm that contains six interrelated basic assumptions. The first assumption is: *football is played with rationalism.* This assumption permeates the whole culture as both the discourse and the actions on and off the field point to this state of mind. The title of the autobiography of the Italian player Pirlo underlines this: 'I think therefore I am' (Pirlo and Alciato 2014). The second assumption reveals what characterizes a winning team; *a winning team is a good defensive team.* This is strongly coherent with the key espoused value, but it is also evident in terms of numbers of scored goals compared to Brazil. A study by Filho and colleagues found that in 80 years the Brazilian team had scored in average 2.0 goals per match, whereas the Italian team had scored 1.6 goals per match. Similar tendencies were also found at national league level in both the countries (Filho et al. 2013). We derive the third assumption from document analysis and find it to be: *A winning team wins by any means necessary.* For instance, 'An Italian crowd would applaud the kind of challenge that saves a goal even at the cost of a yellow card, even a red card …' (Goldblatt 2008). However, the external communication we found in the video analysis does not indicate such hardiness. Instead, the actions' analysis points to a development in the Italian national team from a somewhat hard external communication in 2010 to a more shifting tendency in 2014. Therefore, the basic assumptions found in the document analysis are not found to be especially coherent with the observed action artefacts.

The fourth assumption, *football is about winning*, is closely connected to the fifth assumption that states what is most important in football: *The result of the game.* This manifests the core of the culture, which the three levels centre around. The effort to win becomes dynamic, as there is no specific way to achieve this. However, the sixth assumption, *collectivism*, is a dogma to proceed to win. This dogma seems to be quite stable in both our video analysis and document analysis, which underline the cultural value of collectiveness that seems to exist within the Italian football culture and also in the Italian national team. The maintained collective rhythm indicates a strong cultural norm within the national football culture, whereas the other categories to some degree have altered in the four years between the World Cups. We find that the action artefacts from the World Cup 2010 to some degree are consistent with the basic assumptions. The action artefacts for the World Cup 2014 shift remarkably, which indicates clear alterations in playing style at national team level, but not directly as a change in consistency with most of the basic assumptions.

To sum up, the organization culture of Italian football and her national team is characterized by some degree of coherence between the different cultural levels in the World Cup 2010 and 2014. There are, however, discrepancies such as the hardness of the external communication, which could be a result of a cultural change or as a tactical adaptation from the national team. The action artefacts of the national team have to some degree shifted in between the World Cups. The considerable change in actions on the field may be a result of a cultural change, which a change in the positttion of national coach could indicate. Yet, this could also be a result of a conscious change in team tactics, which is consistent with most of the basic assumptions derived.

Organization football culture: Brazilian football culture and the national team

Artefacts
An essential verbal artefact is *Joga Bonito* (i.e. playing beautifully) that expresses a saying that also reflects the espoused values (Filho et al. 2013). However, we do not find this particularly coherent with the playing styles observed in both the World Cups. In 2010, the team played mostly collective, whereas in 2014, the team played with a tougher playing style. To some extent, these actions are incoherent with the espoused value and therefore incongruent with the national football culture. Furthermore, we find the central action artefacts to have both consistent and shifting action artefacts between the World Cups in

2010 and 2014. The Brazilian national team consistently plays in small areas and generally the ball moves at ground level in both the World Cups, which to some extent is coherent with the verbal artefact *Joga Bonito*. However, our analysis also shows a shift from a collectivist rhythm in 2010 to an individualist rhythm in 2014. This is an interesting change when compared to the changes found in external communication. We find that the external communication adjusts from medium to hard, which indicates a move towards a tougher playing style. Together with the shift in tempo from changing to fast and the movement of players towards goal, the action artefacts indicate a somewhat cultural shift in the playing style, not altogether in line with verbal artefacts and espoused values and basic assumptions as we will show in the next few paragraphs.

Espoused values

The key espoused value in Brazil is said to be: 'The best defence is a good offense' (Filho et al. 2013). This state of mind creates a clear emphasis on the offensive aspect of the game. The value is difficult to decipher directly from our action artefact analysis, but may be a state of mind of the team tactics and within the actions.

Basic assumptions

From our document analysis, we find the national football culture in Brazil to contain five interrelated basic assumptions characteristic of this cultural paradigm. The first assumption, *Football is played with aesthetics,* is in line with the action artefacts such as the individualistic rhythm from the World Cup 2014 and the espoused values. The second assumption, *A winning team is a good offensive team,* is coherent with the verbal artefact *Joga Bonito,* since the focus lies on the expertise with the ball. The third assumption, *Football is about displaying skills,* is found in the Brazilian writer Freyre's description of Brazilian football: '... Our passes ... our tricks... that something which is related to dance, to capoeira, mark the Brazilian style of football' (Brown 2014). The fourth assumption, *The beauty of the game,* indicates what is seen as the most important aspect of the game, which recurs in artefacts and espoused values. The individual offensive performance in the game is necessary to create the aesthetic demand, which leads us to the last and fifth assumption that a team is characterised by *Individual qualities.* However, as seen in the analysis of action-oriented artefacts, the rhythm of the game is characterized by both an individualism and collectivism, which indicates a discrepancy between action artefacts and basic assumptions. Additionally, the adjustment to a tougher playing style in 2014 is not found to be representative in the document analysis as well and therefore not congruent with the national football culture.

Although the organization of the Brazilian football culture and the national team overall seem to be characterized by a coherence between the different levels, certain characteristics are somewhat inconsistent with the national culture. The move from collective to individualized rhythm is a move towards the derived basic assumptions, but it also indicates a dynamic relationship with the actions on the field. Another inconsistency is how the tougher playing style in the 2014 World Cup to some degree interferes with the basic assumptions related to aesthetics. This may be regarded as a minor cultural adjustment, but it can also be viewed as a culturally adapting playing style, that to some extent is in contrast to the basic assumptions derived from the national football culture in Brazil. However, it may also be a dynamic shift in the basic assumptions at the national football culture of what Brazilian football is, how it is played and what Brazilians think football is.

Discussion

The cultural analysis of the two national teams and football cultures revealed findings that may be summarized as follows.

National teams as playing dialects

We have found that the action artefacts clearly show changes in both national teams, but mostly moderate changes. Furthermore, the empirical analysis also illustrates that football dialects are based on different assumptions and understandings of the game, resulting in distinct actions on the field between the selected nations. This indicates that the national teams to some degree are adapting their playing styles from the two World Cups and therefore to some degree also culturally develop in time. In spite of the variations in action artefacts, the cultural analysis reveals some cohesion between basic assumptions, espoused values of the national football culture and the actions found in the national teams' playing style. The empirical analysis also shows differences between the national football cultures and national teams in the actions and understanding of football, which supports the notion that the playing styles can be understood as dialects within the language of football. International sport is said to be a national struggle in which national teams symbolize the nations: 'The imagined community of millions seems more real as a team of eleven named people. The individual, even the one who cheers, becomes a symbol of his nation himself.' (Hobsbawm 1990) The national symbol is not just about winning or losing the game, but also about displaying a specific national identity in an international tournament setting. In spite of the global time – space compression, our results indicate that national identity is still to some extent being expressed through the symbolic action artefacts that the players construct through their movements on the field. This process may be kept somewhat stable because other language users such as coaches, spectators, commentators etc. also co-construct the symbolic actions on the field and thereby stabilize basic assumptions.

Dynamic and stable national team cultures?

The revealed dialects within the language of football, however, do not seem to be stable cultural blueprints, but rather more dynamic cultural actions that mostly seem to operate within a set of espoused values and basic assumptions from the national football culture, that in some cases are found to be incoherent with these. For instance, we did not find a distinct individualistic rhythm in Brazilian football in the analysis of the actions on the field in 2010, which could indicate a shift in the actions as well as in the basic assumptions of the national team. We can only speculate as to why this shift is found in the analysis. One suggestion might be that the Brazilian national team in 2010 had intentionally adapted a more European playing style. The renowned Brazilian sociologist and writer Gilberto Freyre already proclaimed this as a necessary evolution: 'we need to conciliate the [Brazilian] individualism with the [European] discipline.'(Maranhão 2007) Interestingly, if the European dialect is understood as a collective rhythm, the quote may be quite precise, since Italy as an European representative in our analysis plays with a collective rhythm in both the World Cups. The Brazilian shift may have occurred because of the demands from the general public that emphasize performance as important, thus creating the possible alteration of playing style and understanding of the game. The cultural shift may have become acceptable within the language users, even though it alters the foundation of the Brazilian game – and therefore the basic assumptions, thereby to some degree creating a form of dichotomy between the national team culture and national football culture. However, according to our analysis, the European collectivistic trace was altered in the Brazilian team in 2014, since they seemed to return to more individual actions, which better resembles a Brazilian playing style according to the national football culture. Nevertheless, both national teams appear to have changed their dialect and therefore to some extent have created a cultural adaptation. The reasons for these cultural adaptations are numerous and our analysis does not allow us to give a precise answer. However, one possible explanation on the variations on the field is the change of leaders in both the national teams. Between the World Cups in 2010 and 2014, Italy changed their national coach from Marcello Lippi to Cesare Prandelli, while Brazil changed from Carlos Albert Parreira to Luiz Felipe Scolari. Since we have found that all language users co-construct the symbolic actions, a cultural transformation is rather difficult. However, Schein argues that leaders and cultures are particularly interwoven in both the organization and the culture, which makes coaches and managers the likely frontiers in the cultural evolution of the game (Schein 2010). Therefore, changing the national coach may create possibilities of altering actions on the field. Still, the national football culture possibly creates underlying cultural goals to be achieved in the game besides winning the game. These cultural goals could be characteristics such as aesthetics, hard work and collective rhythm within the playing style, which to some extent creates a cultural framework that the new national coaches may operate within.

Migration or homogenization

As of today almost all the Brazilian players in the national team live their daily lives in European countries and are consequently exposed to European assumptions about football. Thus, the shift to a more individualistic rhythm from the World Cup in 2010 to 2014 is even more interesting because it contradicts the obvious homogenization towards a more European playing style within the Brazilian national team. We observed the Brazilian national team in the World Cup 2010 to have a collective rhythm opposed to the described national football culture. Somehow the rhythm changed to mostly an individual rhythm, which points to a change in culture between the World Cups. The observed change in the rhythm between the World Cups can be characterized as a kind of *cultural looping*; the national team moved away from the perceived football culture, only to return to this playing style or dialect during the 2014 World Cup. The question is why the probable cultural looping occurs between the World Cups. The exposure to European football could unintentionally have altered the playing style in 2010, but the lack of contented results in 2010 might have pressured the national federation in Brazil to select a national coach, Scolari, with a more Brazilian playing style. It is also possible that the role as the host of the 2014 World Cup forced the federation to select a national coach with a more traditional Brazilian playing style, because this would display a more 'true' Brazilian football culture and bring more possible support to the language users.

Both the Brazilian and Italian national football teams seem mostly coherent with the national characteristics. Although both countries have had an excessive influx of foreign players to the national leagues (Maguire and Pearton 2000), both countries seem to have been able to remain a dialect, thus preventing a homogenized international playing style. In our cultural analysis, we find the national football cultures to inspire the observed national team football cultures even though there are variations in the action artefacts. The reason why that is the case may be the high pressure on results at national level, the players available to recruit from and also the leaders' cultural background. These factors may replace an idealized national football culture to a more short-term national team culture that includes a cultural adaptation in order to compete internationally.

Conclusion

In spite of the globalization and migration trends, our cultural analysis indicates that the national football culture and the national team remain rather stable, which to some extent coherently allow us to view the different playing styles as dialects within the language of football. This suggests that football as a language still has dialects that appear symbolically through the distinct movements on the field. However, some cultural inconsistencies were found between the Brazilian football culture and national culture, which may be a result of globalization or migration trends. Thus, in a globalized world, national teams may not function as representative of the national football culture, but as a more or less coherent symbolic artefact within the national football culture. This leads us to believe that one should look towards football club cultures for a dialect representation of national football culture instead of looking at national teams. However, when applying our methodology, the difficulties arise if the club cultures are less documented.

Keeping the cultural perspectives in mind would allow football coaches and managers to act accordingly to the underlying cultural assumptions. This may constrain alternative approaches to the style of play. The cultural insight may also ease transitions from one national league to another, allowing players to adapt to the cultural understanding of football in a given country with more ease than what has previously been the case.

Acknowledgment

We would like to thank Mads Lange Møller-Larsen to his contribution in our data analysis and to Diana Stentoft who revised an early draft of the paper.

Disclosure statement

No potential conflict of interest was reported by the authors.

ORCID

Niels N. Rossing ⓘ http://orcid.org/0000-0003-0271-0682
Lotte S. Skrubbeltrang ⓘ http://orcid.org/0000-0001-7419-1856

References

Almind, K., and K. L. Madsen. 2003. "Boldspil – I Clinch Med Kroppen Og Kulturen." [Ballgames - Going into clinch with the body and culture] In *Idrætpædagogisk Årbog*, edited by K. Lüders and N. Vogensen, 119–147. Aarhus: Klim.

Archetti, Eduardo P. 1992. "Argentinian Football: A Ritual of Violence?" *The International Journal of the History of Sport* 2: 209–235.

Armstrong, David, Ann Gosling, John Weinman, and Theresa Marteau. 1997. "The Place of Inter-rater Reliability in Qualitative Research: An Empirical Study." *Sociology* 31: 597–606. doi: 10.1177/0038038597031003015.

Auerbach, Berthold. 2013. *On the Heights a Novel*. London: Forgotten Books.

Berg, Per Olof, and Kristian Kreiner. 1990. "Corporate Architecture: Turning Physical Settings into Symbolic Resources." In *Symbols and Artifacts: Views of the Corporate Landscape*, edited by Pasquale Gagliardi, 41–67. New York: Aldine De Gruyter.

Brandt, Keri. 2004. "A Language of Their Own: An Interactionist Approach to Human-horse Communication." *Society & Animals* 12 (4): 299–316. doi: 10.1163/1568530043068010.

Brown, Matthew. 2014. *From Frontiers to Football: An Alternative History of Latin America since 1800*. London: Reaktion Books .

Bryman, Alan. 2012. *Social Research Methods*. 4th ed. Oxford: Oxford University Press.

Chihara, C. S., and J. A. Fodor. 1965. "Operationalism and Ordinary Language: A Critique of Wittgenstein." *American Philosophical Quarterly* 2: 281–295. http://www.jstor.org/stable/20009178.

Danesi, Marcel. 2003. *Second Language Teaching: A View from the Right Side of the Brain*. Dordrecht: Kluwer Academic .

Ericsson, K. Anders, ed. 1996. *The Road to Excellence: The Acquisition of Expert Performance in the Arts and Sciences, Sports, and Games*. New Jersey: Lawrence Erlbaum Associates.

Filho, Edson, I. Basevitch, Yanyun Yang, and Gershon Tenenbaum. 2013. "Is the Best Defense a Good Offense? Comparing the Brazilian and Italian Soccer Styles." *Kinesiology* 45 (2): 213–221.

Foot, John. 2007. *Winning at All Costs: A Scandalous History of Italian Soccer*. New York: Nation Books.

Frick, B. 2009. "Globalization and Factor Mobility: The Impact of the 'Bosman-ruling' on Player Migration in Professional Soccer." *Journal of Sports Economics* 10 (1): 88–106. doi: 10.1177/1527002508327399.

Gagliardi, Pascal. 1990. *Symbols and Artifacts: Views of the Corporate Landscape*. Edited by Pascal Gagliardi. New York: Aldine De Gruyter.

Galeano, Eduardo. 2013. *Soccer in Sun and Shadow*. London: Nation Books.

Gillespie, Alex, and Flora Cornish. 2010. "Intersubjectivity: Towards a Dialogical Analysis." *Journal for the Theory of Social Behaviour* 40: 19–46. doi: 10.1111/j.1468-5914.2009.00419.x.

Goldblatt, David. 2008. *The Ball is round: A Global History of Soccer*. London: Penguin.

Gullestrup, Hans. 2007. *Kulturanalyse: En Vej Til Tværkulturel Forståelse*. 4th ed. København: Akademisk forlag.

Harris, Roy. 1988. *Language, Saussure and Wittgenstein – How to Play Games with Words*. London: Routledge.

Hobsbawm, E. J. 1990. *Nations and Nationalism since 1780*. New York: Cambridge University Press.

Holt, Richard. 1989. *Sport and the British: A Modern History*. Oxford: Oxford University Press.

Huberman, Michael, and Matthew B. Miles. 2002. *The Qualitative Researcher's Companion*. London: Sage.

Kvale, Steinar. 1996. *Interviews: An Introduction to Qualitative Research Interviewing*. London: Sage.

Larsen, Janne, and Majken Schultz. 1990. "Artifacts in a Bureaucratic Monastery." In *Symbols and Artifacts: Views of the Corporate Landscape*, edited by Pasquale Gagliardi, 281–302. New York: De Gruyter.

Lever, Janet. 1995. *Soccer Madness: Brazil's Passion for the World's Most Popular Sport*. Illinois: Waveland Press.

Maguire, J. 2000. "Globalization and Sport." In *Handbook of Sport Studies*, edited by Coakley, Jay and Eric Dunning, 356–369. London: Sage.

Maguire, J., and R. Pearton. 2000. "The Impact of Elite Labour Migration on the Identification, Selection and Development of European Soccer Players." *Journal of Sports Sciences* 18 (9): 759–769. doi: 10.1080/02640410050120131.

Maranhão, Tiago. 2007. "Apollonians and Dionysians : The Role of Football in Gilberto Freyre's Vision of Brazilian People." *Soccer & Society* 8 (4): 510–523. doi: 10.1080/14660970701440790.

Martin, Joanne, and Caren Siehl. 1983. "Organizational Culture and Counterculture: An Uneasy Symbiosis." *Organizational Dynamics* 12 (2): 52–64. 10.1016/0090-2616(83)90033-5

Mead, George Herbert. 1967. "Wundt and the concept og the gesture". Chap. 7. In *Mind, Self, and Society – From the Standpoint of a Social Behaviorist (Works of George Herbert Mead)*, edited by Charles W. Morris, 42–51. Chicago: The University of Chicago Press.

Pirlo, Andrea, and Alessandro Alciato. 2014. *Andrea Pirlo: I Think Therefore I Play*. Milano: BackPage Press.

Pollard, Richard, and Miguel A. Gómez. 2009. "Home Advantage in Football in South-West Europe: Long-term Trends, Regional Variation, and Team Differences." *European Journal of Sport Science* 9 (6): 341–352. doi: 10.1080/17461390903009133.

Schein, E. H. 1990. "Organizational Culture." *American Psychologist* 45: 109–119. doi: 10.1037//0003-066X.45.2.109.

Schein, Edgar H. 2010. *Organizational Culture and Leadership*. 4th ed. New York: John Wiley and Sons.

Tangen, Jan Ove. 2004. *Hvordan Er Det Mulig? Skisse Til En Idrettssosiologi* [How is it possible? Drafts toward a sports sociology]. Kristiansand: Høyskoleforlaget.

Tomlinson, Alan, Andrei S. Markovits, and Christopher Young. 2003. "Introduction: Mapping Sports Space." *American Behavioral Scientist* 46 (11): 1463–1475. doi: 10.1177/0002764203046011001.

Wagner, Eric A. 1990. "Sport in Asia and Africa: Americanization or Mundialization?" *Sociology of Sport Journal* 7 (4): 399–402.

Wagner, Ulrik, and R. K. Storm. 2013. "Sport as a Communication System." In *The Routledge Handbook of Sport Communication*, edited by M. P. Pedersen, 46–55. London: Routledge.

Conflicting traditions: the FIFA World Cup, Australia and football identities

Binoy Kampmark 🆔

ABSTRACT
Demonstrable sectarianism and severity towards the sport of soccer in Australia has not prevented the country from reaching the FIFA World Cup tournament on several occasions. The national team, the Socceroos, have made qualification something of a normality. Despite reaching a position of some prestige in the social and cultural landscape, the sport finds itself in an unusual situation in Australia: a global enterprise that continues to struggle against rival and entrenched sporting codes despite its universal message; and an assortment of ethnic and cultural associations saddling it. In this, the game faces various challenges, with its supporters attempting to show its global appeal while trying to avoid suggestions of parochialism. Brazil 2014 provided the ideal platform for that demonstration.

'It's football, but not as you know it.'

A-League Slogan, August 2005

Introduction

Australia shares with the United States, and other historical 'white' dominions of the former British Empire, a common suspicion, or at the very least a disregard, for soccer over other sporting codes. For a sport considered the unquestionable 'global game', battles to entrench it in such societies as Australia have proved challenging for the game's custodians. In Australia, it has been deemed a 'wicked foreign game', though evidently such wickedness has been confined to the men's game, rather than the women's, where they have excelled (Hay 2006). Administrative bodies of rival sporting codes have taken aim against the game over decades, guarding any advances made by the sport, with at times ferocious dedication.

Such dedicated sectarianism and severity towards the sport, however, has not prevented Australia qualifying for the FIFA World Cup on several occasions, making the achievement even more impressive. The national team, the Socceroos, have made qualification something of a norm; much of this is, however, due to a reorientation of the qualification process in the Oceania region.

Despite gaining some prestige in the current social and cultural landscape, the sport in its Australian variation finds itself in an unusual situation: a global enterprise that continues to struggle against local codes despite its universal message, and an assortment of ethnic and cultural associations saddling it. In this, the game faces various challenges, with its supporters attempting to show its global appeal while trying to avoid suggestions of parochialism. Brazil 2014 provided the ideal platform for that demonstration.

Football wars

Where is soccer to be found, as Ian Syson puts it, in Australian cultural life? Australia's relationship with the game, suggests Syson, is a complex one, a combination of flat denial of its appeal, and obvious attraction on the other. It amounts to something of an ugly secret and rude confession – shunned in some circles yet embraced with need in others. For one, it is old – at least 125 when it comes to being first played in Victoria, and even older in New South Wales. Syson sees a range of reactions to the sport, many conflicting in nature. '[P]roponents of the game have constantly to justify themselves in watching, playing, preferring this supposedly "new" Australian sport'. (Syson 2009) It has been seen at stages as 'a menace to Australian masculinity and life in general' (Syson 2009).

Syson elaborates a particularly illuminating discussion that took place on a June 2009 instalment of Radio National's *Australia Talks*, including such soccer personalities as Andy Harper, John Kallinikios, Bonita Mersiades and Geoff Miles. Of greatest interest was a radio call from a member of the public 'Nicholas in Geelong'. Nicholas was keen to illuminate what he regarded as the essentially superior fitness and skills of the Australian Rules Football (AFL) players, notably such a player as Aaron Davey. 'Week in, week out Davey did things with the ball that would make Ronaldinho's jaw drop'. Indeed, Nicholas was cheeky enough to suggest that the team selectors had made a mistake overlooking Davey for the Socceroos (Syson 2009). Such presumption was telling, and even suggestive of deep insecurity: we have a local game superior in fitness and aesthetics to the global game. We simply have to remind people about it.

Such sentiments have been common. The strategy of those following the AFL code has been one of creating tradition, but more to the point, one that displaced, rather than grew out of, the soccer tree. Readings of football matches during the 1850s in Victoria were not necessarily suggestive of Australian Rules – they might just as well have been soccer itself. Such has been the lure, and threat, of soccer.

Australia's performances in getting to the World Cup are all the more impressive given the domestic battles waged by various codes, notably of the footballing variety, against soccer. The sport's attraction was always affected by the winter games of Australian Rules and Rugby. Cricket posed less of a threat than other codes, being ascendant during the summer months. But the greatest rival, notably in Victoria, was AFL. The editor of *Soccer News*, V. J. M. Dixon, would comment in 1954 that, 'The usual panic is on in on the home of another code [AFL] and all the clubs are combining to make sure "Our Wicked Foreign Game" shall not use any of their hallowed ovals'. (Dixon 1954, in Hay 2006) When soccer was not being considered a menace to supposedly indigenous sporting traditions, it was deemed a menace to itself, self-defeating in its existence. As Syson notes, the feuds within Australian soccer have been many, and 'unfathomable incompetence' frequent.

The historical flavour in this regard is intense and extensive, and suggests how the sport has survived, and at stages even expanded. The 1950s and early 1960s saw extensive growth in Melbourne, while, interestingly enough, Australian football in the Victorian Football League saw a modest decline (Kallinikios 2007). But the game remained persistently marked by the stereotype of 'wogball' (Warren, Harper, and Wittington 2002). It was axiomatic that the wogball tag suggested migrant associations (another way of referencing new migrants, notably of the non-Anglo base), and all that came with that.

Studies of violence and ethnicity have been made on perceptions demonizing soccer as exceptionally susceptible to attracting specific followers prone to exceptionally violent tendencies (Vamplew 1996; Danforth 2001). Specific ethnic groups have also been saddled with the label, locating the experience of soccer within a specific migrant experience (Hay 2001). The terminology is coded and loaded, tending to ignore the 'wider situation' which 'manifests itself along the fault line in a particular society' (Wen 2014). Such perceptions have been shown to be off the mark, with soccer violence in Australia being no less spectacular from other codes (Adair and Vamplew 1990). Distinctions matter: soccer is the foreign agent, and a point of juxtaposition that can be deemed 'un-Australian' (Hay 1994). Minor altercations and disagreements with fans see descriptions of 'soccer riot' or 'brawl' used. 'This mentality, this deep seated prejudice still lives and breathes in our country and there is no sign it is going away anytime soon'. (Murray 2012) The push towards de-ethnicization of Australian soccer, for that reason, became a consciously adopted policy to push the sport into mainstream attention (Hughson 2001).

The challenges proved formidable. Johnny Warren knew exactly what he was up against when he took part in a Socceroo motorcade through Sydney, one which saw beer-swilling patrons at a pub screaming extreme profanities and being told 'go back to where you came from' (Murray 2012). The fact that the team had just returned from Vietnam on a goodwill tour showed the dispiriting nature of the venture. Warren seemed to be a one-man army preaching for soccer in the antipodes, and not necessarily feeling he was getting anywhere. In doing so, he made it clear he was proselytizing with some fervour – after all, football was a passport, a global identity. It was part personal mission, but with an obvious suggestion: soccer, given the power of assumption as a global sport, had to be cultivated in the antipodes. Embracing it awoke 'the world citizen inside me' (Warren, Harper, and Wittington 2002).

In spite of this negativity, studies on Australian attendance for competitive international soccer matches, notably World Cup qualifiers, have shown persistently healthy numbers. FIFA World Cup qualifiers against Iran in 1997 and Uruguay in 2001 drew capacity crowds at the large Melbourne Cricket Ground. But such interest in the sport was far more enduring, stretching back to days when the game was not officially feted. As Hay notes, the Olympics Games soccer final in 1956, held in Melbourne, drew over a hundred thousand (Hay 2006).

Through the 1980s, efforts were made to drag the sport into prominence. This proved to be a challenge. An account in *The Canberra Times* on an international between Australia and England in June 1983 might as well not have happened for the sake of the sport. Ian Warden lamented that coverage of the game was not only abysmal in its scope, but primitive in the attention it was given. It was also appallingly staged, played in what were seemingly substandard conditions. 'Any Australians who were on the brink of urging their kiddies to break from tradition and play soccer instead of one of the more "manly" codes and who saw Sunday's exhibition will have retreated from the brink and will be buying their Brads and Jasons their mouthguards and their rugby boots after all'. Rex Mossop, one of the commentators moonlighting in a soccer role, could only lapse into rugby lingo and terms of reference. 'It's gone out on the full', he noted at one point. 'He got the names wrong and called passes "shots" and contributed to a dismal afternoon by not bothering to sound especially interested in the match'. (Warden 1983) A radio commentator, Peter Wilkins of the ABC, was thrilled that the match had somehow 'exploded' at some point, ignited by bursts of talented displays. Warden resoundingly disagreed, with the match being well and truly 'soporific'. Wilkins was seeing 'explosions' of good play everywhere, despite the fact that England had barely managed a shot on goal.

Broadcasting wars

Soccer has also faced another, pressing obstacle: battling competitors for a slice of the broadcasting market. Round-the-clock exposure, ever the watchword of publicity-driven sport, has been the historical Achilles heel of the soccer establishment in Australia. With such entrenched fixtures as AFL, Rugby League and Rugby Union, the competition has always been stiff, sometimes ruthlessly so. When Channel Seven acquired TV rights to Soccer Australia's properties, notably the Socceroos and the NSL on a 10-year contract, in 1998, there were suggestions that the sport would edge through, finding a suitable place on the broadcasting scene and decent exposure on pay television. There was a catch. 'Seven, then an aggressive competitor for the AFL rights, appeared to quite deliberately bury the game from public view just to appease the Aussie rules governors'. (Murray 2012)

In a 2005 court case, one in which Seven sued such companies as Foxtel partners, News, Publishing and Broadcasting Ltd and Telstra, the plot was shown to be well and truly thick. In attempting to show that its pay TV channel C7 had been driven out of business in being refused NRL or AFL rights in December 2000, Steven Wise, executive in charge of the venture, showed frustration at not being acknowledged for his work in frustrating soccer's coverage in the country. The suggestion was that the rights were purchased in order to be snuffed.

All of this seemed a far cry from Brazil 2014. The World Cup affirmed the sport's importance to Australians, enrapturing audiences, garnering unprecedented ratings. As broadcast rights and popularity of sport tend to be intimately connected in the Australian sporting landscape, football executives were relieved, and some even thrilled, to secure the $160 million contract for rights between Fox Sports on SBS TV. Rivals in other sporting codes could only watch with a degree of trepidation.

To understand the financial victory made by Australia's soccer authorities in the broadcasting stakes, one has to understand the domestic revolution in football that was initiated the same year Channel Seven was initiating its own legal skirmishes. 26 August 2005 saw the launch of the new soccer competition, which was purposely termed a football league. It had the support of such business figures as Westfield co-founder Frank Lowy, who combined faith and money in supporting the competition. Lowy himself came in with the findings of the Crawford review of Australian soccer in 2003 which found that 'the current structure of soccer in Australia is ineffective, does not work and needs changing' (Crawford 2003).

The effort to use the 'football' tag was revolutionary and suggestively calculating. As Buck Clifford Rosenberg argues, the battles surrounding football were very much matters of branding – notably the use of the term 'football' for soccer (Rosenberg 2009). According to Rosenberg, the soccer fans in Australia were very much part of a cultural battle of localization and globalization, typified by 'the religiosity of soccer and the discourse of destiny invoked by soccer fans in Australia about its inevitable popularisation as a visual culture' (Rosenberg 2009).

AFL writer Martin Flanagan was all too aware in the 'football wars' about the use of the term when writing about the subject that year. The side using that term 'to some extent owns the future'. The soccer aficionados might well think their game appropriate of being called football, but, 'What we call our game is very much our business. Our game [Australian rules] was seen as football' (Flanagan 2005).

Typically though, the globalization narrative in sport is constructed around suggestions of a universal appeal – merely playing a sport embraced by the global community somehow suggests a world identity, cosmopolitan in nature and scope. This was Warren's unchanging view, as, indeed, many Australian soccer fans who have taken to popularizing the notion as a weapon against seemingly more parochial counterparts and codes. In its own way, it was a method of dealing with the cultural cringe, to bring Australia, deemed historically one of soccer's distinct backwaters, onto a global stage. The social institution of sport, however, can also act as a singular counter, a repudiator of cultural globalization itself (Rowe 2003). Such universalism, in other words, can be pure illusion, the mask that merely hides a form of tribalism.

Other codes, notably AFL, reacted with suspicion to the new competition in what was perceived as a rival tribal challenge. AFL commentator and radio host Graham Cornes saw a threat around the corner readying to harry the complacent. 'There have been a series of minor skirmishes and several subversive actions, but we Aussie Rules fans, are sitting blissfully unaware that our great game is about to be challenged seriously by soccer. For heaven's sake, they're already trying to call it football'. (Cornes 2005)

Even seven years after the establishment of the A-League, veteran soccer commentator, Les Murray, would still find the curse of anti-football prejudice stalking the land. It was a neurosis, seemingly unshakeable. 'So just ask yourself, where would the A-League's popularity be if there was a more realistic, not to say more just distribution of media space and the league got the allotment appropriate for it? Where would it be if it got, say, four full pages of coverage per day to the NRL's five?' (Murray 2012)

This was particularly difficult for Murray, who shared, with Warren, assumptions about the place of soccer, its obvious merits, and most importantly, the message of pluralism it entailed. The FIFA World Cup was its own indisputable brand, one so much more than 'a bunch of football matches strung together'. It was a 'party', one signifying 'the world at play', one of celebrating 'global diversity – amongst countries, races, religions, languages, traditions, all sorts of things'. (Les Murray in Holmes 2014) Soccer (which he repeatedly makes a point of calling football, and the world game) is a mirror, a cultural reflection.

Such worries on the part of Murray are starting to seem dated, given recent threats posed by soccer to the AFL code. The enduring hostility shown by coaches and administrators to any prospect of encroachment by soccer has come to verge on caricature. But at the heart, they remain serious concerns. Former AFL player Kevin Sheedy could not resist remarking in May 2013 that the success of the A-League club Western Sydney Wanderers was somehow linked to the Immigration Department. Inadvertently, he had opened the debate up to the seemingly irrepressible appeal of the game. 'We don't have the recruiting officer called the immigration department recruiting fans for the West Sydney Wanderers'. (Wu 2013) His own AFL side, the Greater Western Sydney Club, had suffered a resounding defeat to Adelaide, further spoiled by the turnout of a mere 5830 fans. It was the lowest turnout to a regular season AFL match since the final year of Fitzroy's existence in 1996. A beleaguered Sheedy surmised that, 'All I said was that Wanderers have an advantage because most people that migrate to Australia know soccer – it's a world sport'. Western Sydney was receptor and breeder of soccer followers, a gathering of fans that had challenged the supremacy of the AFL. 'Because that's what happens when you bring a lot of people through, channel into a country and put them in the west of Sydney and all of a sudden they build a club like that in one year and all of sudden they've got probably 10,000 fans and 20,000 going to a game'.

Sheedy's remarks were hardly exceptional, typified by such observations as those of AFL club Collingwood's president Eddy McGuire, who suggested that western Sydney was the 'land of the falafel'. Such comments give the impression that soccer is stomping its way through the sporting codes. Sheedy had various supporters, more for the fact that he had, in fact, been an anti-racist advocate and recruiter of indigenous talent for the AFL. Such an attitude did not suggest a desire to smear the soccer cult. In the business of race, he was admirably embracing. 'He was equally proud to have names like Misiti, Alessio and Mercuri on his Essendon premiership team sheets'. (Hinds 2013) The suggestion, then, was that he was a competitor. As a competitor, he, and the sport of his life, was losing ground to the very game that had been estranged to so many. As a posted comment in response to the article noted, 'One can see how AFL maintained its tight grip on the southern capitals'. The erosive and conquering influence of another sport is thus becoming all too evident. 'Bit by bit, Melbourne, Adelaide and Perth are developing a taste for some of the global games. Sheedy is typical of the "stalag" mentality from these states that maintained a "vice-like" grip on their codes dominance, and their derision for those who pursued other games'. (Comment by Cros, Wahroonga, 13 May 2012, available at: http://www.theage.com.au/afl/afl-news/sheedy-links-wanderers-success-to-immigration-department-20,130,512-2jgnj.html). Whatever this "stalag" mentality might well have been, soccer was not merely becoming popular, but seemingly unimpeachable. The fans and investors and sponsors were turning up and putting in. Simon Hill of Fox Sports took note of Manchester City's investment in the game, showing that the Australian soccer market had become attractive. 'The news that Manchester City – the world's wealthiest sporting club – has chosen to invest in the A-League, must have come as a brutal shock to those crowing about sagging fortunes, in the face of cricket's onslaught'. (Hill 2014)

Bids corrupt and pure

The corruption scandal behind the award of hosting rights for the 2022 FIFA World Cup to Qatar offers a backdrop to Australian attitudes to the game. The publication in the British paper, *The Sunday Times*, had revealed documentation suggesting that former FIFA vice-president and Qatari national Mohamed bin Hammam had dolled out $US5 million through a private company to various African officials to secure the bid.

While Australia was never a genuine contender, self-assuming confidence on winning hosting rights was prevalent. According to FFA chief executive David Gallop, 'If we can get the World Cup in Melbourne and Victoria we would put our hands up – it's a great world event as we will see it in Brazil'. (Bossi and Ward 2014) Former England striker, Gary

Lineker, seconded the suggestion, claiming that, 'The best candidate for 2022, given 2018 is in Europe, was, and still is, Australia' (Bossi and Ward 2014).

After the expenditure of $45 million for the failed bid for the 2022 rights, Lowy of Football Federation Australia expressed his fury (AAP 2014a). This betrayed as much the naiveté of the moment as the illusion of prowess. If Australia can host the Olympic Games, then it can surely front up to the podium for hosting the World Cup. The language used by Lowy after the Australian snub, and the emergence of claims of corruption regarding the winning Qatari outfit, was minted in the language of universal appeal. It was inconceivable to him that Australians would not have wanted to back the bid. The taxpayer, in short, had to be refunded for the debacle. 'Australia invested heavily in the World Cup process and the entire nation was behind the bid. Since December 2010 Australia has been careful not to let its misgivings about the process be interpreted as sour grapes'. (Lynch 2013) For one, it demonstrated a generic obsession with sport, of which soccer had become a key expression – that any tournament could not be staged more professionally than in an Australian environment. If soccer was the game with heralded global credentials, there was no reason why Australia could not colonize it, or at the very least incorporate it into its own schedule of sporting events.

Other commentators preferred to douse the flames of indignation with another, sobering perspective on the governing authority and the world game. 'Don't worry, its only soccer', claimed one commentator after Australia lost the bid to host the 2022 World Cup (Murray 2012). Bernard Keane of *Crikey* could barely contain his indignation, hoping to disturb the seeming erosion of contempt, let alone opposition, to soccer in Australia. 'I despise the World Cup. Not dislike it. Not hate it. But viscerally loathe it'. (Keane 2014) It was specifically 'silly' – thank goodness for the evolutionary steps made by such individuals as William Webb Ellis picking the ball up at Rugby School in 1823. Keane's detestation was, however, more focused on the politics of it. FIFA 'is probably the world's most corrupt organisation'. The 'Blattercrats' were reaping a tax-free windfall, while states hosting the particular tournament in question were being rendered indigent.

Some Australian soccer followers conceded to certain merits in Keane's sniping, but noted such movements as ChangeFIFA as an 'example of how fans are trying to express their desire to change the organisation' (The Accidental Australian 2014). Keane may well have preferred his winter 'being dominated by AFL/NRL talk without this huge soccer Behemoth', but the reality was that all soccer fans, many Australian amongst them, similarly loathed FIFA. 'We can't hate the game because of FIFA'.

Notwithstanding such a dismissive attitude, the political establishment and various administrators saw a chance with the Qatar corruption scandal to swoop in on the spoils, should the tournament be prized from the state's hands. Even players such as the usually outspoken Mark Schwarzer would argue that soccer matches should, as a general rule, be banned from countries in the Middle East during summer (AAP 2014b). For Schwarzer, the issue was also FIFA corruption, evidenced by the Garcia report into the affair, which the authorities refused to release. A moral message was embedded in this – the game could not continue at the mercy of such officials. 'It is such a shame to see football being run how it's being run, with so little trust'.

Historical acceptance

Australia's first World Cup qualification came in 1974 with the Socceroo side coached by Rale Rasic. Eleven qualifying matches had been played, with Australia beating South Korea in the Asian zone final play-off. Culturally, Rasic's team found themselves in the identity debates not merely where soccer stood as a sport, but how various cultural motifs operated. Gough Whitlam's reforming Labour government favoured a new national anthem – that of Advance Australia Fair. The conservatives and monarchists preferred the status quo God Save the Queen (Gorman 2014). It was the attitude of 'nationalism that allowed for internationalism', to use the words of historian Stuart Macintyre, that prevailed. Central here was the enduring conflict between the Imperial memory of God Save the Queen, and the supposedly more representative Advance Australia Fair. For Rasic, the meanings of soccer in the Australian setting were fundamental. Like Warren, he saw it in metaphorical terms of mobility, a 'vehicle'. He insisted that his team sing the national anthem, or at the very least stand still at its playing. 'The national anthem is a bible for all of us Australians, and you must obey that', he commandingly told the skipper, Warren (Gorman 2014).

Even as this cultural battle was taking place, the Australian Socceroos were engaged in a pay and bonus dispute with the Australian Soccer Federation over their World Cup engagements in West Germany. Players were expecting $5000; the actual total was a considerably lower $1000. The federation had its eyes on the bank balance, fearing moving into the financial red. Rasic, in the meantime, was furious at club coaches who had proven negligent in keeping their players in peak physical condition. The national coaches of all countries in the world, except Australia, fumed Rasic, did 'not have to worry about physical fitness when players report to represent their country'. (The Canberra Times 1974)

But it was only when Lucas Neill tripped Italy's Fabio Grosso in the penalty box in the Round of 16 at Fritz Walter Stadium in Kaiserslautern, that World Cup football assumed a spot worthy of heated nationwide discussion. Italy won the match 1-0, and would go on to win the 2006 tournament. This noisy and lingering anguish showed that the Australian soccer appreciating public had come of age – or at the very least, engaged. Just as Diego Maradona's 'hand of God' in the 1986 tournament had made English fans apoplectic, Grosso's dive would enrage Australian followers. Grosso was pilloried – he had been all too cavalier about being 'tripped', and claimed that, while not being 'glamorous', the incident could hardly have been deemed a 'scandal'. Responses from spectators were deemed naïve for ignoring the one man advantage Australia had after the 50th minute when Marco Materazzi was sent off. 'Listening and reading the responses to the debate four years on presents a fascinating portrait of Australia's naivety when it comes to the nuances of the world game'. (Musolino 2010)

The dive did, however, have another impact. It made moralists of Australian sporting followers. It gave some pause to wonder about the ethical standing of the game. Football, for one Roar commentator, would only 'ever become the number sport in Australia' if football players and fans tapped into the values of 'the Australian fans sporting psyche'. This would require stamping out the habit of 'diving' or 'simulation'. 'It is under-handed, weak, cowardly, to put it more simply, cheating'. (Knight 2010) Responses on the forum to the article lauded its accuracy, but noted that 'football wasn't always like this'. The football of the Anglo tradition had been 'robust and manly'.[1] Nostalgia mixed with a more contemporary suggestion: clean the sport's dishonesty, and win Australian admiration.

Brazil 2014

The Australian campaign for Brazil 2014 had shown how the sport had aged, even if it had not aged in the way some if its proponents had wanted. Tensions between the old guard and the approaching new were becoming apparent. As ever, the old head of bad selection decisions reared, with the campaign stuttering in the first part of 2013. A 2-2 draw with Oman in March that year left the Socceroos third in their group, with commentators such as Andy Harper concerned that the chickens had 'come home to roost with this current team because of the constant refusal to blood young players' (Brodie 2013). The coach, Ange Postecoglou, seemed to respond with that bravest of gambles, cleaning out the stables, stripping the altars and going for a lean enthusiastic side heavy in their salad days. The new coach did have the feeling of being rushed, having replaced Holger Osieck after the Socceroos' pummelling in friendlies with Brazil and France in October 2013. Both losses had been disorienting, pushing back much of the gains gotten after Australia's 2006 performances. Football Federation Australia's interest in the Dutch and German strand of coaching, after a period of serious courtship, was at an end (Mark 2014a). 'I was trying to do a lot in a short place of time and I didn't, right from the start, want to discount World Cup as some sort of building exercise or experimentation'. (Mark 2014b.)

Australian goalkeeper Mark Schwarzer was amongst the critics, suggesting that Australia's new coach was playing with an 'experimental team'. 'My biggest concern is that I don't think we've picked the best players that we have available right at this moment in time to go to the World Cup. And at the World Cup you need your best players'. (Triple M Radio (Melbourne) 2014) Another goalkeeper – Zeljko 'Spider' Kalac, also a former backup keeper for Italy's AC Milan – expressed even stronger views. He had in mind the Socceroos performance against Bafana Bafana, which earned both teams a 1-1 draw with open play and a range of attacking options. That particular style of play, notably with an inexperienced team, was bound to land the team in trouble in the upcoming tournament. 'A lot of the pundits out there are saying it was a great Ange-style of football and an attacking brand of football. Yeah, an attacking brand of football against a third rate team that's not even going to the World Cup. God give us strength against teams that are fully prepared like Chile, the Netherlands and Spain'. (Four Four Two 2014)

The tournament provided Australian followers of the game with a vantage point of reflection, though some were disappointed with the 'Be There With Hyundai Contest' which sought slogans for each of the 32 teams. The Australian winner came in with 'Socceroos: Hopping Our Way Into History'! Others were somewhat more poignant and reflective – Algeria's was a more eloquent 'Desert Warriors in Brazil'.[2] Veteran commentators preferred something less fluffy, urging a reconsideration of the first side which qualified. Football columnist Craig Foster argued that the event 'should be used to connect the game back to Germany 1974, and also our rich indigenous ancestry' (Foster 2013). More to the point, it was time to accept a gritty egalitarianism. Football representatives 'without any history of football' were suggestive of only one thing – 'that the game is still a playground for the rich'.

Australian celebrities were also busying themselves with promoting the team. The highly billable Hugh Jackman enthused about the World Cup and Australia (FIFA TV 2013). Indeed, FIFA ran a campaign featuring Jackman as the person who, while excelling on the acting side of things in Hollywood, had actually had 'dreams of excelling on the pitch' (FIFA.com 2013). Jackman says all the appropriate things about the World Cup, including the rather ham necessities of how a character he plays on screen might treat soccer. Would he, asks the interviewer, be a good goalie? No, the violent, impulsive figure of Wolverine, a character he made famous in the Marvel Comic series of X-Men, would 'keep popping and slashing the ball'. Like other followers of the game in Australia, Jackman resorted to the cult of the pure, evoking a depth that supposedly no other game has. Football is a game of 'pureness' unlike others, who are the mere pretenders before the global sport. He speaks of his son playing it, of assisting him in a coaching sense. Then, there is Australia, perennial underdog, a state of affairs he does not mind. 'I think it's good to be the underdog in every situation'. (FIFA.com 2013)

Even the Australian Prime Minister, Tony Abbott, found himself making statements on the Australian presence in Brazil, though he did so with a degree of confusion. Draped in a team scarf, Abbott released an awkward YouTube message to the team, in which he claimed that, 'Ange, Mike [sic] and the Socceroos, in this World Cup you have the opportunity to make the world game our national game'. (AAP 2014c) The error-prone Abbott had decided not to check the accuracy of the skipper's name, calling Mile Jedinak 'Mike'.

The group draw saw the Socceroos pitted against Chile, the Netherlands and the holders Spain. If shock treatment was what the Australian side needed, then it had certainly gotten it. 'I am of the mindset', wrote John Camburn, 'that this is exactly what the doctor ordered for Australian football as we need a wake-up call to find what is missing in the development of our players and national team'. Japan was being seen as the 'superior' side in Asia. Golden age players were being put out to pasture, or at the very least having their 'golden years' (Camburn 2013).

From the start, it was acknowledged that the Socceroos had been lumped with a formidable set of countries. Reaching the elimination stage was going to be the tallest of orders, with 'the holders Spain, European giants Holland and South American qualifiers Chile' (Smithies 2013). Will Brodie adduced a range of studies suggesting why Australia should have been worried about their placing in the group. He dipped into a study about the David and Goliath complex. He dipped into university studies about luck, citing the Socceroos as the least lucky (with 0%), to that of Mexico, with 99%. 'In concrete terms', claimed *The Times*, 'Australia will need to beat out two of the world's 15 highest-ranked teams in order to advance'. (Brodie 2014) For all of that, Australia's embrace of the 'underdog' tag was 'a major luxury going into the World Cup' (Brodie 2014).

Australia would lose to each of these countries, though if the commentary was to be believed, the losses concealed as much as they revealed. The most glowing praise for the Australian performance was something outside their on-pitch display – it was the acceptance that soccer was here to stay. The juggernaut of the world game had finally arrived, as had Warren's posthumous global passport. The Midfielder, a regular contributor to the popular Roar sports site, found the coverage of the World Cup an indication that the winds, or at the very least streams, had changed, showing 'football treated as a mainstream sport for the first time in Australia' (Midfielder 2014).

The usual hunger for highlighting negative stories regarding the sporting tournament was ignored in favour of those of greater uplift. There were no reports of diving, disaster and few on corruption. Even such journalists, whose teeth had been cut on the hard yards of AFL for years, succumbed to its allure. 'The sense of drama that imbues a World Cup final', argued one such writer, Martin Flanagan of *The Age*, 'comes precisely from the fact that it is a world title. It's a distinction, a sense of honour, that boxing shared in the days when there were undisputed world champions'. (Flanagan 2014) Indeed, Flanagan had had something of a revelation, a psychic readjustment that reflected on the company he was sharing, when watching the final between Argentina and Germany. He saw melodrama, poetic material, tragic loss. The stuff, indeed, he might have linked to the more traditional Australian codes. His fellow spectators, being an Argentinean family, were watching a global event, and the culmination of a global event at that. The Villarubia family, were his football spectator companions, and in them, he saw something else: 'I watched last Monday's World Cup final with the Villarubias and I could see the way Nico's big shoulders quivered with excitement and apprehension, and how much the game meant to him'. (Flanagan 2014) The experience moved Flanagan so much he had a confession to his readers. 'What struck me coming back from watching the World Cup is that Australian football is a world-class game. It is the duty of its administrators to ensure that it remains one. Meanwhile, I'll be returning to the Villarubias to watch a Collingwood game'. (Flanagan 2014)

The tournament itself drew a few bubbly responses from the press at Australian stoicism and bravery on the field, a sort of repackaged set of cultural themes from brave Australian warrior fighting the odds (Gallipoli) to plucky upstart facing the world in general. It might have seemed foolish, but it was certainly brave. Against the Dutch at the Estadio Beiro-Rio, Australia got two goals against Holland's winning three. 'Defeat to the Netherlands by 3-2 in Porto Alegre wasn't unexpected, but the way they lost captivated the world'. (Smithies 2014) The language of fate proved essential – Australia, brave, but ultimately undermined by a series of errors, with chances that were not taken, and misses that proved crucial.

Cahill proved grittily skilful. The Australian media was convinced that he had executed 'what could prove the goal of the tournament', and the assumption was not necessarily misplaced. 'With one sensational touch', wrote Chris Greenberg in *The Huffington Post*, 'Tim Cahill made everyone a Socceroo'. (Greenberg 2014) Battle against the Dutch was undertaken with 'power and poise, reducing the Oranje to uncertainty with the directness but also the precision of their football' (Smithies 2014). The Dutch only got past the Australians because they were 'ruthless'.

On returning from the tournament, Postecoglou urged a shedding of 'our negative attitude and I think that's an important part of our education as a football country'. The search for a local Australian brand of football was essential. 'From my perspective it's not about playing the type of football most people externally and here in Australia think we can't play but about showing our players they can do it'. A few shots were also aimed at the cultural cringe, that which condemns the local as invariably inferior to the overseas variant. 'As an Australian I don't think I should be measured any less than anyone else and I don't see myself as any less than any other international coach'. (Micallef 2014b) David Davutovic of the Newscorp Network gave the team only a modest dust up – the three defeats were not calamitous, nor did they need to induce crestfallenness. 'Those suggesting Australia disgraced itself are naïve'. For Davutovic, the very act of getting to the FIFA final stages of the World Cup, one featuring scores of nations, was remarkable. Those who did not make it had been an illustrious, even immodest sampling – the self-confident Zlatan Ibrahimovic, or the Real Madrid star Gareth Bale (Wales). 'The lack of world-class quality in the Socceroos squad is a by-product of neglect in the junior ranks and this is something that has and must continue to be rectified'. (Davutovic 2014) Despite stuttering and collapsing in the tournament, the unorthodox performances of such players as Cahill sent ripples of enthusiasm through the crowds.

The background discussions about Australian football after the World Cup had an optimistic murmur, though the sources on that optimism vary. Cahill was most enthusiastic at all, dismissing the naysayers. Did Australia lose any goodwill after losing three on the trot, with a final drubbing by Spain? 'No chance, we can't let it, because when you look at the bigger picture we probably could have set up and parked the bus and hit them on the counter but you have to go out and try your best'. (Gatt 2014) Cahill was mechanical and reductive in his assessment; differences between the contesting sides had been minimal, a matter of a few stunning players and the occasional, critical faux pas. The difference in the match against Chile was forward Alexis Sanchez. The second, it was the hurling speed of Holland's Arjen Robben and Robin van Persie. For all of that, 'We've pretty much changed the footprint of football, the way played, the style'.

Former Barcelona footballer, Guillermo Amor, was another to add confidence to the post-cup wash-up, even if his own view was shaped by harvesting the fruit of his old club's rewarding tiki-taka style. Getting his sense of the Australian footballing environment in his stint helping Reds coach and former Barcelona player Josep Gambau impressed him. 'Style' and 'level of performance' of the Adelaide players was encouraging. 'I can see that Australian players are good professionals who work hard and are keen to do well'. The image of the Australian footballer as an unsubtle brute, one 'basically physical and competitive' was mistaken. (Micallef 2014a)

Brazil 2014 had even propelled some interest in Australia's own domestic competition. The A-League received an immediate spike of interest after the Socceroos performance against the Netherlands. Perth Glory's Dutch winger Youssouf Hersi took note: 'Now you can see David Villa is coming here and Damien Duff, and may other players too'. With confidence, he could assert that, 'football is actually taking off here and if the salary cap opens up, better academies… there'll be a big boost for the game'. (Ormond 2014)

Concluding remarks

Few countries boast the same array of 'football' codes Australia does, of which soccer has been a historical struggler and straggler. What the World Cup has become to Australian sport has been a confrontation of symbols and temptations, the sense of an invader that had to be resisted, but eventually took ground. While it became a fashionably manufactured nonsense, football became specific to local sporting codes, and specifically indigenous, while soccer, a game that had nestled quite comfortably in the Australian sporting landscape, assumed an alien form.

Australians involved in the World Cup, and in soccer, positioned the sport as a global one, central to various battles of identity, viewed through the prism of local challenges between the footballing codes. The conflict has come in stages. Warren gave the impression of fighting a lonely battle, but the appeal of FIFA's game was such that it was finding a foothold, however unsettled it might have seemed. To call the rising enthusiasm for soccer in Australia, with the influence of FIFA's tournament, a revolution is to ignore what was already there. While the game suffered structurally, association football never left once it found some form in Australia, even despite near fanatical resistance by other administrations. The cultural battles over the game, however, remain. The attitudes of such figures as Sheedy are probably more honest than most. The game is not merely here to stay, but has become a genuine rival. The foreign game has been tamed of its wickedness.

Notes

1. Post by 'Roger Rational' to 'Why football struggles for support in Australia,' 11 April 2010, http://www.theroar.com.au/2010/04/11/why-football-struggles-for-fans/.
2. Winning slogans available at: http://www.fifa.com/worldcup/games/be-there-with-hyundai/winning-slogans/index.html.

Disclosure statement

No potential conflict of interest was reported by the author.

ORCID

Binoy Kampmark ⓘ http://orcid.org/0000-0002-4171-0645

References

AAP [Australian Associated Press]. 2014a. "Final Lap for the Man Who Saved Soccer." October 9.
AAP [Australian Associated Press]. 2014b. "Mark Schwarzer Slams FIFA over Qatar Decision." October 10.
AAP [Australian Associated Press]. 2014c. "Tony Abbott Gets Socceroos Skipper's Name Wrong." *The Age*, June 14.
Adair, Daryl, and Wray Vamplew. 1990. "Not So Far from the Maddening Crowd: Spectator Violence in Britain and Australia: A Review Article." *Sporting Traditions* 1: 95–103.
Bossi, Dominic, and Roy Ward. 2014. "Australia Ready to Host 2022 World Cup." *Sydney Morning Herald*, June 2.
Brodie, Will. 2013. "Socceroos in Deep Hole: Harper." *Illawarra Mercury*, March 27.
Brodie, Will. 2014. "Underdogged: Will Socceroos Embrace Their World Cup Status?" *Sydney Morning Herald*, June 10.
Camburn, John. 2013. "FIFA World Cup Draw." *Team Mates Australasia*, December 11. http://teammatesaustralasia.com.au/fifa-world-cup-draw-11th-december-2013-0002/.
Cornes, Graham. 2005. "Football or Soccer? Speaking in Code." *The Advertiser*, October 22.
Crawford, David. 2003. "Report of the Independent Soccer Review Committee into the Structure, Governance and Management of Soccer in Australia." April. https://secure.ausport.gov.au/__data/assets/pdf_file/0008/153818/Crawford_Report_2003.pdf.
Danforth, Loring M. 2001. "Is the World Game an Ethnic Game or an Aussie Game? Narrating the Nation in Australian Soccer." *American Ethnologist* 28 (2): 363–387.
Davutovic, David. 2014. "Australia's World Cup Performance at the FIFA World Cup." *Herald Sun*, June 27.
FIFA TV. 2013. "Hugh Jackman Talks World Cup, Socceroos." October 7. https://www.youtube.com/watch?v=GBz6dLB46XU#t=299.
FIFA.com. 2013. "Jackman: I Love the World Cup." October 7. http://www.fifa.com/worldcup/news/y=2013/m=10/news=jackman-love-the-world-cup-2190620.html.
Flanagan, Martin. 2005. "Footy Should Stand by Its History." *The Age*, December 10.
Flanagan, Martin. 2014. "World Sport Codes Battle in the Same Lounge Room." *The Age*, July 18.
Foster, Craig. 2013. "Time to Upgrade Legends like Rasic to Business Class." *Sydney Morning Herald*, December 14.
Four Four Two. 2014. "Kalac: Naïve Socceroos Face World Cup Mauling." May 28. http://www.fourfourtwo.com/au/news/kalac-naive-socceroos-face-world-cup-mauling?utm_source=www.footballtoday.com.au&utm_medium=referral&utm_campaign=www.footballtoday.com.au.
Gatt, Ray. 2014. "World Cup 2014: Tim Cahill's Vision for the New Socceroos." *The Australian*, June.
Gorman, Joe. 2014. "The Forgotten Story of … Advance Australia Fair and the Socceroos." *The Guardian*, April 24.
Greenberg, Chris. 2014. "This Brilliant Goal Might Be the Best of the World Cup." *The Huffington Post*, June 18.

Hay, Roy. 1994. "British Football, Wogball or the World Game? Towards a Social History of Victorian Soccer." In *Ethnicity and Soccer in Australia*, edited by John O'Hara, 44–79. Campbeltown: Australian Society for Sports History.

Hay, Roy. 2001. "'Those Bloody Croatians',: Croatian Soccer Teams, Ethnicity and Violence in Australia, 1950–1999." In *Fear and Loathing in World Football*, edited by and Richard Giulianotti, 77–90. Oxford: Berg.

Hay, Roy. 2006. "'Our Wicked Foreign Game': Why Has Association Football (Soccer) Not Become the Main Code of Football in Australia?" *Soccer & Society* 7 (2–3): 165–180.

Hill, Simon. 2014. "Manchester City's Investment in Australian Football Shows How Our Game is Only Getting Bigger." *Fox Sports*, January 23.

Hinds, Richard. 2013. "Missionary Sheedy Deserves to Be Judged by His Actions." *The Age*, May 13.

Holmes, Tracey. 2014. "On the Ball: Les Murray, 68, Soccer Presenter." *The Saturday Paper*, June 14.

Hughson, John. 2001. "'the Wogs Are at It Again': The Media Reportage of Australian Soccer 'Riots.'" *Football Studies* 4 (1): 40–55.

Kallinikios, John. 2007. "Soccer Boom: The Transformation of Victorian Soccer Culture, 1945–1963." Walla Walla Press Sports History Dissertation No.2., Sydney: Walla Wall Press.

Keane, Bernard. 2014. "I Despise the World Cup, and I'm Not Ashamed to Say It." *Crikey*, July 9. http://www.crikey.com.au/2014/07/09/i-despise-the-world-cup-and-im-not-ashamed-to-say-it/.

Knight, Luc. 2010. "Why Football Struggles for Support in Australia." *The Roar*, April 11.

Lynch, Michael. 2013. "Frank Lowy Demands FIFA to Compensate for 2022 World Cup Time Shift." *Sydney Morning Herald*, September 17.

Mark, David. 2014a. "In an Ange We Trust." *ABC News*, May 26. http://www.abc.net.au/news/2014-05-26/in-ange-we-trust/5732790.

Mark, David. 2014b. "World Cup 2014: Socceroos Coach Ange Postecoglou Felt His Campaign Was Rushed." *ABC News*, June 26.

Micallef, Philip. 2014a. "Amor Extols Virtues of Australian Mentality." *The World Game*, SBS, September 2. http://theworldgame.sbs.com.au/article/2014/09/01/amor-extols-virtues-australian-mentality.

Micallef, Philip. 2014b. Postecoglou Calls for Belief in Socceroos. *The World Game*, SBS, August 21.

Midfielder. 2014. "How Will the FIFA World Cup Affect the a-League?" *The Roar*, July 25. http://www.theroar.com.au/2014/07/25/will-fifa-world-cup-affect-league/.

Murray, Les. 2012. "Sheilas, Wogs and Apologists." *The World Game*, SBS, January 20. http://theworldgame.sbs.com.au/blog/2012/01/20/sheilas-wogs-and-apologists.

Musolino, Adrian. 2010. "Australians Need to Get over the Italian Dive of 2006." *The Roar*, April 18.

Ormond, Aidan. 2014. "Dutch 'Googling' a-League after Socceroos Heroics." *Four Four Two*, September 17.

Rosenberg, Buck Clifford. 2009. "The Australian Football Wars: Fan Narratives of Inter-Code and Intra-Code Conflict." *Soccer & Society* 10 (2): 245–260.

Rowe, David. 2003. "Sport and the Repudiation of the Global." *International Review for the Sociology of Sport* 38 (3): 281–294.

Smithies, Tom. 2013. "Socceroos Land in FIFA World Cup Group B alongside Spain, Netherlands and Chile." *Fox Sports*, December 7.

Smithies, Tom. 2014. "Australia Beaten 3-2 by the Netherlands in World Cup Classic, but Threatened Much More." *Newscorp*, June 19.

Syson, Ian. 2009. "Shadow of a Game: Locating Soccer in Australian Cultural Life." *Meanjin* 68 (4). http://meanjin.com.au/editions/volume-68-number-4-2009/article/shadow-of-a-game-locating-soccer-in-australian-cultural-life/.

The Accidental Australian. 2014. "Don't Worry – Mr. Keane. It's Almost over (but We Are Sad)." *Blog Post*, July 9. http://accidentalaussie.wordpress.com/2014/07/09/dont-worry-mr-keane-its-almost-over-but-we-are-sad/.

The Canberra Times. 1974. "Socceroos Embroiled in Dispute." 18, March 5.

Triple M Radio (Melbourne). 2014. "Mark Schwarzer Critical of Socceroos World Cup Squad." June 5. http://www.triplem.com.au/melbourne/sport/soccer/news/2014/6/champion-aussie-goalkeeper-mark-schwarzer-critical-of-socceroos-world-cup-squad-/.

Vamplew, Wray. 1996. "Wogball: Ethnicity and Violence in Australian Soccer since the Forties." *Australian Studies* 10: 119–129.

Warden, Ian. 1983. "Soccer Coverage to Put the Game Back 20 Years." *The Canberra times*, June 16.

Warren, Johnny, Andy Harper, and Josh Wittington. 2002. *Sheilas, Wogs and Poofters: An Incomplete Biography of Johnny Warren and Soccer in Australia*. Sydney: Random House.

Wen, Tiffanie. 2014. "A Sociological History of Soccer Violence." *The Atlantic*, July 14.

Wu, Andrew. 2013. "Sheedy Links Wanderer's Success to Immigration Department." *The Age*, May 13.

Amnesia and animosity: an assessment of soccer in the States

David Kilpatrick

ABSTRACT

The twentieth FIFA World Cup Finals, hosted by Brazil in 2014, provides perspective on the game's global growth since the inaugural tournament held in Uruguay in 1930. The fifth such tournament since the United States hosted in 1994 and the tenth in which the United States has participated, the status of the sport there remains anomalous, with compromised if not marginalized status. Elite levels of the sport, especially the Men's National Team, historically struggle for relevance in popular culture – despite widespread youth participation and the record of success achieved by the Women's National Team. This essay seeks to identify the current state of the sport in the United States as characterized by amnesia and antagonism, a conflicted blend of cultural superiority and inferiority complexes played out every four years when the nation asks itself if soccer matters.

Introduction

'Where soccer is religion': how Americans describe all other countries.

Soccer's struggle for relevance in the United States is oft-cited by scholars and proponents of American exceptionalism (either as uniqueness or implied superiority) as a sporting example of the nation's self-conception (Markovits and Hellerman 2001). That soccer is popular as a participatory sport now in the United States is beyond question, as millions of American children have been raised as registered players in the various youth-level governing bodies beneath the United States Soccer Federation (USSF) umbrella. While the signing of Pelé by the New York Cosmos in 1975 is arguably the most significant effort to bring the association football code into mainstream American life, the revolution promised by the Cosmos Country phenomenon didn't manifest in sustained interest in domestic elite professional play, as both the Cosmos and the North American Soccer League (NASL) suspended play within a decade of his arrival, after the 1984 season. Hosting the FIFA World Cup in 1994 brought the sport once more to the forefront of popular culture, with the expectation of sustained interest in elite soccer. While the single-entity Major League Soccer (MLS) moves towards its second decade and a revived NASL (including the Cosmos) is in competition, the question of if or when soccer will truly become an integral part of the fabric of American life remains, the debate revived and amplified in the popular media every four years with each FIFA World Cup.

The state of the game in the States may be understood in terms of amnesia and antagonism or ignorance of the sport's history and conflicts, both external and internal. While the Football Association celebrated 150 years, the USSF celebrated its centenary in 2013. Much of the history of the sport prior to the 1994 World Cup has been neglected if not forgotten as the small band of US soccer historians engage in the scholarship of discovery more than integration or innovation.[1] Turf wars fought over access to play space as well as media coverage continue, as soccer's foreign-ness is used as an excuse to preserve and protect interest in the more mainstream pastimes of baseball and gridiron football. Although American identity is often understood as always already hyphenated, rejection of the global game has long been part of cultural assimilation, soccer often characterized as an ideologically corruptive influence. Meanwhile, infighting among those who are entrusted as custodians of the game in the States continues among those who adopt a defensive, apologetic stance to justify soccer's lingering marginal cultural status.

Despite the successes of the United States Women's National Team since the first FIFA Women's World Cup was held in 1991,[2] in this essay I will focus on the status of the men's game in the United States. While American girls enjoy bragging rights over boys in terms of World Cup glory,[3] and the question concerning sport and gender is especially interesting given nearly equal levels of participation in youth soccer,[4] interest in elite women's soccer is even lower than the men's game.[5] Since the quadrennial FIFA World Cup for men's football is the highest profile event in global sport (arguably more important at present than the Olympics), the significance of this tournament in the United States is my primary concern with this essay.

By exploring the amnesia, animosity and apologetics surrounding soccer in the States, the cosmopolitan/post-nationalist potential of the global game will be viewed as an (inevitable?) antidote to this case of sporting exceptionalism, with consideration for how current modes of the game's governance constrain growth. If success is measurable, it must be done in terms of both the athletes and their audience.

Amnesia

Sesquicentennial celebrations in 2013 marked the formation of the Football Association and the codification of the association football code.[6] Simultaneously, the USSF marked its centennial. The casual observer would be excused for assuming, on the basis of these celebrations, that the sport is a half-century younger in the States, but, as David Wangerin notes, 'soccer has existed in America for much longer than many give it credit for'(Wangerin 2008, 12). Embroiled in Civil War when the *Laws of the Game* were established in England, they were published in New York as early as the spring of 1866,[7] as the nation underwent Reconstruction and an American sporting culture began to emerge. While various games of football may be cited as the first played by the association code, the first recorded match of soccer in New York's Central Park was played on 24 October 1885 (*New York Times*, 25 October 1885, 10). That reference to this match in the annals of *Spalding's 1904–05 Soccer Guide* would erroneously date this a year later (Hurditch 1904–1905, 19) is evidence that much of the game's early history was quickly forgotten. As C.P. Hurditch concedes,

Association foot ball is by no manner of means a new game in this country, for though statistics are lacking which would afford interesting data on the subject, still it can be said that more or less, it has been played for a number of years, and the words "more or less" just about explain the situation. (Ibid., 7)

The formation of the United States of America Foot Ball Association (the USSF's first name[8]) at the Astor House in New York City on 5 April 1913 was a merger between rival factions, the American Amateur Football Association and the America Football Association (AFA), the latter having been formed in 1884, prior to the formation of the first non-British European football associations in Denmark and the Netherlands. The AFA's authority was grounded with an affiliation with the FA in England, unofficial at its inception and formalized in 1908. The first international match for a team representing the United States was a loss in 1885 to Canada, but because this was under the auspices of the AFA and prior to the 1913 formation of what would become the USSF, it is not recognized as official. Although it never strove for a truly national reach, the AFA may be credited with several innovations now taken for granted in the game, such as nets on goals, penalty kicks and forbidding referees from placing bets on games they oversee (Allaway 2005, 36).[9] As Tom McCabe notes, 'Tinkering with the rules would become a tradition in American soccer' (McCabe 2013, 38).

The 2014 tournament in Brazil serves as perhaps the ultimate contrast for a status report on American soccer. For more than any other country, as David Goldblatt notes, 'Brazilian football has become, in the collective imagination if not the daily practice of professional football, the gold standard of the game' (Goldblatt 2014, xii). When one considers that 1894 is Brazilian football's 'Year Zero' (Bellos 2014, 27), it is all the more startling to discover the first professional soccer league in the United States was launched that same year. The American League of Professional Foot Ball Clubs was a short-lived initiative of north-eastern-based National League baseball clubs, disbanding within 17 days of the kick-off that October (Foulds and Harris 1979, 11–16).

It wasn't until 1921 that another professional soccer league was launched in the United States. Lasting just a decade, the American Soccer League (ASL) was more successful than its short-lived predecessor of a quarter-century prior. Just as the innovations of the AFA have been forgotten, so too the ASL may lay claim to experiments adopted decades later elsewhere. Beginning in 1926, the league allowed player substitutions (Montgomerie 1927, 4), almost 40 years before they were allowed in England. A June 1927 friendly between a mixed New York Soccer Giants and Bethlehem Steel side facing a touring Hakoah Wien side was played at night beneath floodlights with a white ball, likewise decades before becoming customary worldwide.

The standard of play and wages in the ASL meant the States were an attractive option for top European talent in the 1920s. As the country slipped into the throes of the Great Depression, the league sunk into decline, but nevertheless, it was this competitive land-scape that spawned the side that would represent the United States in Uruguay, reaching the semi-finals at the inaugural FIFA World Cup. Many have dismissed the success of the United States Men's National Team [USMNT] in the first World Cup as a fluke, but the 'implication that the United States' excellent performance in the 1930 World Cup was tainted by the use of a bunch of ringers simply isn't true', observe Roger Allaway and Colin Jose. 'The strength of American soccer in 1930, a result of the ASL of the 1920s, is forgotten'. (Allaway and Jose 1995) Indeed, all of the 16 players in the squad and of the 11 who saw action in Uruguay were experienced ASL players, but George Moorhouse is the only one to have played professionally elsewhere, making two appearances for Tranmere Rovers in 1921–1922 (ibid.). The Liverpool-born fullback was a star for the New York Soccer Giants since 1923, so Moorhouse had become a naturalized US citizen well before becoming the first Englishman to appear in a World Cup when the USMNT opened with a 3-0 win over Belgium. But he died in obscurity, the posthumous awarding of membership in the US Soccer Hall of Fame erroneously identifying Moorhouse's death nearly 40 years after his passing (Jawad 2014, 6).

Bert Patenaude was an established goal-scoring star with the ASL team representing his birthplace, the Fall River Marksmen, when he went to Uruguay. FIFA didn't officially recognize him as having scored the first hat-trick in World Cup history until 2006, nearly 22 years since his death in 1974, 76 years after scoring all of the goals in the USMNT 3-0 win over Paraguay (Barboza 2010). The 6-1 semi-final loss to Argentina may suggest a reality check for the Americans, but it is interesting to note that finishing the match with just eight fit players (Jawad 2014, 4) would have been most unusual to the Americans, who had likely grown accustomed to substitutes from the ASL's innovation.

Along with its innovations, the ASL was gone by 1932, replaced by another entity bearing the same name, but semi-professional and intensely ethnic, listing the Kearny Irish-Americans of 1933 as their inaugural champions. Historian Colin Jose was surprised to learn four decades later that another ASL had existed from 1921 to 1932. 'How could this be', he wondered, 'there was an American Soccer League before 1933, but no one seemed to know a great deal about it' (Jose 1998, ix). Given the league was almost forgotten, small wonder the context for the first USMNT squad at the inaugural World Cup is oft-neglected or misunderstood. It was not as if US soccer had started from scratch.

The US–Mexico rivalry is the most heated in Central and North America but few know their first encounter was played on Italian soil as a qualifying match for the 1934 World Cup. The USMNT won 4-2 but lost their opening match to the hosts, 7-1.

When the USMNT next appeared in FIFA World Cup finals 16 years later in Brazil, the American players were unaware of their forebears (Personal interview with Walter Bahr, 28 July 2014). It was as if US soccer had to start from scratch. Facing a highly favoured England side appearing in its first World Cup, the USMNT's success 20 years prior was forgotten and the outcome of the contest was a foregone conclusion. But a slight deflection off the head of Haitian-born Joe Gaetjens from a cross sent by Philadelphia-native Walter Bahr was the sole goal of the match. The 1-0 shock defeat of England in 1950 remains one of the few fabled moments in US soccer history but is often dismissed as luck, the unpredictable nature of the sport or a consequence of English hubris. The David v Goliath narrative was told and sold for the big screen, Geoffrey Douglas's 1996 book on the match, *The Game of Their Lives*, 'a celebration of forgotten things' (Douglas 2005, ix), was made into a feature film and released in 2004. But as David Wangerin notes, the film 'proved to be a box office disaster […] the nation was not the slightest bit interested' (Wangerin 2008, 81).

The USMNT would not appear in a World Cup Finals tournament again for another 40 years. It wasn't that US soccer disappeared or suspended play in the interregnum. It had, though, retreated into an isolated, insular and mostly ethnic marginalized status on the periphery of the American sporting landscape, no longer commanding the column space in newspapers as it had in the 1920s or 1890s. So when Pelé signed for the New York Cosmos of the fledgling NASL in 1975, the occasion was hailed as soccer's arrival. He joined a side of part-timers with day jobs to cover their rent. But all that quickly changed and the

Cosmos quickly became the league's biggest draw and not only reclaimed the column space for soccer lost a half-century prior but also commanding headlines. As Pelé recalls, 'Every time we went to a new city, and people came out to greet us, it felt like we were planting our flag, the flag of soccer, never to retreat again' (Pelé 2014, 233). With the addition of Giorgio Chinaglia the next year, and then Franz Beckenbauer and Carlos Alberto in 1977, the Cosmos Country phenomenon caught hold and soccer muscled its way into the public eye. The first Galácticos, the Cosmos drew crowds of more than 30,000 in 70 consecutive home league games from 1977 to 1981. As David Wangerin notes, 'We still hear claims that Pelé's time with the Cosmos represents the "true birth" of the American game – a spurious assertion' (Wangerin 2008, 11). And Wangerin is right. It wasn't as if the Cosmos and the NASL had started from scratch. Founding General Manager Clive Toye began the club by establishing partnerships with the existing local semi-pro ethnocentric clubs in New York. But just as spurious is the notion that the Cosmos exploited foreign talent at the expense of developing the domestic game as well as the accusation that the club's overspending was to blame for the just-as-sudden collapse in interest by the early 1980s.

The Cosmos always featured their share of the finest domestic talent in the starting XI, such as USMNT stalwarts Bob Smith (Cosmos 1976–1979, USMNT 1973–1980) and Rick Davis (Cosmos 1977–1984, USMNT 1977–1988). Although they were starters for club and country in those years, USMNT records indicate just 18 caps for Smith and 36 caps for Davis. Numerous appearances for the USMNT never credited as full-internationals mean forgotten matches. Run from a small office at the Empire State Building, the US operated on a shoestring budget, so the USMNT was ill-prepared and unable to overcome a dominant Mexico side for the CONCACAF spot in World Cup Finals. According to Smith, 'We would train for maybe a week or so, a couple days maybe before qualifying games, and just play' (Kilpatrick 2013a). The difference between the Cosmos and the USMNT was, recalls Davis:

> Night and day. You couldn't compare. With the Cosmos, we traveled first-class. When we went to hotels, our meals were all set up for us with no expense spared in terms of the quality. We traveled with more players than we needed, with a traveling secretary, with multiple trainers, with an equipment guy. The national team was clearly not at that level. With the national team, half the time we were being brought together the day before. So there was a big difference. (Kilpatrick 2013c)

As the league began to see attrition from its franchises and the USSF became frustrated by its inability to get past Mexico in World Cup qualifier, a unique experiment was attempted with the formation of Team America in 1983. With the absence of a local franchise in the nation's capital after the folding of the Washington Diplomas in 1981, it was decided to place the USMNT as a team there to compete in the NASL. This would mean draining the best domestic talent from each of the league's clubs and some players were unwilling to leave their teams, such as Davis. But Cosmos' defender Jeff Durgan left for Team America and became the team's captain, embracing the 'last-ditch effort to try to feature American players and energize the national-team program' (Quoted in Bell 2013, 7). Team America finished the 1983 season with the worst record in the NASL and promptly folded.

The NASL of 1968–1984 and the Cosmos have been demonized for raising false hopes and delivering failure, a retirement league that was all show with no substance, dismissed as 'a fun diversion [...] but not serious soccer' (Hopkins 2010, 7). Such misunderstanding and oversimplification discredits the profound efforts of not just Pelé but an entire generation of players, management and fans. While the league and its teams did indeed retreat, the flag planted by Pelé remained firmly at the grassroots with the establishment of a youth soccer infrastructure and its attendant industry. Where there were just fields for baseball or gridiron, there were now fields for soccer.

Since the NASL suspended play after the 1984 season, when FIFA awarded the 1994 World Cup to the United States, many predicted failure for a country without a fully professional league, seemingly indifferent to the global game. FIFA hoped for 'an upswing in terms of football quality and interest in the land of unlimited possibilities' (FIFA Technical Study Group 1994, 161). This dual challenge in terms of athletes and audience is arguably reciprocal – everyone loves a winner but losers are rarely lovable.

The squad that qualified for Italy's 1990 tournament were relative unknowns with an average age of 23 (Bolster 2014). It was as if US soccer had to start from scratch. 'Everyone kind of forgets about the 1990 team' admits defender Steve Trittschuh, 'we can look at ourselves as pioneers. It's kind of special, but like I said, a lot of people forget about it' (ibid.). Three losses in the opening group round meant a quick exit. Although a 1-0 loss to the hosts seemed more respectable than the 7-1 drubbing to them in 1934, there was little in the USMNT's performance to suggest success was on the horizon.

If 'World Cup 94 had to turn America into a nation of soccer fans' (Hopkins 2010, 69), the squad would have to improve.[10] Six of the players remained on the squad four years later, and in order to strengthen the side, 'all over the globe an eye was kept open for players with American ancestors'. One late addition to the 1994 squad, defensive midfielder Thomas Dooley, was the German son of an American serviceman who didn't speak a word of English when he joined the USMNT (FIFA Technical Study Group 1994, 161), reminiscent of accusations of 'foreign ringers' (falsely) levelled at the 1930 side and the implication that American players weren't good enough to compete on the world's stage.

The short-term objective of the tournament was achieved. People cared. In terms of audience reception, the 1994 World Cup was wildly successful. More than three and a half-million fans attended the 52 matches, establishing a new attendance record for the World Cup, with the global television audience surpassing 31 billion viewers, (ibid., 8) including 8.76 million Americans watching the home team play Brazil on the nation's birthday, the Fourth of July (ibid., 46). That the hosts faced Brazil in the second round was evidence of improvement. 'Good morale, the will to win, tactical discipline and good physical shape were the characteristics of this American team', according to the FIFA Technical Study Group (ibid., 161), 'but a lack of creativity in attack was one of their weaknesses' (ibid., 166). Characters emerged with the likes of Alexi Lalas, Tony Meola, John Harkes and Tab Ramos, as the popular media embraced local heroes from the global mega-event. Meola and Harkes were ballboys for the New York Cosmos as children but now they were in need of a league of their own to further their development and that of the domestic game.

The FIFA Technical Study expressed cautious optimism that the start of a new league in 1995 would further the long-term aims of the tournament, saying 'It would be a great pity if American football sank back into anonymity after the national team put up such a fine show' (ibid.). Despite the opportunity posed by a Major League Baseball strike in 1995, Major League Soccer (MLS) would not commence play until 1996.

Was the rough start of MLS a contributing factor in the USMNT's poor showing in the 1998 World Cup? The scapegoat for the team's failure in France is often defender David Regis, who grew up in France and played in Germany when identified by USMNT management as married to an American and therefore eligible for US citizenship. His insertion in the squad was at the expense of the popular Jeff Agoos, just one of the sources of internal turmoil on the side but the one most obvious to fans and media. In another controversial move just before the tournament began, USMNT Captain John Harkes was dismissed from the squad and Thomas Dooley, who six years prior didn't speak English but by 2007 was playing in MLS, was given the captain's armband. Regis went on to earn 27 caps in five years with the USMNT, but never played in MLS. In an interview given April 2014, he laments having no contact anymore with 'a soul involved in American soccer' (Freedman 2014). In the case of Regis, or at least with the USMNT campaign in France 1998, it is as if there's an effort to forget.

The USMNT opened the 2002 World Cup with a 3-2 win over Portugal. A draw against South Korea was enough to survive group play, despite a 3-1 loss to Poland in the third match. A 2-0 win over regional rivals Mexico set up a quarterfinal against Germany. Arguably the better side in a 1-0 loss to the eventual runners-up 1-0, the quarterfinal exit in 2002 was the best showing for the USMNT since the 1930 World Cup.

Expectations for the USMNT heading into the 2006 World Cup in Germany were at an unprecedented high, ranked 5th in FIFA's rankings (FIFA Technical Study Group 2006, 277). But an embarrassing 3-0 loss to the Czech Republic in the opening match revealed the side were overrated 5th in the FIFA rankings. The second match, a 1-1 draw against Italy, suggested both short-term and long-term progress. The only team not to lose to the eventual champions in 2006, the draw showed definite improvement compared to the losses against Italy in 1934 and 1990. But a 2-1 loss to Ghana meant a first-round exit.

Heading into the 2010 tournament in South Africa, expectations were higher than ever for the USMNT, having finished an impressive second in the Confederations Cup the year prior, defeating Spain 2-0 before losing 3-2 to Brazil in the final. Winning their qualifying group with draws against England and Slovenia and a win over Algeria, the USMNT lost to Ghana in the round of 16 knockout stage, 2-1 after extra time. The 2010 tournament was regarded as another sign of progress if not yet triumph for the United States, well enough to earn the team a respectable post-tournament ranking of 12th in the world (FIFA Technical Study Group 2010; 153). Despite the loss to Ghana, in terms of domestic interest, the USMNT were winners with an unprecedented audience of 19.4 million tuning in to watch the quarter-final on television, the same number of viewers averaged for the six games of the 2013 Major League Baseball World Series (Sandomir 2010). At last, it seemed the USMNT had broken through to mainstream American popular culture, on par with America's sporting pastime.

As part of US Soccer's celebration of '100 Years of American Soccer' in 2013, a Centenary XI was selected. Remarkably, all players picked have played or are playing in MLS (United States Soccer Federation 2013b). No Rick Davis or Bobby Smith. No Walter Bahr or Joe Gaetjens. No George Moorehouse or Bert Patenaude. It was as if all the National Team players prior to 1994 were forgotten.

Perhaps the single most telling symptom of US soccer's amnesia is the National Soccer Hall of Fame. Opened in Oneonta, New York on 12 June 1999, within a decade, the Hall announced it would close, doing so in 2010. The Hall and its contents are now housed in a basement in Hillsborough, North Carolina (Morris 2013).

Animosity

Soccer's struggle for relevance in the United States has always been marked by animosity. George Vecsey grew up playing the game in multi-ethnic Queens in the 1950s, poorly by his own humble account. Reflecting the cosmopolitan mix of his neighbourhood, 'players had different styles, which led to chaos on the field' (Vecsey 2014, 9), the game itself a sign of identity crisis. So he had some knowledge of the game as he switched from covering religion to soccer (if one considers that a switch) for *The New York Times*, falling more and more in love with the sport as he covered eight World Cups, beginning with Spain in 1982:

> The geometry of the game, the space, the freedom of choice for footballers who suddenly come into possession of the ball – all of these made me love soccer. But even as my appreciation grew, I could not help noticing the disdain from friends of my generation, who clearly hated the idea, the very existence, of the sport. [...]

> Soccer seemed to remind Americans of something they instinctively feared – foreign languages, foreign influences. (Ibid., 17)

This disdain, this hatred for a sport considered foreign, is all-too-familiar for aficionados in the States. By 1911, US soccer fans had to concede that 'The average American regards the game as a foreign game played by foreigners' (Wangerin 2011, 38). A soccer writer for the *Daily Express* before he came to the States, Clive Toye was acutely aware of the animosity facing the sport among journalists as he fought to draw attention to the Cosmos, one young reporter relating to him what he was told by the sports editor at the *New York Daily News*, 'Don't waste your time on soccer young man; it's a game for Commie pansies' (Toye 2006, 113). This view did not disappear with the arrival of Pelé and may have intensified with the 1994 World Cup.

Soccer was, and is, a threat to the hegemonic forces in American sport, a potential distraction from the established industries of baseball and gridiron football. One particularly vitriolic attack was launched in 2006, the day after the USMNT was eliminated from the. World Cup in Germany:

> DESPITE HEROIC EFFORTS [*sic*] of soccer moms, suburban liberals, and World Cup hype, soccer will never catch on as a big time sport in America. No game in which actually scoring goals is of such little importance could possibly occupy the attention of average Americans. Our country has yet to succumb to the nihilism, existentialism, and anomie that have overtaken Europe. A game about nothing, in which scoring is purely incidental, holds scant interest for Americans who still believe the world makes sense, that life has a larger meaning and structure, that being is not an end in itself, being qua being. (Cannon and Lessner 2006)

The negative consequences of this sporting xenophobia are many. While acknowledging sport as both culturally formative and reflective, asserting soccer's foreignness and rejecting it as 'un-American' promotes an isolationist ideology of nationalism that sees cosmopolitanism as morally corruptive. This animosity is popular not only among right-wing bloggers, it persists among the popular media, still more likely to report on overseas results via wire reports than assign a writer to cover the local soccer beat. The growth of the women's game has done little to counter such bias, perhaps even reinforcing the notion that soccer isn't macho. The struggle for media attention is no less contentious than the battle for the allocation of resources, as the multi-sport landscape means soccer must compete with other ostensibly indigenous sports for access to play space. As soccer has grown from a marginalized activity among the insular ethnic communities of hyphenated-Americans to become a favourite suburban family pastime, this conflict has become more pronounced.

As interest in the 2014 World Cup reached new levels, popular right-wing blogger Anne Coulter revived the xenophobic attack on soccer:

> I've held off on writing about soccer for a decade – or about the length of the average soccer game – so as not to offend anyone. But enough is enough. Any growing interest in soccer can only be a sign of the nation's moral decay. […]

> If more 'Americans' are watching soccer today, it's only because of the demographic switch effected by Teddy Kennedy's 1965 immigration law. I promise you: No American whose great-grandfather was born here is watching soccer. One can only hope that, in addition to learning English, these new Americans will drop their soccer fetish with time. (Coulter 2014)

One needn't be a tenth-generation descendant of Massachusetts Bay colonists to take offence to such an outrageous assertion. But this is precisely the kind of nativist rhetoric that informs the anti-soccer bias that persists in the United States.

In addition to the antagonism soccer advocates continue to face from those opposing the sport as a corruptive foreign influence, internal antagonism has always plagued the game's growth in the States throughout its history. The first attempt at a professional soccer league was hindered in 1894 by the AFA, which banned players planning to play on the eve of the league's launch ('League Players Barred' 1894, 3). Writing a decade later, C.P. Hurditch would blame the investors: 'the base ball leagues thought the time was ripe to exploit the game, and selecting the best players from various clubs, placed four [sic] professional teams in the field, and thus weakened and disorganized the amateurs' (Hurditch 1904–1905, 7).[11] Ignoring the financial crisis of the 1890s altogether and excusing those still associated with the game's governance, the short-lived experiment with professional soccer was demonized, a scapegoat to take the blame for the sport's relative irrelevance in the States: 'Association foot ball received such a shock that it took years to recover, in fact, it looked at one time as if it had died a natural death' (ibid., 9). One cannot help but consider what might have been, had there been collaboration rather than competition between the association and the league in 1894.

By 1910, the AFA could not escape blame, *The New York Times* acknowledging that 'the influence of the A.F.A. management is limited to the Eastern and New England States, and even there it is not recognized by the entire soccer fraternity' (*The New York Times*, 26 January 1910, 10). With the AFA aligned with England's FA, there were both resentment towards excessive foreign influence and accusations that the self-appointed custodians of the game were more interested in exploiting their authority than promoting the sport. This came to a head when England's Corinthians arrived for a tour in 1911 but local teams were banned from playing them by the AFA, on orders from the FA (Wangerin 2011, 37–40).

Although Edward Duffy would proclaim with the formation of the USSF in 1913 that 'peace now reigns where disorder and enmity once dwelt with all their chaos' (Duffy 1913, 23), the driving force behind the association, the New York-born, St. Louis-raised, 'Forgotten Founder' (United States Soccer Federation 2013a, 147), Thomas Cahill, found his role as Executive Secretary fraught with conflict, no more so than the infamous 'Soccer War' of the late 1920s. Having apparently forgiven or forgotten baseball's 1894 dalliance with soccer, Cahill courted baseball owners for the ASL but came to regret their investment when they seized control of the ASL and refused to compete in the National Challenge Cup (now known as the Lamar Hunt US Open Cup). This sparked the 'Soccer War' of 1928. The ASL banned prominent teams such as the New York Soccer Giants and Bethlehem Steel that wanted to continue with both competitions and Cahill formed a rival league, the Eastern

Soccer League, to compete against the league he had formed. By the time a resolution was reached, the Great Depression had struck and the financial damage to the game was done, the ASL folding in 1932.

When the 1966 World Cup in England seemed to spark of revival of interest in elite soccer in the US, two rival factions the United Soccer Association (USA) and the National Professional Soccer League (NPSL) competed for attention in 1967. In New York, the USA's Skyliners and NPSL's Generals had to share Yankee Stadium. The NASL was formed from a merger of the USA and NPSL in 1968. But the success of the league in the late 1970s was challenged by the Major Indoor Soccer League (MISL), promoting a fast-paced arena version of the sport supposedly better suited to American sporting tastes (Kilpatrick 2013b). Distracting from the outdoor version of the sport, the MISL outlasted the NASL but would downscale by the mid-1980s before folding in 1992.

While opponents of soccer continue to push their xenophobic sporting agendas, internal animosity facing the game's growth is every bit as hostile, if not more so, within advocates of soccer, reflected in the competing organizations governing the game at all levels. Beneath the USSF umbrella alone, there are five professional leagues and four youth organizations competing for the American soccer dollar. Three different organizations offer coaching certifications that do not align or reciprocate with each other or the USSF's coaching licensure program (currently under another reconstitution). The ostensible USSF-sanctioned professional pyramid does not allow promotion and relegation. The single-entity MLS, sanctioned as the first division, competes against the revived NASL, while the sanctioned third division United Soccer League covets the second division status the NASL shuns. Meanwhile, the MLS Commissioner Don Garber publicly scolded USMNT Head Coach and Technical Director Jürgen Klinsmann for disparaging comments on the standard of play in MLS. Garber threatened Klinsmann and all dissenting voices, saying, 'I insist that all of those people who are paid to work in this sport – that they align with the vision that has been established', by MLS (Carlisle 2014). Garber also expressed his frustration over the proliferation of foreign soccer on US television as a threat to MLS (Harris 2013). Indeed, the Internet and the access to live matches on television, especially the UEFA Champions League and English Premier League, have had a profound impact on soccer's growth since the mid-1990s in the US. But advocates of MLS often dismiss supporters of foreign clubs as unpatriotic Anglophiles or Europhiles hindering the game's domestic growth.

The words of C.P. Hurditch written in 1904 ring true today: 'just when it would appear that the game was booming, petty quarrels and the inevitable spectator stepped in, newly organized [sic] clubs lost interest, and spasmodic was the life of this, one of the grandest […] sports' (Hurditch 1904–1905, 7). The complicated and antagonistic infrastructure of US Soccer is a consequence of its history and remains an obstacle that impedes the game's growth. As Gary Hopkins argues,

> the status quo and insular nature of American soccer needs to change, with new structures and a new focus considered. […] The silos that divide soccer in America need to be pulled down for the good of the player, the professional game and ultimately for the US National Team and by doing so everyone in the game will benefit. (Hopkins 2010, 230, 231)

With the Mexican National Team the most popular soccer team in the US, it is clear that circumstances can be improved and that much more needs to be done, not just in terms of player development, but also to ensure stronger identification with representative teams.

Assessment

An assessment of soccer in the States, like FIFA's mandate when awarding the 1994 World Cup, must be twofold in that both the athletes and their audience must be considered. Twenty years after losing to Brazil on 4 July, 64 years after defeating England in Brazil, 84 years after the USMNT competed in the first World Cup and more than a century since the sport's governing body was founded, the 2014 World Cup in Brazil, the USMNT's tenth World Cup Finals appearance, provides an ideal frame of reference for an appraisal of both the USMNT and the US soccer fan base.

Despite the millions of American children learning soccer with the various organizations affiliated with US Soccer, and much to the chagrin of those responsible for the development of domestic talent, Klinsmann has intensified the search outside that talent pool in the quest to strengthen the USMNT, reviving the accusation that the programme relies on foreign ringers (Cotorno 2014; Freedman 2014; Oshan 2014).

Tasked with surviving the dreaded 'Group of Death', arguably the most competitive three matches in opening round-robin group play, survival equates with success for the USMNT's Brazilian campaign, defeating Ghana, drawing against Portugal and losing to Germany in the first round, losing 2-1 to Belgium after extra time in the round of 16 elimination match. The matches themselves were entertaining, dramatic affairs. The *2014 FIFA World Cup Brazil: Technical Report and Statistics* cites the USMNT's athleticism, 'hard-working players' who showed 'determination' (FIFA Technical Study Group 2014, 274). Statistics support this assessment. The USMNT ran more than any other side in Brazil with an average of 124 km per match, more than four km on average distance covered than the next closest team, champions Germany (Knowlton 2014). Midfielder and playmaker Michael Bradley ran more than any other player in the opening three matches (Itel 2014). The standout performer for the USMNT was unquestionably goalkeeper Tim Howard. Praised for athleticism and effort, the USMNT didn't stand out for style or technique, content to cede possession and rely on the counter-attack. An enhanced quality or standard of play, however, was not evident. Ranked 15 out of the 32 sides at Brazil (FIFA Technical Study Group 2014, 151), at the time of writing this essay, the most recent ranking shows the USMNT has slipped to 31st.

But in terms of audience, the 2014 World Cup in Brazil can only be assessed as a tremendous success. While 1363,179 or about 60% of tickets were purchased by Brazilians, the United States had the second-largest number of fans attending with 196,838. Argentina with 61,021, Germany with 58,778 and England with 57,917 round out the top-five nations in terms of fans in the stands. Domestically, television ratings were unprecedented. 24.7 million viewers watched USA versus Portugal and 26.5 million watched the Germany versus Argentina Final. Average viewership for all 64 matches increased 39% since the 2010 World Cup in South Africa (ESPN Staff 2014). These ratings don't factor the numerous public gatherings in pubs and fan-fests nationwide.

Conclusion

Americans care, but still have much to prove. Is soccer a religion for Americans? For many, more than ever, yes. Soccer is more relevant than ever in the United States, though it is still far from becoming the most popular national pastime. Has soccer arrived? Its arrival is unquestionable and should really be dated back well before the century celebrated by

US Soccer. While amnesia allows those in power to take credit and avoid blame for the sport's failings in the States, an historical perspective provides a more honest assessment, identifying the antagonisms that have kept soccer from becoming as popular as it is in the rest of the world. While there's no shame in a second-round exit to Belgium, when one considers the USMNT result against Belgium in the first World Cup, it is clear there have been as many steps back as steps forward in terms of the standard of play on the global stage. But the enthusiasm of US soccer fans at home and abroad during the latest World Cup is proof there is reason for profound optimism when considering the future of soccer in the United States.

Notes

1. The Society for American Soccer History (SASH) was chartered in 1994. After a promising start, such as the *SASH Historical Quarterly*, SASH suffered from neglect, but was revived in 2014.
2. The USWNT has won the FIFA Women's World Cup twice, 1991 and 1999, losing the 2011 Final to Japan on a penalty shoot-out. The United States has hosted the Women's World Cup twice, 1999 and 2003.
3. When the USWNT gathered at the White House for the obligatory photo-op with the president, George Bush quipped, 'Leave it to an American Women's team to win our first world soccer championship ... for the sake of male ego I hope the men start catching up', qtd. Hopkins, *Star Spangled Soccer*, 194.
4. By the 1990s, 45% of an estimated 16 million youth soccer players in the United States were girls (ibid., 195).
5. When I gave the presentation that is the basis of this essay at the *FIFA World Cup and the Nation* conference at Oxford, several attendees conveyed the expectation that a paper on soccer in the States would focus on the women's game and surprise that my talk would focus on the men's game and its reception.
   The question concerning soccer and gender and the United States is highly complex and doubtless worthy of careful consideration but is not my concern with this essay. Without exploring reasons why in this essay, I will simply note the failure of two leagues, Women's United Soccer Association (2000–2003) and Women's Professional Soccer (2007–2012) and the struggles of the National Women's Soccer League (2012-present) to survive.
6. Cf. the *Football 150* conference http://football150conference.wordpress.com and the subsequent special issue of *Soccer & Society*, Vol. 16, Nos. 2–3.
7. Henry Chadwick published the fifty-page *Beadle's Dime Book of Cricket and Football, being a Complete Guide to Players, and Containing All the Rules and Laws of the Ground and Game* on 31 May 1866, on sale in New York on 2 June 1866, less than 14 months after General Lee surrendered his Confederate forces to General Grant and the Union and the assassination of Abraham Lincoln.
8. The organization currently marketed as US Soccer but known officially as the USSF has gone through several rebrandings since its inception. Formed as the United States of America Football Association, it quickly became known as the 'USFA', but changed its name to the United States Soccer Football Association in 1945 and then became the USSF in 1974, embracing the 'US Soccer' brand as part of the preparations for hosting the 1994 World Cup. Clubs and franchises have similarly undergone various iterations and rebrandings.
9. The AFA created the first quasi-national competition with the American Cup but the competition and the organization fell into 'something of a hiatus' in 1899, revived in 1906 after interest in the sport was rekindled with a tour featuring an English side known as the Pilgrims in 1905 (Allaway 2005, 47–50).
10. The negative tactics that plagued the 1990 tournament were another aesthetic concern, addressed by modifications to the *Laws of the Game*.

11. There were actually six teams, not four as Hurditch falsely recalls, competing in the ALPFC, backed by half of the clubs in baseball's National League. The eastern clubs (Baltimore, Boston, Brooklyn, New York, Philadelphia and Washington) fielded sides while the western clubs (Chicago, Cincinnati, Cleveland, Louisville, Pittsburgh and St. Louis) abstained.

References

Allaway, Roger. 2005. *Rangers, Rovers and Spindles: Soccer, Immigration and Textiles in New England and New Jersey*. Haworth, NJ: St. Johann P.

Allaway, Roger, and Colin Jose. 1995. "The Myth of British Pros on the 1930 U.S. Team." *SASH Historical Quarterly*, Spring. Accessed July 23, 2014. http://www.rsssf.com/usadave/usawc30.html

Barboza, Scott. 2010. "Credit for Patenaude Long Overdue." *ESPNBoston.com*, July 12. http://sports.espn.go.com/boston/columns/story?id=5370416.

Bell, Jack. 2013. "Team America". *Howler*, Summer: 46–47.

Bellos, Alex. 2014. *Futebol: The Brazilian Way of Life*. New York: Bloomsbury.

Bolster, John. 2014. "The Unheralded Heroes of American Soccer at the 1990 World Cup." *MLSSoccer.com*, June 5. http://www.mlssoccer.com/news/article/2014/06/05/unheralded-heroes-american-soccer-1990-world-cup-word.

Cannon, Frank, and Richard Lessner. 2006. "Nil, Nil." *The Weekly Standard*, June 23. http://www.weeklystandard.com/Content/Public/Articles/000/000/012/384qgmke.asp.

Carlisle, Jeff. 2014. "MLS, US Soccer Don't Have to Always See Eye-to-Eye on Everything." *ESPNFC*, October 15. http://www.espnfc.us/major-league-soccer/19/blog/post/2090859/mlsus-soccer-dont-always-have-to-see-eye-to-eye-on-everything.

Chadwick, Henry. 1866. *Beadle's Dime Book of Cricket and Football, Being a Complete Guide to Players, and Containing All the Rules and Laws of the Ground and Game*. New York: Irwin P. Beadle.

Cotorno, Steve. 2014. "Are There Immigrants on the 2014 U.S. Men's World Cup Team?" *PolitiFact.com*, June 19. http://www.politifact.com/truth-o-meter/statements/2014/jun/19/nancy-pelosi/are-there-immigrants-2014-us-mens-world-cup-team/.

Coulter, Anne. 2014. "America's Favorite National Pastime: Hating Soccer." June 25. http://www.anncoulter.com/columns/2014-06-25.html.

Douglas, Geoffrey. 2005. *The Game of Their Lives: The Untold Story of the World's Cup's Biggest Upset*. New York: Perennial Currents.

Duffy, Edward. 1913. "Causes Which Led to the Formation of the United States of America Foot Ball Association." *Spalding's Soccer Guide*: 23–35.

ESPN Staff. 2014. "World Cup Final Sets U.S. TV Record." *ESPN FC*, July 15. http://www.espnfc.us/fifa-world-cup/story/1950567/world-cup-final-most-watched-soccer-game-in-us-historymore-than-26-million-viewers.

FIFA Technical Study Group. 1994. *FIFA World Cup USA '94* (Technical Report). http://www.fifa.com/mm/document/afdeveloping/technicaldevp/50/08/62/wc_94_tr_part1_272.pdf.

FIFA Technical Study Group. 2006. *Report and Statistics: 2006 FIFA World Cup Germany*. http://resources.fifa.com/mm/document/afdeveloping/technicaldevp/50/08/32/fwc_2006_germany_1_2_262.pdf.

FIFA Technical Study Group. 2010. *2010 FIFA World Cup South Africa: Technical Report and Statistics*. http://www.fifa.com/mm/document/affederation/technicaldevp/01/29/30/95/reportwm2010_web.pdf.

FIFA Technical Study Group. 2014. *2014 FIFA World Cup Brazil: Technical Report and Statistics*. http://www.fifa.com/mm/document/footballdevelopment/technicalsupport/02/42/15/40/2014fwc_tsg_report_15082014web_neutral.pdf.

Foulds, Sam, and Paul Harris. 1979. *America's Soccer Heritage: A History of the Game*. Manhattan Beach, CA: Soccer for Americans.

Freedman, Jonah. 2014. "What the Legacy of David Regis Says about the USMNT's Julian Green." *MLSSoccer.com*, April 19. http://www.mlssoccer.com/news/article/2014/04/18/what-legacy-david-regis-says-about-usmnts-julian-green-word.

Goldblatt, David. 2014. *Futebol Nation: The Story of Brazil through Soccer*. New York: Penguin.

Harris, C. 2013. "Don Garber Complains There's Too Much Soccer on TV; Wants NFL Model." *EPL Talk*, April 26. http://epltalk.com/2013/04/26/don-garber-complains-theres-too-much-soccer-on-tv-wants-nfl-model-instead/.

Hopkins, Gary. 2010. *Star-Spangled Soccer*. New York: Palgrave Macmillan.

Hurditch, C. P. 1904–1905. "Association Foot Ball." *Spalding's Soccer Guide*: 7–25.

Itel, Dan. 2014. "World Cup: USMNT Midfielder Michael Bradley Ranks No. 1 in Ground Covered through Three Games." *MLSSoccer.com*, June 27. http://www.mlssoccer.com/worldcup/2014/news/article/2014/06/27/world-cup-usmnt-midfielder-michael-bradley-ranks-no-1-ground-covered-through.

Jawad, Hyder. 2014. "Captain George." *Backpass* 37: 4–6.

Jose, Colin. 1998. *American Soccer League 1921–1931: The Golden Years of American Soccer*. Lanham, MD: Scarecrow P.

Kilpatrick, David. 2013a. "Bob Smith in Conversation: Jersey Boy and the Cosmos' Hard Man." *NYCosmos.com*, October 9. http://www.nycosmos.com/article/uuid/1c51eh0x1bo51dw9ks82p69ze/bob-smith-inconversation-jersey-boy-and-the-cosmos-hard-man.

Kilpatrick, David. 2013b. "Cosmos Indoor." *NYCosmos.com*, December 29. http://www.nycosmos.com/article/uuid/1ju4khzvs63zt1bqo1t8d5whpw/cosmos-indoor-part-one-the-big-bang.

Kilpatrick, David. 2013c. "Rick Davis in Conversation, Part One: Club and Country." March 26. http://www.nycosmos.com/article/uuid/ov6hfoag5mut158zgfod1kzji/rick-davis-in-conversation-part-one–club–country.

Knowlton, Emmett. 2014. "The US Team Ran the Farthest of Any Country at the World Cup." *Business Insider*, July 18. http://www.businessinsider.com/ranking-the-distance-covered-by-each-team-at-the-world-cup-2014-7.

"League Players Barred." 1894. *The New York Times*, September 18: 3.

Markovits, Andrei S., and Steven L. Hellerman. 2001. *Offside*. Princeton, NJ: Princeton UP.

McCabe, Tom. 2013. "Loose Threads". *Howler* Summer: 38–39.

Montgomerie, Captain Jim. 1927. "Substitute Rule in Soccer." *Soccer Pictorial Weekly* 1 (6), October 14.

Morris, Neil. 2013. "Who Knew That America's Soccer Legacy Was Stored in Hillsborough?" *Indy Week*, August 14. http://www.indyweek.com/indyweek/who-knew-that-americas-soccer-legacy-was-stored-in-hillsborough/Content?oid=3695636.

Oshan, Jeremiah. 2014. "Jurgen [sic] Klinsmann is Actually Making the USMNT More American." *SBNation*, June 6. http://www.sbnation.com/soccer/2014/6/6/5766076/us-soccer-german-americans-jurgen-klinsmann.

Pelé. 2014. *Why Soccer Matters*. New York: Penguin.

Sandomir, Richard. 2010. "World Cup Ratings Certify a TV Winner." *The New York Times*, June 28. http://www.nytimes.com/2010/06/29/sports/soccer/29sandomir.html?_r=0.

Toye, Clive. 2006. *A Kick in the Grass*. Haworth, NJ: St. Johann P.

United States Soccer Federation. 2013a. *100 Years of Soccer in America*. New York: Universe.

United States Soccer Federation. 2013b. "U.S. Soccer Names All-time Men's National Team Best XI." *USSoccer.com*, December 20. http://www.ussoccer.com/stories/2014/03/17/13/45/131220-mnt-best-xi.

Vecsey, George. 2014. *Eight World Cups: My Journey through the Beauty and Dark Side of Soccer*. New York: Henry Holt.

Wangerin, David. 2008. *Soccer in a Football World: The Story of America's Forgotten Game*. Philadelphia, PA: Temple UP.

Wangerin, David. 2011. *Distant Corners: American Soccer's History of Missed Opportunities and Lost Causes*. Philadelphia, PA: Temple UP.

The art of goalkeeping: memorializing Lev Yashin

Mike O'Mahony

ABSTRACT

Lev Yashin remains, in the eyes of many, the greatest goalkeeper, ever to have played the game of football. Since his death in 1990, coinciding with the dying days of the Soviet Union, his legacy has played an important role in post-Soviet history, a factor that is gaining more importance as Russia prepares to host the 2018 World Cup tournament. Yashin's memory is notably being maintained in the public perception not least through the material form of two key sculptures erected in Moscow in the late 1990s. Yet these works, part of a wider international trend to memorialize footballers in the form of public monuments, offer more than a unique insight into Yashin's career, status and reputation. They also address concerns about the relationship between art and sport as it emerged historically in the Soviet Union and how that cultural legacy is being re-explored in a post-Soviet context. Accordingly this essay examines these two key examples of football statuary as significant case studies through which issues relating to Soviet sport, history and art can be more widely analysed.

The death of a legend

On 20 March 1990, Lev Ivanovich Yashin, the man adjudged by many to be the greatest goalkeeper ever to have graced a football pitch, died in a Moscow hospital. He was just 60 years of age. During his career, Yashin represented the Soviet Union in no fewer than four World Cup tournaments (1958–1970) and, to this day, remains the only goalkeeper ever to have been named European Footballer of the Year (1963).[1] He recorded over 150 penalty saves and kept over 270 clean sheets for both club and country. More importantly, he revolutionized the role of the goalkeeper by regularly advancing from his penalty area to adopt the position of a sweeper, a practice that has become standard in the contemporary game. Perhaps surprisingly, given Yashin's legendary status within the footballing world, his death was not widely reported outside of Russia. In 1994, however, Fédération Internationale de Football Association (FIFA) honoured Yashin by naming him the sole goalkeeper for its fantasy 'World Cup All-Time Team'. This posthumous recognition was further reinforced with FIFA's simultaneous instigation of the Lev Yashin Award for the best performing goalkeeper at a World Cup tournament, later, more prosaically, renamed the Golden Glove. In 1998, Yashin was once again selected by FIFA as the goalkeeper for the notional 'World Team of the Century' and has continued to occupy that position in poll after poll.

Yashin's death was, immediately, and more keenly, felt within his home nation where his career achievements and reputation had long been celebrated.[2] In 1967, for example, Yashin was awarded the highest civil decoration, the Order of Lenin and was later installed as Vice-President of the Football Federation of the Soviet Union. Yet, these official accolades, these State sponsored prizes and honorary positions, went somewhat against the grain of Yashin's personality. For amongst Soviet football fans his high status was accorded not only to his sporting prowess, but also to his somewhat eccentric personality, certainly in Soviet terms, and his reputation as a lovable rogue who notoriously claimed that his pre-match routine included having a cigarette to calm the nerves and a shot of vodka to tone the muscles. In Moscow, Yashin's death prompted an outpouring of grief and his funeral brought parts of the city to a standstill. Here, it is notable that this tragic event came in the midst of major political turmoil. The fall of the Berlin Wall had taken place just four months earlier, and just a matter of days before Yashin's funeral, 6 of the 15 Soviet republics elected to withdraw from the Union. In this context, Yashin's life and career could be seen to be following a similar trajectory to that of the Soviet Union itself. A child of the revolutionary 1920s and 1930s, Yashin had endured the privations of the conflict known in the Soviet Union as the Great Patriotic War and risen to global fame during the cold war era when the Soviet Union's status as one of the two Super Powers was at its apex. The decline in his physical well-being, from the mid-1980s onwards, now echoed a similar decline in the Soviet Union's international prestige, whilst his death came less than 18 months before the collapse of the Soviet Empire. Accordingly, Yashin's death came to symbolize far more than just the passing of a great sportsman. It potentially symbolized the passing of the Soviet Union itself.

In the decade that followed the dissolution of the Soviet Union in December 1991, the Russian nation underwent a dramatic social, political and economic transformation. Attempts at a transition to a free market economy, sporadically supported by Western governments, generated a host of economic and political crises, and the euphoria that had broadly greeted the overthrow of Communism rapidly turned into a nightmare, for all but the few newly emerging beneficiaries. As one Soviet historian wrote in 2002, the first decade after the collapse of the Soviet state might best be described as 'a story of political short-sightedness, unprincipled political struggle, ill health, greed and bad fortune' (Graham 2002). In the city of Moscow, the old capital of the now New Russia, these changes were not only political and economic. New cultural transformations contributed to an extensive reconfiguration of the city's urban landscape. Under the leadership of Moscow's controversial Mayor Yurii Luzhkov, new architectural temples dedicated to commerce cropped up throughout the city, epitomized by the huge scale, four-storey, underground shopping centre built beneath Manezh Square, the very area where both military and sporting masses had gathered in Soviet times, immediately before marching through Red Square at the annual parades (Boym 2001). The revival, and rapid expansion, of the Russian Orthodox Church further contributed to this physical transformation, perhaps most famously through the rebuilding of the grandiose Cathedral of Christ the Saviour, the very architectural monument that had been destroyed under Stalin's orders in 1931 to make way for the never-to-be-built Palace of the Soviets (Boym 2001). But it was not just new buildings that contributed to this transformed urban infrastructure. The first decade following the collapse of the Soviet

Union, also witnessed the appearance of a whole host of new public monuments springing up throughout the liberated capital. Old heroes, revered by the pre-revolutionary Russian establishment, but despised during the Soviet era, now acquired a new-found status amongst a Post-Soviet generation as statues dedicated to orthodox saints, Tsars and nineteenth-century military heroes now adorned the streets, squares and tree-lined avenues of the new Moscow, replacing those dedicated to Soviet leaders that had been removed in the wake of the infamous events of August 1991 (Forest and Johnson 2002). Yet, amongst this plethora of newly celebrated heroes, one individual, perhaps above all others, continues to represent the glory days of more recent, Soviet history, seemingly bridging the gap between those who hanker nostalgically for a collective Soviet past and those who celebrate the individuality and 'freedoms' of Russia's capitalist present and future. For strikingly, during the late 1990s, not one, but two new public monuments dedicated to Russia's famous goalkeeping son, Lev Yashin were erected in Moscow. The first of these was installed in the parklands surrounding the Luzhniki stadium in the south-western district of Moscow in 1997 (Figure 1), the second alongside the Dinamo stadium in the north-western outskirts of the city just two years later (Figure 2). Both are the work of Aleksandr Rukavishnikov, one of the most prolific Russian sculptors of the post-Soviet era. In this essay, I want to focus attention on these two works, to examine them in detail both as individual works and within the wider context of post-Soviet public memorial sculpture, and consider how an emphasis on memorializing Yashin interestingly reflects contemporary concerns regarding sport, and football

Figure 1. Aleksandr Rukavishnikov, *Monument to Lev Yashin*, Luzhniki Park, Moscow, bronze, 1997. Photo: Nathan Gray

Figure 2. Aleksandr Rukavishnikov, *Monument to Lev Yashin*, Petrovskii Park, Moscow, bronze, 1999. Photo: Regina Konovalova

in particular. At the same time, I want to consider how the visual languages used in the production of these two strikingly disparate works address wider cultural concerns, drawing attention to post-Soviet attitudes towards the cultural history of the Soviet Union, and not least debates concerning both avant-garde and Socialist Realist practices in an earlier era and their legacies for the present day. Thus, a key goal of this study will be to bring together sport and art, two vital forms of cultural practice that in the West, at least, are frequently seen as uncomfortable bedfellows. Here, however, the Russian context will be important. For whilst a notional distinction between the so-called 'high' culture of art and the more 'popular' culture of sport has led many Western critics to separate maximally these two forms of cultural practice, in Russia, and particularly during the Soviet period, a fusion of sport and art was widely practiced. Sport, football in particular, was a common subject for Soviet painters, sculptors, print-makers, designers and film-makers, a fact that can be attested to by any survey of Soviet art produced from the Bolshevik Revolution right through to the dying days of the Communist state (O'Mahony 2008). Accordingly, this post-Soviet revisiting of the sporting legacy, epitomized in Rukavishnikov's dual monuments to Yashin, thus not only reflects contemporary sporting interests, but also reinforces a dialogue with Russia's sporting and cultural past.

Football in the USSR

In Russia, the social identity and practice of football was radically transformed over the course of the last century. Beloved of supporters since the pre-Soviet nineteenth century, the game underwent considerable developments throughout the Soviet era.[3] During the 1920s, for example, revolutionary groups had criticized the sport specifically on the grounds of its pre-revolutionary, and thus to their mind, bourgeois, roots. Similarly, its competitive nature, not least its physicality and consequent potential to cause injury, was regarded as a suspect and potentially detrimental form of social practice for those revolutionaries who advocated collaboration and celebration as an important mode of new Soviet leisure. Football, it seems, whether played, or simply watched, risked corrupting revolutionary development (Riordan 1977). But football was also popular, particularly amongst the urban workers in whose name the revolution had been waged, and spectator attendances at matches during the 1920s made the sport far too popular for the Soviet authorities to resist (Edelman 1993). Thus, despite demands from the more extreme left revolutionary groups to ban the game, the Soviet authorities instead sought to transform its meaning and significance, proposing instead that both playing and watching football was an appropriate socialist activity to inspire workers to improve their health and fitness. The expansion of international competitive football during the inter-war years provided another challenge for the Soviet authorities. Though initially hesitant to participate in what it regarded as a 'bourgeois' expansion of sport, the Soviet authorities early recognized how football could be deployed as a state-sponsored tool for international diplomacy. During this period, international fixtures were mostly confined to teams representative of international left-wing Worker organizations, as the Soviet Union refused to participate in the competitions organized by the International Olympic Committee (IOC) and FIFA. Following the Second World War, however, and with the emergence of the cold war, the Soviet authorities increasingly recognized the potential benefits of competing on the international sporting stage. The Soviet Union football team first announced itself on the world stage when it appeared at the 1952 Olympic Games in Helsinki. Four years later, in Melbourne, the Soviet team was victorious and subsequently competed at the World Cup tournament in Sweden in 1958, reaching the quarter-finals at its first attempt. By 1960, at the inaugural European Championships in France, the Soviet Union was once again victorious raising its first, and as things would turn out, only international trophy. Although the Soviet team would never reach the heights of the major international footballing nations, its performances at tournaments, throughout the 1950s and 1960s in particular, escalated the footballing reputation of the state. And it is no coincidence here that much of this occurred during Yashin's tenure as goalkeeper. Yashin's retirement from international football in 1970 certainly coincided with the beginning of a decline in the Soviet Union's footballing status that characterized the final two decades of its existence. Following an unsuccessful appearance in the finals of the 1972 European Championships, the Soviet team failed to qualify for the next three tournaments. They fared little better in the World Cup, being disqualified from the 1974 competition for refusing to play Chile in the aftermath of the Chilean coup d'etat, and again failing to qualify in 1978. In 1982 and 1986, they were eliminated in the second round. Politically, the Soviet Union remained a dominant superpower throughout this period, but political and economic failings in the later 1980s would contribute to its eventual collapse. The harsh economic realities of the post-Soviet transition to capitalism in the early 1990s inevitably impacted seriously on Soviet football, generating what historian Robert Edelman has described as a 'brawn-drain', the exodus of footballing talent to clubs beyond Russian (and former Soviet) territory (Edelman 1993). In recent years, however, this trend is being increasingly reversed as Russian oligarchs pour money not only into clubs based in Europe, but increasingly into Russia's domestic programme. Major international footballing talent can now increasingly be seen in the Russian league. The imminent staging of the World Cup in Russia in 2018 will doubtless contribute to a further resurrection of football in the nation, perhaps bringing crowds back to the stadia, if not guaranteeing international success and here, once again, football will be deployed as a state-sponsored tool for international diplomacy.

In this context, a focus on the representation of the Soviet Union's greatest footballing hero, Yashin, in Rukavishnikov's two monuments might be read as inspiring reflections on the gains and losses that this Post-Soviet transformation has brought about. Yet, it should also be recognized that Rukavishnikov's broader emphasis on the sportsman as a suitable subject for sculptural memorialization in the public arena is far from being simply a local phenomenon. As Chris Stride, John Wilson and Ffion Thomas have demonstrated through their World Football Statues Database (part of the wider *Sporting Statues Project*), monumental sculptures dedicated to footballers can now be found across the globe from Algeria to Venezuela (http://www.offbeat.group.shef.ac.uk/statues; accessed 28 January 2015). Most of these, as Stride and Thomas amply demonstrate, are part of a relatively recent phenomenon, the majority having been erected since the 1990s (Stride, Wilson, and Thomas 2013). This period has witnessed a vast expansion of the deployment of sports figure, and footballers in particular, as the new, publicly acceptable face of monumental sculpture. Part of the explanation for this may well be a shift in an academic, and wider popular, engagement with sport's history and individual memories, reflected not least in a growth in publishing in this area as well as the foundation and expansion of museums dedicated solely to sport (Moore 2012). The growing celebrity status, and wealth, of footballers, particularly following the emergence of dedicated sports channels and the global provision of up-to-the-minute sports news through online web sources and social media has further contributed to the elevation of the football superstar to iconic status. The concomitant decline in social respect for the monarchs, politicians and military leaders, the conventional models for monumental figurative sculpture throughout much of Europe during its heyday in the Victorian and Edwardian eras, has thus left a vacuum that, if the activities of the last 25 years are anything to go by, a consuming public certainly wants filled. In this context, Rukavishnikov's new monuments to Yashin conform to this global expansion of the sporting hero and thus need to be considered as both influenced by, and contributing to, this wider global phenomenon.

The principal aim of what follows will be to examine both these works as case studies, to consider what issues are raised not only by the decision to memorialize Russia's famous goalkeeping son, but also to explore the significance of the siting of these monuments, as well as examining the distinctive artistic styles adopted by their creator. Indeed, these works, despite representing the same subject and being produced just two years apart, might be considered as radically different in conception and execution, thus facilitating very distinctive potential interpretations. Here, addressing two key issues might help to elucidate the wider socio-historical and cultural significances of these works. The first of these concerns the wider impact of the goalkeeper within Russian, and specifically Soviet, sporting history. The second, as an extension of this, will elaborate further on the important relationship between sport and art, and specifically the representation of the goalkeeper, as this emerged in the early Soviet period and how this might contribute to a wider understanding of the significance of Rukavishnikov's more recent interventions.

The goalkeeper in early Soviet culture

As Jonathan Wilson has rightly claimed, 'No nation idolizes its goalkeepers as Russia does' (Wilson 2013). Yet, whilst Yashin's reputation has doubtless gone some considerable way towards reinforcing this paradigm, it should also be noted that a strong emphasis on the importance of the goalkeeper in Russian culture preceded Yashin's appearance by some years. Indeed, the prominence of the goalkeeper can be identified not only in early Soviet sporting history but, more significantly, in the cultural sphere, in early Soviet literature, film, music, painting and sculpture. This early focus on the goalkeeper as archetypal hero can here be briefly demonstrated by reference to just a few of these early interventions. The first of these to make a significant impact took place in 1927, fully two years before Yashin's birth, when the satirist and sometime sports writer Yurii Olesha published a highly influential novel entitled *Envy* (*Zavist'*), initially serialized in the Soviet literary magazine *Red Virgin Soil* (Olesha, 1988). Olesha's novel is not fundamentally about sport. Rather, it acts as a satirical attack on the continuing influence of a bourgeoisie who refuse to accept the changes introduced by the new Soviet state, clinging instead to outmoded capitalist values. Notably, the key character introduced to contrast with this recalcitrant and anomalous presence, and to symbolize an emerging and transformed socialist mentality, comes in the form of a young goalkeeper named Volodya Makarov. This upstanding, hard-working, team-spirited and loyal character, a literary cipher for the Soviet New Man, notably carries explicit military connotations built on his duties as a metaphorical defender of Soviet ideological and geographical integrity. In a key episode within the novel, Makarov's heroic defence of his goal-line against the onslaught of a visiting foreign team, notably German opposition, explicitly forged an association of the goalkeeper with borderland defence. Olesha's emphasis on the goalkeeper as a signifier for the exemplary Soviet citizen in this widely read and officially praised novel thus established the groundwork for the status of the goalkeeper as a new archetypal hero in Russian and Soviet culture.

Over the next few years, Olesha's novel effectively acted as a catalyst for the further development of this conception of the goalkeeper and perhaps its most famous manifestation in Soviet popular culture. In 1936, the box-office hit of the Soviet cinematic season was, notably, a musical-comedy directed by Semen Timoshenko and entitled *The Goalkeeper* (*Vratar'*).[4] Trading on the widespread popularity of football in Soviet society, this film, like Olesha's novel, sought to foreground the goalkeeper as far more than a skilful sportsman, becoming instead a suitable hero of the modern Soviet era. Indeed, like his literary predecessor, Volodya Makarov, the hero of Timoshenko's movie, Anton Kandidov, is representative of the new Soviet citizen, a figure transformed by the changed political and ideological circumstances brought about by the Revolution. This concept is clearly mapped out in the final scene of the film as Kandidov, having initially lost the respect of his team-mates after falling victim to self-conceit at his growing celebrity status, redeems himself by saving the day during a match played by a Soviet team, once again against German opposition. Predictably, the narrative concludes with Kandidov saving a penalty in the final minute of the game and thus preventing his team's ignominious defeat. Not content with this heroic exploit, Kandidov follows this up by throwing the ball up the field, chasing after it and scoring the winning goal against an opposition goalkeeper whose hesitation and indecision serves to reinforce the superiority of Soviet goalkeeping technique. Here, victory is truly snatched, however improbably, from the jaws of defeat. Timoshenko's film was intended to be read as far more than, simply a celebration of the goalkeeper as the much-loved playing position of Soviet football fans. Rather it reaffirmed the metaphorical concept of the goalkeeper as the last line of defence, stoutly protecting the borderline as a means to ensure ultimate victory, a notion that resonated with the socio-political anxieties of the mid-1930s when fear of invasion from growing National Socialist forces was an all-too-real concern. And lest such a message be overlooked by cinema-goers of the time, a constant musical refrain played throughout the movie reinforced this message, the lyrics leaving little doubt of the import of the goalkeeper in a wider sociological contest: 'Hey you, goalie, prepare for battle!/ You're a watchman by the gate!/Just imagine that behind you/The borderline must be kept safe'.[5]Notably, the impact of this light, musically insubstantial tune extended well beyond the context of the film for which it was written, becoming a major popular hit of the era sung by performers in nightclubs and by people on the streets long after the initial screenings of *The Goalkeeper*, thus keeping the concept of the goalkeeper as metaphorical defender of the Soviet state, and faith, firmly in the public consciousness. Yashin, of course, was a mere seven years old when Timoshenko's film was first released. He later acknowledged, however, that seeing *The Goalkeeper* as a child impacted significantly on his decision, along with that of countless other Soviet youngsters of the time, to dedicate his life to becoming a goalkeeper.

This popular, heroic image of the goalkeeper would also extend beyond literature, cinema and music to play a significant role in Soviet art as painters similarly responded to this growing characterization of the goalkeeper as the archetypal hero of the Soviet Union. This can briefly be demonstrated by reference to two strikingly different works produced either side of the conflict known in the Soviet Union as the Great Patriotic War. In 1934, Aleksandr Deineka, one of the Soviet Union's most famous artistic exponents of the sports theme, produced a large-scale canvas dominated by the colossal figure of a diving goalkeeper (Figure 3). Here, Deineka focused explicitly on the representation of the gravity-defying leap of the goalkeeper, a notable emphasis at a time when the Soviet aviation programme was at its height. Exhibited at his one-man exhibition in Moscow and Leningrad in 1936, and reproduced in the art journal *Iskusstvo* that same year, Deineka's work further contributed to the conception that sport could not only serve as an appropriate subject for Soviet artists, but also that it could stand metaphorically for wider sociological concerns (O'Mahony 2008). This notion was further reinforced in a different context in 1949 when Sergei Grigorev produced a sentimental vision of post-war Soviet society again articulated through an emphasis on the goalkeeper (Figure 4). Situated on a piece of unidentified scrubland on the margins of an unknown city, Grigorev represents children indulging in a game of football watched by what appears, from the medals on his jacket, to be a demobbed, decorated war hero. The

Figure 3. Aleksandr Deineka, *The Goalkeeper*, State Tretyakov Museum, Moscow, oil on canvas, 1934.

Figure 4. Sergei Grigorev, *The Goalkeeper*, State Tretyakov Gallery, Moscow, oil on canvas, 1949.

bandaged knee of the youthful goalkeeper, like the scarred land on which this game is played, serves to remind the viewer of the price paid in defending Soviet lands from its wartime enemies. The opponent, presumably about to take a penalty or shot at goal, is completely excised from the image, despite the fact that the gaze of every character within the scene is focused firmly on this absent figure. Here, once again it is defence that counts and despite the obvious support of his comrades, it is the goalkeeper who must face this opposition in his duty to defend the wider collective (O'Mahony 2008).

To return to Rukavishnikov's more recent representation of Yashin, it is of course important to consider what precedents had been established specifically in sculptural practices. Once again, it was during the inter-war years that the goalkeeper emerged as a significant figure within this artistic mode. In 1928, a young, avant-garde inspired sculptor, named Iosif Chaikov, produced a fascinating small statuette representing two footballers tackling for a ball (Figure 5). Although executed in a loosely defined style both figures appear to represent outfield players. The timing of the production of this work suggests that it was a direct response to the staging of one of the Soviet Union's most significant, early international sporting events to feature football. The First Workers' Spartakiad, held in Moscow that year, was staged by the Red Sport International and notably planned to compete with the Olympic Games in Amsterdam (Riordan 1977). Football, always the most popular spectator sport in Russia both before and after the Bolshevik Revolution, proved to be the major attraction in terms of crowd attendance and press coverage (Edelman 1993). Local interest was further ensured by the organization of the competition which created two groups; the first consisted of international sides, including workers' amateur teams from Uruguay, Spain and Switzerland alongside Soviet Republics such as Georgia and Ukraine; the second only Russian teams. As both group victors would play in the final, a Russian presence was thus guaranteed. The tournament ended with a combined Moscow team defeating a Ukrainian national side 1–0. But it is Chaikov's material response to this that is of most interest here, not least as an early intervention that explicitly brought together two distinct forms of practice, art and sport. In stylistic terms, Chaikov's *Football Players*, though figurative in form, openly embraced many of the values of the early Soviet avant-garde.

Figure 5. Iosif Chaikov, *The Football Players*, State Tretyakov Gallery, Moscow, plaster, 1928.

Here, the anonymous sporting figures create a whirling, spiral, geometric form evoking movement and interpenetrating space and a sense of weightlessness. Significantly, all of this came at a time of intense cultural debate between supporters of an artistic avant-garde and those who sought to introduce a more legible, popular and realist approach to art practices. In this context, Chaikov's work sought something of a compromise, advocating a new cultural model that retained some of the formal, experimental stylisations adopted by the early Soviet avant-garde yet simultaneously foregrounding figuration and a popular subject to make the work accessible to wider audiences. The Soviet art critic Aleksandr Romm notably designated this stylistic compromise, 'constructive realism', thus bringing together what many art critics at the time regarded as opposing forms of cultural practice (Romm 1933). Chaikov's seemingly oxymoronic synthesis of avant-garde and realist styles proved, however, to be somewhat ill-timed. By the early 1930s, the avant-garde had largely been rejected by the Soviet authorities and in 1934, Socialist Realism was declared the only official form of culture acceptable to the State. Chaikov's 'constructive realism' was thus largely abandoned as a project, though not entirely and not for long. Four years later, in 1938, Chaikov was awarded a prestigious commission to produce an over life-sized statue to be displayed in the Soviet Pavilion at the 1939 World's Fair in New York. Intriguingly, he decided to rework his earlier representation of football players. In this new version of the *Football Players*, however, the lower of the two figures became more explicitly defined as a goalkeeper, identifiable as such by the costume details of gloves and woollen jersey (Figure 6). Chaikov's new version aptly captured the sense of movement and dynamism typical of sporting practices and proved popular in New York. On its return to Moscow, too, it was widely celebrated and installed in a prominent public position outside the Tretyakov

Figure 6. Iosif Chaikov, *The Football Players*, State Tretyakov Gallery, Moscow, bronze, 1938.

Gallery. Here, like Rukavishnikov's monument to Yashin, it became an integral material artefact within the urban landscape of the city, explicitly reinforcing links between the practices of art and sport.

Rukavishnikov's interventions

But what significance might this wider history of the representation of the goalkeeper in Soviet visual culture carry for Rukavishnikov's more recent monuments to Yashin? Here I want to turn attention first to Rukavishnikov as an artist, and then to offer a more detailed analysis of the two monuments erected in the late 1990s, in particular, giving consideration to the differences between the first and second versions.

Aleksandr Rukavishnikov's family background may well have predisposed him to a career as a sculptor. Both his great-grandfather Mitrofan, and grandfather Iulian were sculptors, as were both his parents, his father, Aleksandr and mother, Angelina Filippova-Rukavishnikova (Rozhin and Glibota 2009). Thus, from an early age, the younger Rukavishnikov was exposed to a variety of sculptural traditions dating back through the entire history of the Soviet Union and to the pre-revolutionary period. The stylistic transitions from nineteenth-century academic sculpture, through the early post-revolutionary avant-garde to the official Socialist Realism of the post 1930s Soviet Union, were thus familiar to Rukavishnikov not only though an education in sculptural history, but also directly though his family heritage. Whilst there is no evidence to suggest that any of Rukavishnikov's forbears produced works on the sporting theme, his mother did produce sculptures of dancers and ballerinas, and Rukavishnikov himself produced at least two works referencing sport several years before producing the Yashin monument. In 1977, for example, his Cubist-inspired work dedicated to the famous karate Instructor Vitalii Pakwas purchased by the Tretyakov Gallery in Moscow and at around this time he also produced a white marble sculptural portrait of the Russian athlete Tamara Bykova (Rozhin and Glibota 2009). But it was in the later 1990s that Rukavishnikov's attention was first focussed on football and the Soviet Union's goalkeeping legend.

Notably, the 1997 Yashin monument was not a single commission, but rather one of three works dedicated to famous Moscow-based Soviet footballers, all produced by Rukavishnikov between 1996 and 1998.Along with the other two works, dedicated to Spartak's Nikolai Starostin and Torpedo's Eduard Streltsov, the Yashin monument was thus part of a triumvirate with all three monuments situated within close proximity to each other in the parkland surrounding the Luzhniki stadium. Thus, in order to understand the significance of this first Yashin monument, it needs to be considered within the context of this wider collective. The earliest of these, both in terms of completion (1996) and subject matter, represents the eldest of the four famous Starostin brothers, all of whom played for Spartak, Dinamo Moscow's biggest rivals, during the 1930s (Figure 7). Spartak had been formed in 1934 and came to prominence after the formation of an official Soviet league two years later. Notoriously, the success of Spartak, generated largely by the participation of the Starostins, and later the leadership of Nikolai, drew the ire of the head of the Soviet secret police, Lavrentia Beria, not least as it was his Dinamo team that mostly suffered at the hands of Spartak's success. This probably contributed to the arrest and exile of all four footballing brothers, none of whom were released until after the death of Stalin in 1953. The now 40 year-old Nikolai was sent to the Siberian Ukhta camp, which reportedly witnessed 40 deaths a day (Edelman 2009). But how might this historical context impact upon an engagement with

Figure 7. Aleksandr Rukavishnikov, *Monument to Nikolai Starostin*, Luzhniki Park, Moscow, bronze, 1996. Photo: Nathan Gray

Rukavishnikov's monument? Here, the emphasis is not on Starostin at a moment of play. Rather he is represented seated on a bench with his shirt and one boot already removed and a towel drapped, scarf-like, around his neck. In this way, the monument notably foregrounds physical exhaustion, thus alluding to camp labour whilst simultaneously emphasizing the side-lining of Starostin; the player is literally benched whilst looking on with a dignified, yet wistful, expression to an imagined game (Edelman 2009)[6] Rukavishnikov's monumentthus references the tragedy of the camp imprisonment and the lost years of Starostin and his brothers, and by extension, countless victims of the late Stalinist period.

Rukavishnikov's monument to Streltsov was the last of the three monuments to be completed and also represents the youngest of the Soviet footballers in this triumvirate (Figure 8). Streltsov shot to fame in 1955 when he made his international debut at the age of just 18, having already played two seasons for Torpedo Moscow. The following year he was part of the famous Soviet Union squad, alongside the more senior Yashin, that won gold at the Melbourne Olympic Games, scoring the vital equalizing goal against Bulgaria in the semi-final. By 1957, Streltsov was being hailed internationally as one of the best players in Europe. That same year, however, he was arrested and charged with the horrific offence of raping a young woman at a team party. He was swiftly sentenced to 12 years imprisonment. Various conspiracy theories have been put forward in the post-Soviet era to explain this incident, some arguing that Streltsov was set up after refusing to transfer his allegiance from Torpedo to Dinamo, others that his refusal to marry the daughter of a high-ranking official put him in the firing line (Edelman 2009). Whatever the truth behind the story, Streltsov served a five-year term, and returned to play for Torpedo in 1963, helping an already successful team win the Soviet championship in his first year back. But Streltsov was far from rehabilitated in the State's eyes. Having missed both the 1958 and 1962 World Cup tournaments as a consequence of his incarceration, he was now prohibited from participating in the 1966 World

Figure 8. Aleksandr Rukavishnikov, *Monument to Eduard Streltsov*, Luzhniki Park, Moscow, bronze, 1998. Photo: Nathan Gray

Cup, although he was finally allowed to return to the national team the following year. Thus, Streltsov's sporting career, similar to Starostin's, might be characterized as one punctuated by absence, interruption and a failure to participate on the biggest stage. And once again, Rukavishnikov's monument makes an interesting allusion to these circumstances. Unlike the 'benched' Starostin, Streltsov is represented in action, his deft body-swivel suggesting a moment of dynamic action on the field of play. The form is loosely based on a photograph featuring Streltsov playing for his country (Figure 9). However, the differences between the original photograph and the final monument are telling. In the monument, the ball is tucked beneath Streltsov's feet, whilst his gaze is distracted away from the immediate action. Here, Streltsov's contact with the ball seems perhaps more clumsy than poised, more hesitant than sure, as if the player is captured at a moment of transition, at a crossroads in his career. Does this potentially imply a moment of distraction for the player, whether conceived as relating to the horrific incident that led to his arrest, or indeed of an offer to change clubs? However interpreted, Rukavishnikov's monument to Streltsov nonetheless seems to suggest a lost opportunity more than a moment of triumph and ultimate victory.

Rukavishnikov's first monument to Yashin should thus be read within the context of these accompanying works, the famous goalkeeper being framed by Starostin and Streltsov both in terms of his age and career, as well as the date of production of each work. But what does the form of this monument tell us about Yashin? Firstly, it presents him in a very down-to-earth manner. Although represented as over-life sized, the goalkeeper is here shown at an ordinary, even passive, moment, perhaps in a game, perhaps in training. Though dressed in a football kit he appears as if strolling nonchalantly through the parkland in which the monument is sited. As with the monuments to Starostin and Streltsov, Yashin is not presented on a plinth, the conventional means by which monuments are literally, as well as metaphorically, elevated above the mundane physical world. This reinforces the notion of Yashin as an ordinary, approachable, everyday citizen, a characterization in stark contrast to the celebrity-driven, alienated and remote identities of modern-day footballers. Here, it as almost as if the spectator has accidentally bumped into Yashin, whilst he is playing a casual game in a public park. In contrast to the physical exhaustion of Starostin, and the

Figure 9. Eduard Streltsov (photograph).

dramatic change of direction of Streltsov, Yashin is presented in an upright posture, reflecting a solidity, confidence and groundedness that seems to belie the athleticism and acrobatic skills for which Yashin was so renowned in his career. Indeed, the only significant reference to his outstanding abilities as a goalkeeper might be seen in the secure grip with which his huge hands contain the diminutive ball. Rukavishnikov overtly emphasizes Yashin's heavily strapped knee, reinforcing the notion that this is Yashin towards the latter part of his career. Certainly Yashin suffered from knee injuries and frequently appeared with one, or even both, of his knees heavily strapped. This emphasis on Yashin's strapped right knee foregrounds the less than ideal physique of the world's greatest goalkeeper, emphasizing his frailties. Significantly, this draws attention to an aspect of Yashin's later life widely known throughout Russia. Following his retirement, Yashin's less than healthy lifestyle, his propensity to smoke and drink vodka, finally caught up with him when, at the age of just 50, the blood vessels in his right leg became gangrenous as a consequence of a blockage widely believed to have been caused by his excessive smoking habit. By 1984, it became necessary to amputate the leg. In this context, Rukavishnikov's 1997 monument carries a biographical point of reference, foregrounding both the humanity and the tragedy of Yashin's later life and eventual early demise. Indeed, the stiffness of the strapped leg in the monument seems almost to prefigure the later physical demise brought to bear on Yashin. At the same time this allusion to injury, and indeed foreshadowing of later amputation, reaffirms the militaristic associations so typically embedded within earlier conceptions of the goalkeeper as defender of the borderline. Rukavishnikov's first monument to Yashin thus emphasizes the modesty, humanity and physical vulnerability of an individual, in preference to representing a heroic individual capable of extraordinary physical exploits. Like the companion-piece monuments to Starostin and Streltsov, this work carries overt connotations of tragedy and loss, emphasizing the footballer as having both suffered through, and risen above, the trials and tribulations of Soviet history.

Shortly after the unveiling of Rukavishnikov's first monument to Yashin, the sculptor was commissioned to produce a second work, this time to celebrate the 70th anniversary of Yashin's birth. This monument, initially erected alongside the north stand of the Dinamo stadium, the home ground where Yashin played the majority of his games throughout his career, presents a striking image of the Soviet goalkeeper somewhat at odds with the earlier version. Here, Yashin has notably been rejuvenated, presented as he appeared in his early career, wearing the workers' flat cap and ordinary gloves typical of this time.[7] The vulnerability of his physique is no longer in evidence here. Indeed, Yashin is depicted at the very apex of a gravity-defying leap, his right fingertips making just sufficient contact with the ball flying above him to convey to the spectator the idea of a glorious save. As in the earlier work, the people's goalkeeping hero is presented without a plinth, though this time the figure is notable elevated, held in mid-air by the metal, netted structure that evokes the goal that Yashin is ostensibly defending. And yet, this very structure signals something of a problem. If read literally, as the post, crossbar and net of a goal, then Yashin's efforts seem, at best, superfluous. After all, if the ball is going wide and above the goal, Yashin's save might thus be read as unnecessarily giving away a corner. But here it can be argued that the inclusion of this, at first glance, peculiar structure operates on several metaphorical levels, simultaneously signifying a number of potential ideas relating not only to football, but also, once again, to a wider cultural and artistic heritage. At a basic level the pyramidal structure evokes a mausoleum, an evocative form frequently deployed in funerary sculpture. In art historical terms, perhaps the most important manifestation of this is Antonio Canova's pyramidal mausoleum in the Basilica of Santa Maria Gloriosadei Frari in Venice, originally designed as a funerary monument to commemorate the great Italian Renaissance painter Titian. After Canova's death, however, the work that had not been completed in his lifetime was constructed as a tomb in which the sculptor's own heart was interred. Whilst this early nineteenth-century Italian cultural precedent may seem a little remote, when considering the memorialization of a Soviet goalkeeper, a more resonant context might also be introduced here. In contemporary Russia, debates still rage regarding the continuing presence of Lenin's corpse, in its pyramidal mausoleum situated at the heart of the capital. Since the collapse of the Soviet Union, and the subsequent removal of countless public monuments to representatives of the Soviet state, the position of Lenin's corpse has generated constant controversy. In 1999, fully eight years after the collapse of the Soviet Union, and notably the same year that Rukavishnikov's second monument to Yashin was unveiled, the Russian President Boris Yeltsin publicly intervened to call for Lenin's corpse to be removed from the mausoleum and buried alongside his mother at the Volkov cemetery in St Petersburg (Forest and Johnson 2002). Yeltsin's argument that it was 'neither humane nor Christian' to display Lenin's corpse in public, outraged many former communists and the President quickly backed down (http://www.theglobeandmail.com/news/world/vladimir-lenin-in-peril-of-red-square-eviction/article534038/ Accessed January 29, 2015). When Vladimir Putin succeeded Yeltsin, that same year his support for the retention of the mausoleum effectively put an end to the debate, although polls conducted since 2011 suggest that the tide of opinion is now turning towards the removal of Lenin's corpse form Red Square (*The Guardian*, 15 May 15, 2013). In this context, Rukavishnikov's decision, in 1999, to represent the figure of Yashin floating effortlessly above this evocative pyramidal, funerary form seems, at the very least, a nod to Soviet history whilst simultaneously evoking the post-Soviet revival of religious orthodoxy. Yashin's ascension alludes to his almost saint-like qualities. Yet, this ambiguous form also allows for other alternative interpretations. For example, the elongated form of the net itself, with its narrow entrance and tunnel-like depth, might perhaps also be read as suggestive of a dangerous trap, even a spider's web, inhabited solely by the figure of Yashin himself. This clearly echoes one of Yashin's most famous nicknames, the 'Black Spider', alluding not only to the black goalkeeping jersey he usually wore when playing, but also to his capacity to scuttle across the goal and keep out shots with both his arms and legs. But to consider the wider potential significance of the monument it might also be useful to explore more deeply the geographical location of the monument and to consider further the important relationship between sport and art in the Soviet Union.

Positioning Yashin directly outside the Dinamo stadium made straightforward historical sense. After all, he was a one-club man, born in the Soviet capital just one year after the stadium was opened, and who spent his entire career playing for Dinamo Moscow. However, the Petrovskii Park region of northern Moscow, in which the Dinamo stadium and Yashin's monument still stand, has a wider history that intriguingly unites both sport and art practices. In the 1920s, this region was developed specifically to facilitate the building of Russia's first major stadium, the constructivist masterpiece, Dinamo stadium, opened in 1928 in time for the aforementioned First Workers' Spartakiad. But this was always designed to be far more than just a sport stadium. Indeed, the whole surrounding area included sports fields and training facilities, making the region something of a sport city, an enclave designed specifically for the practice, as well as the spectatorship, of sport. Within a decade, a new

Metro line had been completed to connect the centre of the city to its sporting region with no expense spared on the marble-clad design of the new Dinamo metro station (O'Mahony 2008). Coinciding with this development of the Petrovskii Park sport space, another series of buildings was also being erected just across the road on Ulitsa Verkhnyaya Maslovka. Pursuing an idea initially proposed by the writer Maksim Gorkii and the painter Isaak Brodskii, this area was specifically designated as an artists' community and included studios, apartments and even an official *Dom Khudozhnikov* (House of the Artists). Shortly after its completion, the famous constructivist and avant-garde artist Vladimir Tatlin became one of the area's newest residents. Over the ensuing years this region, widely described as a 'ship of the arts', became home to the majority of the Soviet Union's most famous painters and sculptors. Intriguingly, like Dinamo stadium itself, many of the new buildings deployed a constructivist-inspired architectural style widely embraced throughout the 1920s, though rejected from the 1930s onwards.

All of this offers a historical context in which the form of Rukavishnikov's monument acquires a more complex significance. Like Chaikov before him, Rukavishnikov's second monument notably deploys a conventional figurative style in its articulation of Yashin. At the same time the more abstracted geometric forms that define the goal area simultaneously reference early Soviet cultural experiments, not least those associated with the works of the Constructivist movement of the 1920s. Where Romm had earlier defined Chaikov's hybrid style as 'constructive realism', Rukavishnikov, as Ivitsa Radinovich has pointed out, has adopted a similarly hybrid term 'free realism' to describe his own practice (Rozhin and Glibota 2009). The siting of Rukavishnikov's second monument to Yashin thus reinforces this allusion to Constructivist history, and notably at a time when Constructivist works, consigned during the late Soviet era to museum basements, were themselves being largely rehabilitated in post-Soviet museum displays. In this context, the second Yashin monument might usefully be read as a nostalgic reflection not just for Soviet sporting history, but also for a wider history of Soviet culture and art.

Moving forward to Russia 2018

In 2008, less than a decade after the unveiling of Rukavishnikov's second monument to Yashin, Moscow's Dinamo stadium was officially closed as plans were put in place to demolish the old stadium to make way for a new multi-billion dollar sports complex surrounded by cafés, restaurants, shops, offices, apartments and a pedestrian zone. Sponsored by Russia's second largest bank, the new complex will be named the VTB Arena, although there have been suggestions that the stadium may also be named in honour of Yashin (http://itar-tass.com/en/sports/758,418. Accessed 29 January 2015). Of the original Constructivist design, only the West Stand with its famous façade will be retained within the newly configured stadium complex. As work commenced on the demolition of the old stadium, the monument to Yashin was removed to a nearby spot away from what has now become a building site and amongst the trees of Petrovskii Park. Whether it will be returned to its original site nearer to the new arena once this has been completed remains to be seen. Russia's bid to host the 2018 World Cup tournament was likely a key factor in the decision to rebuild the former Dinamo stadium and indeed the planned VTB Arena was written into the original FIFA bid. However, in September 2012, Russia announced the list of venues to host the tournament and, perhaps surprisingly, the VTB Arena was not amongst the two stadiums in Moscow designated to stage matches (*The Guardian*, 29 September 2012). There can be little doubt, however, that Yashin's name, and his importance for the history of Russian and Soviet soccer, will play a large part in the publicity surrounding the competition both in Russia and internationally. In April 2013, for example, Putin proposed to no less an institution than the Russian parliament that a feature film dedicated to the life of Lev Yashinbe made to coincide with the build up to the tournament. Despite original objections from Yashin's widow, Valentina Yashina, the project is reportedly going ahead with plans to premiere the film at the VTB Arena on 22 October 2017, Yashin's birthday (http://en.vtb-arena.com/press/news/film-about-lev-yashin. Accessed 29 January 2015). At the time of writing, the completion and release of this film is by no means certain, though the publicity value makes this highly likely. What is clear, however, is that as the world's attention focuses on Moscow for the duration of the 2018 tournament, the name of Yashin will once again ring loud across the global media. And this author, for one, predicts a strong media focus on Rukavishnikov's monument as a fittingly complex, rich and visually engaging material manifestation of the links between a history of football in Russia and its significant representation in the field of art.

Notes

1. Though selected for the USSR squad, the then 40-year old Yashin did not play at the 1970 World Cup finals in Mexico, though his experience was regarded as invaluable as a squad member.
2. At least three biographies of Yashin have been published in Russian in recent years. These include Asaulov 2008; Galedin 2014; and Soskin 2014.
3. For an overview of football in the late Tsarist period see McReynolds 2003.
4. For a critical analysis of this film, see Haynes 2007.
5. Lyrics reproduced in von Geldern and Stites 1995.
6. It should be noted, however, that Starostin was protected from the worst excesses of camp life as a consequence of his footballing reputation; the football-loving camp commander instead recruited Starostin to coach the local football team.
7. As Yashin's widow ValentinaYashina has indicated, Yashin's famous black jersey was in fact dark blue, and the famous flat cap he wore in his early days was stolen by a spectator during a pitch invasion following the Soviet Union's victory in the 1960 European Championship final (Rabiner 2013).

Disclosure statement

No potential conflict of interest was reported by the author.

References

Asaulov, Viktor. 2008. *Lev Yashin: Russkii Genii* [Lev Yashin: Russian Genius]. Moscow: Vagrius.
Boym, Svetlana. 2001. *The Future of Nostalgia*. New York, NY: Basic Books.
Edelman, Robert. 1993. *Serious Fun: A History of Spectator Sports in the USSR*, 1993. Oxford: Oxford University Press.
Edelman, Robert. 2009. *Spartak Moscow: A History of the People's Team in the Workers' State*. Ithaca: Cornell University Press.
Forest, Benjamin, and Juliet Johnson. 2002. "Unraveling the Threads of History: Soviet–Era Monuments and Post–Soviet National Identity in Moscow." *Annals of the Association of American Geographers* 92 (3): 524–547.

Galedin, Vladimir. 2014. *Lev Yashin*. Moscow: Molodaya Gvardiya.

von Geldern, James, and Richard Stites, eds. 1995. *Mass Culture in Soviet Russia: Tales, Poems, Songs, Movies, Plays and Folklore*. Bloomington: Indiana University Press.

Graham, Thomas E. Jr. 2002. "Fragmentation of Russia." In *Russia after the Fall*, edited by Andrew C. Kuchins, 39–61. Washington: Carnegie Endowment for International Peace.

Haynes, John. 2007. "Film as Political Football: The Goalkeeper (1936)." *Studies in Russian and Soviet Cinema* 1 (3): 283–297.

McReynolds, Louise. 2003. *Russia at Play, Leisure Activities at the End of the Tsarist Era*. Ithaca, NY: Cornell University Press.

Moore, Kevin. 2012. "Sport in Museums and Museums of Sport: An Overview." In *Sport, History and Heritage: Studies in Public Representation*, edited by Jeffrey Hill, Kevin Moore and Jason Wood, 93–106. Woodbridge: The Boydell Press.

O'Mahony, Mike. 2008. *Sport in the USSR: Physical Culture – Visual Culture*. London: Reaktion Books Ltd.

Olesha, Yurii. 1988. *Envy*. Translated by J. C. Butler. Moscow: Raduga.

Rabiner, Igor. 2013. "The Jersey That Wasn't Black." *The Blizzard* 9.

Riordan, James. 1977. *Sport in Soviet Society*. Cambridge: Cambridge University Press.

Romm, Aleksandr. 1933. "On the Creativity of IosifChaikov." *Iskusstvo* 3.

Rozhin, Alexander, and Ante Glibota. 2009. *Alexander Rukavishnikov*. Milan: SkiraEditore.

Soskin, Aleksandr. 2014. *Lev Yashin: LegendarnyiVratar'* [Lev Yashin: Legendary Goalkeeper]. Moscow: Algoritm.

Stride, Chris, John Wilson, and Ffion Thomas. 2013. "From Pitch to Plinth: Documenting the UK's Football Statuary." *Sculpture Journal* 1 (22): 146–161.

Wilson, Jonathan. 2013. *The Outsider: A History of the Goalkeeper*. London: Orion Books.

Politics and international fandom in a fringe nation: *La Albiceleste*, Maradona, and Marxist Kolkata

Sarbajit Mitra and Souvik Naha

ABSTRACT

Despite India's disappointing position in the FIFA rankings and the nation's failure to make it to the biggest stage of Soccer, it has a rich historic tradition in the field of football. With India never competing in the World Cup, it was with the giants of Latin American football, Brazil and Argentina, who the fans from Kolkata developed a sense of bonding with. In Pelé and Maradona they discovered heroes who they could identify, worship and empathize with. This essay will focus on how after the departure of Pelé the *La Albiceleste* or Argentina successfully penetrated the 'Brazilian colony' of Kolkata. The essay concentrates on the figure of Maradona and examines how, for more than a decade, Kolkata's passion for him was built around his football ability, personal life and political beliefs, by analysing literary output and support activities. It concludes with a study of Maradona's visit to Kolkata in 2008. It thus shows to what extent do the reception of world football and global icons provide a unique opportunity to understand the complexity of fandom as a global process.

Introduction

On the eve of the quarter-final match between Germany and Argentina in the 2010 FIFA World Cup, I had a social media debate with some of the senior students at my university. I support Germany in international football, and did not make an exception this time. However, a few of the seniors, all supporters of *La Albiceleste*, which is the official nickname of Argentina meaning 'the white and the sky blue', tried coaxing me to change my position. Though I was not ready to follow their line, what intrigued me were the arguments that they came up with. In tune with their political activities for the college union, they felt that an Indian should empathize with a nation that was almost in the same boat in terms of economic conditions and raise his or her voice for them (even for a game of football). They went on to add that one should support Argentina even more because they were coached by someone who had not only been the most graceful and effective footballer ever but was also the one who dared to speak out against the establishment. The match itself turned out to be an anti-climax as Maradona's Argentina lost by a shattering 4–0 margin. These arguments, however, stayed with me and I came to realize that they revealed, in a way, how fans around the world develop identities with a football entity (a nation or a club) or personality located thousands of miles away and how the charismatic appeal of heroes transcends boundaries and resonates with people they are not even aware exist. (Sarbajit Mitra)

Every four years, the same passion and excitement for the FIFA World Cup bring the state of West Bengal, located to the east of India, to carnivalesque frenzy. In Kolkata, the capital city, or for that matter in entire Bengal, the most vociferous support is traditionally reserved for the two South American giants, Brazil and Argentina. The success of the European powerhouses in the last few World Cups or the non-stop television coverage of the European soccer leagues has dented but still has not usurped this support base. During the World Cup, a sizeable part of the city literally wraps itself in the colours of Brazil and Argentina. The cricket icons are stashed away and cut-outs of footballers, mostly from South America, dominate the city's lanes and alleys. It would not be an overstatement to suggest that football frenzy subsumes every sphere of the city's life for these two months. Football jerseys of the participating nations and other accessories are sold in great numbers. Publishing houses release informative and commemorative books while the newspapers bring out especially dedicated supplementary issues. The matches are telecast live at various restaurants, hotels, shopping malls and nightclubs. Some of the premier restaurants and hotels organize special buffets laying out experimental menus (Naha 2014). Such display of exuberance in a nation which has never made it to the biggest stage, which lies at the bottom of the FIFA table, is indeed extraordinary. The World Cup thus provides an interesting field for studying fan culture of a fringe football nation. While much has already been said about how Kolkata transforms into an effective 'Brazilian colony' during the World Cups (Majumdar 2002) or has been Pelé's kingdom (Naha 2014), this essay will focus on how the Argentines made serious inroads into this Brazilian bastion.

India ranks around 160th internationally and has little chance of a World Cup appearance in the near future. Hence, the football followers in India are left with little option than to find temporary 'refuge' among the bigger powers of world football. What is indeed striking is the nearly singular devotion towards South American football teams. The positive image of Latin American football, one could argue, was generated by the local media and certainly not by transnational communication, which was embryonic when the proselytization began. Tom McPhail's theory of Electronic Colonialism (1981), about how modern media can influence attitudes on a global scale, could be invoked to justify the recent rise in support for European football, but not the earlier wave of Latin American fandom. Formation of a local group identity in response to a global phenomenon (such as Latin American football) can be somewhat understood through the concept of 'flow' which Arjun Appadurai (1996, 48–49) developed to examine global circulation of cultural products, people and services. He observed that this flow operates across a number of 'scapes' which are no longer strictly territorialized. Giulianotti (1999, 24) has added 'soccerscape' to the list to understand similar circulation, 'of players, coaches, fans and officials, goods and services, or information and artefacts', across the football world. Michael Schatzberg (2006) called for addition of indigenous appropriator culture as an ideational dimension of soccerscapes. Despite its sweeping theoretical charm, the term soccerscape has not been applied as much as one would expect, but its basic formulation has been used extensively, primarily in the context of the social-cultural-political circumstances of the diffusion and appropriation of sporting practices. Some of the recent works on transnational fandom (Hognestad 2006; Moniz 2007; Ricatti and Klugman 2013; Akindes 2014; Onwumechili and Oloruntola 2014; Bi 2015) have tried to make sense of what determine various fan groups' interpersonal relationship with foreign clubs or foreign presence in local clubs. Among the reasons offered by the authors, mediated understanding of one's location within a football culture seems a key issue in appropriation models.

To what extent was the flow of information along a mediascape significant in the production and persistence of Argentine football in the Kolkata? The process arguably began with Argentina's triumph at the 1986 World Cup. Diego Maradona's exploits at this tournament and later on inspired a generation of football fans to shift allegiance from Brazil to Argentina, thus heralding a rivalry which often turned violent. Since Maradona or a full-strength Argentina had never played before an Indian audience, the only 'flow' to have informed the adoption of new identity was the circulation of news. The analytical usefulness of the devices used by the local media to seduce susceptible football fans is not limited to understanding of identity discourses or capitalist-political enterprises. Rather, the circular loop of mediation, exemplified by dynamic textual construction of events in tandem with the producer's marketing philosophy and cultural preferences, offers a promising perspective from which this essay studies personality cults in fan culture in an international context. Structural similarities of the game's development in Argentina and India was one of the reasons of the fans' attachment, which was cemented by Maradona's playing years and even by his suspension for failing a dope test in 1994. But how were the aesthetic properties of Argentine football circulated? To what extent were they consumed? This essay reviews some of the literary and journalistic productions about different stages of Maradona's career from the 1986 World Cup to his Kolkata tour in 2008. The Bengali media's engagement with global sports, particularly with Maradona as its star, provides the production narrative. When studying reception, one should begin by asking, as Rajagopal (2000, 260) writes, the 'norms and values' defining the field under scrutiny. The public's level of convergence with the media's story can be somewhat gauged from the readers' letters published in editorial pages. Somewhat, because the letters cannot be accepted unproblematically as the media's agency in their selection is overtly visible. The consumption question can be partially settled by the postmodern logic of imagining it as part of the production (Hall 1980). Though there can always be a disjuncture between the meanings encoded in the text and the meanings decoded by the reader, the 'norms and values' can be read into the text as part of the author's intended meaning. This approach, in a way, is more useful in studies of societies without concrete audience reception data than the Frankfurt School method (Horkheimer and Adorno [1944] 1972) which advocates a combinatorial approach to text and audiences located within specific social relations. Hence, this study approaches *Aajkal* and *Anandabazar Patrika*, two major Bengali daily newspapers with vastly different political leanings, along with several works of fiction, to analyse Kolkata's Argentina fans.

La Albieceleste, criollo *and el* Pibe de Oro

The English community had a strong presence in Argentina from the middle of the nineteenth century as the newly independent nation's leading trading partner. They formed a football club in Buenos Aires in 1867. The club was short-lived, but their identical venture in Kolkata – the Dalhousie club, formed in 1878 – still exists (Majumdar and Bandyopadhyay 2005). The real transformation of Argentine football from a spare time activity of sailors and railway construction workers to a culture grounded in the education curriculum began with the arrival of Alexander Watson Hutton in 1882. Hutton founded the English High School in 1884 and introduced football as compulsory physical education (Duke and Crolley 2001). By the 1890s, there were around 40,000 expatriates who had established their own schools, churches, hospitals and clubs (Mason 1995). The English influence in football promotion continued through such schools and the railway workers (Giulianotti 1999), culminating in formation of the Argentine Association Football League (AAFL) in 1891 and the clubs River Plate (1901), Racing (1903), Indipendiente and Boca Juniors (1905) (Mason 1995). Meanwhile, football in Kolkata started outgrowing the ambit of the English educational institutions and became a mass spectator sport (Majumdar and Bandyopadhyay 2005). In Argentina, the English influence declined by 1912 when the AAFL's English name was formally changed to *La Asociación Argentina de Football* as the sign of being taken over by the Spanish-speaking locals (Mason 1995), and it was the final time when an English-dominated club, the Quilmes Athletic Club, won the Association Championship (Duke and Crolley 2001). Incidentally, it was around the same time, in 1911, when the Mohan Bagan club of Kolkata won the Indian Football Association (IFA) Shield. With Mohan Bagan's victory, the European Clubs began to lose interest and hold over football administration (Bandyopadhyay 2008). The theory of coincidental development ends here, as by the 1960s Argentine football soon established itself as one of the best in the world, whereas Indian football started declining to a point of no return. Despite Uruguay and Argentina's success in world football, football fans in Kolkata understood Brazilian football as the representative of the Latin American style of play till the middle of the 1980s (Majumdar 2002; Naha 2014), specifically until they saw and read about Maradona's triumphant campaign at the 1986 World Cup. *Fútebol arté* was now replaced by *criollo*, similar in spirit but advanced in terms of its high priest's skill level.

The *criollo* style of football developed gradually and can be understood only in the context of Argentina's history in the early decades of the twentieth century (Duke and Crolley 2001). Eduardo Archetti (1994) highlights the crucial role played by football in shaping a national identity for Argentina following the massive influx of Italian, Spanish, Jewish and East European migrants during the 1910s–1920s.As the dispute over who or what constitutes Argentineness intensified, in the public debates about national identity was incorporated, as a marker of identity among other qualities, a distinguishable style of playing football. The traditional and popular print media houses of Buenos Aires championed the style of free-flowing football, in which the ball is not hit, but 'strummed as if it were a guitar, a source of music' (Galleano 1997). This style, dubbed as *criollo* or *creole* style, which referenced the Spanish-Americans of Spanish ancestry, was soon projected as the symbol or hallmark of Argentine football. The *creole* style evoked the imagery of a *pibe* (young kid) with a knack for *viveza* (cunning tricks) playing on the *potreros* (abandoned dusty fields) of Buenos Aires. This 'undisciplined' approach was projected as a statement against the more 'methodical' British public school style. The success of the Argentine team in the Olympic Games in 1928 and the inaugural FIFA World Cup in 1930 further reaffirmed the faith in the *creole* style of play. *Creole* thus constituted a distinct cultural product in the context of emerging Argentineness (Sibaja and Parrish 2014). In the next decades, coaches often doubted the style's productiveness at the world stage, but Brazil's success in the 1960s made the Argentines realise the need to effectively integrate the more practical demands of modern football with their traditional style of play as the Brazilians had done. Finally, their failure to qualify for the 1970 World Cup led to a return to the traditional *creole* style. Cesare Luis

Menotti, who as coach of Huracán enjoyed great success with attractive football, was given over the reins of the national team after the 1974 World Cup (662). Eventually, relying on the philosophy of *criollo*, he fulfilled Argentina's long cherished dream of winning a World Cup, in 1978, and the country went on to establish itself as one of the major powerhouses of world football. It was the matrix in which Maradona developed his playing style.

Maradona would have made his debut in the 1978 World Cup had Menotti not decided to hold him back for future. He could never accept Menotti's decision and continues to hold grudge. He eventually played in the 1982 World Cup in Spain, which was also the first World Cup to be transmitted live in Indian television. However, for Maradona and his team, the tournament ended tragically as Argentina was knocked out early with Maradona sent off the field against their arch rival Brazil. Four years later, Maradona etched his name permanently in sporting folklore by leading Argentina to their second World Cup victory. His performance came to be mythologized to the extent of creating the image of him having 'alone' won the tournament for his country (Archetti 1998). With this victory, Maradona's popularity skyrocketed, and comparisons started to be made with Pelé. Weber's concept of charismatic authority can be invoked here to comprehend Maradona's global popularity. According to Weber (1947, 358), charismatic authority rests on attachment to 'extraordinary sanctity, heroism or exemplary character of an individual', which the followers often presumed to have been endowed with supernatural or superhuman qualities. We have seen how his fans endowed Maradona with supernatural skills after he dribbled past five English players and scored a legendary goal in the quarter-finals of the 1986 World Cup. Maradona's apotheosis was complete a few days later when he brought the Cup home. It can also be argued, following Paul Gilchrist's (2005) study of sporting heroes, that the reverence shown towards Maradona by his fans all over the world was guided by a kind of totemic logic. By totemic logic, Gilchrist (110–111) meant superstitious, mysterious reverence for the totem and an almost quasi-religious relationship with the totem which may carry moral and political implications. This quasi-religious relationship became apparent when the Church of the Religion of Heart and Passion in Rosario was dedicated to Maradona on the occasion of his 38th birthday and a new religion, Iglesia Maradoniana, was formed (*The Telegraph*, June 21, 2014). The followers of this cult count time since Maradona's birth in 1960 and name their first sons Diego. Jimmy Burns (2010, 4) refers to a story that narrated how knowing Maradona's name could save a tourist from being robbed in a foreign land (Burns 2010). As he rightly observes, for Maradona, talent forms only part of the story. Compared to his contemporary Michel Platini's 312 goals in 580 club games, Maradona scored 311 in 589, whereas in their international careers Platini's 41 goals in 72 games outdid Maradona's 34 in 91 games. During his two-day trip to Kolkata in 1984, Bobby Moore had said to the future AIFF secretary Priyaranjan Dasmunshi, 'Maradona is a player, but Platini is an artist' (*Khelar Asar* 7 (43), 1984). Yet, neither Platini nor any of his other contemporaries scarcely measured up to Maradona when it comes to global recognition, particularly after the latter's escapades in the 1986 World Cup. This is where the dynamics of mythmaking takes over. Thereafter he became the national symbol of Argentina. When he was expelled from the 1994 World Cup, the national image of Argentina went down with him, so much so that the country declined to its "traditional and scarcely relevant position of food producer and weak exporter of cheap commodities" (Alabarces and Rodriguez 2000, 128).

In addition to his prodigious ball skills, Maradona's inspirational rags to riches story endeared him to football followers, particularly to those from the economically handicapped nations. Most of the Latin American footballers came from underprivileged backgrounds, never having the opportunity to undergo systematic training like their European counterparts (Majumdar 2002). The Argentines thus automatically depended on their self-cultivated *creole* style of play. For both the Brazilians and the Argentines, who based their play on self-cultivated styles, the Europeans represented the 'other' who were only capable of using their body as machines. The unique Latin American style was hence administered in this symbolic space of nationalist sentiments, but which resulted in Latin American football easily grabbing attention of football followers everywhere, India included. Though Argentina was comparatively richer, the people of Kolkata found a parallel between the story of their own footballers with those from Argentina in terms of their underprivileged backgrounds and progress through a society crippled with problems of unemployment and unrest. The advent of television in the 1980s allowed the people of Bengal to watch in earnest Maradona's triumphant campaign at the 1986 World Cup in Mexico. Thus began the Maradona mania, which is analysed in the next section to understand how mediation of a charismatic authority led to formation of an international fan base.

Maradona's populist, Left-oriented, anti-capitalist political character, exhibited time and again while taking a stance against the establishment or supporting a cause, gave him a unique position. Sergio Levinsky, an Argentine journalist, dedicated an entire book, *Maradona, Rebelde con Causa* (Maradona, rebel with a cause), to explore Maradona's rebel image (Tobin 2002). Levinsky observes that Maradona's criticism of the men in power was not limited to FIFA alone. Maradona had never hesitated to voice his opinions publicly on the more volatile international issues. Besides continuously attacking neo-imperial motives of the movers and shakers of world politics, particularly the USA, he also never hid his admiration for the Cuban leader, Fidel Castro. Maradona's left leg bears a tattoo of Castro, while a visage of Che Guevara adorns his right arm. Castro was a guest in an episode of his television show *La Noche del 10*, (https://www.youtube.com/watch?v=27Nc4QijGhU) and was one of the people his autobiography *El Diego* was dedicated to. He condemned America's expansionist policies in the Venezuelan president Hugo Chávez's television show *Aló Presidente*, (http://www.dailymotion.com/video/x2skn0_maradona-en-alo-presidente_news). He spoke against the north–south determinism in European foreign policy too. Levinsky, however, observes that Maradona's rebel image was not grounded in a consistent political position. His struggles against the established order never developed coherently. Burns (2010, 206) made a similar observation that Maradona's repeated charges against the football authorities – club managers or the Argentine Football Association or FIFA itself – were not unjustified, but his radical, revolutionary image was forged by a combination of unsubstantial political ideas and volatile temper, both of which were vulnerable to arguments. The Conservative political columnist John Tierney (2005) blasted Maradona's rally against free trade in Buenos Aires, referring to the latter's $5 million salary in Europe, fee of $32,500 per exhibition match in the Arab countries and annual income of $10 million for endorsing multinational corporations such as Puma, Fuji-Xerox and Coca Cola. Equally true was the fact that in 1987 Maradona had refused a $100 million deal with the sport management group IMG since the corporation wanted him to become a dual citizen of Argentina and the US (Abilash 2006). Maradona's political statements resonated well with the Kolkata public who were governed by a Communist regime from 1977 to 2011. Hence, Maradona's political self arguably became a transnational property which moved among soccerscapes and was appropriated as per the requirement of the receiving culture.

An Argentine in Kolkata: in writings

The Communist alternative to liberal governance was quite prevalent in the Third World countries in the rapidly decolonising world of the 1960s–1970s. India was no exception. Jawaharlal Nehru, India's first Prime Minister, sought to initiate international cooperation to ensure mutual benefit and peaceful coexistence for countries not diplomatically involved in the Cold War. A conference of Asian and African countries in Bandung in 1955 launched a formal group of countries, which by 1961 expanded into the Non-Aligned Movement – a design to assert a common identity for the Third World nations (Arnold 2006). Though the bigger Latin American nations, Brazil and Argentina, never formally became a part of the movement, they remained as 'observer countries' (Arnold 2006). Nevertheless the political leadership in these countries had much in common with those of the major NAM nations, so were the economic challenges and modes of production. Anti-capitalist uprisings spread across both Latin America (Argentina, Bolivia, Colombia, Peru) and India (Bengal, Kerala, Telengana) in the 1960s, encouraged by the success of a peasant-based revolution in China, the Cuban revolution, and the emergence of Che Guevara and Mao Tse Tung as iconic symbols of Communist ideology (Krishna 2009). The Left Front, led by the Communist Party of India (henceforth CPIM) came to power in Bengal following a landslide election victory in 1977, the year Maradona made his international debut against Hungary.

Bengal has a long history of radical movements. Since the late nineteenth century the state had been the base from which secret revolutionary societies operated against the British colonial rule. It was in Bengal in the 1930s and 1940s that Marxism found a broad base among the middle-class (Sartori 2008). The socioeconomic problems generated by the migrant crisis following partition of India threw the nascent nation into turmoil, particularly Bengal which was the site of immigration. The Communists found steady support from the immigrants from East Pakistan (Chatterji 2007), and grew from strength to strength to finally win the state election. In 1979, while Maradona prepared for and won the FIFA World Youth Championship for Argentina, beating the Soviet Union in the final, the West Bengal government was busy resolving the decade-long food and labour problems, political crimes, industrial stagnation, communal and caste conflicts (Mitra 2006). During Maradona's stints with Barcelona and Napoli in the 1980s, the Bengal government was consolidating its 'ideological platforms for mobilizing the socio-economically marginalized sections' (Chakrabarty 2014) in opposition to the reform ideas articulated by American democrats and their Indian followers. Hence, in a state which had been historically susceptible to anti-formalism, in which criticism of neo-colonial powers had been part of the state rhetoric, it is not difficult to see why football followers empathized with Maradona's rebellious persona. With nobody pointing out the shortcomings in his political stands, his Bengal followers, primarily the youth, disgruntled with deprivation, looked up to Maradona's radical image. The government started following neoliberal tenets of development in the 2000s as the state's economic stasis reached alarming proportions. The people of Bengal, however, fed from above the same ideology that Maradona believed in, found in him a kindred spirit. Additionally, from a sporting perspective, Maradona's inspirational rise, powered by nothing but a natural gift for the game, offered much hope to the aspiring youths of Bengal. Bengali newspaper reports, letters to the editor and even fictional works from this period are rife with such sentiments.

The vernacular production of Maradona's celebrity status began during the 1986 World Cup in Mexico, the first World Cup that was followed in much detail by the local vernacular newspapers. *Anandabazar Patrika*, a major Bengali daily, published basic match reports, with little analysis, and hence hardly reflected the shift in fan sentiment. *Aajkal*, the other leading Bengali daily, with a Leftist alignment, spent considerable newsprint in sports reporting which mirrored the changing fan mentality. For instance, after Argentina's controversial quarter-final match against England in 1986, Pelé criticized Maradona for his 'hand of god' effort and called him a cheat. The next morning most of the major Bengali sports journalists and former footballers came out in support of the Argentine star in their respective columns (*Aajkal*, June 23–24, 1986). Until then this was something unthinkable, since Pelé had been the sovereign king of football as far as Bengal was concerned (Naha 2014). A supportive editorial in *Aajkal* concluded that such statements revealed Pelé's insecurity at Maradona's success (*Aajkal*, June 24, 1986). On the eve of the final, Amiya Tarafdar, the photojournalist sent to cover the World Cup, presented Maradona with a *namaboli*, an auspicious cloth worn by the followers of the Vaishnavite sect, inscribed with the name of Lord Krishna, as a good luck gesture on behalf of his supporters from Bengal (*Aajkal*, June 29, 1986). A report compared Maradona's preparation for the final to that of Arjuna, the warrior hero of the Indian epic *Mahabharata*, getting himself ready before the battle of Kurukshetra (*Aajkal*, June 29, 1986). Argentina's victory after a thrilling final was celebrated with much pomp. Processions were brought out with cut-outs of Maradona, joined by even Brazil fans, to salute Maradona's triumph (*Aajkal*, June 30, 1986). Leading Bengali poets such as Nirendranath Chakraborty, Purnendu Patri, Amitabha Chowdhury and Samarendra Sengupta wrote poems on his success in the autumn annual festival edition of the Bengali sports weekly *Khela* (*Sharadiya Khela*, 1393 [1986], 35–36). Maradona's first biography in Bengali was published soon afterwards. Authored by Santipriya Bandopadhyay (1996), the book was titled *Sonar Chele Maradona* (Maradona: The Golden Boy). Bandopadhyay, who had written biographies of Pelé, Stanley Mathews, Frank Worrell, Mansur Ali Khan Pataudi and other sportspersons before, presented Maradona as a humble boy, who made it big despite hardships in early life. The book stressed on Maradona's dedication to his parents and family and readiness to serve his nation, making him an inspirational figure who was not lured by fame or money. Chiranjib (1987), a Bengali sports journalist, too came up with a book titled *Mexico 86*. However this book offered merely basic reports for all of the 52 matches played in the tournament.

The matches Maradona played for Napoli were not shown in Indian television except for occasional highlights. So the public waited another four years to watch him play live, expecting a rerun of the fortunes of 1986 in Italia '90. Any chance of repeating the glory was brought to a cruel end by the awarding of a controversial penalty kick, which decided the final in Germany's favour. The fans did not hide their disappointment and grief. A section of them felt that Maradona's Argentina had fallen victim to a conspiracy hatched by the Italian mafia, though most of the football experts agreed that the Germans were the team of the tournament and deserved victory (*Aajkal*, July 9, 1990). In the autumn annual edition of *Khela*, Timirbaran (1990) wrote the short story 'Bishu, Maradona O Protarona' (Bishu, Maradona and cheating). Maradona himself did not feature in this story directly. The story focuses on the life of Bishu and his friends. Despite showing high promises early in their football life, they fail to fulfil their potential and become victims of the circumstances. Underprivileged origins (just like their hero, Maradona) force these young players to use unfair means in local tournaments to earn quick money. Their dream journey to emulate Maradona is cut short when organizers notice their activities.

The euphoria reached its height during the next World Cup in 1994. The international media created a huge hype over Maradona, who made a comeback from retirement to take part in this World Cup. The Bengali newspapers followed suit, investing a lot of newsprint in the build up to this tournament, particularly on Maradona. Two journalists along with a few former footballers were sent from Kolkata to cover the tournament in the USA. Argentina started the World Cup raising high hopes, thrashing Greece 4–0. However, an anti-climax was to follow in the very next match. Against Nigeria, Argentina won the match 2–1, but after the match Maradona underwent a routine dope test, which he failed and was suspended from the tournament (*New York Times*, July 1, 1994). The decision stunned the entire football world. Kolkata went into an effective state of mourning. *Jugantar* was the only newspaper to publish the news the day after it happened as the story arrived from Reuters very late at night. When the concerned subeditor Surojit Sen barged into the press and demanded the story to be included as stop press, he was told by the machine operator, 'We can't be concerned about those fancies of rich men. I could have considered had the prime minister died. It is too late for the schedule of editions which will be circulated far away' (Sen 2014). It took a liberal dose of threats for the printer to agree, but in the context of the frenzy that was to follow his initial nonchalance seemed to have stemmed from either support for Brazil or a genuine lack of interest in football.

Maradona fans were very critical of FIFA, the European nations and even their former golden boy Pelé. The Sports Minister of West Bengal, Subhas Chakraborty, issued a statement against Pelé and FIFA (*Aajkal*, July 1, 1994). Most of the Bengali media followed the same line. Expressing their support for Maradona, they presented him as a victim of a possible conspiracy. Former Indian footballer Surajit Sengupta felt that if Ephedrine, the banned substance which led to Maradona's suspension, can ensure such superhuman skills and ball control, then its consumption must be made compulsory to make the game more exciting for fans (*Aajkal*, July 1, 1994). Fans showed their solidarity in a variety of ways. In addition to protest marches where effigies of FIFA officials were burnt, many public buses were painted with slogans like 'Long Live Maradona' or 'Maradona, we are with you'. Across the border, in Dhaka, a demonstration was staged after the day of suspension, with almost 20,000 protestors chanting, 'Dhaka will burn unless Maradona is allowed to play' (Burns 2010). The Bangladesh Football Association sent to FIFA a petition for withdrawing Maradona's suspension, and the Dhaka film industry too made an appeal in a press conference (*Aajkal*, July 4, 1994). A Bangladeshi fan even committed suicide after Argentina was knocked-out from the tournament (*Anandabazar Patrika*, July 6, 1994). Another interesting area where the reactions of the fans were registered was the letters to the editor column in the various Bengali dailies. Debapriya Sengupta appealed to the media to launch an investigation and reveal the truth before the world (*Aajkal*, July 4, 1994). Pradip Dutta suspected in his letter that Maradona was a victim of the conspiracy by some influential drug cartel. Bikash Ray, writing to the editor of *Aajkal*, went ahead claiming that FIFA in itself was a puppet at the hands of these drug cartels (*Aajkal*, July 8, 1994). Another fan, Prasanta Sengupta, pointed out that FIFA had always been antagonistic to socialist states. None of the Socialist countries ever had the opportunity to host the World Cup. Hence, FIFA was always uneasy with Maradona's criticism of the USA's imperialist motives and his association with the Cuban leader Fidel Castro. Sengupta drew a parallel between Che Guevara's assassination by the Bolivian army to Maradona's suspension from the World Cup, both falling prey to neo-colonial forces (*Aajkal*, July 8, 1994). Arindam Chakraborty, also writing to the *Aajkal* editor, suggested that the AIFF, the governing body of Indian football, should withdraw their membership from FIFA in protest against this disgraceful decision (*Aajkal*, July 8, 1994).

Anandabazar Patrika presented a more balanced view of the entire episode. A few days before the fateful Nigeria match, the newspaper tried to gauge the fascination of the Bengalis over Maradona in a couple of articles. Sabyasachi Sarkar (*Anandabazar Patrika*, June 28, 1994), in his article 'Maradona vs Brazil', showed how the man with the magical left foot had won over the city's Brazil fans and converted them to die-hard Argentines. The author Dulendra Bhowmik (*Anandabazar Patrika*, June 28, 1994), in his fictional write-up 'Mama O Maradona' (Uncle and Maradona), presented the stereotypical character of an uncle, who coming from an underprivileged background identified himself with the early years of Maradona's struggle. He felt that Maradona's success will remain as a source of inspiration for youths from developing or economically backward nations like India. After FIFA suspended Maradona from the tournament, *Anandabazar Patrika* did briefly support him. Former India captain Chuni Goswami expressed solidarity (*Anandabazar Patrika*, July 1, 1994). In another report, a suggestion was put forward to consider doping henceforth as a legal part of game strategy (*Anandabazar Patrika*, July 5, 1994). However, the readers of *Anandabazar Patrika* reacted very differently from those of *Aajkal*. Probably they did not, but that is not what the selection of letters show. Runa Bandopadhyay, writing to the editor, criticized the Bengali media for supporting a man who had flouted the game's ethics. Kamruddin Ahmed applauded FIFA for maintaining a firm stance regardless of the fans' emotional outbursts. Arupratan Aich felt that Maradona had not only committed a breach of trust but also set a bad precedence before thousands of aspiring youngsters who idolised him (*Anandabazar Patrika*, July 9, 1994). On the basis of a survey done in Kolkata by an organization called 'Mode', the newspaper concluded that the number of fans who felt that the right decision had been taken were not far behind the number of fans who believed Maradona had been wronged (*Anandabazar Patrika*, July 5, 1994). *Anandabazar*'s position was crystallized into the title of their leading sport journalist Goutam Bhattacharya's (1995) book about Maradona – *Digbhrasta Rajputra* (Fallen Prince) – a genius gone wrong. Apparently, *Aajkal*, presumably guided by its Marxian grounding, was more taken up with Maradona's image as a champion of the Third World than *Anandabazar Patrika*, and more committed to preserving Maradona's iconicity. Selection of readers' letters depends on the media's editorial policy. This instance was a clear indication of whose loyalty lay where. However, that year's autumn annual of the *Khela* magazine did not publish anything about Maradona. The longer a good dream lasts, the more unbearable the pain becomes when it breaks maybe.

A number of fictional and non-fictional works on Maradona came out soon after the dope scandal. Supriya Sen wrote a short-play, titled 'Death to Maradona' (*Aajkal*, July 9, 1994), which was immediately published in *Aajkal*'s Sunday supplement. The plot of the play involved a fictional meeting between Sepp Blatter, the then FIFA General Secretary and representatives of Italian drug-mafia with business interest in the Americas and how the plan of Maradona's suspension was concocted in the meeting. Saha (1995), who covered the 1994 World Cup for the Bengali daily *Anandabazar Patrika* came up with a short story on Maradona's dope scandal. As the title suggests, 'Maradonar dosh nei' (Maradona is innocent) tried to defend Maradona's position by showing that he was a victim of a conspiracy. Instead of the predictable culprits such as FIFA or CIA, Saha's thriller presented a big Argentine media house as the culprit, which sought to take revenge after Maradona refused to sign a contract with them before the World Cup. The cover of the book in which the story was latter collected, keeping in tune with story, presented Maradona as a Christlike figure awaiting crucifixion. Later he wrote *Bidrohi Maradona* (Maradona, the Rebel) in the World Cup special issue of the children's magazine *Anandamela* (1998). In this non-fictional account Saha followed Levinsky's argument that Maradona's rebellions or protests were mostly ad-libbed and had little logic or cause. Saha felt the only good that such his shenanigans did was to promote an image of a tragic hero, like that of Karna, Arjun's arch rival in the epic *Mahabharata*, before his fans and followers.

Maradona became a referential character in a Bengali romantic novel as well. Written by Subroto Sengupta (1996), *Maradona Hey* (Oh Maradona) tells the story of a young couple in Kolkata who bonds over their shared admiration for Maradona. When circumstances pull them apart, it is their shared concern for Maradona, after the hero fails the decisive dope test, which brings them together again. The novel ends on a positive note with the couple hoping that someday the Kolkata *maidan* will be fortunate enough to witness Maradona's magic.

An Argentine in Kolkata: in person

The dream of the young couple from *Maradona Hey* did never materialize. However, Maradona did visit Kolkata on a brief tour in 2008, long after he had hung up his play-ing boots. The excitement that the tour generated among the city's football enthusiasts reflected Maradona's popularity long after his retirement. The then state government of West Bengal, ruled by the CPI (M), invited Maradona to a two-day tour of the city (*Aajkal*, December 6, 2008). Shamik Lahiri, a CPI (M) member of the parliament, was instrumental behind this 'historic' tour. According to reports, he contacted Maradona's agent the Balwens group and ex-wife Claudia, and was granted an appointment with Maradona for 10 min. He went all the way to Buenos Aires to convince him. Apparently, Lahiri's affiliation to a communist outfit and invitation to visit the Missionaries of Charity to pay respect to Mother Teresa persuaded Maradona to agree to the tour in no time (Bhattacharjee 2008). The tour was announced briefly after Maradona took over as the coach of the Argentine football team, which further added to the excitement of the Argentina fans in Kolkata. The tour became uncertain following the 26/11 terrorist attacks in Mumbai (*ndtv.com*, November 28, 2008). Maradona was reportedly appre-hensive about his safety but finally went ahead with the schedule. The city began to prepare for his visit since the evening of December 5. A number of business houses used the occasion to promote themselves, making use of Maradona's image. Advertisements welcoming Maradona to the 'city of joy' came up not just in the print media but also on billboards across the city. The Bengali folk band Dohar (https://www.youtube.com/watch?v=hBrIMOhqTBc) released a song in praise of Maradona. The fans began to con-gregate in the airport long before Maradona's flight was due. When he arrived, youths in bike, clad in Argentine colours, escorted his car to his hotel. The tour organizers kept a tight schedule for Maradona in the following days. After a token visit to the Missionaries of Charity, he met senior Communist leader and former chief minister of the state, Jyoti Basu. He did find some common grounds with the elderly Communist leader, who had been an old acquaintance of Fidel Castro (*Aajkal*, December 8, 2008). However, the journalists waiting outside Basu's residence ran out of patience and started jostling for vantage positions outside the gate, leading to clashes with the police. Five journalists were injured; one of them was admitted to the hospital. A visibly agitated Maradona left before the scheduled press conference (*Aajkal*, December 7, 2008). The coaching clinic that Maradona's was supposed to supervise at the Mohan Bagan club grounds also had to be cut short. He did set the foundation stone for the Mother Teresa Football Academy at Maheshtala, located a few kilometres off Kolkata. The exhibition match between Chief Minister's XI and the Foreign Minister's XI organized at the occasion of Maradona's felicitation at the Yuva Bharati Krirangan was also successful, according to the organizers. Before leaving the city Maradona promised technical assistance for the proposed Academy, of which nothing more was ever heard (*Aajkal*, December 7, 2008). In an interview given to Kolkata TV, he admitted that after the fanatical celebrations in Naples after their maiden national championship win, this was the biggest reception he had received (https://www.youtube.com/watch?v=ESv0de76gx0). Asked about Castro, terrorism, poverty and food crisis at the same show, he lived up to the public's expectation by reprising his persona of an activist footballer. True to his spirit and to the delight of his Communist hosts, Maradona strongly condemned America's designs in Afghanistan and Iraq, harshly criticizing the former US President, George Bush (*Aajkal*, December 7, 2008).

A part of the media was sceptical about Maradona's tour leaving any positive imprint and generating any potential benefit for Indian football, and later branded it as over-hyped. It was alleged that the CPI (M) organized the tour to gain political mileage at a time when its popularity among masses was dwindling. The people who organized the visit were aware of the immense impact Maradona the player had on the local people and exploited the fandom skilfully (*Goal.com*, December 7, 2008). The organizers were criticized by a section of football enthusiasts too, for shifting an important Federation Cup match to a lesser stadium in Barasat in order to accommodate Maradona's felicitation programme at the Yuva Bharati (*Goal.com*, December 6, 2008) Bob Houghton, the-then coach of the Indian football team, felt that the amount spent on the tour should rather have been invested in providing better facilities at the sub-junior level (*Aajkal*, December 7, 2008). Bhaichung Bhutia, the Indian football legend, who did not hide his excitement of meeting Maradona in person, admitted, '… his being here will not change things. We need to have a long-term place for the coaching centre and develop it accordingly. We need to do the follow up' (*The Indian Express*, November 11, 2008).

The tour however, gives a glimpse into how Maradona's football career morphed into an afterlife in which the footballer's aura, far from being diminished, intensified into the frame of a global celebrity with an extended public lifespan. Maradona never ceased to be involved with football after retirement; he was announced as the Argentine national team's coach months before his Kolkata tour and continued till the 2010 World Cup. Secondly, as discussed before, to his followers Maradona was much more than a skilful footballer; he was an outspoken revolutionary. The rebel, politically entangled image, cultivated by the media across regions, perpetuated his aura among the younger generation. Circulation of selective images in the mass media, evident in the different modes of representation adopted by two rival newspapers, allowed for the reinvention of the legend of Maradona. The tour clearly reflected that Maradona continues to be a source of inspiration among the youth and the aspiring footballers in Kolkata even almost two decades after his retirement.

Conclusion

In recent years, the proliferation of satellite television and easier access to the internet has deeply affected the demography of football supporters in Kolkata. With wider coverage of European leagues and the success of the European teams in the recent World Cups, cracks have become apparent in this little stronghold of Latin American football. However, public exuberance during Maradona's tour or even during the Argentina–Venezuela friendly tie played in Kolkata in 2011 showed that Kolkata's affinity to Argentina or its eternal rival Brazil is far from being diminished.

This essay has made an attempt to locate the origins and map the dimensions of Kolkata's fascination with Argentine football. Maradona's exploits during the 1986 World Cup certainly inspired a generation of football enthusiasts to convert to the white-and-blue. A reading of media narratives, however, reveal that football is only the surface for Kolkata's love for Maradona; the myth of the pocket dynamo lay in his political convictions, which were largely identical to what the province's government and its majority of voters believed in theory. These narratives not only reinforced the popularity of Maradona and the Argentina football team, but also ensured that the future generations continue to dismiss national boundaries and embrace the totemic importance of foreign stars and teams. Fandom is a highly political act in terms of how they negotiate the power and control which the government and the mass media try to exercise upon them. Additional political meanings are often interpolated into the thought process of fans, creating a rhetoric of ideological following that extends far beyond the football field. Politics ceased to be extraneous and became an inalienable component of the Maradona mythology in the mediation techniques of *Aajkal*, evident in its mode of reporting and selection of reader letters. This is also a telling commentary of how a newspaper can uphold its version of a sportsperson's image for a period of over twenty years and yet manage to retain the same belief in fans/readers.

A tempting counterfactual question would be whether Maradona would have enjoyed as much fan following had the CPI (M) been unseated from power in the 1990s, or earlier? Definitely hard to estimate, but politics was a major factor indeed. Is Maradona as much popular in other Indian states too? Probably no, but then few other communities in the world measure up to the football obsession manifested in West Bengal. If we are to consider the English newspapers exclusively to understand the Maradona mania, would the findings be similar to what the Bengali sources reveal? This is certainly a project for the future.

Acknowledgements

We are thankful to Debasis Mukhopadhyay for giving us access to the *Aajkal* Newspaper Archives.

Disclosure statement

No potential conflict of interest was reported by the authors.

References

Abilash, N. U. 2006. "Maradona's Second Coming." *The Hindu*, February 12. http://www.hindu.com/mag/2006/02/12/stories/2006021200060100.htm.

Akindes, Gerard. 2014. "From Stadium to Bars: Transnational Media and African Fan Identity." In *Identity and Nation in African Football: Fans, Community, and Clubs*, edited by Chuka Onwumechili and Gerard Akindes, 214–235. Basingstoke: Palgrave Macmillan.

Alabarces, Pablo and Maria Graciela Rodriguez. 2000. "Football and Fatherland: The Crisis of National Representation in Argentinian Soccer." In *Football Culture: Local Contests, Global Vision*, edited by Richard Giulianotti and Gerry P. T. Finn, 118–133. London: Frank Cass.

Appadurai, Arjun. 1996. *Modernity at Large: Cultural Dimensions of Globalization*. Minneapolis: University of Minnesota Press.

Archetti, Eduardo. 1994. "Masculinity and Football: The Formation of National Identity in Argentina." In *Game without Frontiers: Football, Identity and Modernity*, edited by Richard Giulianotti and John Williams, 225–243. Aldershot: Arena.

Archetti, Eduardo. 1998. "The Meaning of Sport in Anthropology: A View from Latin America." *European Review of Latin American and Caribbean Studies* 65: 93–103.

Arnold, Guy. 2006. *A to Z of the Non-aligned Movement and Third World*. Lanham, MD: Scarecrow Press.

Bandopadhyay, Santipriya. 1996. *Sonar Chele Maradona* [Maradona, the Golden Boy]. Kolkata: A. Mukherjee.

Bandyopadhyay, Kausik. 2008. "'The Nation and Its Fragments': Football and Community in India." *Soccer & Society* 9 (3): 377–393.

Bhattacharjee, Kashinath. 2008. "How Maradona Was Lured towards India." June 12. http://archive. mid-day.com/news/2008/dec/061208-Shamik-Lahiri-Bhaswar-Goswami-Diego-Maradona-Buenos-Aires-football.htm.

Bhattacharya, Goutam. 1995. *Digbhrasta Rajputra* [Fallen Prince]. Kolkata: Bikash Book Agency.

Bi, Yuan. 2015. "Integration or Resistance: The Influx of Foreigncapital in British Football in the Transnational Age." *Soccer & Society* 16 (1): 17–41.

Burns, Jimmy. 2010. *Maradona: The Hand of God*. London: Bloomsbury.

Chakrabarty, Bidyut. 2014. *Communism in India: Events, Processes and Ideologies*. New York: Oxford University Press.

Chatterji, Joya. 2007. *The Spoils of Partition: Bengal and India 1947–1967*. New York: Cambridge University Press.

Chiranjib. 1987. *Mexico 86*. Kolkata: Nath Brothers.

Dasmunshi, Priyaranjan. 1984. "Maradona Is a Player, but Platini Is an Artist: Bobby Moore." *Khelar Asar* 7 (43): 10–11.

Duke, Vic, and Liz Crolley. 2001. "Fútbol, Politicians and the People: Populism and Politics in Argentina." *International Journal of the History of Sport* 18 (3): 93–116.

Galleano, Eduardo. 1997. *Football in Sun and Shadow*. London: Fourth Estate.

Gilchrist, Paul. 2005. "Local Heroes and Global Stars." In *Global Politics of Sport: The Role of Global Institutions in Sport*, edited by Lincoln Allison, 118–139. Oxford: Routledge.

Giulianotti, Richard. 1999. *Football: Sociology of the Global Game*. Cambridge: Polity Press.

Hall, Stuart. 1980. "Encoding/Decoding." In *Culture, Media, Language*, edited by Stuart Hall, Dorothy Hobson, Andrew Lowe, and Paul Willis, 128–138. London: Hutchinson.

Hognestad, Hans K. 2006. "Transnational Passions: A Statistical Study of Norwegian Football Supporters." *Soccer & Society* 7 (4): 439–462.

Horkheimer, Max, and Theodor Adorno. [1944] 1972. *Dialectic of Enlightenment*. New York: Herder and Herder.

Krishna, Sankaran. 2009. *Globalisation and Postcolonialism: Hegemony and Resistance in the Twenty-first Century*. Lanham, MD: Rowman & Littlefield.

Majumdar, Boria. 2002. "Kolkata Colonized: Soccer in a Subcontinental 'Brazilian Colony.'" *Soccer & Society* 3 (2): 70–86.

Majumdar, Boria, and Kausik Bandyopadhyay. 2005. "From Recreation to Competition: Early History of Indian Football." *Soccer & Society* 6 (2): 124–141.

Mason, Tony. 1995. *Passion of the People?: Football in South America*. London: Verso.

McPhail, Tom. 1981. *Electronic Colonialism: The Future of International Broadcasting and Communication*. Newbury Park, CA: Sage.

Mitra, Subrata. 2006. *The Puzzle of India's Governance: Culture, Context and Comparative History.* London: Routledge.

Moniz, Miguel. 2007. "Adaptive Transnational Identity and the Selling of Soccer: The New England Revolution and Lusophone Migrant Populations." *Soccer & Society* 8 (4): 459–477.

Naha, Souvik. 2014. "Of Magic and Mania: Reflections on the Fan following of Brazilian Football and Pelé in Calcutta." *Soccer & Society* 15 (5): 804–821.

Onwumechili, Chuka, and Sunday Oloruntola. 2014. "Transnational Communications, Attitudes and Fan Identity: Studying Nigeria Post-media Reform." *Soccer & Society* 15 (3): 389–410.

Rajagopal, Arvind. 2000. "Mediating Modernity: Theorizing Reception in a Non-western Country." In *De-westernizing Media Studies*, edited by James Curran and Myung-Jin Park, 260–270. London: Routledge.

Ricatti, Francesco, and Matthew Klugman. 2013. "'Connected to Something': Soccer and the Transnational Passions, Memories and Communities of Sydney's Italian Migrants." *The International Journal of the History of Sport* 30 (5): 469–483.

Saha, Rupak. 1995. *Maradonar Dosh Nei* [Maradona is Innocent]. Kolkata: Ananda.

Saha, Rupak. 1998. *Bidrohi Maradona* [Maradona, the Rebel]. Kolkata: Ananda.

Sartori, Andrew. 2008. *Bengal in Global Concept History: Culturalism in the Age of Capital.* Chicago, IL: Chicago University Press.

Schatzberg, Michael. 2006. "Soccer, Science and Sorcery: Causation and African Football." *Afrika Spectrum* 41 (3): 351–369.

Sen, Surojit. 2014. "Shohor Sangskaran [City edition]." *Desher Agamikal* 1 (3): 218–243.

Sengupta, Subrata. 1996. *Maradona Hey* [Oh Maradona]. Kolkata: Aajkal.

Sharadiya, Khela. 1986. Kolkata: Aajkal.

Sibaja, Rwany, and Charles Parrish. 2014. "Pibes, Cracks and Caudillos: Argentina, the World Cup and Identity Politics." *Soccer & Society* 15 (5): 655–670.

Tierney, John. 2005. "The Idiots Abroad." *International New York times*, November 8. http://query.nytimes.com/gst/fullpage.html?res=9404E3D6143EF93BA35752C1A9639C8B63.

Timirbaran. 1990. "Bishu Maradona O Protarona." *Sharadiya Khela* 1396: 166–167.

Tobin, Jeffrey. 2002. "Soccer Conspiracies: Maradona, the CIA, and Popular Critique." In *Sport in Latin America and the Caribbean*, edited by Joseph L. Arbena and David G. LaFrance, 51–73. Wilmington: Scholarly Resources.

Weber, Max. 1947. *The Theory of Social and Economic Organization.* Translated by A. M. Henderson and Talcott Parsons. New York: Oxford University Press.

Soccer and the city: the game and its fans in Solo and Yogyakarta

Andy Fuller

ABSTRACT
Football fandom and sports culture are largely neglected in studies of Indonesia. This is despite the highly complex nature of football fandom in Indonesian cities. This essay draws on experiences in two cities in central Java: Yogyakarta and Solo. Contemporary football culture in Solo and Yogyakarta is linked to the policies of decentralization that have emerged in the post-New Order (1998 onwards) and to the deeply contested identity politics. The essay privileges the perspective of a *capo* (dirigen, conductor) from Solo in articulating the experience of identifying with a particular football club (Persis Solo) and that of an ex-player of PSS Sleman from the province of Yogyakarta. It explores how football culture plays a vital role in the establishment and maintenance of, and contestation over city and urban identity.

Introduction

Soccer/football/*sepakbola* is an intrinsic part of everyday life in Indonesia. Soccer[1] is extremely contested: between clubs, between supporters and between leagues, so much so that it is impossible to talk of a single 'Indonesian soccerscape': It is fluid and diverse. A term introduced by Richard Giulianotti (1999), I use soccerscape(s) as a broad term that incorporates the coverage of soccer, the playing of soccer at an amateur level, the watching of soccer, or the making and consumption of soccer paraphernalia. Soccerscapes exist at many different levels: from being a game played on dirt pitches to a game watched on huge flat screen televisions at luxurious cafes. Soccer in Indonesia, so the cliché goes, is deeply politicized, violent and corrupt. On the other hand, cultures of fandom are increasingly creative, active and productive in terms of their engagement with their team and the city in which the team is based. Although, the jerseys of local teams aren't worn as commonly as those of the (often very poor imitations of) English Premier League (henceforth EPL) teams, the politics of local soccer often breaks into the everyday life of a city.[2]

Talking about soccer is one of the easiest ways of making conversation with strangers, with making small talk and getting into serious discussions. Men who don't use the Internet or smartphones devour daily newspapers such as *Harian Bola* (Soccer Daily) as a means of gaining access to results, debates and controversies in the EPL, La Liga and other international leagues.[3] Cafes and bars in cities advertise their broadcasting schedule of important football games. Men, in their sarongs and loose white t-shirts, at street side stalls, crowd around televisions late at night watching live broadcasts from Italy, England or Spain. Security guards stationed at the entrances of gated communities watch the 4 am Champions League broadcasts in the silence and cool of the early morning. These men, who may have very little formal education, are highly versed in the history and teams of clubs such as Liverpool, Chelsea, Barcelona, AC Milan and others. In recognition of their huge Indonesian supporter base, clubs such as Liverpool and Chelsea have their own official websites in Indonesian (http://indonesia.liverpoolfc.com/ and http://indo.chelseafc.com/). At motorcycle parking lots in provincial Yogyakarta, attendants are dressed in replica soccer shirts. Elsewhere, in fancy cafes in the nation's capital, the young rich gather at supporter clubs for Liverpool, Arsenal, Chelsea, Manchester United and wear the official garments and chant, with utmost devotion their clubs' songs – such as *You'll Never Walk Alone* for those with Liverpool loyalties.

Playing and watching the game are part of the urban fabric of Indonesian cities. Soccer is everywhere: on newsstands, it is in a city's soundscape,[4] in the boutiques of small-time fashion designers, it is evident in the graffiti and murals of city walls. Soccer holds a tremendous grip on the imagination of millions of people – across many apparent social divides. Films, novels and comics reflect the dreams of aspiring, but ultimately unsuccessful footballers. At the same time, soccer fandom, and in some cases, 'activism', represents varying degrees of purchasing power and consumption. My preliminary observations indicate that fandom of the EPL is more widespread than that of domestic soccer in Indonesia. It is not possible to classify the EPL team fans as being 'middle class' and the urban poor as being fans of domestic soccer. Many fans of domestic teams wear the colours of EPL teams when supporting their local team. The high intensity persists despite the continued underperformance of the national team and the disarray of the domestic leagues.[5] But, outside of Indonesia, 'Indonesian soccer' or the 'national team of Indonesia' remains an unknown entity in the World Game. The purpose of this essay is, in part, to articulate the reach of football/soccer in Indonesia and to analyse some of its manifestations. It will analyse some of the scant academic studies of soccer in Indonesia, approach some of the minutiae of 'everyday soccer life' and later, draw some conclusions about what soccer means in Indonesia.

The present study is based on library research conducted in Leiden, The Netherlands, followed by several months of fieldwork in Indonesia, where I worked with football fans in Yogyakarta, Solo and Surabaya. I conducted interviews with former players, aspiring fan-group leaders, team-archivists, supporter-group leaders, chant-leaders, football journalists and football researchers. The time spent in Indonesia, engaging with such a diverse group of football fans, enthusiasts, activists and researchers left me at times despairing, exhausted and cynical, but at other times, being amongst fans at the games was exhilarating, intoxicating and overwhelming. In the context of violent and tense rivalries between fans, I had to manage my engagements subtly, without offending rival supporter groups.

Studying Indonesian soccerscapes: history and culture

The cities of Yogyakarta and Solo are long-established cultural rivals, both claiming to be heirs to Javanese high culture. The tension between the two cities is reflected in football fan rivalries: between the Brajamusti supporters of Yogyakarta's PSIM and the Pasoepati supporters of Solo's Persis Solo. While football supporter culture in Solo is unified behind Persis Solo, fandom in Yogyakarta is much more fragmented, with loyalties being split between PSS Sleman in the north, PSIM in the centre and Persiba Bantul in the south. A study of fan cultures in these cities provides an understanding of how fans create a lively, active football culture as well as use football and fandom as a means of negotiating identity and claiming space (Figure 1).

Soccer in Indonesia has its own language and discourse. The correct spelling of the name for football is itself not agreed upon: it is referred to as both *sepakbola* and *sepak bola*. These are the 'correct' Indonesian terms that superseded the original Dutch name for the game as used in the Dutch East Indies: i.e. *voetbal* (Colombijn 2000). As the cartoonist Muhamad Misrad (2012) has shown in the brief book of illustrations on the vocabulary used by soccer commentators, the terms often evoke other issues in the local social and cultural context. Listening to the commentary of live games and the pre-game and post-match analyses also throws up new opportunities for confusion for the novice. A glossary of soccer terminology is indeed necessary – one that is more thorough than the humorous offering of Misrad: *Kamus Istilah Komentator Sepak Bola* (A Glossary of Football Commentators' Terminology). Misrad's book of illustrations, however, does indicate the degree of traction that soccer occupies in Indonesia. Popular soccer culture is marketable; it sells; it has an audience.

Through listening to regional football commentary in Indonesia, one also becomes particularly aware of the game's globality and how this is reflected through language. Indeed, part of this is indicated through the sheer recitation of the players' names. We hear a combination of Indonesian names – Javanese, Minahasan, Batak, Acehnese, Buginese, Makasarese, Papuan, African, South American and occasionally the familiar name of an ex-EPL player. Some Australian players occasionally play in Indonesia. One of them, Robbie Gaspar, speaks fluent Indonesian and has many thousands of followers on his Twitter account. He remains affectionately remembered as a player and person, across team boundaries. The terms used to describe the action of the game range from direct borrowings from English, to variations and hybrid words that have become standard in the Indonesian (soccer specific) lexicon. For example, the word *catenaccio* is used frequently; the name of the 'conductor' who leads the chanting is called a *dirigen* while the object the *dirigen* stands on is called a *steiger*, coming from the Dutch word for 'scaffolding'.

Figure 1. PSIM mural, southern Yogyakarta, photo by Hayyi Al-Qayummi.

Watching a soccer game thus opens up some possibilities for reconsidering what makes up Indonesia, but also what makes up football – what makes up the practice, creation and playing of football. How is football turned into soccer in the Indonesian context? What does this tell us about the changing patterns, forces and tensions within football more globally? Football in Indonesia is indeed part soccer; whatever its local manifestations, it remains recognizable as a part of the global game of football. Nonetheless, soccer takes on specific local characteristics as it has evolved in its own context; just as there is a soccer that has evolved as a response to the local conditions of Brazil, England, the US and Australia. In this sense, soccer is suggestive of De Certeau's (1984) 'tactics', in comparison to the 'strategies' of football. Supporter groups seek to actively resist the hegemony of the PSSI (Indonesian Soccer Union) as well as that of the management of their own team. Fan groups such as those of the Brajamusti in Yogyakarta belittle Solo's Pasoepati fan groups for their blatant imitation of Italian *Ultra* fans. Instead, they take pride in their own provinciality (Conversation with Unyil, one of the conductors of the Brajamusti supporter group, 17 October 2014, Yogyakarta) (Figure 2).

The essay focuses on two different examples from the Indonesian soccerscape. The first is that of attending a match in Solo; the second case is an overview of issues involving PSS Sleman, a team based in the north of the Daerah Istimewa Yogyakarta (Special Region of Yogyakarta). I presume that soccer in Indonesia is a self-perpetuating, all-encompassing phenomenon, not simply a metaphor for Indonesian politics, culture and society. I seek to follow the example of Pisani (2014), of focusing on a couple of incidents in order to give an indication of a broader picture. Changes in Indonesian soccer reflect the shift towards decentralization and increasingly participatory politics. Tensions often emerge within supporter groups of the one team, based on differences in political party affiliation. One example is the split between PSIM's Brajamusti and The Maident, which is a division between Islamic and secular-nationalist interests. Supporter groups, acting in the names of their clubs, also often change colours while supporting a particular political party or candidate. Some supporter

Figure 2. Fans at the Daerah Istimewa Yogyakarta (Special Region of Yogyakarta) derby: PSS Sleman vs. PSIM Yogyakarta, photo Hayyi Al Qayyumi, 2014.

groups are also active in radical Islamic politics (Interview with Rolly, presidential candidate of Brajamusti, October 31, 2014).

And thus, the study of soccer in Indonesia requires little justification. But this omnipresence of football both at the level of everyday life and of national politics has hardly received the academic attention it deserves. As far as I am aware, no university offers a course on 'the politics of football' or 'football culture in Indonesia'. Solo-based sociologist, Akhmad Ramdhon, is active in promoting the study of soccer and its connection with the urban history of Solo. Fajar Junaedi at the Muhammadiyah University of Yogyakarta also advocates the study of soccer to his students. Aside from these isolated attempts, the general apathy may be a result of cultural snobbery: football may be considered solely as a bodily act of entertainment and thus not worthy of sophisticated intellectual inquiry for fear that the perceived boorishness of the players may infect those who study it. A number of scholars have researched the significance of sport in Indonesian society, however small their number is (Adams 2002; Brown 2006; Colombijn 2000; Flicker 2013; Junaedi 2012, 2014; Lesmana 2013; Moser 2010). Additionally, we find many popular texts on sport (Gunawan 2014; Sindhunata 2002).

The aforementioned omnipresence of football in Indonesia – evident through politics, fashion, the cityscape, popular culture and nationalism – also contrasts with the virtual invisibility of 'Indonesia' as a national team at international level. Within the context of Asia, and even South-East Asia, the Indonesian national team is more of a curiosity to rival nations and source of endless frustration to their tens of millions of fans. Indonesia, despite being the fourth most populous nation in the world, is currently ranked 180th in the world (as of February 2016). It should be noted that Indonesia was ranked in the top 100 in the late-1990s. As Pisani (2012) indicates, sport is one of the clearest examples of how Indonesia has underperformed on the global stage: Indonesia had only two athletes at the 2012 London Olympics.

The performance of the Indonesian national football team at the regional level is equally unflattering. Indonesia was ranked 37th in Asia in February 2016, in between the much smaller nations of Laos and Chinese Taipei). A further insult to national pride is the higher position of regional rivals such as Malaysia (a country frequently considered to have appropriated Indonesian cultural artefacts) and Singapore (a nation which has apparently stolen the nation's best badminton players). Indonesia has participated in the Asian Federation Cup four times and is yet to have progressed beyond the first stage. Indonesia has played in the final of the ASEAN Football Championship four times, but, is yet to have won it. The continual underperformance of the senior national team is one of the reasons behind the celebration of the U-19 Cup which was Indonesia's first 'major' trophy. The story of this team was turned into both a best-selling book and a popular film (*Semangat Membatu*). Much hope was invested in this young team as being 'the future' of Indonesian football. When the players from this team failed to turn into successful senior players, the bureaucracy was blamed for having failed them.

The point of narrating Indonesia's inglorious history as a team on the global and regional scale is not to needlessly point out the poverty of football achievement (who cares?), but rather to indicate that interest in football in Indonesia does not hinge upon national success. The often severely questioned integrity of the domestic league also doesn't seem to affect its popularity; stadiums are often full to the tune of 20,000–30,000 spectators at second division matches (*Divisi Utama*).[6] Football, it seems, might just be popular because football *is*. But, this is also disingenuous: there must be more going on than just the game itself. Something must be at stake for the fans for them to attend the games with such dedication, loyalty and creativity. Even though the number of non-fiction books locally published on football in Indonesian has increased, these works are also largely ignored by scholars located outside the country. Soccer in Indonesia is ignored despite the cross over of politicians into football (Aburizal Bakrie being the most prominent) and the role of supporter groups in strengthening the numbers for political candidates. The lack of success at the national level is contrasted against the massive support the national team always receives, as well as the regional bravado and pride that surround clubs in Indonesia's cities.

Thus, Colombijn's statement that there has been no scholarship on football in Indonesia is, by and large, correct. His article (2000) was seemingly the first to appear in a standard, scholarly journal and to be solely focused on football. Colombijn's call for further studies and his advocacy for sport as a worthy area of study, has at best, been followed by a trickle of articles that have in one way or another addressed matters of sport and society. Indonesian studies conferences largely ignore the area of sports. Talking about media coverage, *The Jakarta Post*, the main English-language daily in Indonesia, routinely ignores the coverage of the domestic leagues – although some 'feature' articles do appear occasionally.

Hence, the question emerges: if one is going to study football in Indonesia, or sport more generally, where does one begin? I am using and focusing on football/soccer as it is the most globalized of games – despite all the local and contextualised adjustments and variations. What is available on football in Indonesia is uneven. There are no established scholars who have taken on 'sport and society', let alone 'soccer and society in Indonesia' as their primary area of research. Fajar Junaedi of Universitas Muhamadiyah Yogyakarta is perhaps, currently the most fervent analyst of local soccer. His work, which primarily revolves on the media coverage and construction of football fandom, includes the book *Bonek: Komunitas Suporter Terbesar dan Pertama di Indonesia* (2012) and a couple of conference papers on *academia.edu*: 'Identitas Sepak Bola Sebagai City Branding' (Soccer Identity as City Branding, 2012) and 'Sepak Bola Sebagai Media Komunikasi Politik' (Soccer as a Media for Political Communication, 2011) (Figure 3).

Figure 3. Photo: Andy Fuller.

An afternoon with the Pasoepati crew

The rivalry between the two central Javanese cities of Yogyakarta and Solo is intense and deeply felt. It is between supporters of the two football clubs, PSIM and Persis Solo that it takes its most violent form. Notable fans of both clubs are reputed to have bounties on their heads; joking or not, these fans make a point of not travelling to their rival city. In order to grasp better the agitation in Yogyakarta and the hatred of Brajamusti fans against their rival supporter group Pasoepati, I had to go to Solo. Although only 40 km away, it would effectively take up most of the day: the trains are slow and suffer from frequent delays.

Before I took a train back to Yogyakarta, my friend Ramdhon said, 'take your t-shirt off – it is better not to wear it in Yogyakarta, or even on the train'. Yogyakarta and Solo are locked in ongoing tensions over claims to be regarded as the legitimate inheritor of ancient Javanese civilization. The conflict comes into sharp focus in the realm of soccer too. So much so, that although both in central Java, they have played in different conferences. The city of Solo is on the rise after having been cleaned up and managed efficiently under Joko Widodoi's (known also as 'Jokowi') years as governor. Jokowi's rise to the presidency is the source of much pride in the city. Key participants in Jokowi's election campaign had developed their skills in mobilizing mass support while collaborating with Pasoepati. Fajar Junaedi argues that the violence that broke out after the Persis Solo–Martapura FC match in Solo on 22 October was linked to Jokowi's inauguration as president. Now that Jokowi was officially president, the behaviour of Persis Solo fans wouldn't threaten his campaign, or be in danger of besmirching his name (Conversation with Fajar Junaedi, 2 November 2014, Yogyakarta).

Ramdhon, a sociologist with a research interest in football fandom, states that Pasoepati generally maintain good relations with supporters of other teams. And in the case of PSGC Ciamis (Persatuan Sepakbola Galuh Ciamis, Galuh Football Club of Ciamis), – them being a small club – there is little cause for tension and animosity. The day's conflict was between the referee and the Ciamis players: the main antagonist being the Dutch player Emile Linkers, who after several and persistent assaults on the referee was belatedly sent off. Ramdhon tells me that it is not possible to send the player off *merely* for intimidating or kneeing the referee in the back of the thigh: this would only be further provocation. Even after the match was halted for player vs referee or police vs player violence, most of the players still shook hands at the games. Ciamis, after being up 2–1 briefly in the second half, were angry at having two goals disallowed and one penalty decision overturned.

This was a game of much tension, excitement and relief for the Pasoepati fans of Persis Solo. The Pasoepati supporter group regarded the protests of the Ciamis players against their goals being disallowed as evidence of the 'exaggerated lack of sportsmanship'. It was only after Persis Solo's home defeats did they cry foul over the lack of fair play. Ramdhon's statement regarding the good relations between Pasoepati and other fan groups is proved questionable after the return leg with Ciamis. The Pasoepati were attacked in Yogyakarta, West Java and in Ciamis in the lead up to the game. This resulted in what the Pasoepati regarded as the 'tragedi Ciamis' (the Ciamis incident; in which tens of millions of rupiah of damage was caused).

One man with his back to most of the action through the game was Andre, the *dirigen* (conductor) of the Eastern Tribune. This stand is also known as being home to the supporters known as Pasoepati B7, named after the main entrance gate to the stand. This stand is also identified as being favoured by the Pasoepati Campus supporters group. In between this Eastern stand and the Northern stand is the corner used by the fans, who identify with (primarily) English hooligan culture. The Pasoepati Campus supporter group is made up largely of students from the Universitas Sebelas Maret, where Ramdhon teaches. Andre and his co-conductor stand atop a makeshift stand known as a *steiger* at the periphery of the athletics track that encircles the football pitch. They share a megaphone, perhaps indicative of slightly different and complementary roles atop their rather loose podium. And just like the conductors of symphonic orchestras, Andre is demonstrative, dictatorial and capable of expressing a wide range of emotions in quick succession. Ramdhon observes, 'these figures are very powerful. They are able to control thousands of people. Today there are about 4000 in this stand – not even the police are able to control them. But these guys are' (Interview with Akhmad Ramdhon, Solo, October 2014).

At the game's conclusion, Andre greeted the players as they did a lap of the pitch to thank the fans. Indeed, three of the four main stands had chanted almost endlessly for 90 plus minutes. Andre is one of the several *dirigen* who play a key role in maintaining and developing the home ground advantage for Persis Solo. This game was part of the play offs to qualify for the ISL and thus victory was particularly sweet as it brought the team a step closer to the highest league. Yet the final whistle was hardly greeted with a specific roar or cheer. Instead, the game's conclusion was marked by flares and the communal singing of their anthem, *Satu Jiwa* (One Soul). The fans stayed to thank the players and receive their gratitude in turn. Only then was the game/performance finished. After exiting the stadium, Andre, and probably other *dirigen* too, were greeted by the rank and file with the same reverence usually reserved only for players. Some had their photos taken with them. Andre talked loudly, but, unsurprisingly was a little hoarse. Andre runs a shop selling Persis Solo and Pasoepati merchandise and as such has a specific interest in galvanizing support for the team and maintaining the unity of the supporter group.

'I have been doing this for some six years. Previously, I was just a rank and file participant in Pasoepati, like all of these young guys. And then one day, I was asked to be the conductor. There was no choice in the matter. Suddenly it was up to me to take on the role. The regular conductor was absent, so someone had to replace him. I started out at the southern stand (tribune, a Dutch word, is the Indonesian word that is most commonly used). But, one time, I was asked to move to the Eastern stand. People were wondering, why is it so quiet? And so, I went there to make it noisy'. Ramdhon, too, is working on shaping the culture of the Eastern stand. Through the *anak-anak B7* (the B7 boys), he is trying to establish a dress code and ethical practice. There is a specific section at the front of the stand for women; crowd members must wear shoes, rather than thongs. At the game's conclusion, when some fans from the other stands ran onto the pitch, the B7 supporters shouted their condemnation. (Figure 4)

> A couple of years ago, when it was already certain that we would be relegated (*degredasi*, in Indonesian) we had 1000 fans still willing to travel to support the team. The journalist who goes by the name Jakarta Casuals on Twitter called us the most loyal fans in Southeast Asia. Having 40,000 to 60,000 or 80,000 fans in a stadium when you are champions is normal. What is extraordinary is when you get 1000 fans still willing to travel when you know that the team will be relegated. I don't use the words 'win' or 'lose'; I simply focus on building the support amongst us fans'. The loyalty of Pasoepati, however, is regarded cynically by their rivals in Yogyakarta. Members of Brajamusti state that Pasoepati have given their support to other teams previously based in Solo (such as Arseto Solo). Thobbel, the conductor of PSIM's supporter

Figure 4. Photo: Andy Fuller.

group, The Maident, states cynically, 'they are no longer virgins. (Conversation at The Maident's headquarters, Kridosono Stadium, November 21, 2014, Yogyakarta)

It is not exactly easy being a conductor of these fans. At every game the crowd is just a little bit different. Our problem is the stadiums that we use. At games in Europe, the same fans sit or stand in the same place for every game, more or less. They know what to sing and how to behave. Sometimes I have to use a strong voice. It doesn't mean that I am angry, it is simply because I have to give more precise and direct instructions. Just think, again, these stadiums that we use are not like those in Europe, where there is a roof over the crowd. Here, the noise goes straight up into the air and dissipates very quickly. If we want to be heard, we have to be organized. If we had a roof at our stadium, we would be on a par with the Kop at Liverpool, no doubt.

A week or so after my afternoon with the B7 section of the Pasoepati crew, I met up with some members of Brajamusti at a soccer discussion held by Football Fandom's founder, Hasby, and Dimaz Maulana of Forum Bawah Skor. The day before the discussion, a photograph had been circulated on Twitter of myself talking with Andre. The Brajamusti diligently follow the Twitter accounts of rival supporter groups and my encounter with them had created some gossip. 'When did you go there?' 'When are you going back?' 'I'm going next Wednesday. Do you have a message?' 'Send them my greetings, from the Number 1 of Brajamusti', Pak Eko says. There is laughter all round, but, the rivalry is undoubted. I went to Solo to participate in the practice of being a fan: given the difficulty of attending games in Yogyakarta, I had to do fieldwork in Solo. The title of 'researcher' doesn't always trump that of 'supporter': one is given loyalties and thus obligations, where one may not necessarily want them. The friends I have made through the Brajamusti supporter group ask what I talked about. I told them, I didn't discuss violence or conflict – only that of their songs and the practice of being a conductor. One of them told me, when it comes to exploring the conflict between Brajamusti and Pasoepati, his information must be 'cross-checked'. This is a moment in which the tension between partiality, trust and insight are threatened. I want both of their stories and I don't care too much for their differences: I want to know what it means to be both Pasoepati and Brajamusti and I believe both of their mutually exclusive truths.

Pak Eko states that PSIM has rivalries with many other clubs and that these are no problem; it is a part of being a PSIM supporter. He states, however, that it is only with

Pasoepati and Persis Solo that Brajamusti and PSIM must remain as enemies. The basis for the enmity is the supposed violence inflicted upon them by the Pasoepati in the past, and that to reconcile with Pasoepati would be to insult the more senior supporters of PSIM, who are referred to as 'forebears'. Being aligned with Brajamusti means adopting the slogan – 'warisan simbah' – the heritage of forebears and thus inculcating the typical Javanese values of showing respect to elders and conforming to the expectations of others. The Brajamusti use Javanese as their primary language, further strengthening their sense of regional difference in a decentralized Indonesia (Figure 5).

PSS Sleman: nostalgia, corruption, violence

Sofyan, an Acehnese man living in Yogyakarta, runs a small stall by the side of *Lapangan Minggiran* (Minggiran Field) in the southern part of the city. His regular customers are largely ex-soccer players from the local leagues. Some are doing it tough, others have regular jobs. He fears for the fate of one of his many old teams, PSS Sleman, from the north of the city of Yogyakarta. He says, 'oh no, don't wipe out the history of my team. It is okay if they are relegated to the Nusantara League, but, don't dismantle them (*tapi jangan dibubarkan*)'. Sofyan has no shirts left from his playing days; he has given them all away. He was carefree with the money he had earnt (he claims to have been well-paid) and went bankrupt in the business ventures he tried to start after his career was shortened by untreated injury. On weekends, he plays casual games with Old Crack Mataram, an informal group of ex-players (*mantan pemain*), many of whom played with PSIM. It is with these ex-players, and some former members of PSIM's old supporter group, that he shares stories with about both 'the good old days' as well as the decrepit state of Indonesian soccer. The roughly middle-aged men, in their early to late 40s, also use each other as informants about where to find work and how to make the most of one's limited opportunities in maintaining a steady income. 'This *warung* (street stall) was rented to me by an ex-player. It was an ex-player who paid for the pavement on which my *warung* stands'.

Sofyan's fear of PSS Sleman's dissolution is a result of the pending punishment for the team's participation in match fixing during a game against PSIS Semarang. Both teams were trying to lose the game so that they wouldn't face Borneo FC in the semi-final of the playoffs to reach the ISL (Indonesia Super League, the highest division). The match saw

Figure 5. Photo: Andy Fuller.

five own goals scored after the 87th minute. Although both teams were not playing to win from the beginning of the game, it was PSS Sleman that scored the first own goal and thus have become most heavily implicated in the drama. The head coach of Sleman has been banned for life, so were some of the key players, while others have been banned for five years or one year. Quite a few have been fined Rp.50 million ($5000). The scandal is known as 'sepakbola gajah', translated as 'elephant football'. This controversy showed up the intricate webs of match-fixing so reportedly common throughout Indonesian football, yet so rarely disclosed and confronted head-on in the football media. The outrageous nature of the game and its clear affront to any notions of sporting integrity polarized supporters' opinions. PSS Sleman's supporters became defensive of their club while attacking the journalists that covered the event and brought it to the international media's attention.

The story of the elephant football incident, however, complicates the earlier smooth trajectory followed by PSS Sleman. Until late in the 2014 Divisi Utama season, commentators, observers and rival fans were convinced of PSS Sleman's eventual rise to the ISL. Their progress was viewed cynically, to say the least, by members of PSIM's supporter group, Brajamusti, as well as that of Persis Solo's Pasoepati. A Yogyakarta-based journalist blatantly stated, 'those who will go up to the ISL are already determined before the start of the season'. However, a turning point came in October 2014, when members of PSS Sleman's supporter group, Brigata Curva Sud (BCS, South Terrace Brigade) were involved in the brutal murder of Muhammad Ikhwanuddin, a PSCS Cilacap supporter, on the main street in front of Yogyakarta's Adisucipto airport at 8:30 pm. The bus on which the supporter was travelling had been chased by a group of 30 or so men on motorbikes for about 10 km. The suspects were apprehended and PSS Sleman was given the light punishment of playing two home games at venues 100 km away from their stadium, Maguwarhojo. One of these games conveniently became a 'walkover' after Persiwa Wamena, claiming not to have the finances to travel, didn't show up for the game.

Responses to the killing of Ikhwanuddin were varied. The brutality of the murder brought the *Divisi Utama* into *Kompas* newspaper, while the sports-focused *Harian Bola* gave little attention it; placing it in the middle pages of the tabloid. Although *Harian Bola* will acknowledge the doubts of supporters' over the integrity of games and refereeing decisions, the newspaper avoids any critical investigation into sports' corruption in Indonesia. *Tribun Jogja* and *Kedaulatan Rakyat* ran the story as front page news. On the one hand, football violence is normal, gang violence, however, can be sensationalized. On Twitter, Brajamusti account holders sent out messages denying their involvement.[7] Further complicating the story was that a Bonek 1927 supporter from Cilacap was injured in the attack on the bus.[8] Some members of Brajamusti expressed their ambivalence over the killing of Ikhwanuddin, stating that it was a risk all supporters participate in, while another member of Brajamusti regretted that it was his friend who was killed. Both of these Brajamusti celebrate their own involvement in violent encounters between themselves and other supporters. Andre Jaran, a conductor of Pasoepati, regarded the killing as an outcome of the lack of discipline within BCS and the inability of its 'respected figures' to assert their authority over their followers (Conversation with Andre Jaran, October 20, 2014, Solo). Dimaz Maulana of Bawah Skor, a PSIM affiliated forum, responded by uploading a short essay on his brief encounter with the victim. BCS and Slemania members stated their undying support for the team and saying that their punishment was merely 'a trial they would have to face before making it to the ISL'.

According to Fajar Junaedi, the rise of PSS Sleman and their supporter groups, Slemania and more recently, BCS, emerged as a result of decentralization in the post-Suharto era. Regional governments were now in greater control of their budgets. Sleman is a part of Daerah Istimewa Yogyakarta (Special Region of Yogyakarta, DIY), and is regarded as having many sources of income. The era of decentralization also saw the rise of a greater sense of identification with one's team, evident in the organization and mobilization patterns of the BCS and Slemania. The BCS became known for their intricate choreographies, chanting and performances during PSS Sleman's games. Ultras websites and YouTube channels feature their ultra-style performances (Ultras Channel Tifo TV: https://www.youtube.com/watch?v=Mc6vRYoaKzc). PSS Sleman were successful in the 'no ticket no game' campaign to encourage supporters to buy tickets, as well as running successful PSS Sleman, BCS, Slemania merchandise shops, with a portion of takings going to the running of the team.[9] The marketability of the club was an essential part of the indication for its readiness for qualifying for the ISL. Moreover, the relegation of Persiba Bantul from the ISL to the Divisi Utama would mean that there were no teams from the DIY in the ISL. PSS Sleman, it was considered by Fajar Junaedi, Dimaz Maulana and Andre Justinus, all of whom held deep scepticism about the fairness of the process for qualifying for the ISL, would be the 'logical replacement' for Persiba Bantul's relegation.

The Brajamusti have been particularly delighted by the controversy of 'elephant football'. Signs have been erected on the streets of Yogyakarta, sarcastically mocking both PSS Sleman and its BCS supporter group. The FIFA's possible ban on PSS Sleman after just less than 40 years since its founding delights Brajamusti as they reinforce the idea of PSIM's own longevity through many murals that state PSIM 1929. The Brajamusti deride PSS Sleman's fans as being both 'glory hunters' and 'soulless' in their pursuit of soccer-euphoria. PSIM's very failure at capitalizing on the decentralization era, and PSIM's supporters' persistent infighting, has led to its inability to reach even the later stages of attempts at qualifying for the ISL. The glee of these supporters contrasts sharply with those of the former PSS Sleman players, who have seen their former team becoming the laughing stock and source of collective shame for Indonesian soccer fans (Interview with Fajar Junaedi, November 2014, Yogyakarta). The BCS and Slemania, however, have struggled to deal with the outcome: seeking in turn to deny that the own goals were deliberate, blame PSIS Semarang for their own corruption, to intimidate the journalists covering the story and more recently, to argue that the real agents behind the drama haven't been punished (Interview with Fajar Junaedi, November 2014, Yogyakarta).

Conclusion

Soccer in Indonesia is engrossing as an area of research. Its everyday reality, however, is often difficult to stomach. It is often difficult to discover the 'soccer' behind the many layers of corruption, violence and well, gross-mismanagement. In many cases, it is impossible to attend games as they have either been moved to an undisclosed venue, or, are being played locally, but are barred to spectators. The domestic leagues are sites of intense battles along city and regional identifications. Supporter groups mobilize their creative energies in the name of supporting their club: this is evident through practices of making street murals, performing punk songs, researching their club and city's archives, and of course, performing choreographies or chants on game days. Soccer, for all its carnivalesque and macabre daily realities, is arguably the most intensely fought over cultural product in contemporary Indonesia. It is the intersection of main stream politics, identity politics, negotiations of hetero-normative masculinity, as well as being the playing field for a diverse range of religious and youth gangs managed by a broad spectrum of *preman*. Indonesian soccer fans contribute significantly to a 'critical reading' of their sport and city; moreover, many – such as the Brajamusti of PSIM and the Pasoepati of Persis Solo – act as de facto staff for the club and perform vital tasks to maintain their clubs' name and public visibility. This extremely complex area of struggle and celebration[10] is yet to be given attention by scholars in Indonesian or sports studies.

Notes

1. I primarily use the word 'soccer' over 'football'. For my purposes, 'soccer' is the term for 'football' in a specific, local context, in comparison to the game of 'football' that is understood at a global level.

2. Fights often break out between rival supporter groups on the streets of Yogyakarta, or as fans travel between cities. In the aftermath of the PSS Sleman–PSIS Semarang 'elephant football' (match-fixing scandal) fans of PSIM erected provocative banners showing their pleasure at the penalties handed out to the neighbouring PSS Sleman.

3. The largest national newspaper, *Kompas*, has a relatively short sports section. It gives little coverage to the ISL and as good as none to the Divisi Utama. The main domestic sports news stories are reserved for badminton players and the national football team. Otherwise, sports coverage prioritises more global sports, such as English Premier League or Formula One.

4. For example, crowds of football fans make their way through city streets while revving their engines.

5. To many fans' embarrassment, the national team lost 0–4 to the Philippines during the 2014 AFF tournament in Vietnam. This loss meant that Indonesia couldn't qualify for the knockout stage of the tournament. In 2002, Indonesia beat Philippines 13–1 in Jakarta. While watching the Indonesia–Philippines game, I was immediately told that the Philippines players weren't real Filipinos, but, were all imports.

6. The doubtable integrity of the competition, however, does affect the mood of the crowd. One of the roles of the conductors during the Persis Solo games at Manahan Stadium which I attended was to make sure that the crowd presented a united showing in accusing the referees of cheating. Once the conductors (two each at the north, south and east stands) were given the go-ahead, the masses of supporters waved rupiah notes while chanting, 'the referee has been bribed'. Conversation with Andre Jaran (conductor of Pasoepati, B7), 20 October 2014, Solo.

7. I would later find out through conversations with members of The Maident that members of BCS had asked them whether or not they would be involved in 'sweeping' against PSCS Cilacap fans as they passed through Yogyakarta on their way back from Solo. They replied that they wouldn't be doing any sweeping. The members of The Maident informed me that BCS wanted to check with them because they were fearful of confronting them on the streets of Yogya.

8. This led to another series of Twitter conversations. Anom, a renowned Yogya-based Bonek and brawler, was quickly using Twitter and SMS to determine the 'official' stance that Bonek 1927 would take against BCS. Bonek 1927 supporters are 'supporters without a team', according to the Yogya-based Bonek, Cak Tulus. As such Bonek 1927 often attend games with other supporters, as a means of enjoying soccer, but, also of creating stronger alliances in their ongoing conflict with the PSSI.

9. In the wake of PSS Sleman's punishment of two 'banishment games' (*partai usiran*), fans bought virtual tickets for the games as a means of making up for any lost takings.

10. 'Celebration' is used by Fajar Junaedi in the title of his book: *MerayakanSepak Bola : Fans, Identitas dan Media*. From August to December 2014 in Yogyakarta, Solo and Surabaya, I witnessed far more signs of struggle, incomprehension, disillusion and disappointment amongst soccer fans.

References

Adams, I. 2002. "Pancasila: Sport and the Building of Indonesia – Ambitions and Obstacles." *The International Journal of the History of Sport* 19 (2–3): 295–318.

Brown, C. 2006. "Playing the Game: Ethnicity and Politics in Indonesian Badminton." *Indonesia* 81: 71–93.

Colombijn, F. 2000. "The Politics of Indonesian Football." *Archipel* 59: 171–200.

De Certeau, M. 1984. *The Practice of Everyday Life*. Translated by Steven Rendall. Berkeley: University of California Press.

Flicker, T. 2013. "Framing Corruption and Nationalism in Indonesian Soccer: A Case Study of Media Reporting." Honours Thesis, Monash University.

Giulianotti, Richard. 1999. *Football: Sociology of the Global Game*. Cambridge: Polity Press.

Gunawan, F. X. R. 2014. *Semangat Membatu: Official Story, Timnas U-19*. Yogyakarta: Bentang.

Junaedi, F. 2012. *Bonek: Komunitas Suporter Pertama dan Terbesar di Indonesia* [Bonek: The Largest and First Supporter Group in Indonesia]. Yogyakarta: Buku Litera.

Junaedi, F. 2014. *Merayakan Sepak Bola* [Celebrating Football]. Yogyakarta: Buku Litera.

Lesmana, T. 2013. *Bola Politik dan Politik Bola: Ke Mana Arah Tendangannya?* [Political Football and Football Politics: Which Way will the Ball be Kicked?]. Jakarta: Kompas Gramedia.

Misrad, M. 2012. *Kamus Istilah Komentator Bola; Football's Coming Home (A Dictionary of Football Terminology)*. Jakarta: Octopus Garden Publishing.

Moser, S. 2010. "Creating Citizens Through Play: The Role of Leisure in Indonesian Nation-Building." *Social and Cultural Geography* 11 (1): 53–73.

Sindhunata. 2002. *Bola-Bola Nasib: Catatan Sepakbola Sindhunata* [Balls of Fate: Sindhunata's Notes on Football]. Jakarta: Kompas.

Websites

Aremania.net: website for Arema Cronus (Malang) fans.

Bawah Skor Mandala: bawahskor.wordpress.com.

Sambernyawa.net: website for Persis Solo fans, known as Pasoepati.

Jakmania.asia: website of Persija fans.

Nobartv.com: live streaming of Indonesian soccer games.

Bolatotal.com.

Women's time? Time and temporality in women's football

Kath Woodward

ABSTRACT

Time is central to sport, not least football, through measurements and memories. The sophisticated technologies of recording time matter in training and on the pitch, the intensity of spectatorship at the stadium or watching the big screen and memories of being present at big games generate what makes football the beautiful game. What does a focus on time and temporality tell us about the women's game? Does the Super League mean that this is women's time? Or are women excluded and marginalized through persistent invisibility? How are the links between past, present and future experienced in women's football? This essay explores time and temporality in football by looking at some of the transformations, representations and experiences of women's football.

Introduction

Football is, as they say, a game of two halves. Sometimes you have a storming first half and it looks as if this time your team is really on top. Then, there is a complete failure in the second half and it all goes wrong: another dreadful defeat. It can go the other way of course, but usually for fans, especially if, one supports a team that is often struggling, all the hopes and dreams of a good start are more often dashed. These tensions, which are so often experienced by football fans, are reflected in this essay. The only difference is that for fans at a game, the two halves are chronological; one follows the other. In this essay the two halves, the one positive and something to celebrate, and the other, a depressing manifestation of failure and the repetition of old mistakes, are happening at the same time.

> Time matters in sport, as does the experience of time (Adam 1994, 2004; Woodward 2012c; Chasing Time 2014–15)

Time is not just a matter of progressing from A to B and, in sport measuring the time that takes; a game of two halves and the full 90 min. The passage of time is also experienced differently in different contexts. Time involves the past, the present and the future, and the passage of time is constitutive of change, not only within the game but over longer periods, for example, of transformation or maybe of continuity. In this paper, some of the possibilities of women's time in football will be explored. Is the culture of football changing? What does the increasing popularity of the sport among women at grass roots as well as at competitive, international levels (UEFA Women 2015), tell us about how football both globally and locally, is gendered? Is football becoming a more equal and democratic playing field in terms of gender politics and opportunities? The popularity of soccer, for example, among young women and in colleges and schools is one thing, but the enduring manifestation of traditional forms of masculinity and the reiteration of misogyny and social exclusion tell a different story and these are stories being told at the same time.

This essay, which is based on a talk that the author of it gave at a conference held in Oxford on 23–24, July 2014 (Oxford Conference 2014; Taylor and Francis 2014) just after the men's football World Cup in Brazil in 2014, uses an exploration of the state of play for women in football in such a big year for the sport, which saw the advent of the FA Women's Super League (Super League 2014) 2014 was the men's competition, but did it augur any cultural change for the women's World Cup in 2015 (Women's World Cup FIFA's 2015)? Could we be moving into women's time in football with greater recognition of the part played by women at all levels in the sport?

The focus of this essay is upon a particular timescale and draws upon a range of evidence from coverage of football during a limited period of time which, nonetheless cannot be seen as isolated, because the present although it carries distinctive features, is always informed by the past, and, in football always looks to the future. Change may not be entirely transformative, but the progress of time usually includes elements of continuity and change, and the purpose of this paper is to explore the extent of change and what form that change may take in relation to the sexual politics of football.

Sporting times

Time is central to sport, not least football, through measurements and memories. The sophisticated technologies of recording time matter in training and on the pitch, the intensity of spectatorship at the stadium or watching the big screen and memories of being present at big games generate what makes football the beautiful game. There is also the amount of time athletes are able to devote to training and to improving performance (Chasing Time 2014–15). What does a focus on time and temporality tell us about the women's game?

The advent of the English Football Association Super League (FA WSL) in 2011 meant that the women's sport was being taken seriously and for the first time women would be paid, albeit and rates which bear no comparison to the men's football league; the top four players in each team being initially paid £20,000 a year. The WSL, which replaces the FA Women's Premier League as the highest level of women's football in England and Wales, currently has two leagues. Sixteen clubs applied to join the WSL at the outset and a single league was created, with the expansion into two competitive women's leagues for 2014, with the aim of further expansion, with the increasing popularity of women's football in the UK, for example, as manifested in England's bronze medal in the 2015 Women's football World Cup in Canada. The WSL delivered some of the players who not only achieved so highly in the 2015 competition, but also led to women footballers becoming known and recognized in the UK media. The Super League might herald at least some incremental move towards women's time (Super League 2014), even if it is, as yet, early days. Alternatively, old values might be further entrenched through the exclusion and marginalization of women through their persistent invisibility, for example, in lack of mainstream media presence. This is beginning to change, for example, with Sky TV's ongoing coverage of women's games, and in 2015, the BBC's commitment to broadcasting the women's FA Cup final at Wembley, but print media remain intransigent about including reports and comments on sports pages, which are dominated by the men's game. Even lower league men's matches gain precedence over any women's games, including international events. The connections between past, present and future are experienced differently in women's football from men's, not least because of the legacy of memories of the pivotal moments, record breaking displays and the construction of male heroes of the sport in the history of the men's game in public narratives, which are largely absent in women's football, as in many other sports. It will take time to build these memories and to put the women's game into discourse (Foucault 1981), although part of this process is recognizing the role of women's participation in the past (Hargreaves 1994).

Time and temporality are central to football in exploring some of the transformations, representations and experiences of women's football. A focus upon temporality in sport is particularly pertinent because understanding of how memories make experience, and how past present and future can be condensed in the 'real time' of spectatorship provides explanation of enduring inequalities. It is through time that heroes are made as well as records established and broken. Brazil's disastrous early exit from the 2014 competition was so much more painful and distressing because of the legacy of football in that nation; a legacy generated and sustained over time. Similarly, when Argentinian Lionel Messi gets the ball, for example in recent games for Barcelona, the excitement (or fear if you support the opposing team) of the spectator and engagement in the real time of the present is enormously intensified because we know what he has achieved in the past; this is a moment which has a history and a hero and goes beyond the embodied practices on the pitch, however skilful they may be. It is memories of past performance, future projections and the embodied practices of the present, including recovery of form in the real time of the game being watched, which generate debate about whether or not Messi might be the greatest player of all time.

The most obvious relevance of time to sports is through measurement of time and the increasingly precise mechanisms of setting records. As stated at the start of this article, football is a game of two halves and time and expressions of temporality permeate the game; the full 90 minutes, extra time, injury time, playing for time, time out; in international competitions, there is talk of it being a particular nation's time to succeed. Time however is always moving and always carries hopes for the future.

Past achievements are central to football culture and football fandom, for example, current engagement in the action on the pitch connects to the promise of future success (or the threat of future failure and relegation to a lower division or league). Past records and performances are especially important in football and the past makes memories as well as generates expectations for the future. Memories connect people in the culture of football; fans recall past glories and even if they were not actually present at the game, much store is placed upon remembering where you were when it happened. This to and fro between past and future is also what makes the present so exciting; the confluence of times enhances the experience of the game you are watching. It is not only the players who are immersed in the operation and experience of time on the pitch; spectators too are in a constant conversation with past and future in the real time of actually watching the game, whether in the flesh or virtually, for example, on television or the big screen (Woodward 2015). Legacies of the past performances create expectations and fears in the present as well as the hierarchies of success and failure, promotion and relegation also particularly what makes the men's game. Women's football has fewer legacies and heroic narratives from the past expressed within the public arena upon which to draw. This is why visibility is so important to effecting change. Visibility and audibility have to be appropriate, however as I argue in the article. There is much more to a good second half and for the sexual politics of football than numbers of women playing and women being included in the coverage of competitions. In order for any claims for the emergence of women's time in the twenty-first century, women have to be serious contenders in the sport, not just appendages, in the field of vision.

An exploration of temporality also raises questions about equalities and inequalities, not only about whose past counts and is recounted, and whose is silenced and made invisible (Woodward 2012a). Sport and politics are closely enmeshed, and this is as true of football as most other sports (Woodward 2012b). The management and organization of football manifests inequalities at many different levels and thus, football reflects and reproduces wider socio-economic imbalances and social inequalities, many of which are particular to specific periods of time (Goldblatt 2015).

The passing of time may be inevitable and relentless, but not everyone experiences time in the same way. Some athletes report timelessness or being lost in time especially when they're 'in the zone' (Chasing Time 2014–15; Woodward 2015). This experience of timelessness and of being totally immersed in time is not available to everyone, and access to the heightened state of peak performance of being in the zone may not be entirely democratic.

In this essay, I use the social dimensions of temporality and some of the ways in which time creates intensities to evaluate the extent to which changing times in football are possible, and whether such changes might be redressing some of the imbalances of gendered time. The 2012 London Olympics were described as 'women's time' (Woodward 2012, Woodward 2012a, 2012c). One example of this in 2012 was the inclusion of women's boxing in the games. Attention would be drawn to the way the sport was covered during the games and in the aftermath. In spite of tedious reiteration of old arguments about women's fragility, the dangers of voyeurism and the replacement of some of the men's events by women's, the outcome was mostly serious, informed discussion and commentary, and some very entertaining boxing (Woodward 2014).

The Olympics are much more egalitarian in terms of sexual politics than soccer, with almost equal participation for women and men, which is very different from football, but nonetheless the development of grass roots interest and of systems like the Super League and, for example, the positive encouragement of Premiership clubs like Arsenal (Arsenal Ladies 2015); women are still called ladies, long after the category of gentlemen has been abandoned, even in cricket) nonetheless suggest changing times. For example, in the Football League, women are no longer classified, as in the bureaucratic structures of individual clubs, under the umbrella of community, within a charitable discourse of those who are in some way disadvantaged, for example, on the grounds of race, ethnicity or disability, or as deviant (Woodward 2007), but as real players, even if they are called ladies, who enjoy the game and want to play competitively and not as some form of therapy or in the promotion of social inclusion. Maybe the times are changing and it could be 'women's time, when the Women's World Cup in Canada in 2015 was not only anticipated in at least some respects more like the 2014 Men's but also received media coverage which engaged spectators and fans?

The Men's World Cup 2014: time for change?

The men's World Cup in 2014 might have signalled some small-scale transformations in the binary logic of sex and gender, which operates so powerfully in football. Not only is the sport divided into the men's and the women's games in the actual practice of the sport at all levels, but also its culture is dominated by patriarchal values and a traditional hegemonic masculinity (Connell 1995; Woodward 2012a). Hegemonic masculinity refers to a social and cultural version of masculinity which is constructed through associations with male, especially patriarchal, power which values traditionally the male qualities of aggression and force, which are exercised not only over women, but also men who do not concur with its values and prescriptions. Hegemonic masculinity operates through networks and cultural practices, which in the contemporary world can include those of journalists and commentators as well as the governance of sports and players themselves.

Even though it was the men's competition in 2014, it might have been possible to see some evidence of change. Women were included, if not in commentating on games, as experts who could be interviewed about the national team's prospects. There was the usual discussion of players' sexual partners under the category of wives and girlfriends, who even in 2014 were called WAGS (World Cup. "Wags" 2014), sex workers (McKenna 2014) and the customary visibility of attractive reporters who, unlike the vast majority of male commentators, tend to be appointed for their appearance, and clear enunciation, rather than experience of playing the game or particular expertise. Although all mega events attract some discussion of the working opportunities afforded by the presence of large groups of men a long way from home, in a configuration of hegemonic masculinity which is embedded in the culture of football, one hoped for change in 2014 and there were some glimmers of light, and there was some evidence of incremental change.

These issues raise dilemmas for the football fan, who has a commitment to equality, not least in the negativity of such inequitable forces, such as those which sexualize women and deny them the right to be taken seriously as players, commentators or indeed fans, which might be destroying the enjoyment of the beautiful game (Woodward 2012b). Some blogs have debated the extent to which feminists could support the men's World Cup and have engaged with discussion of the extent to which expressions of enthusiasm constitute collusion with women's exclusion and oppression (fbomb 2014). Whilst critical analysis is central, such an approach might be posing the wrong questions and a false set of alternatives. The point must be to continue to enjoy football and all the excitement it offers and to argue for change, which can make the sport more socially inclusive and broaden its base and widen its appeal (McKenna 2014). The Women's World Cup in 2015 offered hope for the future of football, through its excitement and competitive spirit, based on performance on the pitch, rather than narratives of celebrities and, sometimes, aberrant behaviour.

The year 2014 was certainly not all negative; there were opportunities and possibilities, which promised transformations or at least marginal incremental shifts. This time women's presence at the men's World Cup was not without acknowledgement of expert knowledge. Women, such as statistician Dr Susan Bridgewater, were recruited as expert commentators, not on actual games, but in the run up, for example by the BBC, prior to the big event itself (Bridgewater Sue 2015). Women footballers were also interviewed in the sports media. For example, Arsenal player, Rachel Yankey, was invited to comment on England's chances before the competition, as a serious pundit (Yankey 2014) and there was some, if limited recognition that women contributors might have expertise.

Overall, 2014 showed little departure from previous masculine dominated mega football events, however, and the culture and practices of hegemonic masculinity remained pretty entrenched on the pitch and in the sociocultural context and location of the competition. There were some great games and a focus upon the game itself, but any aberrance was attributed to provocation or deviation and some of the greatest football players in the world fought and bit their way through the tournament without any comment from sports commentators based on the analysis of the enactment of embodied masculinity. This tournament, like many mega events, suggests that gender in sport is more an outcome of masculinity than femininity. The resistance to women's time in football might be less attributable to particular (Woodward 2009) practices such as tackling like a girl to paraphrase Iris Marion Young's essay *Throwing Like a Girl* (Young 2005), but more about kicking (and biting) like a boy. There is a case to be made that in evaluating the extent to which women's time is a possibility in soccer, attention should be focused upon masculinity rather than assuming the 'problem' to be femininity or that gender is just about women and in particular, about empirical evidence of participation in the sport. The popularity of football and increased numbers of women who play is enormously important in democratizing the sport, but a concentration upon numbers is not the whole story of changing times. Nonetheless, football is very popular at all levels and its growth across the globe is encouraging for wider participation.

Women's football worldwide

World cups, which are the top-ranking competitions of national teams, as well as indicators of the development, performance level and the global spread of a sport, are also indicative of the extent to which women are playing greater roles in soccer worldwide. In the USA, women's soccer has had a sustained presence in recent years, with the US women's team having won more international competitions than any other national team with 10 million registered women players (Markovits and Hellerman 2003). Nonetheless, even with extensive media coverage the women's game is still subject to patriarchal and often sexualized constructions in the media. As Markovits and Hellerman argue, soccer in spite of its popularity in terms of numbers of participants, occupies a relatively marginal space in the sports landscape in the USA. Women's presence in international competition, for example, championships in sports, which have a relatively short history, such as women's soccer is also largely unremarked, but nonetheless of considerable significance. The Women's World Cup, which has been organized by FIFA, since 1991, attracts an increasing number of teams, which participate in the qualification matches. The number of participants and their performance demonstrate that women's soccer has now spread to many parts of the world (Williams 2007), including China where there has been considerable recent growth (Hong and Mangan 2003). Recent estimates suggest that there are 26 million women and girls now playing soccer worldwide at some level (FIFA Women 2015). However, the recognition and support given to women's soccer, as well as its organizational bases, vary considerably from country to country; for example, although there were 120 football federations listed in the FIFA Women's World Ranking with an active national squad in 2013, women's soccer leagues exist in only 61 countries (Williams 2013).

With an estimated 26 million female players globally and 6 million based in Europe, the numerical evolution of football has been dramatic. Growth in the women's game has led to more widespread player migration as new forms of professionalism emerge (Williams 2013; Pfister, Klein and Tiesler 2014).

The increases seen in the number of registered female players, the number of national associations organizing a national women's league, the number of football academies dedicated to girls and the number of associations adopting a strategy for women's football are all further signs of the steady progress that is being made (UEFA Women 2015). The FA WSL has only just begun, but following the Women's World Cup in 2015 some the players' names, like captain Steph Houghton, goal keeper Karen Bardsley and star of the tournament, right back Lucy Bronze are being put into popular sporting discourse in the UK for example, and footballing times are changing.

More media coverage is promised. For example, in 2015 the FA Women's Cup final between Chelsea and Notts County on Saturday, 1 August, was held at Wembley (BBC Women Wembley 2015) for the first time in the competition's history and shown live on the BBC, having previously been covered by Sky. This is the beginning of mainstreaming and all part of incremental shifts towards the integration of the women's game into the centre – and the location of sporting events as part of the traditional national calendar and part of the flow of changing times.

Unlike in the men's game, the professionalization process in women's soccer however, is in an incipient stage and the sport is thus, not dominated by the global sport media nexus, which shapes developments in the men's game to a large extent, which may have advantages as well as disadvantages, for example, in terms of visibility. The enduring inequalities which include the intersection of race, ethnicity and gender, although gender carries some distinctive aspects (Scraton, Caudwell and Holland 2005), in the men's game through its governance and culture (Goldblatt 2015) might yet invade the women's sport but so far, for women, what matters is performance and opportunities. The women's game, in spite of its popularity at the start of the twentieth century (Hargreaves 1994), in the twenty-first century, is at an early stage.

What is the state of play in the year of the women's World Cup, and in the aftermath of the men's competition in 2014?

A bad second half?

The signs on the pitch are encouraging with the numbers of participating in the women's game increasing, but what about the culture of football? Is there evidence of any cultural shift towards a more inclusive sport or are there still manifestations of hostility to women? Misogyny remains well documented for example, in instances of violence against women (WHO 2015), but one might not expect it in sport. It is one thing to exclude women from participation on the pitch and within regimes of governance and even the public space of media representation, but how far does hostility go? In the wake of the National Football League scandals in the USA in 2014 (NFL 2014), there have sadly been myriad examples of misogyny in football too. In the UK, ongoing debate about the reinstatement at various football league clubs of the convicted rapist Ched Evans through 2014, on his release from prison on licence and cases of what was called sexist chanting at Premiership grounds, suggest that there remains deep antagonism against women in football. In spite of the UK priding itself on anti-racist and diversity policies aimed at promoting social inclusion, the last bastion may indeed be prejudice against women. Apologists for such chanting which has been called 'banter', fail to acknowledge the hatred, which informs and underpins such practices (Gibson 2015). Owen Gibson suggests more female role models and interestingly, highlights the temporal dimensions of contemporary sexist practices, especially in relation to the endurance of an unequal sexual politics. He suggests that the culture of football remains unchanged since the 1970s; it also remains framed by a defensive discourse couched in terms of good humour and the platitude that sexism is somehow a joke and not serious (Gibson 2015). Another aspect of the debate, which demonstrates a conversation with the past is the use of the term sexist, which has largely been abandoned in contemporary gender studies where other axes of power have been identified (Woodward and Woodward 2009; Richardson and Robinson 2015).

The Football Association has called upon fans to report sexist abuse at games after being shown disturbing scenes of women officials and staff being subjected to obscene chants. For example, BBC footage showed Chelsea's doctor, Eva Carneiro and a female assistant referee Helen Byrne suffering taunts and extreme verbal abuse in 2015. FA board member Heather Rabbatts stated that such abuse should not be tolerated and pleaded with fans to report (BBC Sport 2015). Whilst such behaviour is formally unacceptable to clubs, which have a responsibility to implement equality legislation, as with anti-racism programmes there is an element of paying lip service to statutory requirements and failing to address the embedded cultures of social exclusion and prejudice.

The club has no option but to state its opposition as Chelsea did in this case; 'The issue of equality is one that we take extremely seriously at Chelsea Football Club and we abhor discrimination in all its forms, including sexism. We find such behaviour unacceptable and we want it eradicated from the game' (BBC Sport 2015). This is not only a matter of individual responsibility of fans or of clubs; it is also demands an exploration of the persistence of such entrenched attitudes over such a long period of time and their eruption at this moment.

The greater participation of women in football, including line judges and medical staff at the pitch side forces the sport to confront these attitudes. In the 2014–15 English Premier league football season, there have, at the time of writing in March 2015, 25 match-day incidents of sexist abuse have been reported to anti-discrimination campaign group Kick It Out (2015) and equality group Women in Football (WiF 2015), whereas last season, there were only two. No action has been taken by football's governing bodies against the perpetrators due to lack of specific, direct evidence, but my point is that the reporting of these misogynous acts, including the documented abuse through mass chanting of Chelsea medical staff, suggests that this is structural, cultural and enduring, and is a phenomenon which challenges the more positive features of the good first half and increasing popularity of football for women.

Manchester City, the club against which Chelsea was playing when the abuse was so loudly expressed as the doctor ran onto the pitch added that 'A new specific guidance on sexist abuse was introduced from the very next game and a new training programme implemented' (BBC Sport 2015), which suggests, given the length of time that the UK has had anti-discriminatory legislation, either that the club thought battles against discrimination had been won or that gender equality was not something high on the club's agenda. Other clubs have argued that no formal complaints have been made and that consequently they have not taken any action.

Reflections on researching real time

In this discussion of the possibility of changing times in football, I have drawn upon my experience of immersion in the 'real time' of the 2012 Olympic Games (Woodward 2012c Woodward 2012). One of the advantages of this auto ethnographic approach is that it is attentive to the affect and feeling of the process of engaging with the embodied practices of sport in the 'real time' of the moment, which provides a route into understanding at least in part what is so important about sport and for example, why football has such massive global appeal.

I drew upon this experience to inform my consideration of the impact of the men's World Cup and why it is the competition we want to watch, and the one that generates such powerful emotions and passions. I mention this in order to explain the need to incorporate the relationship between spectators and performers in creating the affective event of the sporting mega spectacle. Football demands recognition of its affective dimensions and of some of the ways in which sport combines bodies and body practices with emotions, feelings, personal and collective psychic investments and social, cultural, political and economic systems. All of these elements, including different axes of power, combine and intersect at particular times and in particular places. Temporality provides a connecting strand, which locates culture, including the culture of football. It is impossible to consider the possibilities of women's time without some understanding of the operation and experience of time and temporality in football.

In seeking to make sense of inequalities in sport, conventional social science and sports studies suggests lack of media coverage of women's sport, lack of opportunities, lack of interest by young women (Soccer and Society 2011) demonstrates these reasons and such accounts very well. Also the intersection of gender, class, sexuality, ethnicity and race underpin inequalities in football (Caudwell 1999, 2011. All these factors are relevant but not in equal proportion and I'd like to add time and temporality to the mix. Women's sport has not received anything like the prime time coverage, which men's has, and this absence from the airways has been particularly marked in football. Sometimes women footballers in the news are there for familial reasons; for example the pregnancy of England and Arsenal defender Casey Stoney was described by BBC sport as her imminent transformation from footballer into 'gay mother' in 2014 (BBC Sport 2014). There is often an elision of sex gender and sexuality although they are clearly not the same. Sex and sexuality do share the capacity to generate hostilities and prejudice however. A focus on the real time coverage of football and the lack of support and resource for the women's game is part of an assemblage of factors and of the intersection of power axes in which gender is not just about women and which is located temporally as well as spatially.

However, watching in real time demonstrates time and temporality as factors which play a part in the establishment and entrenchment of inequalities and imbalances of power which can have more purchase in sport because of the emotions and intense feeling a sport like football inspires. The excitement of football is generated in the moment of the event. It is being immersed in its intensities in the real time of the present, which brings together the memories of past performance and the promise of the future. In 2014, the inclusion of a young German team in the men's World Cup invoked a whole new way of expressing support internationally in a new discourse of attachment and affiliation on a stage of global transformation, as well as the setting of records. This was manifested in the language of the commentators on the Germany Brazil game when they expressed the desire for Germany to score even more goals in order to break the record, so that the commentators too could lay claim to being part of the record.

Conclusion

This essay has delved itself in a particular period of time including the period immediately before the men's World Cup in 2014 up to September 2015, in order to weigh up the possibilities of change in the gender politics of global football. Whilst the focus has been eclectic, one has sought to interrogate cultural change and the ways in which new ideas and ways of thinking about the sexual politics of football might have been put into discourse, at least tentatively. The concept of temporality has been used to explore the possibility that the culture of soccer is changing and to evaluate the argument that, as was suggested in the case of the 2012 Olympic Games, this point in the twenty-first century might herald women's time. Women's time is not an alternative to men's time, but might suggest some incremental shifts in the patriarchal framework in which world football operates. Change is slow and marginal, but it has been argued that it is possible if we engage with the inequalities of the present to signpost a more egalitarian future.

It is time, not just the length of time of the competition and the records set but the experience of time, in the present and through memories of the past, which generate the intensity of sport's spectatorship. It is not just the body practices on the pitch, especially at the time when women in football are increasingly skilled and developing more sophisticated skills and tactics, especially in making the sport fast and entertaining, but it is only with time that the women's game will catch up with the commitment and enthusiasm which makes the men's game so powerful. Time is about inequalities in the present and tracing their genealogies in order to redress them in the future, rather than utopian dreams or predictions. It is not a matter of women's time or men's time; football can accommodate people's time and further democratization of the sport can only enhance its excitement and significance.

A celebration of the embodied practices of the beautiful game might be more possible if we can concentrate on what is happening on the pitch unconstrained by hostility and hatred, and a binary logic of sex; the people's game fits well with the beautiful game. Changing times might open up the possibilities of an enjoyment of football unencumbered by some of its current social, cultural and economic constraints, when it might be feasible to focus upon what is happening on the pitch rather than off it.

Disclosure statement

No potential conflict of interest was reported by the author.

References

Adam, Barbara. 1994. *Time and Social Theory*. Cambridge: Polity.
Adam, Barbara. 2004. *Time*. Cambridge: Polity.
Arsenal Ladies. 2015. Accessed March 21. http://www.arsenalladies.com/index.html#IIocJuRTT OP7x2jk.97
BBC Sport. 2014. Accessed March 23, 2015. http://www.bbc.co.uk/sport/0/football/28316160
BBC Sport. 2015. Accessed March 21, 2015. http://www.bbc.co.uk/sport/0/football/31750397

BBC Women Wembley. 2015. Accessed March 10, 2015. http://www.bbc.co.uk/sport/0/football/31798146

Bridgewater Sue. 2015. Accessed March 20, 2015. https://www.liv.ac.uk/management/staff/susan-bridgewater/

Caudwell, Jayne. 1999. "Women's Football in the United Kingdom, Theorising Gender and Unpacking the Butch Lesbian Image." *Journal of Sport and Social Issues* 23 (4): 390–402.

Caudwell, Jayne. 2011. "Reviewing UK Football Cultures: Continuing with Gender Analyses." *Soccer & Society* 12 (3): 323–329.

Chasing Time. 2014–15. Accessed March 10, 2015. http://www.olympic.org/content/the-olympic-museum/explore/press/press-releases/chasing-time/

Connell, R. W. 1995. *Masculinities*. Cambridge: Polity.

FA Women. 2015. Accessed March 10, 2015. http://www.thefa.com/womens-girls-football

fbomb. 2014. Accessed March 20, 2015. http://thefbomb.org/2014/07/sexism-and-soccer-balls/

FIFA Women. 2015. Accessed March 10, 2015. http://www.fifa.com/aboutfifa/footballdevelopment/women/

Foucault, Michel. 1981. *History of Sexuality*. Vol. 1. Harmondsworth: Penguin.

Gibson, O. 2015. "More Female Role Models in Game Can Root out Discrimination." *The Guardian*, March 6, 3.

Goldblatt, D. 2015. *The Game of Our Lives: The Meaning and Making of English Football*. Harmondsworth: Penguin.

Hargreaves, Jennifer. 1994. *Sporting Females: Critical Issues in the History and Sociology of Women's Sport*. London: Routledge.

Hong, Fan, and J. A. Mangan, eds. 2003. *Soccer, Women, Sexual Liberation: Kicking off a New Era*. London: Routledge.

Kick it Out. 2015. Accessed March 23. www.kickitout.org/

Markovits, Andrei S., and Steven Hellerman. 2003. "Women's Soccer in the United States: Yet Another American 'Exceptionalism.'" *Soccer and Society* 4 (2–3): 14–29.

McKenna, Ewan. 2014. Accessed March 20, 2015. http://www.independent.co.uk/news/world/americas/brazils-sex-trade-how-the-countrys-one-million-prostitutes-are-preparing-for-the-world-cup-9457494.html

NFL. 2014. Accessed March 23, 2015. http://gu.com/p/42vht/sbl

Oxford Conference. 2014. Accessed March 17, 2015. http://www.uclan.ac.uk/news/uclan_oxford_football_conference.php

Pfister, G., M. Klein, and N. Tiesler. 2014. "Momentous Spark or Enduring Enthusiasm? The 2011 FIFA Women's World Cup and Its Impact on Players' Mobility and on the Popularity of Women's Soccer in Germany." In *Women, Soccer and Transnational Migration*, edited by S. Agergaard and N. C. Tiesler, 140–158. London: Routledge.

Richardson, Diane, and Victoria Robinson. 2015. *Introduction to Gender Studies*. Basingstoke: Palgrave MacMillan.

Scraton, Sheila, Jayne Caudwell, and Samantha Holland. 2005. "Bend It Like Patel. Centring Race, Ethnicity and Gender in Feminist Analysis of Women's Football in England." *International Review for the Sociology of Sport* 40 (1): 71–88.

Soccer and Society. 2011. Soccer and Society. 12 (6).

Super League. 2014. Accessed November 26, 2014. http://www.superleague.co.uk/

Taylor and Francis. 2014. Accessed March 17, 2015. http://explore.tandfonline.com/page/pgas/fifaoxford

UEFA Women. 2015. Accessed March 17, 2015. http://www.uefa.org/football-development/womens-football/news/newsid=2218440.html

WHO. 2015. Accessed March 23, 2015. http://www.who.int/mediacentre/factsheets/fs239/en/

WiF. 2015. "Women in Football." Accessed March 23, 2015. www.womeninfootball.co.uk

Williams, Jean. 2007. *A Beautiful Game: International Perspectives on Women's Football*. Oxford: Berg.

Williams, Jean. 2013. *Globalising Women's Football: Europe, Migration and Professionalization (SavoirsSportifs/Sports Knowledge)*. Bern: Peter Lang.

Women's World Cup. 2015. Accessed March 10, 2015. http://www.fifa.com/womensworldcup/news/

Women's World Cup FIFA. 2015. Accessed March 12, 2015. http://www.fifa.com/womensworldcup/

Woodward, Kath. 2007. "On and Off the Pitch: Diversity Policies and Transforming Identities?" *Cultural Studies* 21 (4–5): 758–778.

Woodward, Kath. 2009. *Embodied Sporting Practices; Regulating and Regulatory Bodies*. Basingstoke: Palgrave.

Woodward, Kath. 2012. *Sporting Times*. Basingstoke: Palgrave MacMillan.

Woodward, Kath. 2012a. *Sex Power and the Games*. Basingstoke: Palgrave.

Woodward, Kath. 2012b. *Planet Sport*. London: Routledge.

Woodward, Kath. 2012c. *Sporting Times*. Basingstoke: Palgrave.

Woodward, Kath. 2014. *Globalizing Boxing*. London: Bloomsbury Academic.

Woodward, K. (2015). *The Politics of In/visibility: Being There*. London: Palgrave MacMillan.

Woodward, Kath, and Sophie Woodward. 2009. *Why Feminism Matters: Feminism Lost and Found*. Basingstoke: Palgrave.

World Cup. "Wags". 2014. Accessed November 27, 2014. http://metro.co.uk/2014/06/06/world-cup-2014-forget-england-vs-italy-its-baden-baden-wags-vs-2014-wags-4747232/

Yankey, Rachel. 2014. Accessed March 23, 2015. http://sportsvibe.co.uk/sportsvibe-tv/football/stuart-pearce-and-rachel-yankey-with-their-world-cup-predictions-34503/

Young, Iris Marion. 2005. *On Female Body Experience. "Throwing like a Girl" and Other Essays*. Oxford: Oxford University Press.

Making sense of race/ethnicity and gender in televised football: reception research among British students*

Rens Peeters and Jacco van Sterkenburg

ABSTRACT

Most people today watch football by way of the mass media, sites that reproduce and transform ideologies and ideas surrounding racial/ethnic and gender identity. However, still little remains known as to what extent actual football viewers take up or resist these ideas. Drawing on a cultural studies perspective, this study tries to identify the dominant discourses that British television viewers use to assign meaning to race/ethnicity and gender in men's and women's football on television. Eleven focus groups of British students ($n = 44$) were utilized to explore these discourses. Our findings indicate that viewers from various ethnic backgrounds were largely compliant with the hegemonic media discourses about natural physicality in both gender and race/ethnic comparisons. At the same time, multiple negotiated/oppositional discourses were found in relation to women's football that showed how other social practices contributed to such readings. Limitations and possible areas for future research are discussed.

Introduction and aim

Football on television has become one of the most popular forms of entertainment and a primary form of leisure for many people. This also applies to the English context where football constitutes an important part of the nation's cultural identity (Lines 2000). Huge events such as EURO 2012 or the 2014 FIFA World Cup draw millions of viewers and football matches consistently are among the best watched programmes on British television (Conlan 2012). Televised football, by virtue of its massive popularity, functions as a key site where prominent ideas about identity groupings such as nationality, race/ethnicity, gender and sexuality and the differences they entail are reproduced and naturalized. In a multicultural society that has openly began to question the apparent lack of Englishness of its highest national football league with the influx of foreign players, managers and owners (Gibson 2013), the question of how dominant ideas about race and ethnicity inside the

---

*Portions of this work were published in a thesis form in fulfillment of the requirements for a MA degree for the first author (Peeters, 2013).

football media are related to and understood by the television audience becomes all the more relevant. A similar question regarding gender should be pursued, as women have in increasing numbers made their way into the football stadiums, as audiences and as players, making it the most practiced team sport among women in the UK (Women's Sport and Fitness Foundation's 2012).

In the last two decades, textual and content analyses of gender and race/ethnicity representations in the sports media have uncovered a number of transnational trends that are remarkably persistent over time. Although improvements have been visible, sportswomen (especially those performing in sports that are traditionally geared towards men) remain underrepresented in terms of media coverage when compared to sportsmen (Adams et al. 2014). Furthermore, women are often represented in stereotypical ways that trivialize and marginalize their athletic performances and instead focus on their femininity and heterosexuality (Bruce 2013; Pressland 2012). Research has also shown that sport and football commentators (unconsciously) employ racial/ethnic stereotypes (Hylton 2009; McCarthy, Jones, and Potrac 2003), thereby reinforcing long-standing ideas about the natural athletic black body and white cognitive capabilities (Carrington and McDonald 2001).

While these content and textual analyses have certainly provided valuable insights into the discourses provided by the sports and football media, they fail to provide concrete information on the way different audiences receive and interpret these texts. Audience research that investigates the discourses employed by consumers of sport media remains relatively scarce (Bruce 2013; Cooky, Messner, and Hextrum 2013). This is surprising since media scholars agree that media texts acquire meaning in the complex interactions between those texts and their viewers/readers (Hermes 2005). It is of the essence, therefore, to start doing audience reception research. In the present study, we will therefore address the sport media audience and explore:

(1) The discourses television viewers of various ethnic and gender groupings draw on to give meaning to race/ethnicity and gender in men's and women's football.
(2) How viewers' individual receptions and discourses overlap with hegemonic media discourses and strengthen or challenge wider hegemonic discourses and relations of power in multi-ethnic society.

State of knowledge and research question

The few studies that have been conducted in this field show that media consumers don't necessarily comply with the stereotypical representations of ethnic or gender groupings or that they are at least more complex than textual analysis suggests. A study by McCarthy, Jones, and Potrac (2003) shows, for example, how black British viewers frequently rejected stereotypical comments directed at black players by sport commentators. In a similar vein, Knoppers and Elling (2001) reported that immigrants in the Netherlands tend to oppose dominant representations regarding race and ethnicity in the sport media more often than non-immigrants. Regarding the latter finding, several studies from different countries have indicated that white media users more readily employ stereotypical explanations (natural physicality) regarding black athletic performances (Harrison, Lawrence, and Bukstein 2011; Morning 2009).

Regarding the differences between male and female athletes, both men and women are more eager to employ the hegemonic media discourse which emphasizes that men are naturally stronger and tougher than women (Knoppers and Elling 2001; Lines 2000). Even though the media construct men's sport as the norm, viewers do have the capacity to reject this marginalization of women's sport and actively enjoy it, as, for example, Bruce has shown in the case of US women's basketball (Bruce 1998). A recent body of research has furthermore shown that consumers of sport generally prefer to view images of physically able sportswomen, instead of the sexualized representations that permeate the sport media (Kane, LaVoi, and Fink 2013).

While these studies provide useful insights, most of them were conducted in the US context, focussed on either race/ethnicity or gender and examined either men's or women's sport. The present study, on the other hand, aimed to gain more insight into the way British television viewers from different ethnic and gender groupings receive and make sense of race/ethnicity *and* gender representations in men's as well as women's televised football. The question of relevance that we will address can now be formulated as follows: *How do English viewers of various racial/ethnic and gender groupings receive and negotiate representations of race/ethnicity and gender in televised men's and women's football?*

The point of reference in the present study is the English context. The English context can be considered exemplary for some other European countries such as the Netherlands and France in harbouring a mixture of postcolonial migrants and labour migrants. In addition, football consumption constitutes a significant part of the English cultural identity. This also applies to many other countries across Europe and worldwide (Alabarces, Tomlinson, and Young 2001; Lechner 2007). Results are, therefore, not only relevant for the English context but also for other (Western) European countries where similar trends in football media discourses surrounding race/ethnicity and gender are visible as the ones reported here (De Bruycker 2012; Ličen and Billings 2013). We will draw on a cultural studies perspective to further interpret and discuss the hegemonic discourses that the British television viewers in this study used to assign meaning to race/ethnicity and gender in televised football.

A cultural studies approach

Working from a cultural studies perspective, televised sport is understood as a site where discourses concerning race/ethnicity and gender are (re)produced and transformed. Following Hall (1995), the concept of discourse is conceptualized here as a way to construct knowledge about a certain topic (such as race or gender) that opens up and at the same time limits the possible ways to talk about a topic. Discourse then, by producing meaningful knowledge about a subject and having real effects on the social world, is always imbued with power relations (Hall 1995). Hegemonic discourses produced inside the sport media often tend to reinforce the status and position of those in powerful positions which leads Bruce to argue that the sport media 'produces coverage *by* men, *for* men and *about* men' (2013, 28).

The concepts of race and gender are viewed as dynamic social constructs that acquire meaning in and through discourse (Hall 1995; Pfister 2010). However, these terms are often essentialized in society and the sport media by constructing them as a set of binary oppositions (black/white, masculinity/femininity, etc.) whereby difference is fixed and the status quo retained (Hall 1997). But meanings over these terms are always being contested and hegemony is never completely won. The football media is one of the places where such struggles over meaning takes place. Watching televised football means watching filtered representations that audiences can actively use to make sense of the world, themselves and others (Hall 2011). We don't hold the view that the sport media is the *only* site from where people receive ideas about identity and difference, but, as Carrington has noted (Carrington 2011), it is one of the most powerful social institutions through which popular ideas about race are dispersed. Similarly, the arena of sports is one of the very few places in our modern society where segregation along gender lines is still enacted (Pfister 2010).

Viewers are perceived as active in their negotiation with the meanings of the text, but they're limited by the text at the same time, as the text constructs the subject positions viewers can occupy. Reiterating the earlier argument by Bruce (2013), white males are most ideally suited to take up the ideal subject position and read the text according to its preferred reading (Hall 1980). Marginalized groups may instead more often opt to utilize an oppositional or negotiated reading whereby they either reject the dominant discourse or find some middle ground that incorporates both preferred and oppositional elements (Hall 1980).

Methodology

Conceptualizing race/ethnicity

As has been discussed in earlier studies, the conceptualization of race/ethnicity constitutes a methodological challenge in empirical research (e.g. Gunaratnam 2003; McCarthy, Jones, and Potrac 2003). We used the discourse of the black–white binary to both label the respondents and structure most of the questions. Although we realize that the categories of 'black' and 'white' are generalizations lumping together various more specific racial/ethnic groups, this black–white dualism is still very much alive among the general public in everyday British society (Billings and Hundley 2010; McCarthy, Jones, and Potrac 2003; Schönwälder 2010). This was also apparent in the way respondents in our study described themselves, often invoking white-British or black-British. In addition, the use of this binary provided the opportunity to compare our findings with previous studies which generally used a black–white dichotomy to define race as well. In addition to the black–white binary, the respondents had the opportunity to also use and/or discuss other racial/ethnic categories such as the category of Asian footballers which the respondents regularly referred to (see 'Results' section).

Data collection

Data have been gathered through a series of focus group interviews. These interviews were conducted with students at Brunel University and Croydon College (both Greater London) in October 2012. We used focus groups because they reflect as closely as possible the everyday TV talk about football as a site of social interaction where meaning is constructed collectively immediately after the broadcast. Of the 44 young people who participated, 29 were females and 15 were males, while there were slightly more students with a black-British (23) than with a white-British (21) background. Each focus group consisted of 3–5 students. These focus groups occasionally consisted of friends resulting in ethnic and gender homogeneous as well as heterogeneous groups. Ages of respondents ranged from 15 to 22.[2] Viewing behaviour was generally consistent across the focus groups which included many heavy viewers (i.e. watching football every week). Interviews generally lasted somewhere between 40 and 80 min. The interviews were conducted using a semi-structured interview which included predetermined topics based on the available body of literature. This provided the necessary amount of focus, but still left room for additional themes to emerge. The interviews were structured around the following main themes: (1) context of (televised) football involvement, (2) discourses surrounding race/ethnicity and gender in televised football, and (3) perceptions towards the football media's treatment of race and gender.

Data analysis

The analysis undertaken here borrows insights from the grounded theory approach where data give rise to theory (Boeije 2010). A software package was used for the qualitative analysis of the 11 interviews. The first stage of the analysis, using a process of open coding, consisted of identifying themes at the smallest level and concretizing them into comprehensive labels (Strauss and Corbin 1998). Labels that were similar were grouped together in broader categories in the process of axial coding (Strauss and Corbin 1998). We also checked whether the so-formed categories still represented their labels well or that new categories should be created. A third and final step was the integration and refinement of existing categories in a process called selective coding (Strauss and Corbin 1998). The approach required the ability to reverse between steps and question or alter earlier decisions as new themes or concepts emerged from the data.

Results: ethnicity, gender and media commentary

In this section, we identify and categorize the most prominent discourses used by the respondents to give meaning to race/ethnicity and gender in televised men's and women's football. They are structured around the three themes (ethnicity, gender and media commentary) that were dominant in the interviews.

Ethnicity

Natural physicality discourse
Irrespective of their ethnicity or gender, a majority of the respondents used a 'natural physicality discourse'[1] to evaluate black players and differentiate them from other ethnicities. Some respondents used this discourse to explain the apparent over-representation of black players in attacking and winger positions. Black players were often seen as possessing a strong physique and being naturally fast:

> [...] but the black people are more often the ones with the power and the speed in order to like progress up the pitch. [...]. They've got the quick feet, they've got like the speed to get in behind the back four and I think you do see that an awful lot.

The natural physicality discourse was refuted by some of the respondents. Two groups (ethnically and gender diverse) did so explicitly. One male participant remarked: 'I think it has been a big thing for a long time, like about black players have supposedly a genetic advantage of being quick. I think that stereotype just carries'. This stereotype is so ingrained in modern football that it has a major influence on where players are positioned on the pitch, one group argued. Besides, this stereotype wouldn't hold up on closer inspection as most black players wouldn't conform to this stereotype of being big and physical. Other respondents believed that a correlation between positions on the pitch and ethnicity was no longer valid or would over time disappear. White or Asian players were almost never described in terms of a natural physique.

Mental discourses

A second, less prevalent, discourse that was used in some groups involved the evaluation of players on the basis of mental capacities. In a few instances, this discourse was linked to the positions taken up in the field by players of different ethnic backgrounds. Several respondents drew on a discourse to positively assess the mentality of white players. First, white players were described in terms of having a good 'perception' or overall view of the pitch:

> Paul Scholes he is always vision and what he can do with the ball, like the way he spreads the ball across 60 yard passes. Those are the same with Rooney as well.

These players were furthermore deemed to be role models that put the team above anything else and have good tactical knowledge. A few black male students thought that this tactical knowledge could be the reason for the apparent over-representation of white players in the controlling positions of the game, such as central midfield or central backs. These same students argued that black players play in attacking positions because they want to be 'the star of the show', and the people who get in the limelight are usually the one's that make the goals.

Nonetheless, there were some students that used a mental discourse to ascribe black players with positive mental traits such as hard work or leadership qualities. A white female student argued:

> The people that are not English put a hell of a lot more effort into the game, because they actually want to be there. [...]. So if you think Drogba, he sends pretty much half of his wages back to his country, to help them out.

Cultural discourses

The under-representation of Asians in English football was largely explained through the use of a discourse that referred to 'culture'. Asians, by which respondents usually meant people from Indian or Pakistani origin, were seen as not being interested that much in football, but more invested in a sport like cricket. A statement made by a black male student was exemplary for this discourse: 'So, when Indian families come over to England ... even if the child grows up in England, they're going to play cricket. Because that's what their parents or the whole family has been into'. Other arguments included the lack of Asian role-models, the time devoted to religious activity rather than sports and the claim that English scouts didn't scout for Asian players, either because the Asians play in little known separate leagues or because the scouts harboured stereotypical prejudices which say that Asian people are not very well fit for football.

Gender

Physicality and mentality discourse

Although it's difficult to single out a dominant discourse regarding gender, a slight majority tended to view football as a masculine activity. Irrespective of their outlook on football, most students agreed that men are inherently stronger than women. Most respondents believed this to be the main reason that mixed gender teams will probably never happen as the physical difference between men and women is just too large. An argument by a black male student further illustrated this: 'You know, the males [...] their bodies are stronger. The female's legs will get broken, if men never held back when they're playing each other'. Some respondents said that mixed teams would ruin football (as a physical contact sport) and argued that physical contact between men and women wasn't desirable.

There existed a different discourse that was, with a few exceptions, primarily used by female students to argue that mixed teams would be interesting in that they would improve the quality of the female players by increasing the competitiveness of the game. Some respondents steered towards mental differences between men and women as a reason why football is masculine. One white male respondent observed: 'Whereas females still have that [...]. When you are older you have that maternal instinct, so you don't want to hurt anyone'. One male student stated he didn't 'expect a woman to be aggressive' as opposed to men.

Entertainment discourses

A slight majority, a group comprised mostly of male students, found men's football to be more entertaining than women's football, because of its superior quality. Men's football is viewed as being better and more exciting when compared to women's football where 'the quality of the football is not as good as in the men's game'. Respondents argued that women's football has a slower pace, is less technical and players aren't as skilful as their male counterparts. Some respondents found it boring, while others went further as the following comment from a black male student illustrates: '[...] they're [women] not really meant to play. They're not skilled enough'. The students that used this discourse would only watch women's football if it was entertaining enough, meaning that the female players should possess the same qualities that are displayed in the men's game.

By contrast, a slightly smaller group that largely consisted of female students (and some black-British males) also explicitly connected men's football to entertainment, but insisted that this wasn't necessarily a positive thing. This reasoning is explained by one female student who pointed out that men's football is 'all about the media' and that women's football is actually 'all about the football'. Male footballers were deemed to 'play up to the cameras' and when fouled, they would make a fuss about it. On the other hand, women's football was viewed as containing a lot less drama. When a female player gets fouled, she would be 'up and ready to go again' making the game 'flow more'.

Cultural and economic discourses

In some cases, discourses were used that revolve around 'culture' or 'economy' to explain why women's football has a hard time gaining ground. An 'economic' discourse, used by men and women, was connected to the absence of sponsors and the little amount of funding. Consequently, women do not have the best facilities to train or play. An example was given by a female student who discussed the Arsenal women's team that can't play in the Arsenal stadium. Another aspect that was mentioned was that most of the female players have normal jobs as they don't get paid enough to rely solely on their income from football activities. A cultural discourse focused on the way males got more opportunities to play football from a young age onwards as structured in society's institutions and societal norms and values. A female student remarked: 'Boys do their sports, girl do their sports. So, it is kind of how you are brought up in education'.

Media commentary

Masculinity discourse

All respondents, irrespective of their gender or race, acknowledged that women's football gets less coverage than men's football and that only major international and cup final games are shown on television. When women's football is on television, there's hardly any advertising to promote the game and it's broadcast on more obscure channels. The dominant discourse here is that men's football is the norm in the media. A black-British female claimed that in general 'women aren't portrayed in the media as doing sport'. Male and female respondents also stated that the commentary in a female match was often less exciting and that commentators were less critical on mistakes made by female players and thus don't take women's football as serious. One black-British male described this as follows:

> It seems that sometimes commentators, they don't take the women's game as serious when they're commentating. So it's kind of 'aaah she made a mistake,' [...] It's not the same commentating, it's completely different.

This prioritization of men in the media was also witnessed by male and female students in the case of the Sky Sports commentator Andy Gray who made sexist remarks about a female linesman.[3]

Nearly, all groups agreed that women's football could and should get a lot more coverage and that this could increase its popularity. A few male respondents digressed from this by stating that female football just isn't a viable commodity and that more coverage won't change that. This tied in with the more widely accepted idea among respondents that football in the present day is first and foremost a money-making business which is promoted by the media and advertising.

Neutrality discourse

The vast majority of respondents claimed that commentators do not differentiate between players of different racial/ethnic backgrounds. In most groups, the argument was posited that commentators reflect on what happens on the pitch and that ethnicity isn't a focal point. As a white British woman noted: 'I think mainly during commentating it all focuses on individual players' performance, rather than where that player comes from'. In two groups, this seeming neutrality of commentators was explained by arguing that commentators would be prone to a backlash in the media if they made remarks about someone's race or ethnicity.

An oppositional discourse was identified and used to argue that the media do indeed stereotype players based on their ethnic or racial background. This discourse highlighted the fact the media would associate black players with physical qualities and white players with technical abilities. This claim was on some occasions followed by the argument that these kinds of observations do have some basis in reality, but are usually put forward as 'massive blanket statements', as one black participant notes.

Discussion: hegemonic discourses and contradictions

This segment shows to what extent discourses used by students to evaluate gender and racial/ethnic differences in football overlap with hegemonic media discourses. Results are also contextualized by comparing them with findings from earlier studies. As it is impossible to exhaust the whole set of data, the focus will be on hegemonic discourses found in the data including their contradictions.

Confirming the dominant

Regardless of gender or race, a majority of the students used a natural physicality discourse to evaluate black football players. In just a few cases where a possible explanation was given to account for this natural physique, respondents usually pointed to a perceived genetic advantage among black people. This discourse was almost never invoked when the students talked about white or Asian players. White players were more readily connected with positive mental capabilities, although this discourse was less prevalent. Positive capabilities ascribed to white players included a good tactical overview of the pitch, but also terms like teamwork and role model were used. These results are in line with the dominant media discourse whereby black athletes are represented as being naturally gifted athletes, while white athletes are more easily associated with mental and intellectual capabilities (Coakley 2009; Hylton 2009). The relative lack of British Asian players in the English Premier League and the national team was largely explained by reference to cultural inhibitions on the side of Asians. Students stated that Asians either don't play football as they're more invested in a game like cricket, or that they don't do sport at all as they have to attend to religious or educational activities.

Burdsey (2006) shows it is only in the British Asian press that serious coverage is produced, while the mainstream British press usually resorts to irrelevant or 'humourous' coverage that fails to seriously acknowledge the participation of British Asians in the game. Tactics like these produce the effect that British Asians in the game fall outside the scope of the white normative codes inherent in the coverage (Burdsey 2006). White normativity is often silently sustained and normalized through the social construction of whiteness, a set of discourses that produces a privileged and unmarked (i.e. being exempt from race) position from which one can view the world (Hylton 2009). British Asians deviate from this normative standpoint and are either stereotyped and viewed as the other or are completely exempt from the coverage.

A natural physicality discourse was more pronounced in the case of gender, where the majority of students use this discourse to explain the present structuring in football along gender lines. Students that used this discourse construct masculinity with concepts like having a killer mentality and physical presence. Here, an idea of femininity was constructed in the opposite sense and connected with terms pertaining to a maternal instinct and emotional fragility. This natural physicality discourse corresponds with the one practised inside the masculine domain of the sport media where femininity and masculinity are still being constructed along the lines of traditional gender values (Bruce 2013). Many male respondents also used discourses that are congruent with the hegemonic media discourse which constructs male football as the norm and imbues male events with dramatic narratives that acquire a near historical significance (Bruce 2013; Coakley 2009). The fact that football is already structured along gender lines – with a separation between men's football and women's football – might have contributed to the arguments presented by the respondents. Van Dijk has given an account of how social situations (or social contexts) can influence discourse (van Dijk 2009). Likewise, it is also argued that existing gendered structures of professional sport may influence the discourses about gender that media users draw on.

Alternative discourses and internal inconsistencies

The entertainment discourse was, however, also used in a non-hegemonic manner by a group of female students and a few (mostly black-British) male students. Some of these students enjoyed women's football or actually preferred it over men's football. Their approach to football is different than the hegemonic media discourse that aligns football with masculinity (Caudwell 2011). While some of them still believed that men are inherently stronger than women, those who opposed this also recognized the role the media play in constituting this difference by presenting stereotypical ideas about men and women.

Little research is available on how viewers (men and women) interpret women's sport on television, but a study conducted by Bruce (1998) on how women receive representations of US women's basketball does provide a useful comparison. Bruce reports that women took the coverage of the men's game as the norm to make comparisons with the coverage of the women's game (Bruce 1998). They acknowledged that the men's game was a higher valued commodity which in turn framed their expectations of the women's game (Bruce 1998). Students in the present study also argued that the commentary in the women's game is less exciting than it is in the men's game and that coverage of women's football is very different in this respect. Instances of sexualization and trivialization are also commented upon in other groups, coinciding with the discourses identified by Bruce (1998). Students argued that women are either portrayed as wives or mothers and in another group the incident with commentator Andy Gray is put forward as an example of sexism in the media. Students identified the discourses of trivialization and ambivalent representation of female athletes that textual analyses have found, but also show how these can be challenged (Cooky, Messner, and Hextrum 2013; Pressland 2012).

Receiving any form of pleasure from watching a women's football match requires a constant act of negotiation, as preferred meanings that are encoded as such by the media need to be read and reconstructed in an alternative way (Bruce 1998; Hall 1980). Even tuning in to a women's game requires effort as games aren't always announced beforehand or are broadcast on the more obscure channels (Bruce 1998). It's also worth noting that the students who adopt this discourse generally tend to watch much football and some of them played football themselves, as knowledge and experience are considered important parameters in the way viewers read a cultural text (Morley 1980, 1983). Discourses at the disposal of the students might also explain why it's mostly black males that used this specific discourse, because members of minority groups in general are more likely to read dominant texts against the grain (Bruce 1998). In one particular group, this explanation is further reinforced by oppositional readings that call out the media on racial stereotyping.

A couple of male students (with diverse ethnic backgrounds) acknowledged that women's football can be of a good standard and some resorted to the statement that gender doesn't matter. Women's football, it was argued, should receive more attention in the media. Although it might be interpreted as a positive view on the behalf of women's football, these students did eventually fall back on stereotypical views of men and women. Thus, statements such as 'gender doesn't matter' imply a negation of difference and at the same time conflict with the stereotypes used to explain differences between men and women. Such ostensible gender neutrality among males can instead be argued to be a form of gender-blindness (Bruce 2011). Furthermore, these explanations lay bare the inherent contradictory nature of discourses (Morley 1980).

Nonetheless, the much heard argument among women as well as men that women's football should receive more coverage to increase its popularity and the fact that some women as well as men already actively enjoy women's football or even prefer it above men's football, warrants further exploration (Kane 2013). Almost all students were well aware of the fact that sport is a major business and that the media play an integral part in creating or denying opportunities for athletes. While some of these students were thus able to articulate a more comprehensive account of the sport media by seeing how this business model could lead to specific and stereotypical approaches to, for example, women's football, others only acknowledged this point without any further reasoning as to what this actually implied.

An even greater incongruity exists between the hegemonic discourses used by students to evaluate race/ethnicity and the discourses used to evaluate the commentary. Those who were prone to stereotypical approaches to race and ethnicity generally argued that the football commentary is neutral on the topic of race. If pressed a bit further on the topic, some students did acknowledge stereotypes might happen once or twice. Such reasoning was sometimes accompanied with the argument that commentators merely reflect reality and state facts about players. The study by McCarthy, Jones, and Potrac (2003) identified this same ambivalence from the part of white respondents about the use of racial stereotypes in football commentary, stating that 'for the white respondents in this study, only a small discursive space existed between awareness of the black athletic stereotype and acceptance of that stereotype' (McCarthy, Jones, and Potrac 2003).

Skin colour is often deemed insignificant, a non-issue, in light of a player's (or team's) overall quality and skill. This particular account might be indicative of what has been termed 'colour-blind racism' (Bonilla-Silva and Dietrich 2011), an ideology that sees racism and racial stereotyping as something of the past and no longer an issue even though a great variety of studies proof otherwise. Colour-blind racism operates through the denial of the structural character of racism and thereby leaves unequal power relations, white normativity and the invisibility of whiteness unmarked and unspoken (Bonilla-Silva and Dietrich 2011; Hylton 2009). Colour-blind racism was also evident in the statements by respondents who claimed on the one hand that race or ethnicity has nothing to do with how players play while associating, on the other hand, black players with natural physicality and white players with mentality. Again, it shows the contradictory character of discourses that are being used which was also evident in the finding that some black and white students identified and opposed racial stereotypes that circulate in the media and that also persist in sport itself as expressed through trainers and scouts. These findings corroborate those of Cleland and Cashmore who report how this colour-blind ideology remains embedded in football authorities and how sometimes fans are very much aware of the persistent nature of racism in contemporary football (Cleland and Cashmore 2013).

Conclusion

Our findings show that ideas about the natural physicality of the black football player remain firmly embedded in the minds of sport media audiences. This discourse was often complemented with the discourse of colour-blindness which discards racial difference and the structural character of racism and instead champions individual qualities and entertainment. In reality, however, numerous studies show that racism, in whatever form it may take, is still firmly entrenched in British sport. The quest to tackle the myth of the natural black athlete, as was the goal of Carrington and McDonald over a decade ago, remains an ongoing battle (Carrington and McDonald 2001). There may be some reason for optimism though, as some respondents were aware of and opposed the racism that resides in the institutions of modern football. These findings might be indicative of a more conscious awareness among fans (Cleland and Cashmore 2013). Respondents were also equally aware that the sport media are a huge business and often called out the media on their exaggerations. It might prove a potent gateway to educate viewers on how (subtle) forms of racism and stereotyping maintain the status quo.

In the case of gender, more heterogeneous discourses were identified. A considerable portion of the respondents, most of them (though not all) women, presented a negotiated/oppositional reading of women's football which they considered a truer appropriation of the game. These alternative discourses also function as reminders that cultural texts don't exist in a vacuum, but that readings of these texts are interspersed by a variety of external factors (Morley 1980, 1983). A few female students that were actively involved in the women's game used their own personal experiences to provide a very different account of women's football than the one appropriated by the mass media. With the growing popularity of women's football, one might expect that such discourses become more prevalent.

Differences between black or white students were more difficult to single out, although black (male) students were in some instances more eager to draw on oppositional/negotiated readings regarding gender and race in football. However, it does illuminate one of the limitations of the study, it being the specific conceptualization of race. Labelling the students predominantly as either black or white on the basis of their own (brief and sometimes not too explicit) textual introduction, isn't entirely without its pitfalls. Most notably, this conceptualization may sidestep other forms of belonging such as those at the national or local level and proves problematic with the idea of mixed people. The use of these same categories in the topics and questions that were asked during the interviews may also have structured the way respondents use certain discourses although they were free to add their own viewpoints. We suggest, therefore, that future audience research aims to produce a fuller understanding of a participant's sense of belonging that includes various domains of social experience such as national and/or local belongings. This would require a vastly more complex approach in both the focus of the interviews as well as in the analysis of the data and presents the researcher with new and politically infused questions about groupings and racial hierarchies in and through (mediated) football.

Notes

1. The term 'physicality discourse' and terms like 'economic disocurse' or 'cultural disocurse' used later on in this section derive from Van Sterkenburg & Knoppers (2004).
2. The ages of five respondents are unknown, but all fall well within the aforementioned range.
3. Andy Gray is a former Sky Sports commentator who was fired in 2011 after he made derogatory, sexist remarks about a female linesman and towards his female co-presenter.

Acknowledgements

We appreciate the support we received from Brunel University and Croydon College for conducting the interviews, especially Dr. Laura Hills, Dr.Eileen Kennedy and Dr. Alison Mailtand. We also appreciate the support from UEFA as the study has been made possible as part of the UEFA Grant Scheme and has been presented to UEFA (Van Sterkenburg, 2013). Each year, the European Football Association UEFA awards several scholars worldwide to conduct independent research through its UEFA Grant Scheme.

Disclosure statement

No potential conflict of interest was reported by the authors.

References

Adams, C., M. Ashton, H. Lupton, and H. Pollack. 2014. "Sport is King: An Investigation into Local Media Coverage of Women's Sport in the UK East Midlands." *Journal of Gender Studies* 23 (4): 422–439.

Alabarces, P., A. Tomlinson, and C. Young. 2001. "Argentina versus England at the France '98 World Cup: Narratives of Nation and the Mythologizing of the Popular." *Media, Culture & Society* 36 (1): 547–566.

Billings, A. C., and H. L. Hundley. 2010. "Examining Identity in Sports Media." In *Examining Identity in Sports Media*, edited by A. C. Billings and H. L. Hundley, 1–16. Thousand Oaks, CA: Sage.

Boeije, H. 2010. *Analysis in Qualitative Research*. London: Sage.

Bonilla-Silva, E., and D. Dietrich. 2011. "The Sweet Enchantment of Color-blind Racism in Obamerica." *The ANNALS of the American Academy of Political and Social Science* 634 (1): 190–206.

Bruce, T. 1998. "Audience Frustration and Pleasure: Women Viewers Confront Televised Women's Basketball." *Journal of Sport and Social Issues* 22 (4): 373–397.

Bruce, T. 2011. "Shifting the Boundaries: Sportswomen in the Media." In *Communication on the Edge: Proceedings of the 2011 Australia and New Zealand Communication Association Conference*, edited by A. Henderson, 1–16. Hamilton: Australian and New Zealand Communication Association.

Bruce, T. 2013. "Reflections on Communication and Sport: On Women and Femininities." *Communication and Sport* 1 (1–2): 125–137.

De Bruycker, G. 2012. "Zwarte Parels: Een inhoudsanalyse naar het gebruik van raciale stereotypen in Belgische sportkranten [Black Pearls: A Content Analysis regarding the Use of Racial Stereotypes in Belgian Sport Newspapers]." PhD diss., University of Ghent.

Burdsey, D. 2006. "No Ball Games Allowed? A Socio-historical Examination of the Development and Social Significance of British Asian Football Clubs." *Journal of Ethnic and Migration Studies* 32 (3): 477–496.

Carrington, B. 2011. "'What I Said Was Racist – But I'm Not a Racist': Anti-racism and the White Sports/Media Complex." In *Sport and Challenges to Racism*, edited by J. Long and K. Spracklen, 83–99. Basingstoke: Palgrave Macmillan.

Carrington, B., and I. McDonald. 2001. "Introduction: 'Race', Sport and British Society." In *"Race", Sport, and British Society*, edited by B. Carrington and I. McDonald, 1–26. London: Routledge.

Caudwell, J. 2011. "Reviewing UK Football Cultures: Continuing with Gender Analyses." *Soccer & Society* 12 (3): 323–329.

Cleland, J., and E. Cashmore. 2013. "Fans, Racism and British Football in the Twenty-first Century: The Existence of a 'Colour-blind' Ideology." *Journal of Ethnic and Migration Studies* 40 (4): 638–654.

Coakley, J. 2009. *Sports in Society: Issues and Controversies*. Boston, MA: McGraw-Hill.

Conlan, T. 2012. "Olympics and Euro 2012 Triumph over Downton and X Factor to Win TV Gold." *The Guardian* December 12, 16.

Cooky, C., M. A. Messner, and R. H. Hextrum. 2013. "Women Play Sport, but Not on TV: A Longitudinal Study of Televised News Media." *Communication & Sport* 1 (3): 203–230.

van Dijk, T. A. 2009. *Society and Discourse: How Social Contexts Influence Text and Talk*. Cambridge: Cambridge University Press.

Gibson, O. 2013. "Premier League Still 'Quintessentially English', Says Richard Scudamore." *The Guardian*, November 19. Accessed January 24, 2014. www.theguardian.com/football/2013/nov/19/premier-league-english-richard-scudamore

Gunaratnam, Y. 2003. *Researching 'Race' and Ethnicity: Methods, Knowledge and Power*. London: Sage.

Hall, S. (1980) 2005. "Encoding/Decoding." In *Culture, Media, Language: Working Papers in Cultural Studies 1972–79*, edited by S. Hall, D. Hobson, A. Lowe, and P. Willis, 117–127. Reprint, London: Routledge.

Hall, S. 1995. "The West and the Rest: Discourse and Power." In *Formations of Modernity*, edited by S. Hall and B. Gieben, 275–332. Cambridge: Blackwell.

Hall, S. 1997. "The Spectacle of the 'Other'." In *Representation: Cultural Representations and Signifying Practices*, edited by S. Hall, 223–290. London: Sage.

Hall, S. 2011. "The Whites of Their Eyes: Racist Ideologies and the Media." In *Gender, Race, and Class in Media: A Critical Reader*, edited by G. Dines and J. M. Humez, 81–84. Thousand Oaks, CA: Sage.

Harrison, C. K., S. M. Lawrence, and S. J. Bukstein. 2011. "White College Students' Explanations of White (and Black) Athletic Performance: A Qualitative Investigation of White College Students." *Sociology of Sport Journal* 28 (3): 347–361.

Hermes, J. 2005. "Burnt Orange: Television, Football, and the Representation of Ethnicity." *Television & New Media* 6: 49–69.

Hylton, K. 2009. *'Race' and Sport: Critical Race Theory*. Abingdon: Routledge.

Kane, M. J. 2013. "The Better Sportswomen Get, the More the Media Ignore Them." *Communication & Sport*,1–6. Advance Online Publication. doi:10.1177/2167479513484579.

Kane, M. J., N. M. LaVoi, and J. S. Fink. 2013. "Exploring Elite Female Athletes' Interpretations of Sport Media Images: A Window into the Construction of Social Identity and 'Selling Sex' in Women's Sports." *Communication & Sport* 1 (3): 269–298.

Knoppers, A., and A. Elling. 2001. *Gender, Etniciteit en de sportmedia: productieprocessen en publieksinterpretaties* [Gender, Ethnicity and the Sportmedia: Production Processes and Public Interpretations]. Arnhem: NOC*NSF Breedtesport.

Lechner, F. J. 2007. "Imagined Communities in the Global Game: Soccer and Development of Dutch National Identity." *Global Networks* 7 (2): 215–229.

Ličen, S., and A. C. Billings. 2013. "Cheering for 'Our' Champs by Watching Sexy Female Throwers: Representation of Nationality and Gender in Slovenian 2008 Summer Olympic Television Coverage." *European Journal of Communication* 28 (4): 379–396.

Lines, G. 2000. "Media Sport Audiences – Young People and the Summer of Sport '96: Revisiting Frameworks for Analysis." *Media, Culture and Society* 22 (5): 669–680.

McCarthy, D., R. L. Jones, and P. Potrac. 2003. "Constructing Images and Interpreting Realities: The Case of the Black Soccer Player on Television." *International Review for the Sociology of Sport* 38 (2): 217–238.

Morley, D. (1980) 2005. "Texts, Readers, Subjects." In *Culture, Media, Language: Working Papers in Cultural Studies 1972–79*, edited by S. Hall, D. Hobson, A. Lowe, and P. Willis, 154–165. Reprint London: Routledge.

Morley, D. 1983. "Cultural Transformations: The Politics of Resistance." In *Language, Image, Media*, edited by H. H. David and P. Walton, 104–117. Oxford: Basil Blackwell.

Morning, A. 2009. "Toward a Sociology of Racial Conceptualization for the 21st Century." *Social Forces* 87: 1167–1192.

Peeters, R. 2013. "I don't see different colors, different races. I just see eleven people on a pitch". *How British students assign meaning to race/ethnicity and gender in mediated sports*. MA Thesis, Utrecht University, The Netherlands.

Pfister, G. 2010. "Women in Sport – Gender Relations and Future Perspectives." *Sport in Society* 13 (2): 234–248.

Pressland, A. 2012. "'Still Struggling after All These Years?' the Representation of Sportswomen in Middle-brow British Newspapers 2008–2009." PhD diss., University of York.

Schönwälder, K. 2010. "Beyond the Race Relations Model: Old Patterns and New Trends in Britain." In *National Paradigms in Migration Research*, edited by D. Thränhardt and M. Bommes, 109–126. Osnabrück: V&R Unipress GmbH.

Strauss, A., and J. Corbin. 1998. *Basics of Qualitative Research: Techniques and Procedures for Developing Grounded Theory*. Thousand Oaks, CA: Sage.

Van Sterkenburg, J. 2013. *Race/ethnicity, gender and audience receptions of football on television in the Netherlands and England.* A research project financially supported by the UEFA Grant Scheme, for internal use UEFA. Nyon: UEFA.

Van Sterkenburg, J., & Knoppers, A. 2004. Dominant discourses about race/ethnicity and gender in sport practice and performance. *International Review for the Sociology of Sport*, 39, 301–321.

Women's Sport and Fitness Foundation. 2012. *Football Factsheet.* London: Women's Sport and Fitness Foundation.

FIFA, the video game: a major vehicle for soccer's popularization in the United States

Andrei S. Markovits and Adam I. Green

ABSTRACT

Soccer in the United States is undergoing major changes. The game's growth on the fields of the country's suburbs and among its middle class has been nothing short of sensational. Major events such as the World Cup – both Men's and Women's – have gained the sport millions of followers. In addition, a growing number of Americans has come to incorporate Europe's most prestigious tournaments and prominent leagues into its daily sports consumption. Our study analyses how a particular venue – EA Sports' *FIFA* video game series – has contributed to this fascinating ongoing development. While at this temporal stage, soccer's popularity in following (in notable contrast to playing) continues to lag behind that of America's 'Big Four' of football, baseball, hockey and basketball, recent events, aided by the burgeoning proliferation of *FIFA* the video game, may catapult soccer's cultural presence into the Big Four's in coming years.

Introduction: the US soccer fan yesterday and today

The 2014 Men's World Cup was not the first time that Americans had gotten behind their team for the world's biggest soccer tournament and largest sporting event. In 1994, the United States hosted the Men's World Cup for the first time in the tournament's history and the nation did not disappoint on any count: with an average attendance of 69,000 per match, the World Cup in the United States remains to this day far and away the best attended such tournament among the 20 held thus far, with attendance levels that are quite unlikely ever to be surpassed (Carswell 2010). The US team qualified for the Round of 16 in that tournament surely benefitting from playing on home ground (which has proven to be a major supporter for many, though not all, hosts). In the subsequent World Cups, the United States fared poorly in France in 1998, reached the quarterfinals in Japan/South Korea in 2002 (which to date is still the furthest the United States has progressed in this tournament other than reaching the semifinals of the first World Cup in Uruguay in 1930), was once again unsuccessful in Germany in 2006 and acquitted itself solidly in South Africa in 2010. With the United States having qualified for every World Cup since 1990, and with the team steadily improving in its overall presence on the global soccer scene, there developed an unmistakable growth in interest among the larger American public well beyond the soccer community in the consumption of this quadrennial event if not necessarily in the following of soccer on a quotidian basis.

We would be remiss not to mention the growth of women's soccer as a steady contribution to the game's cultural presence (i.e. soccer's existence in the lexicon of 'sports talk' among Americans, as well as soccer players or teams capturing American sports fans in a way that the American Big Four sports teams have) in contemporary America. But here, too, it was almost exclusively the eight Women's World Cup tournaments that proved the contributors to soccer's growing popularity in the United States, with Women's World Cup soccer having been on an upward swing since the early 1990s, especially due to the U.S.W.N.T.'s World Cup-winning performance in the 1999 World Cup, which was hosted by the United States. In fact, the 1999 World Cup final, pitting the US vs. China, drew a robust 90,185 fans, still the most ever in the history of and sport to attend a women's event (Markovits 2015) To prove this hypothesis, one must look no further than the contrast of television ratings between Women's World Cup games and National Women's Soccer League (NWSL) games. The most recent US-Japan Women's World Cup Final held in July 2015 in Vancouver, British Columbia (which the US won by the score of 5–2) averaged a remarkable 25.4 million viewers in the United States, the second-most viewers in the US for a soccer game in history (Ourand 2015), trailing only the 2014 U.S.M.N.T.'s bout with the Portuguese national team. And it wasn't even just the Women's World Cup final that drew fans in the United States to their television sets. The U.S.W.N.T.'s first match of the 2015 tournament, vs. Australia, drew 3.3 million American viewers, more than any other women's soccer game in history up to that point (O'Connell 2015). Meanwhile, women's professional soccer in the US has seen mostly hardships; the first women's professional soccer league, the Women's United Soccer Association, was founded in 2000 and subsequently folded in 2003 (Hays 2003). When the continental governing body for Association Football in North America, known as CONCACAF (Confederation of North, Central American and Caribbean Association Football)attempted to offer a revival of WUSA in 2007 with Women's Professional Soccer, it again failed, with WPS folding in 2012 (Bell 2012). There exists a women's professional soccer league at the time of this writing in early 2016, called the NWSL, but it has virtually zero influence on the American public, as most of its matches are not even televised (but rather streamed via YouTube or the individual team sites), and the select few that are (only 10 matches of the 288 played during the 2015 season were televised) rate very poorly. Last September, the two NWSL semifinal matches (which were broadcast on the middling cable network Fox Sports 1) each registered a 0.0 TV rating among viewers ages 18–49. The two matches combined drew an abysmal 76,000 viewers for both (by comparison, the US Open Men's Tennis final between Novak Djokovic and Roger Federer drew 3.15 million viewers, and even that number paled in comparison to that afternoon's Sunday NFL games). Fan attendance at these women's professional soccer matches hasn't been much better, with the aforementioned two semifinal matches combining for just 8,000+ fans. With no television contract beyond the 2016 season, there are questions as to just how long the NWSL can survive (Kassouf 2015).

Thus, one could well characterize the World Cups'– both men's and women's – cultural presence in daily American life as akin to that of the Olympics – a big event followed by millions every four years with much less interest for the sports' regular seasons. After all, few Americans follow track and field events or target shooting on a daily basis. Even such marquee disciplines as swimming in the summer Olympics and figure skating as well as Alpine skiing in its winter variant fail to constitute a level of quotidian following among the American public that approaches anything comparable to that garnered by the North American 'Big Four' of baseball, football, basketball and hockey. Thus, one could safely characterize the World Cup (both men's and women's) as an 'olympianizing' agent for the sport's quadrennial popularity among the larger viewing public in the United States (Markovits 2015; Markovits and Hellerman 2003).

However, we argue in this study that Americans came to experience the World Cup 2014 in Brazil differently from any of its predecessors (DiLorenzo 2013). On 26 June 2014, at the Arena Amazonia Manaus in Manaus, Brazil, the United States Men's National Soccer team found itself at a crucial juncture in terms of its fate at the World Cup tournament (FIFA. com 2014). Having already picked up three points with a win over Ghana a few days prior, the Americans were looking to get themselves another win and inch a little bit closer to advancing to the elimination round. Their opponents that day were a Portuguese national team that featured some of the greatest players in the world. Portugal was fresh off a humiliating 4–0 loss to Germany (FIFA.com 2014) and was desperate to get a win and earn itself a position in the elimination bracket.

Just 4 minutes and 51 seconds into the match against Portugal, the US committed a defensive blunder that provided Portugal with a golden opportunity that it would not waste. Winger Nani, who played his club soccer that year with Manchester United, put in a goal to give Portugal a 1–0 lead (Clare 2014; FIFA.com 2014). It was at this point that the major difference between today's US soccer consumption and the way Americans followed previous World Cups emerged unmistakably. Even as recently as in the 2010 tournament in South Africa, following a deflating goal the like of Nani's in the 2014 tournament, the casual American viewer would have had to look up Nani on Twitter or Facebook. In the 2006 and 2002 tournaments, probably only soccer's most committed followers in the United States would have checked out Nani on the Internet to find out more information about the early goal scorer: who he was, what team he played for or how he performed for his club team that season, information that even then was basic knowledge to the small circle of the game's most avid followers. Our point quite simply is that in all tournaments prior to the one in 2014, we can surmise with relative certainty that most Americans watching World Cup matches would have had no idea who such a Manchester United star from Portugal was (Ratto 2013). Indeed, Manchester United would not have had anywhere close to the cultural presence then that it gained in the course of the past few years. But today, things are very different. In 2014, after Nani scored, many Americans took to Twitter or Facebook with their frustrations, a typical activity for Americans in the twenty-first century. 'Nani has just matched his goal tally for Manchester United last season', tweeted sportswriter and Oklahoma native Brian Phillips. 'Americans certainly wish they could play with this version of Nani on FIFA rather than the Manchester United version', said Major League Soccer (MLS) analyst (and Houston, Texas resident) Eddie Robinson (Clare 2014). Even US celebrities chimed in on social media. 'What A Game!! #USAvsPOR' tweeted world famous American boxer Mike Tyson (Klein 2014). These tweets proved that in 2014 the discourse about soccer in the United States was different from any previous time both in terms of quantity and quality: for the first time, millions of Americans participated in the public discussion revealing a fine degree of knowledge and awareness. In terms of quantity, tens of millions of tweets were sent out from within the borders of the United States during the US-Portugal match, exponentially more Twitter activity than had ever been seen for a soccer match before (Clare 2014). In terms of quality, in the 2014 iteration of the tournament, Americans had known who Nani was before Portugal had even stepped onto the field that day. They had been following his inconsistent performance with Manchester United all season. In 2014, Nani was no stranger to the large American audience fully conversant with soccer (Clare 2014). Many factors contribute to this change of discourse. One factor, which we argue may well be the most influential, is the soaring rise of the *FIFA* video game series in recent years.

In this study, we trace the growth of soccer's cultural presence in the United States in the course of the past 10–12 years. We argue that one among many decisive factors in soccer's massive consumptive proliferation in the United States has been the *FIFA* video game series. What makes this particular video game's cultural power so interesting in the North American case is that precisely the game that it depicts has lacked any significant cultural presence for well over one century in the United States and Canada. Thus, unlike in Europe or Latin America, for example, where *FIFA*, the video game, reinforces extant tropes in which soccer has been the culturally dominant sport for more than one hundred years, and unlike the *Madden* video game series, which assumes *FIFA*'s exact counterpart in the United States in that it replicates and reinforces a historically hegemonic cultural mainstay in the form of American football, *FIFA* in the United States of America (as well as Canada which, however, will not comprise the subject of our research) performs a culturally pioneering function that goes against type. Thus, a video game – not reality – furnishes a new cultural vehicle that creates a novel lived experience which, in turn, has massively contributed to the changed perception of the very real social and cultural construct of 'soccer' in the United States. It is precisely for this reason that this video game's study is so interesting (Markovits and Hellerman 2003).

Coming to America: the origins of soccer's explosion in the US

Americans were first afforded the opportunity to see Nani and his Manchester United teammates live two years ago, after NBC executives made a decision drastically that would alter the framework of the US sports viewing culture. In 2012, NBC signed a contract to air games of the English Premier League (arguably the most competitive of the Big Five European soccer leagues featuring the largest bundle of teams with a global following) beginning in the 2013–2014 season. The contract initially granted NBC the rights to just six Premier League games per week, but by 2014–2015, its network had expanded the coverage to include up to 10 games per week (Tannenwald 2015). By all accounts, NBC made this move to give soccer such an unprecedented forum in the United States solely on account of wanting to appeal to a younger audience (Kondolojy 2015). Arriving at the decision to feature men's professional soccer of the highest quality made sense for NBC, as among 12–24-year-old American males, men's pro soccer had become the second most popular sport behind only the NFL. According to ESPN.com, among Americans aged 12–24, 24.1% identify NFL football as their favorite sport, and 13.7% accorded professional soccer this position (followed by the NBA at 13.1%, NCAA Football at 8.9%, MLB at 8.1%, NCAA Basketball at 4.8%, and NHL Hockey at 4.3%). Among Hispanics, pro-soccer is in the lead, with a whopping 25.8% responding that the Beautiful Game is their favorite (with NFL in second at 17.9%, followed by MLB at 10.2%, NBA at 9.2%, NCAA Football at 3.6%, NCAA Basketball at 3.1%, and Volleyball at 2.4%). According to the same poll, the percentage of Americans aged 12 or higher, who classify themselves as avid soccer fans, has risen from 2.8% in 2000 to 9.1% in 2012.

In addition, the aforementioned poll (as well as others) indicated that many soccer players, including Cristiano Ronaldo, David Beckham and Lionel Messi were on a list of the most popular athletes in America, even ranking ahead of superstars like the NBA's Dwyane Wade (Badenhausen 2014; DiLorenzo 2013; Luker 2012). This would have seemed far-fetched just 10 years ago and absolutely unfathomable prior to that.

NBC and NBC Sports Network averaged 479,000 viewers per match during the 2014–2015 season, up an incredible 118% from 2012–2013 season, when the Premier League aired on ESPN and FOX, and an increase of 22% from the 2013–2014 season, NBC's debut year with its broadcasting rights (Badenhausen 2014; Gallup 1994; Kondolojy 2015). Supporting this trend, leading EPL clubs such as Arsenal, Liverpool, Manchester United, Tottenham Hotspur and Manchester City have made their summer appearances in North America a virtual must in their annual schedule. Ditto for Real Madrid and its archrival Barcelona, as well as Italian giants Inter Milan, AC Milan, Fiorentina and AS Roma; and, of course, Germany's perennial behemoth Bayern Munich (Badenhausen 2014; Luker 2012). So how did this soccer phenomenon arise in America? There are many contributing factors – some of which have been discussed elsewhere by Markovits as well as other students of the game – but one that has undeniably been very significant is the rise in popularity of the *FIFA* video game series in America.

The first *FIFA* game was released on 15 July 1993 and was notable for being the first video game to have an official licence from FIFA (the Federation International de Football Association, the world governing body of soccer) (Gallup 1994). It was originally called 'International Soccer', so EA could sell the game successfully in Europe. An EA official later conceded that at the time, EA assumed that the company would have no success selling the game in America (Good 2013). Actually, *FIFA '93* became an instant commercial success ranked by Maverick Magazine as the 7th best Mega CD game of all time, though many sales contributing to this ranking must have come well after the game's release due to *FIFA* fans' search for the novelty of the first ever *FIFA* game (Gallup 1994; Good 2013). EA Sports' marketing of the *FIFA* franchise has been nothing short of spectacular, clearly constituting a decisive factor among the many reasons for *FIFA*'s consistent growth almost every year following the game's debut in 1993. There have manifestly been visible improvements in game play with every new release; every single club as well as national team (with a few exceptions due to licencing constraints) – no matter how obscure and seemingly unimportant – has come to be featured, and the graphics are so good that one game reviewer was quoted as saying that *FIFA '15* 'has the greatest presentation in sports game history' (Butt 2015; Meda 2014). 'I'm not a big sports fan, but I love FIFA: it has probably the best graphics of any sports game I've ever played', says Michael Calvas, a University of Michigan senior. However, EA Sports' most powerful marketing technique may have been born from a 21-year-old Japanese cartoonist who did not have much money or experience with video games, but possessed a profound love of sports and a dream.

The *Captain Tsusaba* effect: linking aspects of popular culture

Yoichi Takahashi was born on 28 July 1960, in a small municipality of Tokyo Prefecture called Katsushika. As a boy, Takahashi loved two things: playing baseball in the park with his schoolmates and creating cartoons. Like most young boys, as Takahashi grew up, he began to realize that becoming a professional baseball player was not likely to be his future.

Then, while watching the 1978 FIFA Men's World Cup in Argentina on television during his high school years, Takahashi developed an interest in soccer. He conducted some research on the sport and found out that in Europe, soccer was much more popular than baseball. Takahashi's research also led him to conclude – quite correctly – that soccer, not baseball, was the world's most popular sport (Takahashi 2011). Takahashi had dabbled in base-ball-themed manga before his burgeoning interest in soccer, but other, more established manga artists had already utilized the baseball theme quite impressively. Thus, the aspiring manga artist from Katsushika decided that he would try his hand at soccer-themed cartoons instead (Takahashi 2011). In 1981, he created *Captain Tsusaba*, a story about an 11-year-old elementary school student named Tsusaba Ozora who loves the game of soccer and dreams of one day playing for Japan in the World Cup. Originally published in a magazine, the series was an instant hit, and by 1983 TV Tokyo, one of the major television channels in the country, aired *Captain Tsusaba*. The series exploded from there, reaching television sets not only across Asia, but also South America, Europe and the Middle East. In the course of the 1990s, *Captain Tsusaba* mutated into one of the most watched television programmes in the world, competing with other animation powerhouses such as the popular *Dragonball Z* franchise, which was also originally created in Japan. In 2013, Takahashi's hometown of Katsushika erected a statue of Tsusaba Ozora (Meda 2014).

Captain Tsusaba became the worldwide inspiration for video games, television pro-grammes and cartoons. A poll conducted by TV Asahi in 2005 named it the 41st greatest anime series of all time (Meda 2014) *Captain Tsusaba* assumed such popularity in Japan that it paved the way for the creation of the first ever Japanese professional soccer league in 1992 (known as the J-League) (Bashour 2004). Indeed, Takahashi's video game mutated soccer from a marginal sport in Japan to becoming one of its most popular actually rivaling Takahashi's youthful passion of baseball on many dimensions as the country's most beloved team sport (Meda 2014; Takahashi 2011). If not for *Captain Tsusaba* taking Japan (and the whole world, for that matter) by storm in the 1980s and 1990s, soccer may never have had the kind of cultural footprint in Japan, South Korea or many other countries where children growing up sat at their televisions and watched Tsusaba Ozoro's adventures, that it does today (Meda 2014). In fact, prominent soccer players such as Hidetoshi Nakata, Alessandro Del Piero, Fernando Torres, Zinedine Zidane, Lionel Messi, Alexis Sanchez and Andres Iniesta (among whom only one player, Nakata, hails from Japan, proving the show's global popularity and presence) all credit *Captain Tsusaba* with inspiring them to pursue professional soccer as a career (Northcroft 2006). In 1998, Japan qualified for its first ever Men's World Cup and in 2002 it co-hosted the world's biggest soccer tournament with South Korea featuring the World Cup final between Brazil and Germany in Yokohama. Neither of these things seemed very likely prior to *Captain Tsusaba*'s emergence (Meda 2014). And the legendary show's influence has not abated: kids currently growing up in Japan see soccer not only as their favourite sport, but also as a national pastime (Meda 2014). For all he's done to inspire Japan's youth, maybe a statue in his small hometown isn't enough to properly honour Yoichi Takahashi.

In addition, quite ironically and certainly unintentionally, *Captain Tsusaba* also changed the soccer landscape in America forever. The show's emergence furnished a small contri-bution to a series of many that were to trigger an avalanche of events that created soccer's contemporary popularity in the United States and its expanding presence in the American media (Kessler 2014; Meda 2014; Takahashi 2011). In one of the later episodes of the show airing in the late 1990s, Tsusaba signs a contract with a fictional version of Spain's FC Barcelona and meets a fictional version of one of its great stars, the Brazilian midfielder Rivaldo, without any doubt among the best-known soccer players in the world at that time. (Meda 2014) Due to this twist in the storyline, the fans of the show, which by now included people from all across the globe,[1] developed a newfound interest in following European soccer. Kids saw their favourite player and TV character in a Barcelona uniform, so they started watching the guys in the real Barcelona uniforms (Meda 2014). EA Sports, according to a 2014 interview with former EA CEO Larry Probst,[2] noticed this phenomenon and thought it could apply the principle to its game. (Meda 2014; Probst 2015). Starting in 1998, the year the Men's World Cup was held in France, EA began using different cover athletes for different regions of the world (for example, David Beckham was on the cover in the UK in 1998), putting local male professional players on the game's cover for each region (in the earlier editions of the game, EA used the same cover athlete for every region) (Meda 2014; Probst 2015). EA's strategy worked beautifully: *FIFA '99* became the bestselling video game in the UK that year and sales all across Europe skyrocketed (Meda 2014). In the 2000s, EA began using American born players as cover athletes for games sold in the US. Among the notable Americans used for this purpose were Eddie Pope in 2000, Ben Olsen in 2001, Landon Donovan in 2003, Freddy Adu in 2006 and Clint Dempsey in 2015 (Meda 2014). Although there is no way to know exactly how much the presence of *Captain Tsusaba* (and resulting use of American *FIFA* cover athletes) affected American gamers' usage of American players and MLS teams, we do know that *FIFA*'s sales numbers in the US experienced a drastic increase following the appearance of these country-specific cover athletes (Trefis 2014), as did the usage of MLS teams among *FIFA* video gamers (Luker 2014). With all this evidence, it certainly seems as if at least a moderately strong link of causation can be implied here, if never fully confirmed.

Although it is very unlikely that the appearance of MLS players on the cover of *FIFA '15* leads to gamers (even American gamers) developing the same kind of affective relationship and positive identification with MLS players and teams as they do with European players and teams, the utilization of American born *FIFA* cover athletes has clearly coincided with the rise in MLS' popularity: according to a December 2014 Harris Poll, 6% of Americans chose men's professional soccer as their favourite sport, a percentage which surpassed mainstays of American sports such as professional ice hockey and men's college basketball (Lintner 2015). And *FIFA* gamers are using MLS teams more often than ever; a Richard Luker study estimates that there was a 112% increase in MLS clubs used from *FIFA '14* to *FIFA '15* (Luker 2014). EA even staged a launch party for *FIFA '15* during which it featured a video game tournament in its California headquarters. The tournament's participants were only allowed to use MLS clubs in the tournament and the 'MLS Next' logo, which embodied the MLS rebranding initiative for the coming year, appeared on the screen after every play. This is a marketing strategy which has been proven successful for the following reason: placing an advertisement on the screen of a sports video game (given that the brand being advertised actually exists in the associated sport league thus lending authenticity to the sport video game) causes gamers' cognitive, affective and conative awareness of the advertised brand to increase by 229%, 2.7% and 9.6%, respectively (Cianfrone 2008; Meda 2014). Starting in 2012, EA also began to use popular American celebrities and athletes such as the rapper Snoop Dogg and the two-time NBA MVP Steve Nash to promote the *FIFA* product (Kessler 2014; Meda 2014). EA's strategy of reaching out to people beyond the evident soccer community and the game's core consumers has resulted in even more additions to the following of both the *FIFA* video game and professional soccer in the United States (Meda 2014). Between these types of initiatives and the inclusion of MLS athletes on the cover of *FIFA* games (Clint Dempsey is an MLS player, and more MLS players are expected to be used as cover athletes in the coming years), this may only be the beginning of the burgeoning proliferation of soccer players in the general media landscape of the United States. This attests to two things: soccer's growing acceptance in America's crowded cultural 'sports space'[3] and MLS' snowballing effect on the game's American presence (Meda 2014).

'It's in the game' (or is it?): an in-depth analysis of video game users and their narrative

It could have just been the musings of a technologically challenged older generation, but when video gaming began to become a staple of everyday life, the media, parents, politicians and even academics denounced video games as 'leading to a generation of anti-social, overweight, unhealthy, and aggressive "mouse-potatoes"' (Crawford and Gosling 2009). However, when the research was conducted, there was little direct evidence to suggest that video games led to decreased sports participation, higher aggression levels, or lower sociability (even in the case of the most violent video games). But the academic research hasn't stopped there. Instead, the question that emerges is one regarding the narrative effects of playing video games (and in our case, we will focus on sports video game) on the individual; how, if at all, does playing video games influence a person's 'narrative', both in a social context and in regard to developing interests?

According to some sociologists, a 'narrative identity' is a person's 'storied self', comprised of internal dialogue from the individual, stories told by others, and other, wider social and cultural narratives. Any form of media – including books, television shows, 'shooter' video games, etc. – affects a person's individual narrative. What is unique about sports video games, however, is how they are used as social narratives and have effects on people outside of their time playing the game (Conway 2010; Crawford and Gosling 2009). Much of this is due to the uncanny, almost perfectly life-like, realism present in sports video games in particular; not only are the graphics of today's games so good that the caricatures of the players look like mirror images of the real athletes, but the sports video games provide gamers with a cornucopia of information about the players, clubs, managers, histories, stadiums and more. Also, unlike books, movies and other forms of media, video games are interactive and simulation based, which expands the boundaries of participation and spectatorship of sports: in particular, gamers' increased exposure to the information about their simulated sport of choice ignites a more passionate fandom within those gamers, as they acquire knowledge about the sport and subsequently find an interest in watching the games in order to use that knowledge (Crawford and Gosling 2009, 2011; Conway 2010). Also contributing to the realism of the video game is that frequently sports video games are played in front of an audience (consisting of friends and/or family members gathered around the game room to watch), just as real sporting events are. The presence of an audience then makes the gamers feel a heightened intensity towards the game, and subsequently, the games carry a higher social relevance, as more social pride is on the line: lose and you may get made fun of for weeks. This intense social gravity that exists between true gamers constitutes what makes the sports video game so socially influential, and in turn can lead to that sport encompassing the gamer's entire life (Crawford and Gosling 2009). In other words, if someone is this consumed by *FIFA*, soccer will then likely find its way into other parts of this person's life (Crawford and Gosling 2011). Why not watch the real Liverpool vs. Arsenal match that you've played out in simulation so many times before?

There is an important distinction to be made when classifying how certain people internalize their experience playing a video game into their personal narrative. That distinction is the one between a 'player' and a 'gamer' (Grooten and Kowert 2015). According to some sociologists, a player is defined as 'someone who interacts with a game while the game interacts with them'. In other words, someone is a player the moment they first insert the video game disc into their console. A player does not carry his or her social identity with the game. A loss in front of many people gives a player no angst; that loss will have no lasting social effect on a player. A gamer, by contrast, is 'someone with an identity defined in relation to dominant discourses about who plays games, the deployment of social capital, the context in which players find themselves, and who are the subjects of game texts' (social capital in this case is the ability of an individual to talk about the game in a social context) (Grooten and Kowert 2015). Gamers carry a large portion of their social identity in how they perform in the game, and the game itself has a large influence on their inclusion in social clubs and their interpersonal identity as well. In the later part of our study, when we will refer to certain interviews and poll statistics regarding *FIFA*'s popularity among its users, we will recall the very important distinction between 'players' and 'gamers' to draw a clear line between the resulting interest in and involvement with professional soccer experienced by *FIFA* gamers vs. *FIFA* players.

Some other sociologists disagree with the just-presented interpretation regarding the relationship of sports video games to the personal narrative. Critics of the narratological view counter that this interpretation focuses only on the game itself in a vacuum, and neglects that any individual's brain has a tendency to take experiences from the video game and just add it to the extremely complex personal narrative. Also, some critics contend that the aforementioned view does not account for the fact that the game's social consequences vary in different situations. This argument can also be used to counter the importance of the audience: since the narrative really comes to life in the individual's head, what the audience sees does not necessarily matter, as it is not always what the person playing the game sees (Crawford and Gosling 2011). The many differing views in the relevant scholarship on this topic constitute an interesting amalgam as to how video games truly interact with the personal narrative, but it is clear that as video gaming becomes ever more popular, we will continue to see higher levels of interaction like we have never seen before (Cianfrone, Zhang, and Jae Ko 2011).

'I just can't turn it off': why everyone loves *FIFA*, and video games in general

The *FIFA* game series has enjoyed immense success among its users. It is said to be one of the highest quality sports video games on the market, with many consumers citing its crisp graphics and very realistic gameplay as the game's major attractions. In 2014, *FIFA* scored 87–90.5 out of 100 points from game critics, becoming the highest rated sports video game by US gaming experts (in contrast *Madden* scored between 75 and 85 points, *NHL* 82–88 points and *NBA 2 k* 82–90 points) (Meda 2014). According to one gamer blog, the game features 'honed games, possessing both the simplistic play like shoot or pass, to the more advance through balls, finesse shot, skill moves and many more … I just can't seem to turn it off' (Butt 2015). Stephen Short, a University of Michigan senior, agrees: 'The game has ridiculous graphics and game play: by far the best I've ever seen'. The blog also cites the advantages *FIFA* gains from having every club from every league across the world available for play.[4] This, of course, offers an immensely rare and also welcomed opportunity for fans of even the most remote and least known clubs to play with their favourite team. *FIFA* also updates its squads throughout each year to account for injuries and trades among different clubs and even among different leagues (Weber 2011). In addition to great game-play, the popularity of *FIFA* in the US could also be due to its being different from American kids' daily sports fare. One sports gaming forum suggests that since American youngsters for so long played the traditional sports games representing the Big Four (*Madden, NBA 2 k*, etc.), some might welcome the opportunity to try something different. University of Michigan junior Joe Krieger agrees: he 'followed mostly baseball and football growing up, but started playing *FIFA* in 9th grade because I wanted to try something new, I guess'. Along with (or independent of) motives such as aesthetically pleasing game-play and curiosity, there is also a strong social pressure on children in particular to play the video games that their friends or elders play. In fact, 'The culture surrounding the games is an important means of establishing and sustaining interpersonal relationships – from the swapping of games, advice and "cheats", to … the ongoing social construction of an "interpretive community"' (Radway 1984) – and in this respect, as Jessen (1999) argues,

> video games may be better suited to the pattern of children's play than older media such as books … [since] the videogame console often acts as a site of social contact, bonding and networking (particularly in today's age of online gaming). (Conway 2010)

In other words, when kids start playing a new video game like *FIFA,* any younger children around them will start playing to emulate their older friends (Weber 2011). In fact, says University of Michigan senior Austin Like, 'I started playing FIFA when I was 14 because my older cousins were all playing it'.[5]

There is no doubt that the rise in popularity of the *FIFA* video game series in America has coincided with a rise in popularity of men's professional soccer in the US. The percentage of Americans who identify themselves as avid men's professional soccer fans has grown every year since 2009, as per ESPN.com. (Badenhausen 2014; DiLorenzo 2013; Kondolojy 2015; Luker 2012). In this same period, the popularity of the *FIFA* video game series has expanded rapidly: *FIFA*'s unit sales in the US increased by 35% from 2010 to 2012, reaching 2.6 million in 2012. Each new edition since *FIFA '10* has received ratings of at least 9 out of 10 by some rating system on at least one device (Butt 2015; Higgins 2014; Trefis 2014). *FIFA* has also become EA Sports' bestselling entity, accounting for nearly 25% of its revenue in 2014 (Higgins 2014; Reeves 2012).

Unsurprisingly, the children who play *FIFA* and other sports video games are *not* the same ones who excel at sports on the field playing FIFA and other video games has no tangible effect on sport participation (Crawford and Gosling 2009). In fact, studies show that it might be the opposite: according to one paper published in the scholarly journal *TeachThought*, kids who are not as good at sports tend to have more interest in video games due to not having to spend as much time practising for a less intense league featuring less accomplished athletes while also wanting to project their athletic dreams that they know they will never fulfil on the field or courts onto the screen (Reeves 2012). Video games are a form of escapism for children, and for children who love sports, sports video games fulfil that function perfectly (Markovits and Smith 2008; Reeves 2012; Trefis 2014; Weber 2011). A similar study was conducted in 2003 by Andrei Markovits and David Smith featuring University of Michigan students. The authors concluded that the students who followed professional sports most closely were more likely not to be athletes: rather, they were the quintessential 'sports nerds' or 'sports omnivores' as Markovits has come to label these devoted and knowledgeable sports fans. Indeed, these sports omnivores, almost exclusively male, were real outliers in the study of nearly 400 student athletes and the equivalent number of 'regular' students in that they were markedly different from male student athletes in terms of their respective following and knowledge of sports. Male athletes did not know who the point and shooting guards of the Boston Celtics of the 1960s were, nor did they commit to memory the pitching rotation of the Los Angeles Dodgers of the same era. Tellingly, these athletes did not care to know these sports minutiae. Such knowledge did not constitute a core ingredient of their identity as it most assuredly did for the non-athlete sports omnivores. Although athletes, just like sports nerds or omnivores, love to play sports video games, the two groups do it for different reasons (Crawford and Gosling 2011; Garber 1999). It may well be that athletes enjoy playing themselves on a game system, or that they find that playing a sports video game helps them see different strategies and nuances of the game, as they are approaching it from a different angle than they do in the real contests on the field and the courts. In a notable contrast, sports omnivores derive two very different kinds of pursuit from playing video games: we could call the first a kind of vicarious pleasure, a fantasy pleasure in which they engage in an activity which they know full well will always be way beyond their very own athletic abilities and thus will always be the stuff of wishful thinking and dreaming. We could call the second pleasure an intellectual one in which by playing sports video games the sports omnivores excel at knowing all the players' names, their statistics, their moves on the field, their teams, their transfers, and their accomplishments (Garber 1999; Markovits and Smith 2008). For the sports omnivores in the Michigan study, it was precisely such in-depth knowledge of sports history and details that gave them their social and cultural distinction and constituted their identity (Markovits and Smith 2008).

The 'chicken or egg' question and the growing relevance of MLS

The question remains: does the popularity of the *FIFA* series cause the rise in popularity of men's professional soccer in America, or is it the other way around? Obviously, there are some men's professional soccer fans in the United States that have never heard of *FIFA*, let alone become avid gamers of this video game. But one simply cannot discount the extant, if perhaps not iron-clad conclusive, evidence that at least some of the recent considerable increase in soccer fandom among Americans might also be due to the expanding video game franchise. Per an ESPN.com poll conducted by Richard Luker, 34% of *FIFA* users became big men's professional soccer fans after playing the video game and 50% of users gained at least some interest in men's professional soccer due to their love of playing *FIFA* (Luker 2014). Per the same poll, Americans played FIFA '14 the second most of any country, and there has been a 112% increase in Americans' playing with MLS clubs in FIFA '15 compared to FIFA '14 (Luker, 2014). According to EA Sports sales records, *FIFA* sold nearly 800,000 copies from January to October 2014 (Trefis 2014), meaning that according to Luker's calculations, approximately 400,000 more people in the US gained an interest in watching men's professional soccer in 2014 than they would have without *FIFA*'s impact, and around 272,000 became major professional soccer fans due to the game's influence (Luker 2014). According to NBC viewership numbers, this would mean that approximately 57%

of Americans watching the Premier League games on NBC are people that likely would not have had an interest in professional soccer before *FIFA* emerged[6] (Badenhausen 2014; Collins and O'Leary 2014; Kondolojy 2015; Luker 2014; Tannenwald 2015).

In addition to its effect on the massively growing popularity of European (particularly English) soccer among Americans in the past five years, *FIFA*'s popularity and rapid proliferation have also had a major influence on the men's professional soccer league that is actually based in the US: Major League Soccer (MLS). The idea for MLS was first concocted in 1988, when FIFA agreed to award the 1994 Men's World Cup to the US on the condition that there appear a top-tier men's professional soccer league in the country immediately following the conclusion of this tournament (Eligon 2005; Fraser v. Major League Soccer 2000). This did not happen as originally requested, but after a two-year delay the first MLS game was played in 1996. Although MLS had a small contract to have its games broadcast on ESPN, the league struggled mightily in its initial phase, losing an estimated $250 million over its first five years (Eligon 2005). However, MLS made a noticeable turnaround in the first decade of the twenty-first century due to many factors, including a surprising performance by the US men's national team at the 2002 World Cup in Japan and South Korea (Collins and O'Leary 2014; Fraser v. Major League Soccer 2000), the construction of soccer-specific stadiums in MLS cities (Associated Press 2012; Evans 2015; McMahon 2012), and the successful effort by MLS to attract A-lister European stars, such as French striker Thierry Henry and English midfielder David Beckham (McMahon 2012) to be followed a few years later by the hiring of international stars such as David Villa, Steven Gerrard, Kaka, Frank Lampard, Didier Drogba and Andrea Pirlo (Evans 2015). But no factor may be more influential for the recent rise of MLS than the prominence of *FIFA*. All MLS clubs are available to be played on the video game, and recently, players and gamers alike have shown an increasing tendency to do just that. As mentioned above, according to Richard Luker's research, there has been a 112% increase in MLS club usage by participants of *FIFA '15* compared to *FIFA '14* (Luker 2014).

When considering these television ratings and poll statistics courtesy of Richard Luker, it is important to understand exactly what constitutes a 'fan' of professional soccer and what constitutes 'being more interested' in professional soccer. Different people have different definitions of fandom: Luker's definition of a fan may differ completely from someone else's (he did not explicitly define 'fandom' in any of his published *FIFA* studies (Luker 2012, 2014)). However, there are some published definitions of fandom, and for the purposes of defining fandom in this study, we will utilize them. Possibly the most popular model of defining sports fandom emanates from sociologists Funk and James (2001), who in 2001 came up with the Psychological Continuum Model of fandom, which offers four levels on the spectrum of fandom. They are, in ascending order, from least emotionally invested to most: awareness, attraction, attachment, and then allegiance.

As soccer's popularity has risen, so too has the media coverage (and consequently popularity) of the sport. In May 2014, ESPN, Fox Sports and Univision signed an eight-year contract to retain joint coverage of MLS games (ESPN and FOX will broadcast games in English, while Univision will host telecasts in Spanish). The deal comprises a total of $720 million over an eight-year period. ESPN and FOX are paying a combined $600 million with Univision laying out $120 million. Games not broadcast by ESPN or FOX Sports are broadcast by the regional networks of the respective MLS clubs. This $90 million annual contract represents a 900% increase from MLS's last TV contract, a three-year, $30 million deal with NBC, and constitutes more than a gigantic increase of 8233.333% (not a typographical error) from MLSs' first TV deal, a three-year, $3.25 million contract with AXS TV (Harper 2014; Ourand and Botta 2012).

To be sure, other sports and leagues in America have also witnessed a rise in popularity, most notably the NBA, which is set to sign a TV contract within the next few years that will total $2 billion annually, double the league's last deal with ESPN and TNT (Harper 2014). But no other major team sport has experienced the rate of expansion currently being enjoyed by MLS in such a short amount of time (Garber 1999; Harper 2014; Ourand and Botta 2012). EA Sports' marketing tactics, which we discussed earlier (Meda 2014) have clearly contributed to MLS's growing popularity. As of late 2015, the average MLS team is valued at $157 million as per Forbes.com (a 52% increase from 2013) (Badenhausen 2014; Smith 2015). It is safe to say that much of that value can be attributed to Americans' being attracted to soccer by a video game.

Obviously, we need to consider some confounding variables. Most notably, there is a clear business relationship between EA Sports and MLS. EA could not be faulted for exhibiting selection bias by publishing certain statistics that promote MLS and the *FIFA* series in general, as EA holds stake in MLS' success: the more people like MLS (and men's professional soccer in general), the more will buy the newest edition of *FIFA*. In fact, Richard Luker, whom we have cited numerous times in this paper, is a client of EA (Pekush 2015), and therefore certainly has an incentive to speak highly of *FIFA*. There is also the (very difficult to answer) question as to how much of the increase in the popularity of men's pro soccer in the US is due to *FIFA*'s expansion vs. how much is due to MLS' and European soccer leagues' marketing strategies towards Americans. Notably, long-time MLS Commissioner Don Garber has outlined a detailed marketing plan geared towards creating a phenomenal in-stadium MLS experience (which European teams obviously cannot offer American fans) and expanding the league in order to create more places in which fans can receive that in-stadium experience. Two new franchises (in New York City and Orlando) were added to MLS in 2015 (albeit with one dissolving), and there are plans to add franchises in Atlanta (by 2017), Los Angeles (by 2018), Minnesota and Miami (with unclear timelines for the latter two) (Vaccaro 2014). Meanwhile, many European clubs have played exhibition games all over the United States during the summer, which has undoubtedly helped establish an American fan base for soccer, some of whom most assuredly have never played *FIFA* (Prince-Wright 2014). In addition, games of European soccer leagues have also been broadcast on NBC for the past four years, and on Fox before then. These telecasts have certainly lent those leagues added exposure to American fans as well. Even considering these variables, however, it is hard to deny that there is at least some correlation between *FIFA*'s rise and that of men's professional soccer popularity among Americans. The word 'soccer' was basically alien diction to Americans up until the 1990s. Due to many factors such as suburbanization, the rise of the Latino population, the growing popularity of video games and the changing roles of women, soccer has become part of the American vernacular. It is in this larger context that *FIFA* has clearly contributed to the further growth of soccer. Alas, we remain very skeptical whether any analysis, no matter its quantitative sophistication, could satisfactorily – let alone definitively – enlighten the issue of causation in this larger historical trend. (Markovits and Smith 2008). Although Luker may be a bit biased, the contents of his interviews and public statements give the impression that he has confidence in his data and that his methods for obtaining them are sound (Pekush 2015). Luker's study is the best approximation of FIFA's effect on soccer's popularity in the United States, as there are no credible studies on this issue that were not conducted by an EA employee. We are working on virgin territory here. MLS may have sound marketing strategies independent of *FIFA* which aid its popularity among Americans; but with the success of the 'MLS Next' initiative in 2015 and the increased sales numbers that the *FIFA* series has observed over the past five years, it is hard not to believe that at least some of the staggering proliferation of men's professional soccer's cultural presence in the United States is due to the video game. The same can be applied to the European leagues: in fact, some of the American fans that appeared at EPL teams' exhibition games in American stadiums over the summer may have only been there because they love playing with the European stars in virtual gaming land.

In addition to confounding factors that arise from the marketing and biases of large corporations, there are also contrasting tendencies among gamers themselves which give rise to a correlation vs. causation debate. There are plenty of people in America who love playing *FIFA* but do not pay any attention to professional soccer (men's or women's), at home or abroad. There are also other Americans who love watching professional soccer in the United States, Latin America, Europe or anywhere in the world for that matter, but have never played *FIFA* in their lives. The only way to understand the reasons for this confounding complexity is to understand the individual players (or gamers) themselves. Why do some people love *FIFA* but not professional soccer, and vice versa? One possible reason could be the immensely crowded sports space for the American consumer. An American sports fan already has four major men's professional leagues to follow (NFL, MLB, NBA and NHL, not to mention any women's professional sports that an American may follow) and closely following yet another sport can just be too much of a time commitment. According to University of Michigan senior and avid Big Four sports omnivore Morris Fabbri, 'I love playing *FIFA*, but I just don't follow soccer: any knowledge I do have about the actual players is taken from playing the game'. Another issue might be the population of video game lovers who are athletes. An ESPN study showed that athletes at the professional and collegiate level love playing video games, specifically the video games in which they are included (Garber 1999). This is strongly confirmed by the Markovits-Smith study (2008) which concluded that athletes mainly follow sports which feature strongly in their lives with giving scant attention to others. Thus, for example, many high-level soccer players in the United States, especially on the collegiate level, may love to play *FIFA*, but they likely will not end up closely following the professional game. They don't have the time to do so even if they wanted to, with the highly intensive practice and training schedule that comes with being a high-level athlete.

On the other hand, why do some people enjoy watching professional soccer but do not find joy in playing *FIFA*? According to Markovits and Smith (2008), this faction is more likely to come from the 'sports nerds' or 'sports omnivores' demographic meaning people who love watching myriad sports and get cognitively and emotionally involved with many of them. Americans who follow the four major men's professional sports leagues in addition to European soccer, MLS or both are putting in major hours doing so. It is simply very difficult to spend that much time complementing the watching and following of professional sports with the playing of sports video games. Throw in the time commitment of school, work and whatever else that person is juggling, and it is tough to imagine someone having enough hours in the day to function properly by devoting time to both of these related but separate endeavours. Another possible reason that is unrelated to *FIFA* does in fact pertain to the 'sports space' concept. Since European matches are usually televised in the afternoons on America's East Coast and Middle West, and mornings in its Rocky Mountain area and its West Coast; for Americans, European league soccer fills a space that is – with exceptions, to be sure – unoccupied by other sports, as American Big Four sporting events usually do not take place during the day time. And since professional soccer's main demographic is 12–24-year-old males, which includes high school and college students, a student can watch an EPL game at 2 pm, Eastern Time or 11 am Pacific Time if he or she does not have class that day, or, alas, even if he or she does as many a student has been known to watch a match on his or her laptop during class. This phenomenon isn't directly related to *FIFA*, but it certainly provides a window for people to get hooked on soccer though this modus does not apply to MLS games, which are played during the evenings in America.

Conclusion: growing by leaps and bounds with endless possibilities

The *FIFA* franchise and MLS were both born in the 1990s. At the time, they both had very little in terms of a following, but both were determined to become leaders in their respective areas (Meda 2014). Both have experienced major struggles. MLS's problems in the late 1990s and early 2000s included financial difficulties and very low viewership. It seemed quite likely at the time that MLS would not even survive a 10-year stint (Eligon 2005). *FIFA* generated very poor sales figures in the early years after its inception, and trailed Konami's *Pro Evolution Soccer* in sales through most of the 2000s before a redesign of the game for the 2008 version (which was discussed in detail above) (Badenhausen 2014; Butt 2015). Now, according to Luker, 95% of Americans who play soccer video games play *FIFA*, proving *FIFA*'s market dominance over PES and any other small competitors in the soccer video game market (Collins and O'Leary 2014; Luker 2014). Even after its rebranding in 2008, *FIFA* seemed unlikely ever to approach the sales numbers of powerhouse video game franchises such as *Madden* and *NBA 2 k*. But in 2014, *FIFA* surpassed *NBA 2 k* and, at the time of this writing in January 2016, is rapidly closing in on *Madden* for the title of highest selling sports video game in North America (Meda 2014). It is, of course, already the highest selling game worldwide by a large margin: *FIFA '15* has outsold *Madden '15* 13.6 million to 4.9 million copies as of March 2015, per Forbes.com (Badenhausen 2014).

Both MLS and English Premier League soccer are planting cultural roots in America. They have begun to enter the American sports space in a serious manner. While soccer fandom in the US may not reach the NFL's or college football's astronomical levels for many decades to come, it definitely seems certain that men's professional soccer has found a home in the US and its fans are here to stay. The US-Portugal game from the 2014 Men's World Cup had over 26 million total viewers and is the most viewed soccer game in US history to this point (Collins and O'Leary 2014; Kessler 2014; Weber 2011). In a telling comment on how integral the women's game has become to soccer's presence in North American culture (as opposed to virtually anywhere else in the world), the cover of the most recent *FIFA* game in the United States features the ubiquitous Lionel Messi, the world's greatest player over the past decade, together with Alex Morgan, the heir apparent to Abby Wambach and arguably one of the most recognizable and respected soccer stars of any gender in the United States. In the Canadian edition of *FIFA*'s latest iteration, it is the Canadian female star Christine Sinclair who appears alongside Messi underlining that there, too, just like in the United States, soccer is far from a virtually total male preserve like it still is in most of the rest of the world. In fact, the rise of the women's game is already illustrated in the gaming realm: *FIFA '16* features 12 women's national teams (notably not including the Japanese Women's National Team, the 2015 World Cup runners-up, as Konami purchased the exclusive licence to use the Japanese women in *PES '16*) (FIFA 2015).[7] However, *FIFA 16's* women's national teams have not yet enjoyed frequent usage or any widespread popularity among gamers which may offer further prima facie evidence that women's soccer simply is not popular among the masses apart from the quadrennial events of the Women's World Cup and the Olympics which, unlike in the men's game, matter a lot in the women's (Funk and James 2001).[8] With *FIFA* sales expected to increase exponentially over the next few years (Meda 2014), it is anybody's guess as to how many Americans will tune into the telecasts of the 2018 Men's World Cup (or the 2019 Women's World Cup, for that matter). What the next chapter for soccer in the US holds is a mystery, but in studying the ascension of *FIFA,* we may have found an answer as to how we got here.

Notes

1. By that time, Captain Tsusaba had developed a rabid worldwide fandom, with ratings only approached by Dragonball Z, another popular Japanese Anime television series that was developed into numerous video game spin-offs (Meda 2014).
2. Probst, who served as CEO of EA from 1991 to 2007, said in that interview that 'Marketers … face the challenge of marketing to their specific demographics. We needed to create … a brand story, a brand narrative, a brand voice. At the time we decided that we wanted … to diversify our marketing strategy in the most efficient manner possible in the best interest of our company and our product' (Probst 2015).
3. Markovits defines 'sports space' as that geographic location and cultural construct in which sports assume emotional rather than callisthenic attachments. In other words, it is what people follow, dream about, hope for, get ecstatic over, fall into despair. It is not what they do. This sports space coincides with what Markovits has also called 'hegemonic sports culture'. Like with every space, the one with sports can also be filled. Moreover, early arrivals have a much better chance of assuming long-term positions. Thus, in the American sports space, the four early arrivals of baseball, American football, basketball and ice hockey crowd out newcomers such as soccer (Markovits and Hellerman 2001; Markovits and Rensmann 2010).
4. *FIFA* does not have a licence to use UEFA Champions League clubs. That licence is held by Konami's *Pro Evolution Soccer,* which has been one of *FIFA's* main competitors since *PES's* release in March 2001. In its early years, *PES* actually outsold *FIFA* (Konami 2013), achieving astounding acclaim from game reviewers (Metacritic 2008) and fans alike (*PES 2, 3* and *4* received aggregate Metacritic scores of 93, 93 and 92/100, respectively) (Metacritic 2004). *PES's* early success was also in part due to its having the market cornered on soccer video games made for the PlayStation and PlayStation 2 gaming devices, which at the time controlled the gaming device market (Metacritic 2004). However, *PES's* game-play declined beginning with its 2006 edition (reaching rock bottom in 2008, with *PES 2008* receiving a woeful Metacritic score of 58/100 (a disaster that led to Konami acquiring exclusive rights to use UEFA in *PES* games beginning in 2009) (Metacritic 2008). Due to *PES* fans losing faith in their old friend between 2006 and 2008, EA Sports' revamping of the *FIFA* series' game-play (with a notable change in game-play for the *FIFA '09* edition, which was a nominee for 2009's Best Sports Video Game for Nintendo) (Badenhausen 2014) as well as developing their own tendencies for acquiring exclusive rights for the *FIFA* series (due in part to the influx in cash EA began to see because of the great popularity of *FIFA '09* and *FIFA '10* and relative unpopularity of *PES 2009* and *PES 2010*) (Trefis 2014); *PES* simply cannot compete today with the amount of licences populating the *FIFA* games, with the Premier League and Bundesliga being the most notable absences. Although *PES* may have had a large role in producing the

competitive environment from which the *FIFA* series emerged, *PES* today simply does not have even close to the type of market share and widespread influence that the *FIFA* series do, particularly among Americans.

5. Note that all of the interviews that we conducted were with male students: although we reached out to all students on campus, only male students responded to interview requests for our research. This falls in line with the demographics targeted by EA as well: the company has consistently targeted 18–24-year-old males specifically in its marketing strategies (Good 2013). And for good reason: video games are deeply gendered by virtue of most to technology being associated in all western cultures with masculinity from early childhood (Conway 2010). In a large study of sports video game players, the researchers found that among their 1309 respondents, 98.4% identified as males and only 1.6% as females (Stein, Mitgutsch, and Consalvo 2012).

6. Per an NBC Sports survey, approximately 700,000 Americans consider themselves 'European soccer fans' and watched English Premier League games during the 2014–2015 season, with over 317 million minutes of Live EPL action estimated to be watched by those Americans (Kondolojy 2015). From Luker's 2014 poll, about 272,000 Americans considered themselves to be big professional soccer fans because of *FIFA*. Thus, 272,000 out of 700,000, or about 39%, of the American portion of the English Premier League audience may not have sat down for a Saturday afternoon tilt between Leicester City and West Ham United were it not for their first soccer love: the *FIFA* video game.

7. There was also a controversy regarding the National Collegiate Athletic Association (NCAA) informing EA that six collegiate players from the Canadian National Women's Team would have to be removed from the video game, as their inclusion would violate NCAA rules (not the first dispute between the NCAA and EA, as the NCAA has previously forbidden its players from being paid for their likeness being represented in video games (most notably *NCAA Football* and *NCAA Basketball*)). (Ore 2015) This ruling could potentially set a precedent on the inclusion of collegiate athletes who also play on their country's national team in the video game (one major example is Jordan Morris, a current Stanford University player who also plays for the U.S.M.N.T.). But due to the US college soccer system's lack of adequate training for its players (and their subsequent rare appearance on national rosters, as evidenced by the fact that Morris is the only member of the US. Under-23 squad that plays college soccer (Conn 2015), a large scale controversy regarding a superstar player being left off the national roster in FIFA seems unlikely to occur in the near future.

8. On the other hand, the lack of frequency in which Women's National teams have been used so far in *FIFA '16* could be in part due to the lack of exposure for Women's soccer in non-Women's World Cup years (Goldberg 2015). This pertains well beyond the United States and also holds for such soccer powerhouses as Germany where the women's Bundesliga's attendance records barely reach 2000 spectators for marquee matches and often hover under 1000 for regular games (Markovits 2015). It would be interesting to contrast the frequency of usage for Women's national teams during non-Women's World Cup years and Women's World Cup years (i.e. to see how the usage statistics for the Women's teams compare between *FIFA '19* and FIFA '16, '17 and '18 (provided EA continues to include the Women's national teams in the coming editions).

Disclosure statement

No potential conflict of interest was reported by the authors.

References

Associated Press. 2012. "M.L.S. Continues to Bolster Growing Brand wIth New Stadium in Houston." *New York Times*, May 12.

Badenhausen, K. 2014. "EA Sports' FIFA Video Game Helps Fuel Interest in the World Cup." *Forbes Magazine*, July 13.

Bashour, N. 2004. "TV Asahi Top 100 Anime." Japan: *Anime News Network*, September 23.

Bell, J. 2012. "WPS Suspends Operation." *New York Times*, January 30.

Butt, L. 2015. "Gamer Syndrome." May 19. Accessed June 2015. http://gamersyndrome.com/2015/video-games/fifa-why-it-continues-get-better

Carswell, W. A. 2010. *FIFA.Com*. Accessed June 14, 2015. http://www.fifa.com/mm/document/fifafacts/mencompwc/51/97/30/fs-301_01a_fwc-stats.pdf

Cianfrone, B. A. 2008. "Effectiveness of In-game Advertisements in Sport Video Games: An Experimental Inquirty on Current Gamers." *International Journal of Sport Communication* 1 (2): 195–218.

Cianfrone, B. A., James J. Zhang, and Y. J. Jae Ko. 2011. "Dimensions of Motivation Associated with Playing Sport Video Games." *Sport, Business and Management: An International Journal* 1 (2): 172–189.

Clare, S., ed. 2014. "How Twitter Reacted to USA Vs Portugal Match." United States: *NBC Sports*, June 22.

Collins, S., and M. O'Leary. 2014. "Americans' World Cup Fever Gives Soccer a Leg up in TV Ratings Game." *Los Angeles Times*, June 25.

Conn, J. R. 2015. *Grantland.Com*. October 7.

Conway, S. 2010. "'It's in the Game' and Above the Game; An Analysis of the Users of Sports Videogames." *Convergence: The International Journal of Research Into New Media Technologies*, 16(3), 334–354.

Crawford, G., and V. K. Gosling. 2009. "More than a Game: Sports-themed Video Games and Player Narratives." *Games and Culture* 26 (1): 50–66.

Crawford, G., and V. K. Gosling. 2011. "Game Scenes: Theorizing Digital Game Audiences." *Sociology of Sport Journal* 6 (2): 135–154.

DiLorenzo, G. 2013. "Soccer Steadily Gaining Popularity in United States." *Fordham Observer*, September 9.

Eligon, J. 2005. "For M.L.S., the Sport's Future is in the Eye of the Beholder." *New York Times*, November 11.

Evans, B. 2015. "Frank Lampard, Andrea Pirlo Will Transform NYC FC." *The Sports Journal*, June 10.

FIFA. 2015. *FIFA.Com*, May 28. Accessed January 14, 2016. http://www.fifa.com/media/news/y=2015/m=5/news=twelve-women-s-national-teams-to-feature-in-ea-sports-fifa-16-2609581.html

FIFA.com. 2014. *FIFA.Com*. June 22. Accessed June 14, 2015 http://www.fifa.com/worldcup/matches/round=255931/match=300186483/index.html

Fraser v. Major League Soccer. 2000. *United States District Court, D. Massachussetts*, April 19.

Funk, D. C., and J. M. James. 2001. "The Psychological Continuum Model: A Conceptual Framework for Understanding an Individual's Psychological Connection to Sport." *Sport Management Review* 4: 119–150.

Gallup. 1994. *Official Gallup UK Mega Drive Sales Chart, February–July 1994*. Mega issue: 17–22.

Garber, G. 1999. "Athletes Find Games Virtually Impossible to Put down." *ESPN*, May 17.

Goldberg, J. 2015. "National Women's Soccer League Semifinal Games Draw Weak Television Ratings." *The Oregonian*, September 15.

Good, O. 2013. "How times Change: EA Didn't Give a S–T about FIFA 20 Years Ago." *Kotaku*, August 17.

Grooten, J., and R. Kowert 2015. "Going beyond the Game: Development of Gamer Identities within Social Discourse and Virtual Spaces." *Loading … The Journal of the Canadian Game Studies Association* 9 (14): 70–87.

Harper, Z. 2014. "Report: NBA Nearing TV Deal Extension for over $2 Billion Annually." In *CBS Sports*, edited by M. Moore. September 8.

Hays, G. 2003. "WUSA Collapse Leaves Void in Sports." *ESPN.Com*. Briston, Connecticut, U.S.A. September 15.

Higgins, L. 2014. "FIFA Video Game Taking off in America." *USA TODAY*, June 25.

Kassouf, J. 2015. "NWSL Posts Low TV Ratings, Attendance for Semifinals." *The Equalizer*, September 16.

Kessler, M. 2014. "FIFA Video Game Scores American Soccer Fans." *Only a Game RSS*, July 1.

Klein, J. Z. 2014. "United States and Portugal Play to 2-2 Draw." *New York Times*, June 22.

Konami. 2013. *2012 3rd Quarter Financial Statement*. Osaka: Konami.

Kondolojy, A. 2015. *NBC Sports Group Sets TV and Streaming Records for 2014–15 Premier League Coverage*. May 28. Accessed June 14, 2015.

Lintner, J. 2015. "Soccer Passes College Hoops' Popularity in U.S." *Courier Journal*, January 23.

Luker, R. 2012. Accessed June 14, 2015. http://www.ESPN.com

Luker, R. 2014. *EA SPORTS FIFA and the Growth of Soccer in the U.S. Bristol, CT.*

Markovits, A. S. 2015. "Will Women's Soccer Ever Have a Mass Following Beyond the World Cup?" *The Conversation*, June 9.

Markovits, A. S., and S. L. Hellerman. 2001. *Offside: Soccer and American Exceptionalism*. Princeton, NJ: Princeton University Press.

Markovits, A. S., and S. L. Hellerman. 2003. "The "Olympianization" of Soccer in the United States." *American Behavioral Scientist* 46 (11): 1533–1549.

Markovits, A. S., and Rensmann, L. 2010. *Gaming the World: How Sports Are Reshaping Global Politics and Culture*. Princeton, NJ: Princeton University Press.

Markovits, A. S., and D. T. Smith. 2008. "Sports Culture among Undergraduates: A Study of Student Athletes and Students at the University of Michigan." *University of Michigan Journal of Political Science* 2(9): 1–58.

McMahon, B. 2012. "Has the 'Beckham Rule' Worked for MLS?" *Forbes Magazine*, August 5.

Meda, P. I. 2014. "FIFA 15 and Its Influence in US Soccer." *Soccerly*, September 24.

Metacritic. 2004. "Review of pro Evolution Soccer." *Metacritic.Com*, December 31. U.S.A: AceGamez.

Metacritic. 2008. "*Pro Evolution Soccer 2008 for DS Review*." *Metacritic.com*. U.S.A: GamerBoards. com. March 11.

Northcroft, J. 2006. "I Don't Understand Why People Are Football Fans. I Don't like to Watch Any Kind of Sport." *The Sunday Times*, January 1.

O'Connell, M. 2015. "TV Ratings: Women's World Cup Brings Record Audience with US-Australia Match." *The Hollywood Reporter*, June 9: 1–3.

Ore, J. 2015. "6 Canadian Women's Soccer Players Removed from FIFA Video Game." *CBC News, Sports News, CBC*, June 9.

Ourand, J. 2015. "(Women's) Soccer Nation: USA-Japan World Cup Final Averages Record-Setting 25.4 Million Viewers on Fox." *Sports TV Ratings*, July 6. U.S.A: NBC Sports.

Ourand, J., and C. Botta. 2012. "MLS's Big Play." *Sports Business Journal*, May 14.

Pekush, D. 2015. "How Video Game Technology Creates Sports Fans." *Sports Business Daily*, January 26.

Prince-Wright, J. 2014. "Preseason: US Tour Schedule for Every Premier League Team Heading Stateside." *Pro Soccer Talk*, July 16.

Probst, L. 2015. "2014 IAS: Marketing Leaders on Consumer Engagement." Interview with A. Silverman, May 29.

Ratto, R. 2013. "The Slow Evolution of U.S. Soccer Fandom." *CSN Bay Area*, September 11.

Reeves, B. 2012. *Why People Play Video Games*. TeachThought. GameInformer.com.

Smith, C. 2015. "Major League Soccer's Most Valuable Teams 2015." *Sports Business Journal*, August 19.

Stein, A., K. Mitgutsch, and M. Consalvo. 2012. "Who Are Sports Gamers? A Large Scale Study of Sports Video Game Players." *Convergence: The International Journal of Research into New Media Technologies* 19 (3): 345–363.

Takahashi, Y. 2011. "A Soccer Hero Adored around the World." Interview with I. Yoshihiro, October 18. Nippon Communications Foundation.

Tannenwald, J. 2015. "NBC Sports' 2014–2015 English Premier League and MLS TV Schedule." *The Goalkeeper*, May 25.

Trefis. 2014. "Electronic Arts' FIFA Franchise to Maintain Dominance." In *Sports Genre*, edited by T. T. staff. *Forbes Magazine*, October 6.

Vaccaro, A. 2014. "An Unlikely Case Study in Fast Growth: Major League Soccer." *Inc.Com* The cover of *FIFA '98* copies sold in the UK, featuring David Beckham.January 8.

Weber, L. 2011. "Why People Play Video Games: Top 10 Reason." *Addiction Blog*. April 18.

Stakeholder governance and Irish sport

David Hassan and Ian O'Boyle

ABSTRACT

Within global sport it appears the effective management of the interdependency of national governing bodies, individual clubs and a network of stakeholder interests has never been more widely discussed. It points to a requirement for all sporting organizations to remain sensitive to what is an ever-growing dichotomy between sporting volunteers and professional salaried staff, their competing interests and objectives. It is by no means a straightforward undertaking and is particularly foregrounded in a sporting environment that attaches significance to the preservation of an amateur ideal. As many sports clubs are now faced with the challenge of offering an adequate forum through which to reflect the views of their grassroots members, whilst simultaneously facilitating greater commercial interest in their affairs, the fundamental changes facing Ireland's largest sporting body, the Gaelic Athletic Association (GAA), offers cause for timely reflection. This article argues that only through the introduction of a meaningful stakeholder model can the governance of an organization like the GAA, a social and cultural touchstone unmatched within Irish sporting life, begin to respond to these mounting and competing agendas.

Introduction

In its broadest sense corporate governance addresses two issues; the philosophy of accountability evidenced towards stakeholders and the presence of a management framework that ensures the effective and efficient supervision of an organization (McNamee and Fleming 2007). As such its principal aim is to ensure that high standards of corporate behaviour are retained and the activities an organization undertakes are ethical and transparent. Consequently, corporate governance describes all the influences affecting how an organization executes its business, including those for appointing the controllers and regulators charged with organizing the production and sale of goods and services (Ansell and Gash, 2008).

Of course, viewed in these terms, corporate governance includes all types of businesses whether they are officially incorporated or otherwise. The Gaelic Athletic Association (GAA), Ireland's largest sporting body, as an unincorporated entity, is not mandated to abide by the provisions governing the best practice in the corporate world. Nevertheless, it could be argued that many examples of good practice emerging from the field of business can and should be adopted by all large organizations, including those, like the GAA, operating in the sporting realm.

Within Great Britain and Ireland, stewardship theory is the bedrock upon which most company law is founded. It requires that an individual behaves as if s/he was the principal of the organization and not merely an agent. Of course the willingness of an individual to act as a selfless steward is tied closely to the cultural expectations evident within the respective business (sporting) field. The particular cultural norms and values underpinning the activities of the GAA though make this model an ideal one for the effective regulation and strategic future of the indigenous body, which has over 1 million members in Ireland and even more amongst the Irish Diaspora living everywhere from Sydney to San Francisco.

In the realm of modern sport, the GAA remains something of a cherished entity. An organization founded upon the principles of amateurism and self-sufficiency, it is sustained by an unselfish sense of altruism. It is best described as a 'volunteer led' sporting body, one that is understood as 'membership owned', even if its success has almost necessitated the appointment of a professional management infrastructure to sustain its continued growth. This issue, in fact, goes to the very heart of this article – how do sporting organizations around the world satisfactorily manage the competing demands, expectations and views of an overwhelmingly volunteer membership, upon whom–in the case of the GAA–the entire association's infrastructure depends, with an ever more corporate approach to its business in which the principles of neo-liberalism seemingly hold considerable sway. The latter therefore is increasingly subject to the heightened expectations placed upon it by a form of 'stakeholder governance', defined by the positioning of sport for non-sporting, indeed largely commercial, outcomes.

As such the traditional hierarchical system of sporting authority has come under increasing pressure, mirroring developments in wider policy-making arenas. 'Governance' has been redefined as 'a change in the meaning of government, referring to a new process of governing' (Clarkson, 1995, 31). It is argued that this manifests itself through decision-making networks rather than direct control and an increase in the number of actors in the policy-making process. Henry and Lee (2004) have similarly referred to the notion of 'systematic governance' in which the,

> old hierarchical model of the government of sport, the top-down system, has given way to a complex web of interrelationships between stakeholders in which different groups exert power in different ways and in different contexts by drawing upon alliances with other stakeholders. (Henry and Lee 2004, 24)

In this respect, the concept of 'network' governance provides an appropriate starting point from which to assess the changing nature of control within the GAA. Within the context of elite-level competition, the GAA has had to re-evaluate its relationships with stakeholders who are both part of the GAA sphere (its clubs, wider membership and various levels of management) and external stakeholders with the power to influence (such as the institutions of the State, the increasing media interest in its affairs and wider developments in civic life). If control within the GAA now occurs through a network of influence, as appears to be widely understood, then it is important to appreciate how that network operates as the breakdown of influence will necessarily impact upon the achievement of 'good governance' in the management of Ireland's foremost sporting body. In the context of the administration of the association, this relates directly to the management of revenue (including its maximization), the role of non-salaried 'priority' members (specifically its elite players and managers) and the strategic direction of the GAA in an evolving Irish society where, amongst other concerns, a changing work–life balance and the appeal of global sports are prime considerations for its volunteer-base. Ultimately, an understanding of the GAA governance network, and in a wider sense the challenges faced by a mutually owned sporting body, can be gleaned through analysis of the different dimensions of power and the ebb and flow of the association's transition from a wholly amateur body to the management of one in which the primary means of revenue generation (the elite game) appears to fund what some still regard as an over inflated central operation at danger of losing touch with its volunteer base.

Sport governance

Indeed, in an overarching sense, the sport industry continues to evolve into an evermore professional and commercial entity and, in line with these changes, we are witness to a number of interesting phenomena taking hold within the broad field of sport governance. A previous, comparatively basic, need for governance in a largely volunteer led and wholly amateur context has now evolved into a requirement to adopt a full range of functions and practices synonymous with the corporate or traditional non-profit sectors. Within the contemporary non-profit sporting environment specifically, which best describes the context in which the GAA exists, this has led to tensions between volunteers and the influx of paid staff within the industry and has often resulted in conflict between member–stakeholders and representatives of sporting bodies (Shilbury and Ferkins 2014). Similar issues have also emerged in the for-profit or professional sports governance domain where members and fans of professional clubs and organizations have expressed dissatisfaction with the manner in which their organization is being governed, often leading to calls for wholesale structural changes in the governance systems in place within such clubs.

Alongside the issues outlined here, the question of governance within sports generally is receiving a significant increase in attention within industry and academia over recent times. This may be attributed to the growing number of high-profile incidents of alleged malpractice within sport and similar accusations of corruption, which continue to define some sectors and organizations within the industry. Although governance deficiencies are mostly reported in mainstream media only when they involve high-profile figures, governance is not an area of sport scholarship solely reserved for such individuals or the organizations they are affiliated with. Rather governance is a necessary and institutionalized component of all sporting codes from club level to national bodies, government agencies, sport service organizations and professional teams around the world (Ferkins and Shilbury 2010). The term is often cited in the singular perspective, where one organization's governance practices are brought into sharp contrast. This is often referred to simply as corporate or organizational governance (O'Boyle and Shilbury 2016; Shilbury, Ferkins, and Smythe 2013). However, governance also encapsulates networks of sport organizations, such as those that operate within the non-profit domain, which in turn are often affiliated with regional, national and indeed international governing bodies. This concept is generally defined as systemic, networked or federated governance within the extant literature (Henry and Lee 2004).

Regardless of the type of governance that is being discussed, one aspect of this field of enquiry is clear; governance coheres around the work of the board within a sport organization and their on-going responsibility in ensuring their organization is performing at an optimum level, is in tune with the body's key trading objectives and is operating in an efficient and effective manner (O'Boyle 2012). Hoye and Cuskelly (2007) suggest that the board must establish 'a direction or overall strategy to guide the organization and ensure that organizational members have some say in how that strategy is developed and articulated' (10). The latter is best preserved through a form of mutual ownership or at least the creation of a democratic setting in which grassroots members can exercise their opinions. They add that the board should also control the activities of the organization, its members and staff so that individuals act in the best interests of the organization and are working towards an agreed strategic direction. There is general consensus that one of the fundamental roles of the board within any sport organization is to act in such a strategic manner and thereby demonstrate its overall strategic capability (Ferkins and Shilbury 2012).

Governance in non-profit sport

This focus on the strategic function of the board, alongside its many other roles, has been the primary field of enquiry within a number of studies in the non-profit sport governance domain (Inglis 1997; O'Boyle and Hassan 2014; Shilbury 2001; Yeh and Taylor 2008; Yeh, Hoye, and Taylor 2011). Other areas that have received attention, specifically within the non-profit sporting setting, include volunteer motivations for serving as a board member, board performance and CEO--Chairperson relationships (Cuskelly and Boag 2001; Hoye and Doherty 2011; Inglis 1997; Shilbury and Ferkins 2011; Soares, Correia, and Rosado 2010). These studies have been important additions to this field of study and have assisted our understanding of the intricacies of sport governance challenges that the industry faces and how they may be best overcome. To coincide with studies published in the academic arena, there have also been a number of industry reports that have sought to highlight the challenges associated with effective governance practices and potentially illustrate something of a 'best practice' approach for sport organizations amidst general acknowledgement that each organization can face distinct pressures and challenges in respect of their organizational capacity (ASC 2013; SPARC 2006; UK Sport 2004).

The most recent high-profile industry report addressing sport governance in the non-profit context has been published by the Australian Sports Commission (ASC) and has placed a responsibility on Australia's sporting organizations (both national and regional) to address real and perceived governance deficiencies within their sports. This report, entitled *Mandatory Sports Governance Principles* (2013), requires all ASC-funded bodies to comply with the principles therein or risk a reduction in funding from this government agency in subsequent years. Within the report the ASC states:

> ... the time is now here to raise the bar, recognising that organizations that are managing public investment and member interests must have structures in place that reflect a greater level of professionalism. This is true whether a national sporting organization (NSO) is focused on high performance or participation. Good governance is a necessary condition for success. (1)

The ASC (2013) report appears to capture the major issues facing contemporary sport organizations in relation to their governance, and is a relevant departure point not only for organizations operating within the Australian context, but also for those existing internationally in both non-profit and even, in some instances, within the for-profit sporting environment. The report is delineated into three distinct sections, each focussing upon a multitude of governance challenges; structure for sport; board composition and operation; and sport transparency, reporting and integrity.

The first section, structure for sport, refers to the complex issue of ensuring all affiliated organizations that comprise a sporting network are working towards a common strategic vision and direction, with a shared understanding across the sport. This has been one of the major challenges within the non-profit sporting context in recent times, where often wholly autonomous organizations at regional levels are expected to collaborate and cooperate for 'whole of sport' progression, led by a NSO. This governance issue has also been the focus of a limited amount of academic work, which has investigated how such a sporting network can ensure that all federated bodies are working cohesively and towards such common strategic outcomes (Henry and Lee 2004; O'Boyle and Shilbury 2016; Shilbury, Ferkins, and Smythe 2013).

This federal system of sport governance operates similarly in a host of countries throughout the world, including New Zealand, Canada, the UK and a number of other European nation states. When exploring governance issues within federal models, Shilbury, Ferkins, and Smythe (2013) highlight a series of concerns surrounding these types of networks. These include questions about the suitability of federal models to facilitate a whole of sport perspective, how barriers to collaboration may be overcome and what role leadership plays within governance positions in a federal sporting network. O'Boyle and Shilbury (2016) build on this work when examining the issue of trust within governance networks and have uncovered that pre-histories of conflict and antagonism, and low levels of mutuality between federated bodies was significantly, and adversely, impacting upon the governance function of the sports examined in their research. They also noted that increasing the frequency of face-to-face dialogue between boards in a sporting network and intentionally seeking to become more transparent in decision-making processes could, in turn, elevate levels of trust and therefore collaboration within these systems. Also, coinciding with the findings of Shilbury, Ferkins, and Smythe (2013) and previous work in the public administration domain undertaken by Ansell and Gash (2008), it was found that effective leadership built on an ability to negotiate and communicate effectively was imperative when fostering high-level working relationships and facilitating horizontal cooperation within sport governance networks.

As commentators from both industry and academia begin to afford increased attention to 'structures of sport' in relation to governance, this area of 'collaborative governance' may play an increasingly important role in how we view and understand the relationship between various bodies that are required to work together within these governance systems. Previous studies, outlined above, have typically adopted theoretical frameworks from more established fields of enquiry and these theoretical underpinnings have, at times, had particular relevance to the federal model of sport governance. For instance, institutional theory, resource dependence theory, agency theory, inter-organizational relationships and network theory have all been adopted by researchers in this field and have provided useful results and insights (Dickson, Arnold, and Chalip 2005; Ferkins and Shilbury 2010; Henry and Lee 2004; Hoye and Cuskelly 2007; O'Boyle and Bradbury 2013; O'Boyle and Hassan 2016). An important recent addition to the suite of theoretical frameworks that has been applied within the field is the theory of collaborative governance (O'Boyle and Shilbury 2016; Shilbury and Ferkins 2014). Collaborative governance theory has its origins within public sector administration and until recently studies relating to this position have largely been based within this sector and emerged predominantly from the US (Ansell and Gash 2008; Emerson, Nabatchi, and Balogh 2012). It has been proposed that this theory has particular relevance to the federal model of sport governance as it is an arrangement in which wholly independent bodies are brought together to engage in a 'collective decision-making process that is formal, consensus-orientated, and deliberative' (Ansell and Gash 2008, 544).

Governance in professional sport

Notwithstanding the importance of governance within federal networks, and indeed that of boards operating within these environments (as previously described), governance in this domain is limited to those organizations that operate on a non-profit basis and many face different challenges and pressures when compared to those sporting bodies that exist in a more profit driven environment, as witnessed in a number of professional sporting leagues throughout the world. Examples include many of the professional soccer leagues operating in Europe and, of course, the dominant American sports systems. Within the US specifically, although federalism defines the nation's political make-up, a reflection of this federal system is absent from the sports environment with a significant disconnect between mass participation sport and professional sport is evidenced. The combination of a federalist system of government and an avowedly free-market economy has resulted in a plethora of sport organizations claiming governance over the same sport (Green, Chalip, and Bowers 2013). Furthermore, the lack of a nationalized governance framework within all sports in the US has created an opening for entrepreneurs who own professional sport franchises and who control the leagues in which that team compete. These groups and individuals can present their teams and leagues in any manner they see fit, with the only regulation to ensure that these activities do not contravene American business law. Consequently, each of the major leagues in the US, such as the National Basketball Association (NBA), National Football League (NFL) and Major League Baseball (MLB), have their own rules and systems of governance, even if they do appear to operate in a broadly complimentary fashion.

Taking the NFL as an example of the contrast between governance in the traditional non-profit and for-profit sporting environments, it is clear to witness the contrast in the challenges facing these alternative governance systems. The NFL is a private and wholly for-profit enterprise. The mission of the organization is: 'To present the National Football League and its teams at a level that attracts the broadest audience and makes NFL football the best sports entertainment in the world' (NFL 2015). Much like a traditional corporate entity, the league is overseen by a Commissioner (equivalent to CEO) who reports to the Executive Committee (equivalent to a board) with ultimate responsibility for the welfare of the league (note the emphasis on the product as opposed to the sport). A delegate system of board composition predominates with representation from each of the 32 NFL teams. League policies are brought into effect based on a three-quarters majority of team owners with the overwhelming number of teams owned by individuals or a private corporation, who present a remarkably similar profile of sporting venture capitalism. In contrast to non-profit sporting networks, where members at grassroots level are often referred to as the 'owners' of the sport, this stakeholder group is largely absent from the governance systems that operate in such professional sporting networks. Corporate governance within these types of professional leagues generally involves the adoption of a shareholder perspective – that is to maximize the economic performance of the teams (Senaux 2008).

This is not to imply that all professional sport is governed in a manner that directly mirrors the NFL. Within the English Premier League (EPL), for instance, a more free market-orientated system exists, which has been described accurately by Amara et al. (2005) as 'neo liberal'. Contrasting the NFL and the EPL cases, Gratton and Taylor (2000) described the NFL system as involving much greater intervention and where media rights incomes are shared across the network, recruitment strategies are policed through the draft pick system whilst entry into the market is monopolized by the league itself, where a limited number of franchises exists and rare instances of expansion remain. These 'equalisation' measures are in large part designed to protect the key principle of 'uncertainty of outcome' to sustain interest in the league from fans and, by extension, the broadcast media (Amara et al. 2005). In contrast, the EPL has seen a wide disparity in the income levels of those teams at the top and bottom of its league over recent times and has led to somewhat of a reduction in the uncertainty of outcome within the regular season. Although Gratton (2000) suggests that there is a lack of empirical evidence to argue that the EPL should adopt a more 'equalised' approach, there have been suggestions that a European wide league (distinct from the existing UEFA Champions League) with limited entry could be established, as the various national leagues throughout the continent become evermore predictable and thereby risk the possibility of spectator interest waning over time (Szymanski and Hoehn 1999).

Remaining with the example of the NFL and indeed other professional sport in the USA, the corporate governance nature of these teams and leagues is, as suggested, ultimately to protect the value of the shareholder in every respect. In contrast to this shareholder perspective, the non-profit sporting environment can be understood as adopting a stakeholder view – and indeed some scholars have argued that a number of 'for profit' professional teams and leagues also adopt this perspective (Foreman 2006; Senaux 2008).

The concept of a stakeholder, and the development of the stakeholder model, are attributed to Freeman's seminal publication: 'Strategic Management: A stakeholder approach' (1984). He suggested that the stakeholder is 'any group or individual who can affect or is affected by the achievement of the organization's objectives' (46). Further definitions and descriptions of stakeholders have been offered by numerous other scholars, including Clarkson (1995), who labelled stakeholders as individuals or groups who have put something at risk in their relationship with the organization. Both definitions detailed here evidently rely upon high levels of dependency between organizations and their stakeholders. However, Donaldson and Preston (1995) also add that it is important to establish a clear contrast between 'true stakeholders' and those that simply influence the organization. The media, for example, may influence the actions of a sport organization but one could argue are not stakeholders in the truest sense of the word. Supporters, players, coaches, administrators and competitors, on the other hand, are more closely linked to the definition of a stakeholder from a sporting perspective.

This stakeholder perspective has its roots in the history of European sport, from which the majority of professional teams today have evolved after originally being developed as 'sporting associations', in contrast to the pathway developed by professional sport in the USA. Although professional sport in Europe also now reflects a strong emphasis on economic activity, as one might expect, 'there are still deep heritages which profoundly structured the organization of sport in Europe and somehow explain the existence of complex power games' (Senaux 2008, 67) between professional sport and its stakeholders. The stakeholder perspective in relation to sport governance is therefore relevant to professional sport in this respect where there may be a variety of interests and goals competing, and in conflict, with each other. Of course shareholders also exist in professional sport throughout Europe and therefore cannot be overlooked in any analysis of corporate governance in a professional sport setting. Much like their counterparts in the USA, shareholders can have a number of interests and agendas as capital owners within the organization (but not necessarily owners of the organization itself). These interests may include financial returns, reputation, self-promotion and indeed the 'on field' success of the organization as a result of a sporting passion. One could assume that the interests of shareholders in professional sport are often mixed and not necessarily explicit. Nonetheless, they clearly remain an integral aspect of the governance structure.

There are other primary stakeholders, of course, in professional sport from players, coaches, administrators, supporters and various sporting bodies that impact on the activities of this unique business field. Players, in particular, have become an important group within the stakeholder model of sport governance as player associations and lobbying groups continue to exert an ever-increasing influence on the manner in which professional sport, indeed the same may be true of amateur organizations like the GAA, is presented and governed. Something similar can be said for supporters groups who, in some instances, have even assumed capital ownership positions within professional sporting teams. Senaux (2008) suggested that this focus on players, as an exclusive stakeholder group, risks the alienation of other stakeholder groups who may prove equally significant but perhaps remain less visible. This array of stakeholders makes professional sport an interesting context within which to examine corporate governance, especially in respect of the so-called European model of sport. Furthermore, within the non-profit sporting environment it is accepted, with little dissent, that the owners of sport in these systems are the members or the grassroots community involved in a given sport. The entities that comprise the governance framework in non-profit sport are seen as 'service organizations' to their members in this respect.

It is this issue therefore that continues to define many of the challenges faced by the largest sporting body (in terms of membership and asset base) in Ireland: the GAA. At the turn of the new millennium this organization, founded in 1884, appeared to be at something of a crossroads. Its dilemma was clear – it wished to remain wedded to the principle of amateurism (operationally understood as its players, managers and members continuing to give of their services free of charge) but recognized that significant elements of the association belied this sense of honest, voluntary endeavour and, instead, pointed towards an increasingly professionalised and commercial future for the sporting body. Many of its key personnel were in salaried positions, it owned a stadium (Croke Park) that was the envy of many within European sport, and its leading games were regularly sold out having already attracted more than 82,000 spectators. It was the core question of how to offer the effective governance of a sporting body seemingly committed to two competing objectives – the retention of a long-standing model of 'mutual ownership' and involvement whilst at the same time accepting the reality of just how significant the organization had become in commercial terms – that was in the minds of the GAA's leading officers when it published its seminal Strategic Review document in 2002.

Gaelic Athletic Association

Those behind the publication of the GAA's Strategic Review were clearly concerned at the way in which the organization was being managed, which was at best inefficient, and made specific recommendations on how it might undergo much needed transformation. It recommended that 'Coiste Bainisti (the Management Committee of the GAA) should prepare its proposals in respect of governance, and these should be set out in a document formally approved by Central Council' (GAA Strategic Review, 2002, 161). The GAA's Management Committee is concerned with the day-to-day running of the association. It is at this level that rules and regulations governing the affairs of the GAA are ratified and, if appropriate, implemented. It is also considered good practice under these arrangements to appoint an audit committee to monitor the implementation of such proposals. In most cases, the audit committee would also contain an independent person, someone with the requisite expertise, to provide additional assurances to the network of stakeholders, not least the GAA membership, of the continued practices of the organization.

The strategic review report went further in providing detailed recommendations on how the difficult matters of remuneration and performance were to be handled within the GAA. As the GAA is an organization founded upon its amateur ethos the issue of finance has always been one with which it has experienced particular difficulty. Indeed the question of commerce reflects a clear distinction between the GAA's central operation and its membership 'on the ground'. A view exists that the former has access to considerable amounts of money, whereas the latter is comparatively less well off and indeed is struggling to meet many of its on-going financial commitments. The review body was intent on reflecting the concerns of many rank and file members regarding an apparent self-regulating, relatively autonomous body in which the issue of accountability was never made entirely transparent. Instead, drawing upon examples of the best practice in the corporate and semi-state sectors, the review body made specific reference to the remuneration of executive officers at central level and the need for these to be kept under continual review by a separate committee. This committee may also be involved in compiling criteria for evaluating 'performance' for the ever-growing body of full-time employees within the GAA. The inference was clear; that any GAA policy on governance was either unfit for purpose or that one simply did not exist.

The mechanisms through which the wider GAA membership, not to mention its commercial stakeholders, are integrated into the decision-making process, remain equally dated. One general meeting each year, referred to as the GAA's Annual Congress, constitutes the sole occasion when those who govern the association can be adequately held to account. Even then much of the discussion that takes place at this meeting is pre-established as delegates are obliged to forward motions for debate, many of which are deferred or ruled out of order, often on account of some technical minutia. The picture remains one of an operating environment in which very little effective cross-examination of those in positions of authority within the GAA can take place. It makes for a less than satisfactory state of affairs for the majority of GAA members.

The lack of commercial awareness was equally unsettling for the review committee who recommended that the GAA's annual report 'should outline the (Central) Council's responsibility for the preparation of the financial statements and include a representation on the applicability of the 'Going Concern' basis for the preparation of the financial statements, with supporting assumptions and qualifications, as necessary' (GAA, 2000). It is against this backdrop that wider concerns about the GAA's capacity to cope properly with its increasing commercial workload are being raised. As McGee comments:

> Nobody can blame the GAA for maximising its financial returns which have come about from money well spent on developing grounds, coaching, etc., over many years. But lots of GAA people are worried about the emphasis being placed on making more and more money …. Big money and amateur sport have had a volatile relationship the world over and it's hard to see how it would be any different within the GAA. (McGee 2007, 60)

What ultimately was being proposed by the strategic review body was a form of governance that reflects the best practise in managing large organizations, which prioritises efficiency and foregrounds transparent and effective processes of financial management. To this end the stewardship model sees managers work effectively for an organization with the expressed aim of maximizing return for the shareholders or members (Donaldson and Davis 1994). Built around the suggestion that managers wish ultimately to work for the betterment of the organization, Donaldson and Davis (1994) argue that they should be freed from an essentially subservient role to assume a position on a board of directors, where they can control the direction of the business much more productively. This process can be assisted by the presence on the board of external regulators, whose role is to ensure that the fiduciary duty of the board is carried out to the satisfaction of its stakeholders. This remains valid in the case of not-for-profit organizations that occasionally believe that their responsibilities in respect of the organization's membership need not be as resolutely adhered to.

Governance and the GAA in Ireland

The structure of GAA governance is important to an understanding of the stakeholder network of Gaelic games activity in Ireland. Essentially, this is comprised of a hierarchical pyramid in which representatives of the 32 county boards, that together regulate the GAA at a national level, form the membership of the central regulating authority, the all-powerful GAA Central Council. As such, there exists a potential conflict of interests whereby a select group of people emerge from a broader membership body only, in turn, to seek to exercise authority over this wider grouping. Whilst the structures of the national associations vary, they are largely based on wide representation of individuals, counties and provincial bodies at the various levels of the games. Each of the four provincial bodies, Ulster, Munster, Leinster and Connacht, organizes club and county games within their own geographical area (and have their own staffing structures), whilst the aforementioned GAA Management Committee look after national competitions, including the All Ireland championships, the inter-provincial competitions and other all-Ireland series. The hierarchical integration of the elite and the grassroots of the GAA through a single system ensure that everything from the laws of the game to the organization of leagues and championships operates within one framework. The GAA's Central Council, Management Committee and provincial councils effectively enjoy a monopoly position controlling the regulation and organization of Gaelic games activity. There is a single governing body at county level, a single council in each province sanctioned by the GAA and a single national authority. The rules of the GAA prevent Gaelic games from taking place outside their own structures on a competitive basis, and ensure that leagues and clubs are, theoretically, subordinate to the provincial and national organizations.

This subordination is intended to recognize that in a multi-organizational context, in which clubs and counties compete across levels and defined regulatory areas, and with interdependence between those levels in terms of the development, well-being and provision of players and finance from the inter-county games right down to the grassroots, there should be a body that looks at the overall interests of the games at all levels. Thus, the provincial and national associations are routinely composed of different forms of representative combinations of GAA figures across the various levels. These are typically male, middle-aged and imbued with the guiding ethos and principles of a GAA, which are often located in the past. The structures also reflect the belief that there is a responsibility at the top end of the game to redistribute revenue to other areas of the pyramid. According to the GAA's strategic review document,

> the continued voluntary efforts and commitment of thousands of people who play, mentor, coach or administer in every parish and every community throughout the country, remains a distinguishing feature of the GAA; its clubs have developed into a source of both personal and community pride and identity. (GAA, 2000, 10)

Within the GAA, there remains a strongly held belief that the elite game should continue to make a contribution to supporting other levels of the pyramid.

Nevertheless, divisions within the GAA and its on-going negotiations with key stakeholders may act as an obstacle to radical change, and may be one reason why the organizations like the Gaelic Players Association (GPA), effectively a trade union for GAA players, has so far been unable to transform latent power into sizeable political gains in its quest for greater recognition of its core role as a source of revenue generation. Elite players need a successful and united GAA, and the need for consensus amongst a sufficient number of GAA members and delegates means that changes to directives pertaining to the remuneration of players will require broad support. Of course on a range of issues the GPA has legitimate grounds for protest. Any situation where the primary means of revenue production are inadequately compensated for their efforts is likely to create resentment and quite possibly lead to a withdrawal of their services. The players have common concerns such as dealing with a congested fixture programme, meaning an off-season is considered a luxury rather than a permanent arrangement, a failure to be adequately compensated for unavoidable absence from their full-time employment and the negotiation of commercial contracts. The fact that the players help drive revenue production for the GAA, which ultimately helps subsidize the activities of the GAA on a national level, has led to demands for more direct integration into the decision-making structures of the governing body. To this end the GAA has recently expanded its Central Council to incorporate a representative from the GPA. Conversely, there is a degree of distrust within the GAA about the GPA's motives, fearing its agenda is to create an elitist arm of the association. Whilst the GPA denies this, given its present constitution and similar capacity to attract commercial sponsorship, it would be a natural development were the organization to pursue this at a national level.

Conclusion

In many ways the GAA is a unique sporting organization. For its entire existence of some 130 years the association has expressed its strong belief in the amateur ideal and rejected any movement towards professionalism. Whilst it remained a modest, community-based organization such an approach proved to be very effective and it benefited enormously from considerable levels of volunteerism and financial altruism. Yet, as the GAA has developed into a fully fledged, professional sporting organization it has encountered difficulty in retaining support for its policy on amateurism. As its central and salaried operation grew exponentially, it continued to employ a straightforward administrative model of governance, one that lacked any proper strategic underpinning or financial acumen. Whereas, in the past this was almost a part of the GAA's intrinsic charm, as its central bureaucracy grew so too did calls for the adoption of a more professional operating strategy on the part of the association.

These issues were laid bare following the GAA's own strategic review, published in 2002 but the resonance of which is still experienced to this day. A catalogue of issues that required immediate attention were outlined, with the need for a more efficient and effective form of governance foremost amongst these. The recommendation of this article, a view supported by those charged with the GAA's own review, is that a stewardship model of governance should be adopted by the association. This would involve a streamlining of the GAA's Central Council, to be replaced by a much smaller board of directors who would be appointed on merit and not merely on a representative basis. This imperative is made all the more real when one considers the growing body of internal and external stakeholders the GAA is attempting to engage with. Some of these stakeholders are intent on challenging the GAA's traditional modus operandi, and indeed have negotiated partial acceptance of some of their demands. Finally, what is noticeable (and presumably concerning for the association) is that some of the GAA's fiercest critics have emerged from within its own ranks. It exists as a reminder that even the most benign and erstwhile organizations eventually encounter problems as their mode of governance becomes out-dated and ineffective in the face of demands placed upon it from modern day sport.

In essence, then, any balanced analysis of the regulation and governance of the GAA under its current arrangements suggests that whilst its grassroots membership will play a major role in any future developments, the GAA's hierarchy itself is undermined by the nature of its own composition. The level of exclusivity and the lack of defined and coherent membership criteria pose problems of legitimacy and credibility. Positions of authority are held for considerable periods of time and even in those cases where arrangements of this nature are expressly prohibited; such difficulties are overcome by simply rotating portfolios. The GAA makes much play out of its democratic credentials, but in reality the reigns of power are held by a small group of influential personalities, albeit they rely on the passive consent of a much larger group to carry out their duties. It is unlikely that such an arrangement can continue to prove sustainable going forward. In turn the argument that this situation should be reversed and a professional board of directors put in place has gained considerable traction amongst the GAA's broader constituency.

The existence of various stakeholders with power encourages caution and leads to the view that it is unlikely that any single actor will have a monopoly on change in the period ahead. The GAA, through a policy of limited dialogue and a convolute series of 'select committees', has so far managed developments by integrating players, media and corporate Ireland into the existing system, yet at the same time withholding genuine decision-making power. It remains questionable whether this strategy is sustainable in the long-term, but by opting for dialogue the GAA has positioned itself in direct and regular contact with key stakeholders. The GAA's continued commercial and sporting control of the All Ireland championships means that the organization retains its central role in the regulation of the sport in Ireland. Nevertheless, the latent market power of its elite players is evident. That being so, the inclination of stakeholders to operate (but increase their influence) within the established structures, means that market power is offset by the realities of modern day sport governance. The GAA has gradually attempted to come to terms with this transition, albeit it has had sporadic success in doing so. Its principal difficulty is managing a vibrant, professional and modern sporting body within the confines of a historically determined and fundamentally amateur context.

The level of stakeholder influence is further clouded by legal uncertainty regarding the rules of governing bodies in a self-regulatory framework. Whilst stakeholders are largely inclined to operate within the system, they have also succeeded in altering the system through recourse to outside bodies. The full workings of NGB's and their lack of political and legal standing has occasionally been exposed and the GAA has proved as susceptible to this as any other organization. It must remain mindful of the fact that whilst at one level it is imbued with the right to regulate Gaelic games activity, the full extent of this capacity set against the law of the land often results in its autonomy being compromised. It is not beyond the realms of possibility that as the GAA continues to move ever increasingly in the direction of a fully fledged commercial sports body that it may require a more defined appreciation of its legal and political shortcomings. It is for this reason that a move away from a long-standing administrative approach to managing its affairs is long overdue. Indeed the imposition of a professional board of directors offers the opportunity to at least ensure that the GAA safeguards its current position within an increasingly congested sport and entertainment marketplace.

Disclosure statement

No potential conflict of interest was reported by the authors.

References

Amara, M., I. Henry, J. Liang, and K. Uchiumi. 2005. "The Governance of Professional Soccer: Five Case Studies – Algeria, China, England, France and Japan." *European Journal of Sport Science* 5: 189–206.

Ansell, C., and A. Gash. 2008. "Collaborative Governance in Theory and Practice." *Journal of Public Administration Research and Theory* 18: 543–571.

ASC (Australian Sports Commission). 2013. *Mandatory Sports Governance Principles*. Canberra: Australian Sports Commission.

Clarkson, M. 1995. "A Stakeholder Framework for Analysing and Evaluating Corporate Social Performance." *Academy of Management Review* 20: 92–117.

Cuskelly, G., and A. Boag. 2001. "Organisational Commitment as a Predictor of Committee Member Turnover among Volunteer Sport Administrators: Results of a Time-Lagged Study." *Sport Management Review* 4: 65–86.

Dickson, G., T. Arnold, and L. Chalip. 2005. "League Expansion and Interorganisational Power." *Sport Management Review* 8: 145–165.

Donaldson, L., and J. H. Davis. 1994. "Boards and Company Performance – Research Challenges the Conventional Wisdom." *Corporate Governance: An International Review* 2 (3): 151–160.

Donaldson, T., and L. Preston. 1995. "The Stakeholder Theory of the Corporation: Concepts, Evidence, and Implications." *Academy of Management Review* 20: 65–92.

Emerson, K., T. Nabatchi, and S. Balogh. 2012. "An Integrative Framework for Collaborative Governance." *Journal of Public Administration Research and Theory* 22: 1–29.

Ferkins, L., and D. Shilbury. 2010. "Developing Board Strategic Capability in Sport Organisations: The National–Regional Governing Relationship." *Sport Management Review* 13: 235–254.

Ferkins, L., and D. Shilbury. 2012. "Good Boards Are Strategic: What Does That Mean for Sport Governance?" *Journal of Sport Management* 26: 67–80.

Ferkins, L., D. Shilbury, and G. McDonald. 2009. "Board Involvement in Strategy: Advancing the Governance of Sport Organizations." *Journal of Sport Management* 23: 245–277.

Foreman, J. 2006. "Corporate Governance in the Australian Football League: A Critical Evaluation." PhD diss., Victoria University, Melbourne, Australia.

Freeman, R. E. 1984. *Strategic Management: A Stakeholder Approach*. Chicago, IL: Pitman Press.

GAA. 2000. *Strategic Review*. Dublin: GAA.

Gratton, C. 2000. "The Peculiar Economics of English Professional Football." In *The Future of Football: Challenges for the Twenty-first Century*, edited by J. Garland, D. Malcolm, and M. Rowe, 45–63. London: Frank Cass.

Gratton, C., and P. Taylor. 2000. *The Economics of Sport and Recreation*. London: E & FN Spon.

Green, C., L. Chalip, and M. Bowers. 2013. "United States of America." In *Sport Governance: International Case Studies*, edited by I. O'Boyle and T. Bradbury, 20–36. London: Routledge.

Henry, I., and P. C. Lee. 2004. "Governance and Ethics in Sport." In *The Business of Sport Management*, edited by J. Beech and S. Chadwick, 25–41. Essex: Pearson Education.

Hoye, R., and G. Cuskelly. 2007. *Sport Governance*. Sydney: Elsevier.

Hoye, R., and A. Doherty. 2011. "Nonprofit Sport Board Performance: A Review and Directions for Future Research." *Journal of Sport Management* 25: 272–285.

Inglis, S. 1997. "Roles of the Board in Amateur Sport Organizations." *Journal of Sport Management* 11: 160–176.

McGee, E. 2007. "GAA is Getting Rich Quick but What of Its Poor Relations." *Irish Independent* Sep. (8): 60.

McNamee, M. J. and S. Fleming. 2007. "Ethics Audits and Corporate Governance." *Journal of Business Ethics* 73: 425–437.

NFL. 2015. "Values." http://www.nfl.com/careers/values.

O'Boyle, I. 2012. "The Identification and Management of Fundamental Performance Dimensions in National Level Non-Profit Sport Management." Unpublished doctoral diss., University of Ulster, Belfast, Ireland.

O'Boyle, I., and T. Bradbury, eds. 2013. *Sport Governance: International Case Studies*. London: Routledge.

O'Boyle, I., and D. Hassan. 2014. "Performance Management and Measurement in National-level Non-profit Sport Organisations." *European Sport Management Quarterly* 14: 299–314.

O'Boyle, I., and D. Hassan. 2016. "Board Composition in Federated Structures: A Case Study of the Gaelic Athletic Association." *World Leisure Journal*, 51: 56–74.

O'Boyle, I., and D. Shilbury. 2016. "Trust as an Antecedent to Collaborative Sport Governance." *Journal of Sport Management*.

Senaux, B. 2008. "A Stakeholder Approach to Football Club Governance." *International Journal of Sport Management and Marketing* 4: 4–17.

Shilbury, D. 2001. "Examining Board Member Roles, Functions and Influence: A Study of Victorian Sporting Organizations." *International Journal of Sport Management* 2: 253–281.

Shilbury, D., and L. Ferkins. 2011. "Professionalisation, Sport Governance and Strategic Capability." *Managing Leisure* 16: 108–127.

Shilbury, D., and L. Ferkins. 2014. "Exploring the Utility of Collaborative Governance in a National Sport Organization." *Journal of Sport Management, Advance Online Publication*, 29 (4): 380–397. doi:10.1123/jsm.204-0139.

Shilbury, D., L. Ferkins, and L. Smythe. 2013. "Sport Governance Encounters: Insights from Lived Experiences." *Sport Management Review* 16: 349–363.

Soares, J., A. Correia, and A. Rosado. 2010. "Political Factors in the Decision-making Process in Voluntary Sports Associations." *European Sport Management Quarterly* 10: 5–29.

SPARC. 2006. *Nine Steps to Effective Governance: Building High Performing Organizations*. 2nd ed. Wellington: SPARC.

UK Sport. 2004. *Good Governance Guide for National Governing Bodies*. London: UK Sport..

Szymanski, S., and T. Hoehn. 1999. "The Americanization of European Football." *Economic Policy* 28: 205–233.

Yeh, C., and T. L. Taylor. 2008. "Issues of Governance in Sport Organisations: A Question of Board Size, Structure and Roles." *World Leisure Journal* 50 (1): 33–45.

Yeh, C., R. Hoye, and T. Taylor. 2011. "Board Roles and Strategic Orientation among Taiwanese Nonprofit Sport Organisations." *Managing Leisure* 16: 287–301.

Index

Notes: Page numbers in *italics* refer to figures
Page numbers in **bold** refer to tables
Page numbers with 'n' refer to notes